THE FACES OF POWER

SEYOM BROWN

The Faces of Power

CONSTANCY AND CHANGE IN UNITED STATES FOREIGN POLICY FROM TRUMAN TO JOHNSON

COLUMBIA UNIVERSITY PRESS

NEW YORK AND LONDON · 1968

Seyom Brown is an analyst with The RAND Corporation, and coauthor of *Politics and Government in California* (1959).

Permission to quote is gratefully acknowledged:

The White House Years: Mandate For Change 1953–1956, by Dwight D. Eisenhower. Copyright © 1963 by Dwight D. Eisenhower. Reprinted by permission of Doubleday & Company, Inc., and William Heinemann, Ltd.

The White House Years: Waging Peace 1956–1961, by Dwight D. Eisenhower. Copyright © 1965 by Dwight D. Eisenhower. Reprinted by permission of Doubleday & Company, Inc., and William Heinemann, Ltd.

Kennedy, by Theodore C. Sorenson; by permission of Harper & Row.

The Fifteen Weeks, by Joseph M. Jones; by permission of Harcourt, Brace & World, Inc.

A Thousand Days, by Arthur M. Schlesinger; by permission of Houghton Mifflin Company.

The Missile Crisis, by Elie Abel. Copyright © 1966 by Elie Abel. Published by J. B. Lippincott Company.

For Two Benjamins

PREFACE

This book is addressed to political activists, government officials, journalists, and lay political analysts as much as to students and scholars of contemporary politics. It examines an aspect of political reality that most of us take for granted we already know: the basic policy premises that underlie and are expressed by the international behavior of the United States.

We claim to be in a period of great debate over the premises of United States foreign policy, but this debate more often than not turns out to be a contest between rationalizing platitude and deprecating caricature. Peeling back the rhetoric to examine the operating theories on which critical policy choices are in fact made is a painful exercise for those who must defend existing policy, as well as for those trying to make capital out of the difficulties faced today by the United States Government. For the harassed policy official it means abandoning the defense of simple "pragmatism" and seriously considering major alternatives to established policy directions. For the facile critic it means learning to appreciate the profound sources of current policy, in the nation's history, in its bedrock interests, and in its often noble political philosophy, and to show how alternative courses of action would serve these deeper purposes.

I should not be surprised to find that government officials consider my analyses of the premises underlying their actions and words to be an overly academic attempt to read basic patterns into behavior that is prompted largely by the practical requirements of response to immediate situations. On the other hand, I know that academic colleagues will see too little by way of categorizing, drawing generalizations and deriving theory from the flow of events.

Yet this idiosyncratic book is an expression of perspectives, arrived at from an idiosyncratic vantage (or disadvantage) point. Most of my professional activities in political analysis have been performed in the capacity of a research staff member of the RAND Corporation. As such, I am a research scientist who must often work within the reporting deadlines of a foreign service officer, and a social theorist who must take some responsibility for the action consequences of his speculations.

Consequently, it took considerable courage for the Washington Center of Foreign Policy Research, under the direction of Robert E. Osgood, to support my research and writing during the year's leave I took from RAND for purposes of completing this book. It also took courage on the part of Joseph M. Goldsen, then head of the RAND Social Science Department, to encourage me to accept this opportunity to write a book on a subject so intertwined with the critical policy issues that RAND deals with on a daily basis. He knew that even though the research and writing of this book was done entirely under non-RAND auspices, many readers would be tempted to attribute my opinions, and my shortcomings to the institution with which I am most closely associated.

In an ambitious effort such as this, my intellectual debts are larger than my credits. I owe most to Robert E. Osgood and Alexander L. George. Professor Osgood's counsel on the present manuscript is only the latest phase of his encouragement of my work in U.S. foreign policy analysis, which dates back to 1960 in his graduate seminars at the University of Chicago. Dr. George has been a persistent constructive critic and mentor throughout the period of our professional association at the RAND Corporation. And although this book was written away from RAND, he went beyond the call of colleagueship to share important insights at a critical phase in the writing.

Paul Hammond, Dan Weiler, Corinne Lyman, and Daniel Brown

read the complete manuscript and offered valuable refinements. Useful comments on sections of the work were made by Bradford Westerfield, Arnold Horelick, Alton Frye, Cedric Tarr, Roger Fontaine, and Charles Planck.

Other colleagues and mentors who will recognize some of their insights shaping my analysis are Ross N. Berkes, Morton Kaplan, Herbert Dinnerstein, Morton Halperin, Marshall Shulman, Mohinder S. Bedi, Reginald Bartholomew, R. Samuels Brown, Bernard Brodie, and Leslie Gelb.

I am grateful to Francis O. Wilcox, Dean of the Johns Hopkins School of Advanced International Studies, for providing me with the opportunity of offering a seminar on the subject of the book during the time of its writing. To the vigorous graduate students in this seminar I owe special thanks for stimulating me to sharpen and clarify my arguments.

A good part of my learning experience in this effort has been as a participant in the metamorphosis of the raw manuscript into finished book, under the directorship of Robert Tilley and editorship of Cody Barnard of Columbia University Press.

Steven Darrow and Eliot Abraham provided indispensable research assistance. Elaine Clark, Denise Brinig, Rosalie Fonoroff, and Frances Marra helped in various tasks of manuscript preparation. Miscellaneous environmental stimuli were provided by Lisa Dorthea and Nell Lisabeth.

I will refrain from including a catalogue of my wife's many sacrifices without which the book would have been longer in the writing. The benefits of our domestic partnership are considerable, but time gained is the least of them. Rose is a most stimulating colleague. The opportunity to do much of my work at home during the writing year did not hasten the effort. It enriched the content.

Seyom Brown

Washington, D.C.
November, 1967

CONTENTS

CONTENTS

PART III
THE EISENHOWER ERA

PART IV
THE KENNEDY-JOHNSON YEARS

THE FACES OF POWER

In the words of Edmund Burke, we sit on a "conspicuous stage," and the whole world marks our demeanor.

We have an opportunity to be worthy of that role.

JOHN F. KENNEDY

POWER WIELDED AND

POWER PERCEIVED

Power lies in the eye of the beholder. Its different forms appeal to different men in different measure; we can agree on a broad definition, however.

The powerful are those who have large purposes and can accomplish them.

To accomplish their purposes men usually require some degree of consent from other men. The ability to induce consent from others is the essence of political power. But the ingredients of this ability, and their appropriate weights for each situation cannot be set forth in a tidy formula.

This multifaceted and elusive nature of power is not always taken into account in talking of the power of nations. Often national power is regarded in purely physical terms—the ultimate measure being the nation's potential to inflict destruction upon other nations. We sometimes forget that this physical capability is only one of the attributes of power among nations, since the people to be affected have wills, and these wills may determine action in advance of physical force or despite it. The power of one individual or society over another is determined profoundly by the willingness of each to give in to the desires of the other.

The actual resort to physical force in order to exercise power is of-

1

ten a sign of powerlessness in other means of influence. And in a contest between two men or nations equal in physical force, it will be the additional capabilities for affecting the human will that will determine who is the more powerful. Even those inferior in physical force have sometimes proven themselves superior in overall human power by virtue of their ability to sustain their wills and achieve their purposes against the desires of a physically superior adversary. As in the case of Gandhi, this was done by modifying the will and purposes of the opponent.

Statesmen know that power, to be effective, must be respected, and that respect is accorded out of a compound of reasons—fear of the consequences of opposition, admiration of practical accomplishments, admiration of essential qualities of being, and shared ethical premises. A nation's arsenal of power must have variety if it is to be perceived by other nations as worthy of respect. The most successful statesmen nurture a variegated inventory, and have been as reluctant to deplete its non-physical as its physical components. They have known that one cannot predict which will be the critical ingredients of power in any future conflict of purposes—with traditional friends, implacable opponents, or the initially uncommitted. These other groups of people are the objects in the environment that may have to be influenced for a nation to accomplish its purposes. And they shall not be moved unless they will.

The premise that national power is a many-faceted thing informs the analysis in the pages to follow. My effort is to expose the premises of power held by those entrusted with wielding it internationally on behalf of our society. The central question is: what means have our statesmen considered necessary and most appropriate to affect the international environment so as to realize the nation's basic purposes? My thesis is that the significant changes in foreign policy from Truman to Johnson are attributable, for the most part, to changes in the premises of power, rather than to changes in the concept of the nation's basic purposes. Where the analysis seems to exhibit a critical tone it will be the result of my evaluation that the premises of power held by our foreign-policy makers or suggested by their actions were at the time overly focused on too narrow a set of attributes of the nation's strength and influence. The implied criticism in such cases is not of the purposes and values of the responsible officials, but of their premises of power.

Of course any such analysis of the judgments of the nation's responsible policymakers is tentative and speculative. The public disclosures by officials of *all* the considerations influencing their decisions are necessarily incomplete. Nor is there any logical formula by which one may infer, with a high degree of confidence, the basic assumptions underlying observed official behavior. Thus the analysis in the following pages should be understood to carry, attached to each proposition, the critical caveat:—*assuming* the public record reflects, without essential gaps or distortions, the privately held premises of officials responsible for final decision. This caveat in itself is necessarily imprecise, since "the public record" is not something set forth on parchment with major and subordinate clauses neatly numbered. The record comprises unexplained behavior as well as statements, and the latter emanate from many sources and often seem to contradict one another.

The search for the official premises of power does not stop at the printed word on the public document. It must go behind the words and between the lines to seek out the operational premises, those which operate when important decisions are made, those which *make the difference* at forks in the road. We can observe that certain roads have been taken rather than others, and we can hear the official explanations. But between the official explanations and the observed behavior there often remains a hazy area: the articulated premises do not lead inevitably to the actions taken; one cannot deduce the specific behavior from the stated premises, nor can one infer the premises backward from the particular actions. Many premises remain inarticulated, not necessarily out of any official design to hide them, but because space and time do not seem to permit a statement of their sometimes complicated interconnections, and also because actions by governments, no less than by individuals, are often the result of conditioned responses, of pre-programing, in which the actor "knows" what he should do but is unable to summon forward at the time the complete set of premises governing his immediate response. One of the jobs of the analyst of policy is to search out these "memory tapes" of the official bureaucracy so that we may all become aware of the underlying assumptions of our national acts and ask ourselves, ever anew, whether we buy these assumptions today.

Part I tries to ferret out the constant assumptions of United States foreign policy from Truman to Johnson. A central official assumption

3

will be shown to be that the power of the United States to realize its purposes requires us to assure that no potential adversary or combination of adversaries will gain sufficient power to impose their purposes upon us. In other words, the "balance of power" must not be tipped in our disfavor. Parts II through IV will attempt to show how this assumption, however persistent, has produced significantly different foreign policies from Truman to Johnson. Part of the explanation for change will be traced to changing premises about the capabilities, intentions, and identity of those who would oppose what we want. But accompanying these changing premises, and informing them, is the more subtle, yet potentially more significant fluctuation in the premises about power itself.

In its relations with other nations this country, from its very beginning as a republic, has had one overwhelming direction which it has gone and from which it has never varied.

DEAN ACHESON

A consistent and dependable national course must have a base broader than the particular beliefs of those who from time to time hold office.

JOHN FOSTER DULLES

It is quite true that the central themes of American foreign policy are more or less constant. They derive from the kind of people we are . . . and from the shape of the world situation.

Nevertheless we are today in a highly revolutionary world situation. Change is the dominant theme.

DEAN RUSK

PART I

THE SOURCES AND LIMITS OF CONSTANCY

CHAPTER ONE

THE IRREDUCIBLE NATIONAL
INTEREST AND BASIC PREMISES ABOUT
WORLD CONDITIONS

National interest is more important than ideology.

JOHN F. KENNEDY

Between the lofty reiteration of outworn platitudes and the glib profession of radical alternatives are found the deepest and most persistent reasons for basic United States foreign policy. Those who fear the smallest concession to criticism will topple the whole edifice of postwar foreign policy, and those who are trying to topple it with adolescent iconoclasm, mistake the clichés for the underlying concept of the national interest. This underlying concept was indeed the source of many policy formulations—particularly the rhetoric—now regarded as Cold War clichés. But the concept antedated the Cold War and will likely outlast it. It set the boundaries to and had much to do with shaping the character of the foreign commitments and programs of each of the Administrations described in this book. Without his profound appreciation of this same underlying concept John F. Kennedy would not have been able to accomplish as much as he did in his efforts to pry loose the barnacled formulations of the fifteen years previous to his Presidency. And only such an appreciation will allow current and future national leaders to face squarely the awful choices ahead.

The concept of an irreducible national interest is imprecise, but essential, and deeply rooted in the American political experience.

Each of the men whose constituency has been the national electorate have been intensely aware that they were bound by an historical, Constitutional, and current political obligation to service, first and foremost, at least two basic objectives of the national society: its physical survival; and the perpetuation of something called the American Way of Life—in the familiar words, "to secure the blessings of liberty to ourselves and our posterity."

Although it was fashionable in some circles during the years 1959 to 1961 to debate the proposition "Better Dead than Red" or its converse, highly placed officials were reluctant to enter into the speculative discourse, however morally instructive. The Presidential view of the matter has been constant from Truman to Johnson: the primary task is to assure that such a choice never has to be made. Foreign commitments and national security programs have been constrained by firm insistence from the White House that *both* survival and the non-totalitarian condition of the nation are to be placed ahead of all other objectives.

A third imperative with almost as much compelling force upon highest policy levels has been the injunction to promote the general welfare, or the economic well-being of the whole society. From the vantage point of the Presidency, there is a good deal of political steam in the passion of the populace to have its liberties and eat well too.

The highest officials, in their need to erect their foreign policies on the bedrock of historical consensus, often attempt to show how their actions derive from these Constitutional and constant political imperatives: we seek today, as we did in Washington's time, explains President Johnson, "to protect the life of our nation, to preserve the liberty of our citizens, and to pursue the happiness of our people. This is the touchstone of our world policy." [1] Such resounding claims are more than ritualistic bell-ringing. They are reflective of Johnson's perception that the least common denominator of political demand, from the national constituency at large, is that the President pursue *simultaneously* the nation's interest in its own survival and those conditions which allow for the perpetuation of the nation's essential sociopolitical patterns.

This perception is sustained by the dominant themes of debate between the two great political parties. The party in opposition will often accuse the party in the White House of sacrificing too much of one basic value in the service of another. But the premises of critic and defender alike are that all of the basic values—survival, liberty, and economic well-being—can and ought to be pursued at the same time; and that this irreducible triumvirate of interest must not be subordinated to other considerations.

Thus, the strongest criticisms by Democrats against the Eisenhower Administration involved the charge that the nation's defense requirements were being neglected because of a slavish pursuit of a balanced budget. The President, also fending off those in his own party who wanted to reduce defense expenditures still more, defended the existing size and structure of the armed forces with the argument that "to build less would expose the nation to aggression. To build excessively, under the influence of fear, could defeat our purposes and impair or destroy the very freedom and economic system our military defenses are designed to protect." [2]

The concept of an irreducible national interest provides no specific guidance for its implementation—therefore the debate. The point is that, in the offices of ultimate national responsibility, the concept is considerably more than a cliché. Too vague to determine programs and specific commitments, it nonetheless constrains the range of policy choices. Although the concept is dependent for its programmatic expressions upon the particular Administration's definition of the essential American liberties (how much freedom of enterprise? how much freedom of speech?), premises on what makes the economy tick, and analyses of the capabilities and intentions of potential foreign adversaries, the basic Presidential impulse to lead the nation away from situations where ultimate choices between survival, liberty, and welfare have to be made is in large measure responsible for the central thread of continuity in foreign policy from Truman to Johnson.

No less important a reason for the continuity in foreign policy from Truman to Johnson has been the persistence of the view that the primary threats to this irreducible national interest are the spread of International Communism and another world war. The constancy as well as the changes in foreign policy which have occurred may be read as the theme and variations of the basic objective of avoiding one of these threats without bringing on the other. The two prongs of this basic objective are derived from a set of premises about world conditions, and what these conditions seem to require of the United States in order to perpetuate itself and its Way of Life. This set of critical premises—those which have persisted in top policy levels over the past twenty years and have had a pervasive impact on specific commitments and actions—can be stated as follows:

A. The Soviet Union is motivated (how strongly is a variable) to be the dominant world power, and eventually to fashion the world into a single political system based on the Soviet model. The premise that the Soviets are motivated only to secure their society against outside interference has never been bought at the highest levels of the United States government since the Second World War. However, there has been constant questioning, and occasional diplomatic probing, to determine the extent to which the actions of the Soviets to implement expansionist motives are constrained by their perception that such action may place the security of the Soviet Union in danger and/or take away from their ability to achieve domestic economic and social goals. There apparently has been increasing receptivity in White House and State Department circles, since the Cuban missile crisis, the Test Ban, and the widening of the Sino-Soviet split, toward the premise that the Soviets have seen the futility of expansionist adventures and would now like to turn their energies to domestic development tasks.[3] But varying interpretations are made of the presumed Soviet constriction of their external power drive. It may, as some analysts suggest, be the natural result of the maturing of their sociopolitical system—a supplanting of the revolutionary leadership by a bureaucratic generation most interested in efficiency and political stability. Or, it may be primarily the result of the application of the Leninist stratagem of "two steps forward, one step backward," in the hope that a relaxation of international tension now will lead to a slackening in the West, during which time the Soviet Union will be tending to the reorientation of its economy and technology in preparation for the next phase of hostile competition. There are many versions of these theses, each suggesting a somewhat different set of United States policy responses and initiatives to the Soviet Union. Later chapters will elaborate such attempts by the United States to test the international waters to see if any of these theses should become the operating premise for U.S. foreign policy. For present purposes it is only necessary to take note of this turbulence beneath the surface constancy of the basic premise that the Soviets would be expanding if we, the United States, were not containing them. The desirability of containing the Soviets at least within their present sphere is not in question; but the appropriate role for the United States in this containment function has increasingly become a central issue of policy.

B. Another critical premise underlying the observed constancy in foreign policy from Truman to Johnson has been that in another world war the United States would quickly become a prime target for mass destruction. Early in the period the technology of warfare, plus the obvious strategies deduced from the new technology, were seen to be bringing about a situation in which the United States could not become involved in war against its largest rival without thereby placing the lives of millions of American civilians in jeopardy. By 1948 there was consensus among United States scientists and military planners that it would be only a matter of a few years before the Soviet Union developed such a capability. In the interim the Soviet Union could compensate for its strategic inferiority vis-à-vis the United States (we could already reach the Soviet Union with weapons of mass destruction from our overseas bases) by holding "hostage" the urban populations of Western Europe. By the mid-1950s Soviet thermonuclear developments plus great improvements in their long-range strategic bomber fleet made the vulnerability of the continental United States in a world war an operating premise of military planners and top foreign policy officials. The avoidance of another world war was seen to be equal in importance to preventing the expansion of Communism. "Deterrence" became for a time the magic word, presumably eliminating the potential conflict in priority between preventing strategic attack on the United States and containing the Soviets. But the pursuit of peace could no longer be dismissed as mere rhetoric. World peace, meaning basically the avoidance of general war between the United States and the Soviet Union, had become irrevocably an *essential* policy objective—that is, a necessary means of preserving the irreducible national interest.

C. Yet prevailing premises about the distribution of international power since the Second World War would not allow the pursuit of world peace to take *precedence* over the containment of Communism.

11

The war had left the Soviet Union surrounded by power vacuums where previously it had been hemmed in by constellations of great power. The only source of great countervailing power now was the United States. Therefore, the desire to prevent the extension of Soviet power (assuming the Soviets wanted to expand the territorial basis of their power) carried with it a responsibility for the United States to make its power available to dissuade or block the Soviets. At first, the United States tried to dissuade the Soviets from expanding by appeals to the spirit of the Grand Alliance and the decent opinions of mankind as reflected in the United Nations Charter (there was no expectation that the collective security machinery of the United Nations could be used as a coercive instrument against the Soviet Union). Under the immediate postwar assumption that the Soviets, requiring foreign capital for reconstruction, were anxious to maintain the goodwill of the West, the Truman Administration early tried by tough talk alone to induce the Soviets into a more benign posture. But as it appeared that Stalin was more anxious to take advantage of opportunities to expand his territorial base than to maintain the goodwill of the West, the Truman Administration soon began to seek means of redressing the local imbalances of power around the Soviet periphery. At first, these efforts were concentrated in economic and social measures to reconstruct wartorn Europe and Japan. But Soviet military power plays against Iran, Turkey, Greece, and Czechoslovakia brought into prominence at the White House level premises of the critical effect of military balances, local and global, on the Soviets' propensity to expand. The Berlin blockade of 1948 apparently sealed the case for Truman, and Secretary of State Acheson was given the go-ahead to make explicit in the North Atlantic Treaty the unequivocal commitment of United States military power to counter any Soviet attempts to exploit their military superiority in Europe. In exchange for this commitment of American power the West Europeans were expected to work urgently to build up their own military power, so that the burden would not fall disproportionately on the United States. The willingness to forego even our commitment to world peace, if indeed that were necessary to prevent the Soviets from forcibly adding unto themselves the vast power potential of Western Europe, was by 1949 an explicit premise of United States foreign policy. Such explicitness was possible with respect to Western Europe because its fall to the Soviets could be defined as tantamount to "surrender." The Soviets would become the dominant world power, and could eventually overpower the United States itself.

D. Thus, the "balance of power" became the critical concept for determining the priority to be given in any specific situation to containment of Communism or the avoidance of world war, should these two objectives appear impossible to pursue at the same time. Each of the four postwar Administrations have agreed on at least this much: if a Communist success in a given conflict would critically undermine the power of the non-Communist world to dissuade the Communist world from further advances, then, presumably, the balance of power itself was at stake, and, since, by extension, this meant the survival of the United States, there was no question of where the national interest would lie. In such situations, peace would have to give way temporarily to the active containment of Communism, even if the temporary breakdown of peace would place the United States in danger of direct attack.

E. But none of these premises provided sufficient advance guidance for basic policy in situations where the overall U.S.–Soviet power balance was not thought to be immediately at stake. If the Soviets were only making a limited grab, would it be worth a world war to frustrate them? What if another Communist nation were attempting to extend its power—would we, should we, automatically equate such an attempt with an increment to the Soviet side of the global balance of power? In global balance of power terms, how should we regard the coming to power *within* nations of supposedly indigenous Communist movements? The fact that the United States, through successive Administrations, has not been able to answer such questions *in principle* in advance of unfolding situations has been in large measure responsible for some of our major policy crises over the past two decades. The decision not to bring our coercive power to bear to prevent Mao Tse-tung's victory over Chiang Kai-shek; the expenditure of blood and treasure in Korea to rectify the gross miscalculation of the Soviets that we would not be willing to intervene there to oppose aggression; the Truman-MacArthur controversy; the great debate over "massive retaliation" vs. "flexible response," and particularly its expression in NATO policy; the Quemoy and Matsu crises of the 1950s; the Bay of Pigs, the Cuban missile crisis, and the chronic problem of how to deal with Castro; the Dominican military intervention of 1965; and, of course, Vietnam—all of these have produced as much dissensus as consensus in the nation, precisely because of the existence of varied concepts of international "power."

There has been constancy at one very important level of analysis and policy. Premises of the irreducible national interest, and basic assumptions about world conditions have given persistence to the two-pronged objective of attempting to prevent the spread of International Communism and to prevent the outbreak of a Third World War. As perceived by those responsible for the conduct of United States foreign policy, this has meant primarily influencing the Soviets and the Communist Chinese not to try to expand their territorial base, and influencing other nations to pursue policies that would enhance their resistance to control by these two Communist giants.

But, the major issues have been over means, not objectives. The problem has been essentially a problem of *power*. The difficult question has been what *kinds* of power—what capabilities—are needed to accomplish the agreed upon objectives of the nation. The varying answers given to this question by each of the Administrations and by factions within the Administrations will be detailed in Parts II through IV.

The objectives of containing Communism and preserving peace do not exhaust the range of objectives animating United States foreign policy since the Second World War. These have been emphasized first, however, because they have been generally accepted during the period as practically inevitable derivatives from the irreducible national interest of survival in a non-totalitarian condition.

The nation has also considered itself committed to interests of a more altruistic nature, and much of the story of the past two decades centers on attempts to reconcile the requirements of implementing these altruistic interests with the requirements of self-preservation. But again, the major arbiter of choice has proven to be the concept of the global balance of power.

CHAPTER TWO

LARGER INTERESTS
AND THE BALANCE-OF-POWER
CONSIDERATION

We have no taste for empire. We do not wish to establish a Pax Americana. Nor do we desire to act as the world's gendarme. We do not regard the dominant role of American power in so many parts of the world as a permanent—or satisfactory—state of affairs.

GEORGE BALL

The liberties and well-being of other peoples have been persistent major concerns of United States foreign policy since the Second World War. Officials of the Truman Administration regarded our sponsorship of the United Nations, the Truman Doctrine, the European Recovery Program, and Point IV as consistent with American idealism as well as self-interest. John Foster Dulles preached anti-Communism as a universal moral imperative. President Kennedy, unsentimental realist he is supposed to have been, sounded the trumpet for "a grand and global alliance" against the "common enemies of man: tyranny, poverty, disease, and war itself." His generation of Americans, said Kennedy, felt an obligation to work toward a "more fruitful life for all mankind":

To those peoples in the huts and villages of half the globe struggling to break the bonds of mass misery, we pledge our best efforts to help them help themselves, for whatever period is required—not because the commu-

15

nists may be doing it, not because we seek their votes, but *because it is right*.[1]

And there can be little doubt that Lyndon Johnson believes he is giving voice to the American mainstream when he claims:

> Of course security and welfare shape our policies. But much of the energy of our efforts has come from moral purpose.
> It is right that the strong should help the weak defend their freedom.
> It is right that the wealthy should help the poor emerge from their hunger.
> It is right that help and understanding should flow from friendship and loyalty.
> It is right that nations should be free from the coercion of others.
> That these truths may coincide with interest does not make them less true.[2]

The difficulty, of course, has come not when such moral purposes coincide with interest, but precisely in those situations or programs where they would suggest different policies than what seem to be required by the nation's interest in its own security and welfare.

In the main, our foreign policy leadership since the Second World War has been fortunate in the large measure of coincidence between the nation's self-interest and the nation's altruistic ideals.[3] With the rival superpower propounding a monolithic global society, the traditional American commitment to *national* self-determination, now enshrined in the United Nations Charter, could be used as an ideology to firm up the will of other peoples to resist absorption in the Communist bloc. And with Communist regimes propounding and acting upon the doctrine that a highly regimented populace unquestioningly carrying out policies made at the top is necessary for modernization, the doctrine that governments derive their just powers from the consent of the governed could be one of our most powerful weapons of containment— and possibly even liberation. As Secretary of State Acheson counseled:

> Our first line of action . . . is to demonstrate that our own faith in freedom is a burning and a fighting faith. . . . And we don't restrict this belief to freedom for ourselves.
> If we are clear about this, if we are full of passion about this, then we have in our hearts and minds the most revolutionary and dynamic concept in human history and one which properly strikes terror into every dictator, to every tyrant who would attempt to regiment and depress men anywhere. . . .[4]

Or as put by John Foster Dulles:

The great weakness of despotism has been, is, and always will be its disregard of the rights of man. Despotism can always be routed if free men exploit that weakness. If our example can illumine . . . the great advantages of a free society, then Soviet Communism will lose its deceptive appeal. Furthermore, it will lose its grip upon the enslaved whom it now holds. . . .

. . . I agree with . . . Walter Reuther when he said: "The quest for liberty constitutes the eventual victorious challenge to the totalitarian system."

This quest for liberty must be simultaneously pursued on three fronts—the home front, the free-world front, and the captive-world front.[5]

Characteristically, President Kennedy exhibited a more chastened view: "It is one of the ironies of our time that the techniques of a harsh and repressive system should be able to instill discipline and ardor in its servants—while the blessings of liberty have too often stood for privilege, materialism and a life of ease." [6] Still he had faith that with a national rededication to our deepest ideals, and a willingness to make the hard decisions and sacrifices that such dedication would require, the tide would eventually turn. For in the last analysis, mankind will see that "we can welcome diversity—the Communists cannot . . . we offer a world of choice—they offer a world of coercion. And the way of the past shows clearly enough that freedom, not coercion, is the wave of the future." [7]

Yet at times the magnitude of assistance required to significantly help others pursue their freedom and welfare has appeared too costly. It was 1947 when President Truman proclaimed the doctrine that "it must be the policy of the United States to support free peoples who are resisting attempted subjugation by armed minorities or outside pressures." But the universally-phrased doctrine was applied only in particular cases between 1947 and the summer of 1950. It was applied in Greece and Turkey—the crisis situations which prompted the doctrine. And the $17 billion program for European economic recovery was portrayed as its required corollary. Under cover of the same principle, Berlin was sustained by the American airlift in 1948–49, and the United States committed itself to the defense of Western Europe by the North Atlantic Treaty. But during this same postwar period the Administration did not attempt to apply the Truman Doctrine to events taking place in Eastern Europe or in China.

With respect to Eastern Europe, recalls Walt Rostow, "It was worth protesting diplomatically against Stalin's course of action and maintaining a *de jure* position of opposition to Communist takeover, but it was not worth risking American blood to prevent the outcome." [8] Similarly, a Communist regime in China was not at all desirable to those in control of U.S. foreign policy, and President Truman did all he reasonably could to prevent it. But his liberty to commit American resources to the struggle, Truman felt, was limited. As the situation deteriorated, the only remaining alternative to a Communist takeover appeared to be a large-scale intervention with American forces to bail out Chiang Kai-shek. Truman, certain that "the American people would never stand for such an undertaking," [9] liquidated our commitment, and helped evacuate Chiang to Formosa. After these events, the Republicans blamed the Communist absorption of Eastern Europe and China on the Truman Administration, but the opposition party was notably deficient, at the time of their occurrence, in suggestions for larger United States involvements in either case.

A Republican Administration got its chance during the 1953 East German uprisings, and then again during the Hungarian crisis of 1956, to demonstrate how high a price it would be willing to pay to support the liberty of other peoples. Again, there were certain impassable limits.

These limits are set by the irreducible national interest—the survival of the American Way of Life *here*—and premises about world conditions directly affecting this interest. Our larger interests in the liberties and well-being of other peoples has been pursued where such action is perceived as required by, or supportive of, the basic national interest. We have also expended energy and resources, in limited amounts, to support the liberties and well-being of other peoples, even though not prompted by calculations of self-interest, for the sufficient reason that "it is right." But there has been constancy over the period in Presidential refusals to service these larger interests when the action required was perceived as contrary to policies deemed necessary to secure the blessings of liberty to *ourselves* and *our* posterity.

Thus, although the objective of containment of Communist expansion was often explained to the people as motivated by our deepest desires to preserve and expand the area of freedom, the ultimate calculations underlying decisions to oppose particular Communist provocations have been in terms of the consequences of the contemplated action or inaction for the physical security of the United States, and the freedoms and economic well-being of citizens of the United States.

If the expected costs of United States intervention were very high, and the benefits problematical—as in Eastern Europe, China, and Cuba during the Bay of Pigs—valor gave way, painfully, to inaction dictated by prudence. But, where the consequences of inaction were foreseen as a disadvantageous change in the global balance of power, meaning that the United States might soon lose the wherewithal to secure its own survival in a non-totalitarian condition, decisions to counter the provocation with all that was required have been made, unflinchingly, even though the expected costs in human and material resources have been high, and, on occasion, the irreducible national interest itself has been risked.

The persisting United States commitment to defend a Western presence in Berlin (even though the balance of military force there is against us) and President Kennedy's willingness to establish a very dangerous direct confrontation with the Soviets to compel a removal of their missiles from Cuba are examples of high risks taken in "the defense of freedom" *when* the global balance of power is thought to be at stake. I am not arguing that these decisions were inevitable. I do argue that such decisions are practically inevitable when a President feels the global balance of power is at stake, because a global imbalance against us is regarded as putting our survival at the mercy of our opponents. As there is no absolute measure of power, one President may see the global balance of power at stake in a situation where another may not. Thus the premises of power held by the various Administrations is a crucial variable in explaining the changes as well as the constancy in United States foreign policy.

The more controversial decisions have involved situations where there is a highly ambiguous or tenuous relationship perceived between the liberty and well-being of others and the global balance of power, and where programs thought capable of significantly helping those in need would be very costly.

Such considerations determined the acceptance at the close of the Korean War of a stalemate based on the status quo ante rather than a pressing for "victory" to allow the United Nations to administer nationwide elections and reunify the country. The original decision to intervene to reverse the North Korean drive to take over the whole country, even though this task might be costly for us, was undertaken out of a notion that to allow the Communists to succeed in their invasion would drastically undermine the non-Communist side of the power balance. A weighty ingredient of Western power, particularly as expressed in the new North Atlantic Treaty, was thought to be the faith of our alliance partners that the United States would honor its pledges to oppose aggression. Thus, indirectly, but rather clearly to the American leadership, our own security—dependent upon Western Europe being on *our* side of the balance of power—was seen to be threatened. Consequently, it was very important to oppose the North Koreans with whatever force was necessary to throw them back at least to the line of demarcation. As it began to look as if we could defeat them in the North too, without a significantly larger operation than was already under way, our objective was temporarily expanded to include the freedom and reunification of all of Korea. But the intervention of the Communist Chinese changed the calculations of the cost of implementing this larger interest, which, after all, was not seen to be required by balance of power considerations; indeed, the maintenance of the global balance was thought to require that we husband our resources for the possibility of a greater battle with the Soviet Union over Western Europe (see Part II, Chapter 5).

The lack of clarity over just which American interests were really involved did not prevent the Eisenhower Administration from assisting in the overthrow of a Guatemalan government infiltrated by pro-Soviet Communists. But in this case, the assessment of costs to the United States of the indirect assistance we rendered was made out to be very small. On the other hand, we continued to tolerate the existence of not very "free" regimes and depressed standards of living in many of our southern neighbors, since these conditions did not at the time seem to affect the balance of power, and hence United States security, one way or the other. Moreover, until the Act of Bogotá in 1960, we defended our inaction to support the political liberties and well-being of Latin Americans as consistent with the principle of "nonintervention" (self-determination) as expressed in the Inter-American treaties. The doctrine of nonintervention got fuzzy again as Castro solidified his ties with Moscow. The Kennedy Administration, inheriting the contingency plan of its predecessor, began what it thought was a low-level-of-effort counterinsurgency operation, somewhat on the Guatemalan model. But as a Communist regime in Cuba was not thought to be a crucial factor in the global balance of power, the operation was called off as soon as the costs of carrying it through were seen to have been vastly underestimated. Also, part of the uncalculated cost in the plan as originally handed to President Kennedy was the likely effect on the social reform elements in Latin America whom Kennedy was trying to court; and thus under Kennedy's premises of power, the global balance, if invoked at all as a consideration, might seem to be adversely affected even if the United States were successful in forcibly bringing down Castro.

The ambivalent United States reactions toward prospects of Communist successes in Indochina also illustrate the problems of policy when unclear global power considerations are cojoined with high costs of commitment. We assisted the French effort to keep all of Indochina out of Ho Chi Minh's hands, so long as this involved a relatively small expenditure of our material resources. Later, as the French effort collapsed, the possibility that we might decide to intervene led Eisenhower to talk for a time as if the balance of power itself was at stake —a contention hotly disputed by many of our allies and by the opposition party in Congress. After the 1954 truce, an aid program was reinstituted for South Vietnam, for the ostensible purpose of bringing about conditions that would allow for eventual nationwide self-determination. But the principle of self-determination would have to be postponed until the population could be secured against coercion by Ho's agents. During the Kennedy Administration there was reluctance to define the outcome of the continuing struggle between the Vietnamese Communists and non-Communists in stark balance of power terms. It was "their war," said Kennedy, although we would do all we reasonably could to help the non-Communist side. Furthermore, our aid was conditioned on at least a minimum respect being shown for civil liberties by the South Vietnamese regime. Later, as our help changed into direct United States involvement, carrying with it the implication of our own unlimited commitment to the maintenance of a non-Communist South Vietnam, the Johnson Administration once again defined the stakes of the conflict in global balance of power terms. Yet this definition remained under considerable dispute in the United States as the costs of implementing the commitment rose.

The foreign assistance program as a whole has been operating right in the center of this hazy area, where often the relation of any specific component of the program to basic United States security interests is not at all clear, and therefore the diversion of domestic resources to such foreign ends is disputed by interest groups within and without the government who would like comparable amounts diverted to them.

The Eisenhower Administration, with all its rhetoric about our devotion to freedom as a universal imperative, found a way, temporarily, of avoiding a systematic policy dialogue on the relationships between foreign aid, the character of recipient regimes, political liberty, and basic United States interests by making foreign assistance, for the most part, the reward of military alignment. The military balance of power was easily connected with United States security interests, and military allies were facilely portrayed as weights on our side of the balance. If economic and military assitance was necessary to assure the alignment and security of an ally, no additional rationale was necessary. It was sufficient to argue that, dollar for dollar, X amount given to the recipient allies would result in more military manpower and firepower for the non-Communist world than if that same amount were added to the United States military budget. The case within the Administration, as well as the public rationale, for assistance to regimes who preferred to remain nonaligned in the Cold War remained largely undeveloped. Although the need for such a rationale became evident to Eisenhower and Dulles by the end of their first term, the press of events and the inertia of a bureaucracy already geared to programs based on the older premises put a brake on new initiatives.

It remained for the Kennedy Administration to push with vigor a fresh set of premises on the relationship between assistance from the United States, socioeconomic reform, political democracy, and our own security (see Part IV). Enthusiasm in the White House still had to deal with sluggishness in a Congress responsive to parochial demands, and skepticism from career administrators and diplomats more comfortable in dealings with foreign "Establishment" types than with the bristling revolutionary nationalists of the nonaligned world. The Alliance for Progress and the manifest interest by Kennedy in the new leaders of Africa produced no significant changes in the scale of our overall foreign assitance effort, nor any major reallocation of disbursements within the program. But even if the visible effects of the new orientation to foreign assistance were still primarily on the symbolic level, the realistic joining by Kennedy, MacNamara, and Rusk of our altruistic concerns for the liberties and well-being of others with a sophisticated analysis of international power relationships struck a responsive chord in the country's growing constituency of businessmen and professionals with an active interest in world affairs.

The percolation of these premises to popular levels where they could generate political steam, and therefore appropriations, was another matter. At the time of this writing the popular foreign policy issues were again regressing to "guns vs. butter" simplifications. The dollar and manpower requirements of the Great Society at home were competitive with the dollar and manpower requirements for maintaining our commitment in Vietnam, and the latter were most immediately oriented to military tasks.

The active implementation of our national belief that all men have a right to choose the leaders and the laws by which they will be governed has, at times, involved us in serious disagreement with countries whom we consider allies against Communist forms of totalitarianism. Here too, however, the litmus test for determining our predominant national interest has tended to be the balance of power consideration.

The anti-colonial revolution since the Second World War has for the most part proceeded according to its own inner dynamic, with the United States and the Soviet Union bystanders. However, the pace of adaptations by the old metropolitan nations to the assertion by their former wards of the right to self-governance *has* been subject to United States influence, the outstanding example being the Dutch acquiescence in Indonesian independence. Also, the intensification of nationalist demands for freedom from colonial overlordship was in part a function of the "moral" support given to this global movement by *both* of the superpowers. In practically all of the colonial dependencies there were Communist agents at work, but the successful leaders in most of the new nationalist parties got their revolutionary motivation from studies of the American and French revolutions and learned their socialism from Fabian professors. Lenin's theories of imperialism and capitalist exploitation were only part of the brew, which the Nehrus, the Nkrumahs, and the Sukarnos exploited with telling political effect. Political factions in their countries who were dominated by orthodox Marxist-Leninist beliefs lacked the emotional appeal of the hybrid new nationalistic ideologies. Even the Soviet Union soon recognized this and, by the late 1940s, began to court the non-Communist nationalists, often at the expense of indigenous Communist parties.

Thus, for reasons of traditional sentiment and for the hard-headed consideration of not allowing the Soviets to parade as the sole sponsors of anti-colonialism, the Truman Administration and its successors have felt it necessary to identify the United States with the aspirations of the peoples of the Third World. Each has tried, in its fashion, to give vocal support to the principle of self-determination, and some tangible evidence (in the form of technical and economic assistance) of our determination to have the new nations succeed in their experiments with democratic self-rule. But these genuine efforts to support the new nationalisms of the Third World have been circumscribed, particularly in the Truman and Eisenhower periods, by the emphasis given to the securing of the *military* components of the global balance of power. The military potential of a revived Western European technology, a girdle of military allies to prevent easy expansion by the Communist powers, and a system of far-flung bases to bring our strategic striking power within reach of the Soviet heartland were regarded as priority objectives. As these assets were, in many cases, to be provided by nations with overseas dependencies some deference to the sensibilities and the material interests of the colonial powers was thought to be a requirement of our statecraft.

Fortunately, for this purpose, the ideology of national sovereignty embodied in the United Nations Charter cut two ways: it provided a rationale for mobilizing efforts to combat Communist subversion and overt aggression; it also provided the legal excuse for refusing to take sides in disputes which fell under the "domestic jurisdiction" of another nation.

Moreover, we had a vital interest, professed and real, in reducing the resort to violence as a means of bringing about change. It was by no means clear *who* in any given anti-colonial uprising, say Algeria, was relying most on violence—those defending the existing system of public order, or those trying to overthrow it. In such circumstances our doctrinaire profession of opposition to violent methods of change was able to buttress our propensity to straddle the fence.

Early in his tenure as Secretary of State, Dulles summed up this central dilemma of U.S. foreign policy which, because of the natural course of events, was to become most intense during the late Eisenhower period:

Perhaps some of you feel that your government is not pushing political liberty as strongly as it should. I can say to you three things:

First, we are pushing for self-government more than appears on the surface.

Secondly, where we exercise restraint it is because of a reasoned conviction that precipitate action would in fact not produce independence but only transition to a captivity far worse than present dependence.

Thirdly, we are alert to the possibility that the Communist threat might grow into an excuse for delay, when it is not an honest reason for delay.

There are good and sufficient reasons why the United States desires, in the United Nations and elsewhere, to show unity with its Western allies. But we have not forgotten that we were the first colony to win independence. And we have not given a blank check to any colonial power.

There is no slightest wavering in our conviction that the orderly transition from colonial to self-governing status should be carried resolutely to a completion.[10]

By the time of the Kennedy Administration most of the old colonial empires had been liquidated, so national self-determination could be professed with less qualification. Still, when it came to risking the loss of the strategic base in the Portuguese Azores, prudence prevailed, and Kennedy and Ambassador Stevenson labored to get the African nationalists to tone down demands for the United Nations to apply sanctions against the Salazar regime unless independence was granted to Angola and Mozambique.

Finally, in many of our relationships with the poorer nations our desire to act in accord with our larger altruistic interests—independent of considerations of self-interest or the power struggle vis-à-vis the Communists—produced additional dilemmas of a practical and philosophical nature. When it has come to fashioning concrete policy out of these beliefs, each of the postwar Administrations has been bedeviled by the potential contradictions between:

25

A. our interest in the rights of national societies to determine in their own way their own form of government (a pluralistic world society; Articles I and II of the UN Charter);

B. our interests in social justice based upon a respect for the dignity and rights of each individual human being (Part II, Universal Declaration of Human Rights);

C. our interest in the eradication of those socioeconomic conditions forcing portions of the human race to live in physical misery (Point IV of 1949 Presidential Inaugural Address; Charter of Punta Del Este).

Which of these interests should we put *first?* In our rhetoric these ideals are placed side by side, with the implication that they can and ought to be pursued *simultaneously.* This is a natural extrapolation from our country's own experience, where the demand for self-government was made by men committed to the rights of individuals, and an egalitarian social ethos grew in an environment of abundance.

But many of the poorer nations of the world are run by oligarchies anxious to hold on to their social and material privileges. Economic assistance to such nations without "political strings" attached has sometimes resulted in an increase in a nation's per capita productivity and income; but often it has also perpetuated a system of social injustice. Yet it has been against our inclinations to *intervene,* by withholding or withdrawing economic assistance until major social reforms are first implemented. The Alliance for Progress made a move in this direction, but gingerly.

In other nations there is a commitment to egalitarianism with a vengeance, in which the property rights and civil liberties are trod under heel. Yet with our traditional optimism, we have been receptive to claims that such suspensions of constitutional processes are only temporary, and may—in some cases—be the necessary price for rapid socioeconomic development. We have been less willing to grant the benefit of the doubt to Communist as opposed to non-Communist reformers (such as Ayub Kahn). But even with respect to Communist regimes, as long as they seemed to be refraining from interference in the affairs of other nations, we have increasingly regarded them as fit commercial partners and possibly even aid recipients.

The hopeful "answer" to the potentiality for contradiction between our altruistic political, social, and economic interests—the insistence that all of these ought to be pursued simultaneously—has rarely worked out in practice. In attempting to apply this typically American solution to the problems of national development, Truman, Eisenhower, Kennedy, and Johnson have run up against the hard realization that in most of the poorer nations of the world the human and material resources make for very uneven patterns of progress. In most cases an absolute insistence by us that development in political procedures, civil liberties, social reform, and economic productivity go hand-in-hand would constitute a moralistic criterion defeating progress in any of these areas. A more pragmatic attitude, variously groped for by each of the four Administrations of the period, has been difficult to sell to the Congress, however. The Legislature, acting as the broker for constituent domestic interests jealous of any diversion of resources to foreign objectives, needs either a grand moral crusade or a clear and present danger to the nation to forge a consensus in back of altruistic acts. Unable to provide the former, for the reasons just alluded to, the Executive, from Truman to Johnson, has had to fall back on the national security rationale in order to be granted the wherewithal to influence other nations in directions consistent with our larger interests.

The notion that the United States has been conducting its foreign relations as if it were a global social welfare agency and reform school is a myth derived from a reading of the rhetoric without an inspection of actual programs. As sincere as any Administration has been in professing our larger commitment to the well-being and liberties of all peoples, all have tended to decide major foreign policy questions, ultimately, in terms of the irreducible national interest: how will a given action or program affect the *power of the United States* to secure its way of life for at least its own people? What actions and programs are required in order to keep the *power of potential adversaries* below a level at which they could force the United States to choose between its survival and its way of life?

The limiting criteria for decision have remained essentially constant.

But such constancy only sets the boundary to the story. International "power" is a many-faceted thing. The successive Administrations and factions within them have varied in their premises of power—the essential ingredients and most appropriate uses.

Do not be deceived by the strong face, the look of monolithic power that the Communist dictators wear before the outside world. Remember that their power has no basis in consent.

HARRY S. TRUMAN

The course we have chosen . . . involves building military strength, but it requires no less the buttressing of all other forms of power— economic, political, social, and moral.

DEAN ACHESON

PART II

THE TRUMAN ADMINISTRATION

CHAPTER THREE

THE SHATTERING OF EXPECTATIONS

Force is the only thing the Russians understand.

HARRY S. TRUMAN

United States officials emerged from the Second World War in awe of the physical power nations had been able to develop, but with little confidence in the power of nations unilaterally to exercise the self-control required to channel their tremendous physical capabilities to constructive as opposed to destructive purposes. Throughout the government, there was wide consensus that the survival of civilization required the strengthening of transnational institutions of social control, and also, but with somewhat less conviction, the eventual reduction of the amount of destructive power in the hands of individual nations.

To translate these hopes into reality would require the kind of statesmanship which, in the past, had run afoul of strong American attachments to the value of self-reliance. Remembering the fate of Wilson's sponsorship of the League of Nations, the Administration started early this time to fully prepare the public, and particularly the opposition party leadership, for the premises on which the new postwar diplomacy would be based. Delegations to the founding conferences for the United Nations were carefully selected on a bipartisan basis. And, in an appeal to the patriotic, the successful wartime cooperation between members of the Grand Alliance against the Axis Powers was held up as the embryo from which the new organs of international cooperation would evolve.

The premise of continued cooperation among members of the Grand Alliance had two faces: its internal-governmental aspect, where it was viewed as the *most desirable condition* for the building of the new transnational institutions of control; and its public aspect, where the premise of big power cooperation was viewed as a *prediction* that the presumed existing harmony would last. The more complicated attitudes of those in the government were simplified in their efforts to generate public support.

The essentials of the simplified public version were contained in a set of expectations:

A. the expectation that important international disputes would henceforth be settled by reasoned debate leading to an expression of majority will through the United Nations;

B. the expectation that in important international disputes the Big Five (the United States, the Soviet Union, Britain, France, China) would usually find themselves on the same side—i.e., the veto would be an exceptional, rather than a frequently used, device;

C. the expectation that any required sanctions against international lawbreakers would be organized by this international community.

Whether Truman himself was possessed of these expectations as he assumed the Presidency in April 1945 is of less consequence to an understanding of his pre-Korean War foreign policy than the fact that Truman felt the expectations did place constraints on government policy. Too candid a public presentation of the internal government perception of the Soviet drive for power ascendancy might shock the public into total abandonment of the laborious effort to build up transnational institutions. This would be tragic; since such institutions, if strengthened by support of most of the peoples of the globe, were truly regarded by the United States as the *best* hope for peace. Yet without such candor, the public and their representatives in the Congress would probably not approve the stopgap military and economic measures that might be necessary to induce the Soviets to moderate their power drive and become constructive participants in the building of a world order acceptable to the majority of nations.

The effort by Truman's subordinates to reconcile the President's

fears of shattering public expectations with his belief that standing up
to the Russians now might be a precondition for the eventual realization
of these expectations is the central story of the Truman Administration's early groupings toward a coherent foreign policy.

Truman recalls that during the first weeks of his Presidency he gave
much weight to the analysis of Soviet policies conveyed to him by
Averell Harriman, at that time the United States Ambassador to the
Soviet Union. Harriman was urging a reconsideration of our policy toward the Soviet Union, fearing that to some extent existing policy
might be the product of illusions that the Soviets shared our commitments to an international order based on peaceful national self-
determination.

As recounted in Truman's *Memoirs*, the gist of the Harriman analysis as of April 1945 was that Stalin was misinterpreting our generosity
and our desire to cooperate as a signal that the United States would do
nothing to prevent the extension of Soviet control over her neighbors.
The Soviets, reported Harriman, had no wish to break with the United
States, as they needed our aid for their program of postwar reconstruction; but Stalin would not hesitate to push his political frontiers westward if he felt he could do so without serious political challenge. We
had to disabuse Stalin of his illusion of American softness, counseled
Harriman. We could be firm with the Soviets without running serious
risks, since they could not afford to alienate their only source of help.[1]

Truman claims to have bought this evaluation at this early date, and
was disposed to follow Harriman's advice that the way to exert a positive influence on Soviet policy was to be tough with them on specific
postwar issues as they arose. The assumption was, as Truman put it,
"anyway the Russians needed us more than we needed them." [2] The
Soviets, presumably because of their economic needs, had more to lose
than to gain by the collapse of great power amicability. We wished to
preserve an atmosphere of United States–Soviet cooperation because
this was the key to an effective universal collective security system,
which in turn, it was hoped, would induce more responsible Soviet behavior. It was not yet considered necessary or desirable to be able to
force a general showdown with the Soviet Union over any specific
issue, in the sense of pointing explicitly or implicitly to the military
power at our disposal.

When Truman had his first high-level "confrontation" with Soviet diplomats Molotov and Gromyko at the White House on April 23, 1945, and used language that, according to Admiral Leahy, was "blunt" and "not at all diplomatic," he was evidently still leading from a perceived position of presumed *economic* leverage.[3]

The very next day Secretary of War Stimson wrote an urgent note to the President, requesting "a talk with you as soon as possible on a highly secret matter . . . . It . . . has such a bearing on our present foreign relations . . . that I think you ought to know about it without much further delay." The Secretary of War met with the President on April 25 and told him of the nuclear development program, and that in four months a completed weapon would be ready. The discussion with Stimson, reports Truman, centered on the effect the atomic bomb might likely have on our future foreign relations.[4]

The Bomb was henceforth to be very much a part of Truman's overall calculus of the balance of military power *behind* his diplomacy, both for ending the war with Japan and bargaining with the Soviets over the postwar arrangements. He knew now that if it became necessary to lay all of his cards on the table in a confrontation with Stalin, he could soon do so from a unique position of strength. But the President was evidently unwilling at this stage—although recent scholarship shows he was pressured hard to do so [5]—to make the bomb a visible and immediate part of his bargaining cards in current diplomatic negotiations. At Potsdam in July he could have done so (having received news of the successful Alamagordo test while the conference was in session), but still chose to rely on the Harriman strategy of catering to the Soviet's expected hunger for our economic assistance.

After his face-to-face encounter with Stalin at Potsdam, Truman began to lean toward those in his Administration who believed that a diplomacy characterized mainly by firm *verbal* expressions of disapproval would not disabuse the Soviets of their insatiable appetite for expansion. "I'm tired of babying the Soviets," Truman told Secretary of State Byrnes in January 1946. The past nine months had been filled with what he saw as a series of Soviet power plays.

The Soviet Union's failure to implement the Yalta provisions for freely elected regimes in Eastern Europe was only part of the story, which the President now recounted to his Secretary of State with evident exasperation: the actual disposition of military forces, sheer physical control, was the critical fact for the Soviets in subsequent negotiations over the future of Europe. Under the circumstances, confessed the President, we were "almost forced" to agree at Potsdam to Russian occupation of Eastern Poland and the compensatory occupation by Poland of German territory east of the Oder River. "It was a high-handed outrage." The situation in Iran was another case in point—Iran of *all* places! The friendship of Iran had been critical for Russia's survival in the war; the United States had conducted a major supply operation to Russia through Iran. Without these supplies furnished by the United States, maintained Truman, Russia would have been shamefully defeated. Yet now Russia was stirring up rebellion and keeping troops on the soil of Iran.

Evidently, the original Harriman analysis that the Soviets would respond positively to our blunt talk was inadequate. Stalin, according to Truman's personal reading of events, obviously placed a higher value on expanding the Soviet sphere of control than on maintaining good relations with the United States. The threat of decisive action had to be added to the blunt talk: "Unless Russia is faced with an iron fist and strong language another war is in the making," concluded the President. "Only one language do they understand—'how many divisions have you?' I do not think we should play compromise any longer. . . ." [6]

These developing perceptions of Soviet aims were very much a part of the 1946 Acheson-Lilienthal report to the President on the international control of atomic energy, which became, in effect, the plan presented to the United Nations Commission by Bernard Baruch in June. In contrast to the Soviet plan, which put destruction of existing weapons stockpiles before inspection and controls, the United States plan demanded *prior* establishment of a comprehensive international inspection and control apparatus with access to and authority over all relevant national facilities, including plants where raw materials could be converted into fissionable materials. Moreover, the veto was not to apply to the operations of international control authority. Truman's instructions to Baruch unambiguously outlined the considerations that were to be kept paramount: It was in our interest to maintain our present advantage; thus we should attempt to gain a system of reliable international control that would effectively prevent the Soviets from proceeding with their own atomic weapons development program. And under no circumstances should we "throw away our gun" until we were sure that others could not arm against us. [7]

If President Truman and a few of his official intimates had an early perception of the dominant means by which the emerging political conflict with the Soviet Union would be waged, they were not ready in late 1945 and 1946 to make it the explicit central premise of our foreign policy. To do so would have required a major reversal of the rapid postwar military demobilization already in full gear. It would have shattered the public's expectations, reflected in the Congressional agenda, that the priority business before the nation was to convert to a peacetime economy. James Forrestal's notes of a combined State-War-Navy meeting of October 16, 1945 recount that "it was agreed by all present that . . . it was most inadvisable for this country to continue accelerating the demobilization of our Armed Forces at the present rate." The Secretary of War contended the situation was of such gravity that "the President ought to acquaint the people with the details of our dealing with the Russians and with the attitude which the Russians have manifested throughout." [8]

Appeals to the President for governmental candor with the people about the international situation were made during the next few months by Secretaries Forrestal, Ickes, and others.[9] But Truman apparently needed more than individual instances of Soviet belligerence in order to go before the American people and tell them, brutally, that their fondest hopes for returning to the pursuit of happiness were based on false premises. Even as the increasing newspaper reports of Soviet totalitarianism at home and expansion abroad became a part of the public consciousness, Truman's public posture toward Soviet belligerence continued to stress the mobilization of "world opinion" in back of the principles of the United Nations Charter—issue by issue, situation by situation.

Governmental conceptions of the emerging struggle with the Soviet Union are supposed to have been given new cohesion and direction in February 1946 by George Kennan's eight-thousand-word cable from Moscow. The essentials of the Soviet grand design, the motives (rational and irrational) behind their imperialistic policies, and the meaning of their style of diplomacy were analyzed in historical and psychological depth, and with great cogency (see below, pp. 44–45, for a fuller account). Here was the authoritative and coherent analysis of the Soviet threat that many within the Administration, particularly Forrestal, were looking for. But there is no evidence that these early reports from

Kennan contained, either explicitly or by logical implication, the concrete policy prescriptions Forrestal wanted the President to champion. Kennan did urge, like Forrestal and his colleagues, the importance of having the public "educated to the realities of the Russian situation." And he discounted any deterioration in Russian-American relations that might result from such a campaign. Yet he saw no urgency for paying particular attention to the *military* components of power. "Gauged against the Western world as a whole . . ." observed Kennan, "the Soviets are still [this was early in 1946] by far the weaker force. Thus their success will really depend upon the degree of cohesion, firmness, and vigor which the Western world can muster." [10]

If Truman's *Memoirs* are accurate, he personally, as early as the winter of 1945–46, saw the Russian pressures on Iran and Turkey as an immediate threat to the global balance of power. Russia's failure to withdraw her armies from Iran stemmed from her central geopolitical interests in Iranian oil and control of the Black Sea Straits. Russian possession of Iranian oil, the President was convinced, would seriously alter the world's raw material balance, and would be a blow to the economy of Western Europe. But the power play in Iran was also directly related to the demands the Soviets had been making on Turkey for special privileges and territorial concessions. Turkey had been resisting these demands, but would be in a much weaker position to resist if she were outflanked on the east by Russian armies or a Russian puppet state.[11]

Truman saw Soviet ambitions in Turkey revealed starkly in their proposals to put the Black Sea Straits under joint Turkish-Russian defense. Recalling his own studies of Middle Eastern history, the President recognized in the present Communist thrust a continuation of Czarist Russian attempts to gain control of the strategic exits to the Mediterranean Sea. If they were to succeed now, he deduced, it would only be a question of time before Greece and the whole Near and Middle East fell to the Soviets.[12]

There is evidence that this is more than a retrospective reconstruction by Truman of his perceptions at the time. His January 1946 letter to Byrnes expressing exasperation at the way the Soviets were throwing their weight around contained a bald geopolitical evaluation of Soviet aims: "There isn't a doubt in my mind," he wrote less than a year after the close of the Second World War, "that Russia intends an invasion of Turkey and seizure of the Black Sea Straits to the Mediterranean. . . ." [13]

Moreover, Truman did begin to "show the flag" in 1946 in his dealings with the Russians on Middle Eastern issues. The battleship *Missouri* was sent to Istanbul to demonstrate support for Turkey's refusal to accede to Soviet demands for joint control over the Straits. Truman has divulged, though not until many years later, that he sent Stalin an ultimatum on the issue of Soviet troops in Iran, informing him that the United States would send troops in if the Russians did not get out, and that he had ordered preparations for the movement of American ground, sea, and air forces.[14] But however effective these moves were as gambits in the management of the particular crisis situations, they were not yet presented to the public as parts of a grand strategy toward the Soviet Union, in which the American military potential would be consciously and more or less continuously displayed in back of our diplomatic efforts to moderate Soviet behavior.

Nor was the Administration ready to openly embrace the balance of power ideas Winston Churchill was then advancing. When the British leader delivered his sensational "Iron Curtain" speech in March 1946, with President Truman sitting on the platform, the premises he advanced about Soviet motives and behavior were already widely shared in U.S. policy-making circles. But the main policy conclusion he drew, that there ought to be a long-term Anglo-American alliance against the Soviets, was still not acceptable to the highest levels in the American government.

An early moment of truth was to come shortly for United States policymakers. The February 1947 note from the British government, informing the United States that drastic economic conditions in England made it necessary for the United Kingdom to withdraw all support from Greece by the end of March, provided the need—and the opportunity. The President's top political and military advisers were of the opinion that it was only the presence of British troops in Greece since the war that had prevented that faction-ridden nation from being swept into the Soviet orbit. The prevailing view within the State Department was that unless the tottering Greek government received immediate assurances of large-scale military and financial aid the regime would lose all authority and confidence of the people, and the increasingly successful Communist guerillas would grab control of the country as public disorder mounted. Truman translated the local situation into the starkest global terms: If Greece fell to the Communists, Turkey would become highly vulnerable to Soviet power plays and subversion. Inevitably, the entire eastern Mediterranean would be sealed behind the Iron Curtain.[15]

To save the situation this time more than a White House decision —which had been sufficient for deploying the Navy and sending blunt diplomatic notes in the earlier Turkey and Iran crises—was required. Large-scale economic and military assistance, to be directly administered by American officials, would need Congressional authorization and special appropriations. But Republican majorities had just taken control of both houses, and, according to Speaker Joe Martin, were determined to fulfill election promises for a 20 per cent across-the-board reduction in income taxes with a collateral reduction in government spending. Administration forces, having suffered badly in the Congressional elections, were disposed to regard the Republican spokesmen as, for once, being in tune with popular sentiment. "Now that an immediate peril is not plainly visible," Secretary of State Marshall told an academic audience, "there is a natural tendency to relax and return to business as usual, politics as usual, pleasure as usual. Many of our people have become indifferent to what I might call the long-term dangers to national security." [16]

The stage was set. The national executive considered matters of high national interest to be at stake. But in order to service these interests it would have to ask the nation at large to reorder its priorities. Such a political context (rather than the logic of the international situation) prompts a democratic leadership to call upon the nation for reexamination of existing premises and stimulates it to promulgate new doctrine.

For the public this effort at basic revision of the national premises was associated with Truman's address to the Congress on March 12, 1947 requesting assistance for Greece and Turkey—the so-called "Truman Doctrine." But for many in the Administration responsible for foreign diplomatic, economic, and military programs Truman's formal request of Congress was only the exposed tip of an iceberg of massive intellectual and bureaucratic activity.

The seminal statement for conceptualizing and catalyzing the new orientation was probably neither Truman's address nor Secretary of State Marshall's at Harvard a few months later, but Undersecretary of

State Acheson's effort to educate the bipartisan group of Congressional leaders Truman summoned to the White House on February 27, 1947.

According to a State Department official who was present, the lead-off presentation by Secretary Marshall went very badly. Marshall, rather than expounding on the central strategic importance of Greece and Turkey (a subject on which he was very well versed), conveyed the impression that the reasons for extending aid to Greece and Turkey flowed essentially from humanitarian impulses toward these countries and loyalty to Britain. Many of the Congressional leaders present were not at all impressed, being presently preoccupied with reducing taxes.

Acheson got Marshall's attention and was given the floor. In bold strokes, he displayed for the congressmen the view of Soviet Middle Eastern strategy that for more than a year had prevailed at the White House and top State Department levels. The Undersecretary described the continuing Soviet pressures on Turkey for territorial cessions and for military and naval bases in the Turkish Straits, which if granted would mean "the end of Turkish independence." Soviet pressures on Iran were portrayed as "encircling movements" also apparently focused on the Straits. It was only because the Turks, with strong diplomatic backing from Britain and the United States, had stood up to the Russians that these moves had failed for the time being. As a result the Communists were currently concentrating their pressure on Greece, Acheson explained, where all reports indicated that the Communist insurgents would succeed in seizing control "within a matter of weeks" unless the Government of Greece received prompt and large-scale aid.

This was obviously more than helping the British salvage their interests, said Acheson, building up to his main message. The substance and tone of this message are best rendered in the account of the State Department official whose account is the basic public source for the White House meeting of February 27:

Only two great powers remain in the world, Acheson continued, the United States and the Soviet Union. We had arrived at a situation unparalleled since ancient times. Not since Rome and Carthage had there been such a polarization of power on this earth. Moreover, the two great powers were divided by an unbridgeable ideological chasm. . . . And it was clear that the Soviet Union was aggressive and expanding. For the United States to take steps to strengthen countries threatened with Communist subversion was not to pull British chestnuts out of the fire; it was to protect the security of the United States—it was to protect freedom itself. For if the Soviet Union succeeded in extending its control over two-thirds of the world's surface and three-fourths of its population, there could be no security for the United States, and freedom anywhere in the world would have only a poor chance of survival. The proposed aid to Greece and Turkey was not therefore a matter of bailing out the British, or even of responding on humanitarian grounds to the need of a loyal ally. It was a matter of building our own security and safeguarding freedom by strengthening free peoples against Communist aggression and subversion. We had the choice, he concluded, of acting with energy to meet this situation or losing by default.[17]

Here, full-blooded, were the central premises of what came to be called the Cold War: the two-way polarization of the international system around two great powers; an unbridgeable idological hostility between the two groupings, with the group led by the United States committed to individual liberty and a pluralistic international system, and the group led by the Soviet Union committed to totalitarian statism and a monistic international system organized on the Soviet model; and an intention by the Soviet-led grouping to impose its way of life on the rest of the world.

From these premises it was deduced that any allowance of an extension of Soviet control over additional areas, even if they were limited extentions, would not reduce Soviet aggressiveness, but, on the contrary, would stimulate further aggressiveness by adding to the material and political resources with which the Soviets hoped to impose their will. The policy implications for the United States-led grouping were clear: a balance of power had to be maintained against the Soviet-led grouping, and the intention to apply this power, wherever and to whatever extent necessary, to prevent any further extension of Soviet control had to be unambiguous.

President Truman's address before Congress on March 12, 1947 asking for $400,000,000 in military and economic aid to Greece and Turkey was based on these premises, but he deliberately refrained from making them as explicit as Acheson had done in the private session. A number of statements that emphasized military-strategic considerations were deleted from one of the last drafts of the speech upon the recommendation of Acheson. His view is reported to have been that too much emphasis on the military-strategic considerations might be alarming to the American people, who were not accustomed to thinking in these terms in time of peace. The fact that the recipients of the proposed aid were located close to the Soviet Union would prompt cries of "provocation" and "encirclement" which would be exploited in Soviet propaganda. The emphasis, therefore, in the public approach, was to be on the economic assistance needed by these governments in order to successfully combat subversion: [18]

I believe [Truman told the nation] that it must be the policy of the United States to support free peoples who are resisting attempted subjugation by armed minorities or by outside pressures.
I believe that we must assist free peoples to work out their destinies in their own way.
I believe that our help should be primarily through economic and financial aid which is essential to economic stability and orderly political processes.

. . .

The free peoples of the world look to us for support in maintaining their freedoms.
If we falter in our leadership, we may endanger the peace of the world —and we shall surely endanger the welfare of our own nation.[19]

Similarly, the Marshall Plan for the economic recovery of Europe, announced just four months after the promulgation of the Truman Doctrine, was sold to the public largely as a compound of humanitarian largesse and enlightened economic statesmanship, the latter proceeding from the premise that an economically healthy Europe was a precondition for the world trade required by an expanding United States economy. It was a conscious policy decision to underplay the global balance of power considerations which were very much a part of the impetus behind the Marshall Plan.* In a then-secret memorandum, George Kennan and the Policy Planning Staff recognized that "the communists

* Between Truman's address to Congress in March 1947 and Marshall's speech at Harvard in June, the Moscow conference of Foreign Ministers adjourned in recognized failure to make any progress in resolving the East-West discord over the future of Germany and Austria. "The Americans came home from Moscow," Walt Rostow recalls, "firm in the conclusion that the United States should never again negotiate from a base of weakness. . . . The picture of Europe was one of mammoth slow-moving crisis. There was a growing awareness that something big had to be done in Europe to avoid a disaster to the American interest; that a substantial program of economic aid addressed constructively to the problems of economic recovery was required to deal with the multiple threats to the Eurasian power balance." W. W. Rostow, The United States in the World Arena (New York: Harper, 1960), p. 209.

are exploiting the European crisis and . . . further communist successes would create serious danger to American security." But they advised Secretary of State Marshall that:

American effort in aid to Europe should be directed not to the combating of communism as such but to the restoration of the health and vigor of European society. It should aim, in other words, not to combat communism, but the economic maladjustment which makes European society vulnerable to exploitation by any and all totalitarian movements and which Russian communism is now exploiting.[20]

And significantly, there was a brief separate section at the end of the memorandum advising that:

Steps should be taken to clarify what the press has unfortunately come to identify as the "Truman Doctrine," and to remove in particular two damaging impressions which are current in large sections of American public opinion. These are:

a. That the United States approach to world problems is a defensive reaction to communist pressure and that the effort to restore sound economic conditions in the other countries is only the by-product of this reaction and not something we would be interested in doing if there were no Communist menace.

b. That the Truman Doctrine is a blank check to give economic and military aid to any area of the world where the Communists show signs of being successful. It must be made clear that the extension of American aid is essentially a question of political economy in the literal sense of the term and that such aid will be considered only in cases where the prospective results bear a satisfactory relationship to the expenditure of American resources and effort.[21]

This advice was heeded by the Secretary of State. Launching the program for European recovery at Cambridge on June 5, 1947 he claimed, "Our policy is directed not against any country or doctrine but against hunger, poverty, desperation and chaos." And the offer to join in the cooperative effort was made to *all* European nations.[22] There was considerable disagreement over this formulation. Indeed, many in the United States government and Western Europe were relieved when Stalin prevented the East European states from joining the effort. But the offer to all European nations was genuinely made by Marshall and those like him in the State Department who had a multifaceted view of the relevant balance of power considerations: they felt that the revival of Western European economic vigor, which was based in large measure on manufacturing, would be facilitated by the raw material resources that once again could be tapped in the East European areas. East Europe in turn could provide a market for the West's manufactured goods. To maintain an advantageous balance of power against the Soviet Union the West needed a strong Western Europe; it did not require an unhealthy Eastern Europe. Moreover, there were some in the United States government who felt that an Eastern Europe largely dependent for its own well-being upon economic relations with the West would be less subject to total Soviet control.[23]

But such questions became academic as the Soviet Union moved even more swiftly during the summer of 1947 to transform the lands it had occupied militarily into dependent units of a tightly integrated economic and political system. The last hopes for some preserve of Western liberalism in Eastern Europe died in February 1948 when the Communist leadership in Czechoslovakia, backed by Soviet armed might, demanded, and was granted, full powers of government.

Meanwhile the public dissemination in the summer of 1947, through the medium of *Foreign Affairs* magazine, of George Kennan's analysis of Soviet grand strategy, and his concept of "containment" as a countervailing grand strategy for the West,[24] provided the missing link for policy-oriented intellectuals who were trying to piece together the real basis, as distinct from the surface rationale, for the Truman Doctrine and the Marshall Plan. Kennan's coherent analysis and prescriptions were, of course, only one of a number of alternative formulations of the emerging official premises about United States-Soviet relations. In some accounts of United States Cold War policy the "x" article is treated as the official position of the government. This is incorrect. Many of its premises continued to be debated within the highest levels of the administration. But it did take the public wraps off of a core set of beliefs around which there was already an operating consensus among the responsible decision-makers: the Soviet's "unfriendliness of purpose," as Kennan put it, was "basic." It proceeded from the inner structure of Soviet-Russian society. Soviet policies over the foreseeable future would reflect "no real faith in the possibility of a permanent happy coexistence of the Socialist and Capitalist worlds, but rather a cautious, persistent pressure toward the disruption and weakening of all rival influence and rival power." Consequently, "if the Soviet government occasionally sets its signatures to documents which would indicate the contrary, this is to be regarded as a tactical maneuver permissible in deal-

ing with the enemy. . . ." Moreover, the Soviets believing in the ultimate triumph of their cause, were as patient as they were relentless.
"The Russians look forward to a duel of infinite duration." The implications for American policy needed to be faced: "Sporadic acts" of
standing up and talking tough to the Russians were not enough, even if
they seemed to produce temporary Soviet retreats. "The main element
of any United States policy toward the Soviet Union must be that of a
long-term, patient but firm and vigilant containment of Russian expan-
sive tendencies." This policy would require "the adroit and vigilant application of counter-force at a series of constantly shifting geographical
and political points, corresponding to the shifts and maneuvers of Soviet policy." [25]

CHAPTER FOUR

1948-1950: INTERNAL DIALOGUE ON THE COMPONENTS OF THE BALANCE OF POWER

God knows I am fully aware of the terrific task which this country faces if it is to keep a free economy and a free society. But to . . . deny Marshall the cards to play, when the stakes are as high as they are, would be a grave decision.

JAMES S. FORRESTAL

Kennan's article displayed important premises about Soviet intentions on which there was an emerging consensus among Truman Administration officials. Nor was there any important disagreement with the policy consequences of these premises as broadly formulated by Secretary of State Marshall in a report to the Cabinet in early November 1947. Marshall stated, according to Forrestal's account, "that the objective of our policy from this point on would be the restoration of the balance of power in both Europe and Asia and that *all actions would be viewed in the light of this objective*." [1]

There was still a significant lack of consensus on the *components* of either Kennan's "counterforce" or the "balance of power" that Marshall wanted "restored." The Administration was divided, broadly, between those who regarded the industrial strength of the United States, based on a sound economy, as the weightiest ingredient in the global balance, and those who regarded the extension of Soviet control over new areas of the globe the most important factor. In the pre-Korean War period, the Bureau of the Budget, the Council of Economic Advisers, and the White House staff tended to stress domestic economic considerations, whereas State and Defense tended to emphasize stopping the Soviets.

But even among those who were most oriented toward a global, geopolitical view of the power rivalry with the Soviet Union there was an important divergency of premises concerning both the components of the balance of power and of the American strategies required to stop Soviet expansion. The divergent points of view in 1947–48 clustered around Secretary of State Marshall and Secretary of Defense Forrestal.

Marshall's most passionate commitment now was to the success of the European Recovery Program. But he did concede that a militarily strong Western Europe was essential to right the global balance of power and provide the means locally to dissuade the Russians from attempting an easy fait accompli, either by political subversion or military aggression. Western Europe itself could not contain the Soviets in a major war, but it could provide the front line of defense. The United States would have to come to the direct aid of Europe in any such war, but, as in the Second World War, the full weight of American power would be felt in the later stages of the war as mobilization went into high gear. Marshall favored Universal Military Training in the United States to provide the base for such mobilization should it ever be required, and to signal in advance the refusal of the United States to tolerate Soviet aggression; but he did not view Soviet aggression as sufficiently imminent to require a major increment to ready forces-in-being. Even in response to the Soviet provocations around Berlin in the spring of 1948, and the blockade of 1948–49, Marshall pressed for priority to be given to *European* rearmament. Marshall, of course, was sensitive to the strong political motivations in the White House and Congress for keeping the lid on expenditures, and very likely saw UMT plus European rearmament—neither of which would require any sudden major increases in the U.S. budget—as compatible with continued Congressional financing of the multi-billion dollar project for rebuilding Europe's economy just getting under way.[2]

Secretary of Defense Forrestal gave priority to the rearmanent of the United States as the most effective means of preserving the balance of power against the Soviet Union. To procrastinate on the buildup of an effective United states military posture would be to "deny Marshall the cards to play" in current crisis situations.[3] Strengthening European military capabilities was important, but Forrestal was skeptical of the Europeans' ability to sustain their level of effort on economic reconstruction and simultaneously build the kind of military establishments needed to balance Soviet military power to Europe. In the meantime—he wrote in late 1947—under current budget allocations, reflecting the existing policy of assisting European recovery before American rearmament, we were taking a "calculated risk." That risk involved reliance on the American *strategic* advantage, consisting of: American productive capacity, the predominance of American sea power, and the exclusive possession of the atomic bomb. But the last factor, he warned, would have an "indeterminate" duration. "The years before any possible power can achieve the capabilities to attack us with weapons of mass destruction are our years of opportunity." [4] It was clear that had Forrestal been given his way he would have attached greater urgency to a buildup of a balanced United States military posture, which did not bank too heavily on either the perpetuation of the atomic monopoly or the rapid attainment of a level of recovery in Europe which would allow Europeans to assume the major burden of sustaining the balance on the continent.*

This difference between Marshall and Forrestal over the components of effective international power was in fact resolved in favor of Marshall by the White House and the Bureau of the Budget. Considerations of domestic political economy rather than a systematic analysis of the capabilities needed to carry out the nation's foreign policy commitments seemed to determine the Executive choice to stick with military budgets well below $15 billion a year, until the Korean emergency revised the prevailing priorities.

* There was yet another consideration that may have weighed heavily with Forrestal. In contrast to the services over which he presided (as the first Secretary of Defense), Forestal appeared to be more interested in a general increase in the military budget and capabilities rather than the implementation of any particular strategic doctrine. He seemed to regard some of the esoteric strategic debates of the military as responses to low budget ceilings, and the consequent need to convince their political benefactors that security could be had only through the provision of capabilities required by their particular functions. Apart from this specious quality, these debates were a severe source of embarrassment to Forrestal's attempts to achieve harmony within the Defense establishment. Higher budgets would put him in a position to mitigate the intensity of interservice rivalry.

Actually, a systematic appraisal *was* called for by the President and undertaken by a special State-Defense task force months before the North Korean invasion of South Korea. The Soviet blockade of Berlin during 1948–49 and the collateral negotiations of the North Atlantic Treaty had focused attention in the State Department and the White House on the limitations of the usable military power at the disposal of the West in case of major conflict in Europe. The Soviet atomic bomb detonation in August 1949, three years ahead of United States intelligence estimates, gave immediacy to alarms Forrestal had been sounding on the temporary nature of our strategic advantage. And the final fall of China to Mao Tse-tung the next month, placing the bulk of the Eurasian heartland under Communist control and raising the spectre of a division of the world's population into two halves was suddenly seen by many in the Administration, as it could not be when only hypothetical, as an immense strategic fact of life. The convergence of these events with the need for Truman to say yes or no to an H-bomb program produced a requirement for some kind of coherent doctrine on our military capabilities, just as the withdrawal of the British from Greece in 1947 produced the need for a doctrine on our intentions. Truman's decision in January 1950 to give the green light, tentatively, to the H-bomb program was accompanied by a directive to the Secretaries of State and Defense to make a comprehensive review of United States foreign and defense policies in light of the developments just mentioned.[5]

In the process of preparing the general strategic appraisal called for by Truman a dialogue on the components of the global balance of power, analogous to that conducted between Marshall and Forrestal in the 1947–48 period, was now reenacted within the State Department between George Kennan and Paul Nitze.

Kennan laid greater stress on the nonmilitary components of the bipolar struggle, and felt that the Soviets had such a great reluctance to become involved in a major war against the United States that the most important fact in the strategic equation was a clear *resolve* by the United States not to tolerate piecemeal opportunistic extensions of Soviet control. Translating this into military terms was difficult, and apparently uncongenial to Kennan. However, he is reported to have urged the organization of mobile, quickly deployable United States task forces which could be rushed to the scene of "brushfire" conflicts and thus confront the Soviets with the choice of desisting from their provocation or engaging the United States in a military clash which might expand to a major war. Kennan's analysis of the Soviets convinced him that when confronted with such a stark choice the Soviets would back down. Kennan thus did not feel that a general rearmament program was necessary. Moreover, rearmament would stimulate further the undesirable focusing of national energies on the cruder means of waging the Cold War, in opposition to flexible and subtler forms of diplomacy and stress on improving the quality of life of the Western nations.

Paul Nitze, who was given responsibilities for effecting greater liaison between State and Defense when Acheson became Secretary of State in January 1949, gave greater weight than did Kennan to the overall balance of military force between the Soviets and the United States. As Director of the Policy Planning Staff in 1950, and chairman of the *ad hoc* study group which produced the strategic paper requested by the President, Nitze's views were critical in shaping the advanced planning concepts being developed at the time. Kennan retained major influence as State Department Counsellor, and his knowledge of the Soviet Union was influential in the deliberations of the study group. But Nitze was known to have the full support of Secretary Acheson, who was taking the study very seriously. Forrestal was no longer at Defense, and his economy-minded successor, Louis Johnson, was a weak Secretary who provided little support or guidance to Defense Department participants in the study. Any initiative, or major departures in overall strategic planning, then, would be responsive to the momentum generated by Nitze in fulfilling Truman's desire for a new strategic appraisal.

Nitze felt that the nation's military planning was seriously constrained by the strict budgetary limits imposed by the White House and the Bureau of the Budget. In light of the emergence of a Soviet nuclear striking capability, the United States would need not only to improve its massive destructive capabilities (as was contemplated in the H-bomb program), but also to balance the Soviet capabilities for conventional war. These ideas emerged as major premises in NSC-68 (the paper's file number upon referral to the National Security Council).

But they were only a part of a set of premises designed to give coherence to national security policy. For the first time since the war, military planning concepts were tied to an explicit body of assumptions about the political and technological state of the world. On the basis of an analysis of Soviet economic strengths and weaknesses, the study projected that in four years the Soviets would have a nuclear capability sufficient to neutralize the function of the United States nuclear capability for deterring local wars. Moreover the Soviets would build this capability without any diminution in their local war capability. Thus, by 1954, if the West did not take significant compensating measures, the balance of military power would have shifted in favor of the Soviets. When this happened economic and technical assistance would be insufficient to contain Soviet expansion.

A challenge to prevailing premises about the U.S. economy was also leveled by the Nitze group. They argued that the nation could well afford to devote 20 per cent of the gross national product to national security purposes as compared with the 5 per cent then being spent. In budget terms, defense expenditures could, and ought to, rise to possibly as high as $60 billion a year, from the $15 billion then programed. Nitze and his staff economist, Robert Tufts, had an important ally in Leon Keyserling of the President's Council of Economic Advisers. (Keyserling had been consistently urging "expanisonist" policies against the views of the Council's chairman Nourse. Nourse had resigned in October 1949, and from then on, first as acting Chairman, and as Chairman from May 1950, Keyserling dominated the Council and was an increasingly persuasive force throughout the Administration.) [6] In retrospect it is not possible to say whether this alliance of Nitze and Acheson at State and Keyserling's Council of Economic Advisers would have been able to move Truman away from his natural economic conservatism and political responsiveness to "welfare" demands, and provide a convincing Presidential rationale for *implementing* NSC-68, had the Korean invasion not taken place in June 1950.

Acheson had begun to lay the groundwork with his talks in February 1950 on the need to create "situations of strength" vis-à-vis the Soviet Union prior to attempting any kind of global settlement (as was then being suggested by Churchill). But as yet these declarations did not go much beyond making the aspiration explicit to wider public audiences.[7] An implementation of the aspiration through a diversion of a larger portion of the nation's resources to affect the global balance of military power was still not Administration policy. Truman understood that such a shift in the allocation of resources would have to rest on popular consent; and the people, he believed, did not yet appreciate the current function of the military balance of power in global diplomacy.

The Communist North Koreans, by suddenly taking advantage of a local disparity of military power on June 24, 1950, finally gave Truman a sufficient basis for asking the people to approve militarily "rational" national security policies worked out by his professional foreign policy advisers.

CHAPTER FIVE

THE PRIMACY OF BALANCE-OF-POWER CONSIDERATIONS DURING THE KOREAN WAR

Instead of weakening the rest of the world, they [the Communists] have solidified it. They have given a powerful impetus to the military preparations of this country and its associates in and out of the North Atlantic Treaty Organization.

DEAN ACHESON

NSC-68 became the conceptual framework on which the rapid expansion of United States armed forces was hung during the first months of the Korean War. Before the war was over military spending had reached a peak of $50 billion a year. The 1,461,000 men in the United States armed forces in June 1950 were more than doubled in two years, with the Army accounting for the largest increase. As compared with 48 Air Force wings in 1950, the Korean Armistice in 1953 left the United States with nearly 100 wings, with another 50 expected to come into the inventory over the coming four-year period. The Navy was floating 671 ships on the eve of hostilities in 1950, and over 1100 by the summer of 1952.[1] But merely from the fact that Administration spokesmen before Congress defended their early Korean War budgets with reference to NSC-68, and from the fact that there was an across-the-board doubling of military capabilities, it cannot be inferred that the original premises advanced by the Nitze group about the emerging balance of power now constituted the doctrinal bases of the Truman Administration's new basic national security policy. The Korean War rapidly began to generate its own priority requirements, and the critical question put by Congressmen to any budget proposal was: how does this help us in Korea?

On the more conceptual military planning level, the Korean War heightened differences rather than produced a consensus. For some the Korean War confirmed the thesis that the Western Alliance needed permanent and large-scale conventional armies to deter the Communists from future aggression. This view was reflected most clearly in the NATO force goals formulated during the Korean War, the high point of aspiration being the February 1952 Lisbon ministerial meeting which set the number of divisions to be ready and/or deployable for a European conflict at ninety-six. But the Korean experience also gave stimulus to advocates of the doctrinal antithesis: namely, that Korea was a model of how *not* to fight a war; that to allow the Communists to engage us in conventional land warfare was to allow them to choose the grounds and weapons most favorable to them; that the superior mode of warfare for the technologically advanced West was strategic, relying mostly upon air power to strike deep at the sources of enemy power with weapons of mass destruction; that the way to preserve the balance of power (as the Soviets built up their strategic capabilities) was not to dissipate our resources in an effort to redress the imbalance in armed manpower, but to enhance our capabilities for strategic warfare. The resolution of these antithetical military doctrinal reactions to the Korean War had to await a change in Administrations.

Yet the Korean War—the way it was fought by the United States, and the force-posture planning decisions made at the time—left a material and institutional legacy of programs in-being not significantly different from those implied in NSC-68. And programs in-being tend to shape fundamental policy premises just as much as, if not more than, premises tend to shape programs. The perpetuation of existing programs often becomes a psychological, no less than bread-and-butter, commitment for those with the responsibility for their administration. The fact of the matter was that the Korean War *institutionalized* a set of operational (though not necessarily intellectually held) premises:

A. The Soviet Union would resort to military expansion if it were not checked by visible countervailing military power.

B. Local imbalances of military power which favored the Soviets or a Soviet satellite would lead to further "Koreas."

C. The most appetizing local imbalance to the Soviets was in Central Europe.

D. The global balance of power would shift in favor of the Soviets if they were able to swallow the rest of Central Europe, namely, West Germany and Austria. No other area on the periphery of the Communist world, except for the Greco-Turkish flanks (which were already being buttressed) had such a critical function for the balance of power. The next most critical area on the Soviet periphery was Japan.

E. But while attending to the power ratios focused on the prime military-industrial regions, we must not neglect local imbalances in secondary and tertiary areas. The capability and clearly communicated will to defend whatever area the Communist powers might choose to attack, regardless of its intrinsic geopolitical weight in the overall balance, was necessary to prevent the Communists from picking and choosing easy targets for blackmail and aggression. And a number of small territorial grabs *could* add up to a critical alteration of the global balance. Moreover, our failure to defend one area would demoralize nationals in other such localities in their will to resist the Communists. Even in Western Europe people would wonder under what circumstances we might consider them dispensable.

Similar premises, to be sure, antedated the Korean War. But their existence, even in the person, say, of Secretary of State Acheson, did not make them the basis of government policy. It took the Korean conflict to give "validity" to these premises—not in the sense of proving their correctness, but in making them the assumptions on which important wartime and planning decisions were reached.

The overriding fear in the White House was not simply that the loss of the Korean peninsula would encourage the Soviets to embark on further aggressions. Rather, it was that the Soviets were embarked, *now*, on some pattern of military aggression to pin down the resources of the United States in peripheral battles, and then to move, when the right moment arrived, virtually unopposed into Western Europe.

In his *Memoirs* Truman divulges how the strategic (United States—

Soviet) situation limited his flexibility in the tactical (Korean) campaign. It was his intention, Truman recalls, to take all necessary measures to push the North Koreans back behind the 38th parallel. But he was unwilling to commit the United States so deeply in Korea that we would not have the resources to handle other situations.[2] The strategic prize was Western Europe, with its skilled manpower and industrial infrastructure. Truman was convinced that Europe was still at the center of the Soviet design for world domination, and he, for one, was not going to allow our attention to be diverted from this dominant feature of the global power contest.[3]

When the Communist Chinese armies intervened, the prospect of becoming bogged down in a huge war in Asia became more immediate, particularly in light of pressures from General MacArthur to attack the Communist staging bases in Manchuria, even at the risk of a general war with China. The Administration's view was articulated by Dean Acheson at a November 28, 1950 meeting of the National Security Council. The Soviet Union was behind every one of the Chinese Communist and North Korean moves, said the Secretary of State. We were in competition with the Soviets all around the globe. Thus Korea was a world matter, not merely a regional matter. If we were to lose sight of this fact, he warned, and allowed Russia to trap us on the Asian mainland, we would risk sinking into a bottomless pit.[4]

The American Secretary of State presented a similar case to the British a few weeks later during the President's Washington conferences with Prime Minister Atlee. The central enemy was not China, stressed Acheson, but the Soviet Union. The aggression by the North Koreans was not a local, spontaneous maneuver. It was a part of the larger Communist design to get us preoccupied in Asia so the Russians could have a free hand in Europe. We must not and would not distort our global priorities.[5]

This Europe-first emphasis was of course congenial to the British, who were, if anything, afraid that the United States might have already become overcommitted to an increasingly costly Asian conflict, and might engage in rash action—such as nuclear bombardment of China. Atlee kept on raising reservations about the value of attempting to defend Formosa. Acheson thereupon was forced to refine the Europe-first emphasis, by pointing to strategic interdependencies among the various forward positions then being sustained. He explained to the British leaders that, apart from how we might feel about Chiang Kai-shek, we could not, for geopolitical reasons, allow Formosa to fall into Communist hands. The fall of Formosa would raise severe problems for us in Japan and in the Philippines, contended Acheson; and these countries, being the sites of our bases for conducting operations in the theater, had become essential to our survival as a Pacific power.[6]

General Marshall, present during one of these exchanges, added his weight to the strategic evaluation of Formosa: it was of no particular strategic importance in our hands, but it would be of disastrous importance if it were held by an enemy.[7]

But if hard choices did have to be made in Asia, there was little doubt that priority would have to be accorded the defense of Japan. Such an eventuality was in the minds of the Joint Chiefs during the bleakest days following the Chinese intervention. In the third week of December 1950 they suggested to Truman that consideration ought to be given to ways of withdrawing from Korea "with honor" in order to protect Japan.[8]

The Administration's view of the global geopolitical interests and risks involved in the Korean struggle ran head on with General MacArthur's view that decisive military victory in the theatre of operations was of overriding importance. But this very intensity of the disagreement between Truman and MacArthur had the effect of producing within the Administration a greater self-awareness of its own objectives and the policies it deemed necessary to implement them.

The much-quoted testimony of General Bradley (to extend the fighting to the mainland of Asia would "involve us in the wrong war, at the wrong place, at the wrong time, and with the wrong enemy"[9]) capsules the operational effects on the prosecution of the war itself of the premise that the Soviets really had their military sights focused on Western Europe. The effects on future-oriented military planning and alliance diplomacy were no less significant. As Truman telegraphed MacArthur near the final stages of their controversy: "In reaching a final decision about Korea, I shall have to give constant thought to the main threat from the Soviet Union and the need for a rapid expansion of our armed forces to meet this great danger."[10]

The Europe-oriented consequences of these premises were visible in the rapid efforts to transform NATO from a security guaranty pact into an international regional theatre army, most heavily deployed at the spot of critical vulnerability in the global balance: the Central European front. This in turn meant that our European diplomacy was to be oriented toward gaining acceptance from the North Atlantic Alliance partners of the rearmament of West Germany. And the rearmament of West Germany, in its turn, would require—largely to reassure the French—a United States commitment to the principle of supranational (or "integrated") commands, in which the German units would be unable to take independent action.[11]

Although the stimulus of the Korean crisis was short-lived, and, by late 1951 the Europeans returned to their pre-1950 emphasis on economic recovery, an institutional framework was created for redressing the Central European balance in a future conflict. A Supreme Commander over allied forces was created, and provided with a large international (NATO) staff and planning organization, for the purpose of implementing NATO directives on force posture and strategy. A major responsibility was accorded to Germany for providing troops for a "forward defense" under a multination command directly subordinate to the Supreme Allied Commander (Eisenhower). An American military presence—not just bases for the strategic arm, but an overseas army in the forward defense apparatus—was accepted by United States planners as necessary for the indefinite future. (There was some ambiguity with respect to the function and eventual size of these overseas United States deployments, however. Both General Eisenhower and Secretary of Defense Marshall, in urging Congressional authorization for an additional four divisions for Europe in 1951, attempted to delimit their function as largely that of a catalyst for European contributions to a forward ground defense force, in which the Europeans were expected to assume the major burden.)

Moreover, the United States view of the altered scale of priorities, now giving first place to the military components of the power balance, was made explicit to recipients of Marshall Plan assistance. Further economic assistance was to be made contingent upon the alliance partner's conscientious attempt to fulfill its NATO rearmament obligations.[12] By 1951, the European Recovery program was formally subordinated to "security" considerations under the omnibus Mutual Security Act.

The *way* the United States fought the Korean War—particularly our willingness to allow sanctuary status to Communist China even after she became an active belligerent—did confirm and sharpen the pre-existing official premise that mainland Asia was a secondary weight in the balance of global power as compared with Western Europe. But the fact that we were willing to fight a high-cost war to keep South Korea out of Communist hands also gave impetus to the emerging realization that the power contest could be won or lost in the secondary theatres when there was a stalemate in the primary theatres.

The Korean War thus marked a globalization of containment in terms of operational commitments as well as rhetoric. The United States finally "intervened" phsycially in the Chinese Civil War by interposing the Seventh Fleet between Mao Tse-tung's forces and Chiang's last island fortresses. Despite our anti-colonial protestations, we now put our money behind the French efforts to suppress the Ho Chi Minh Communist-nationalist insurgency in Indochina. And although the United States *formally* intervened in Korea under a United Nations mandate (by virtue of the absence of the Soviet delegate from the Security Council at the time the votes were taken), henceforth our plans and public commitments and material undertakings would no longer convey to our global adversaries the impression that we would hesitate to act unilaterally. As with Europe, Article 51 (the self-defense provision) of the UN Charter now became the operative legal instrumentality of our "collective security" arrangements in the secondary as well as the primary theatres.

The globalization of containment—the notion that practically all pieces of territory now had significant, if not decisive, weight in the power balance, that the reputation for being willing to defend each piece was a critical ingredient of our maintenance of allies and deterrence of enemies—rested on solid bipartisan support. The Republican challenge was not to these fundamental assumptions. Rather, it was a charge that the Truman Administration was first of all too late and then too restrained in countering the threat of Communism in Asia.

The forum for the partisan rallying was the 1951 Senate investigation of Truman's recall of General MacArthur from his command.[13] It was here, for the first time, that the bipartisan Europe-first policy was made the subject of a great debate between the two parties. It was only now that Secretary of State Acheson's January 1950 statement omitting South Korea from our "defense perimeter" in the western Pacific was held up to scorn by the opposition (who neglected to note that General MacArthur traced a similar line in March 1949), the charge being that Acheson's statement constituted an "invitation" to Stalin to attack.[14] It was now that it became a Republican article of party faith that the Truman Administration, out of nearsightedness as to the ultimate power stakes involved, "lost" China to the Communists.

But this breakdown in the domestic consensus over where the stakes in the global power balance lay was a *retrospective* cleavage.

In 1948 no prominent United States politician or China expert rose to challenge Secretary of State Marshall's assessment that:

China does not itself possess the raw material and industrial resources which would enable it to become a first-class military power within the foreseeable future. The country is at present in the midst of a social and political revolution. Until this revolution is completed—and it will take a long time—there is no prospect that sufficient stability and order can be established to permit China's early development into a strong state.[15]

Nor had the critics of the Truman Administration's China policies been willing to go so far as to support United States *combat* operations against Mao in 1948 and 1949 when it became clear that military assistance alone would not suffice. Only marginal increments in aid were offered by Congressmen in the China Aid Act of 1948. The statement of Representative Walter Judd (one of Chiang's staunchest supporters) was typical: "Not for one moment has anyone contemplated sending a single combat soldier in. . . . So it is important to make clear when we speak of military aid . . . it is supplies, training, and advice, nothing further." [16]

This had been the period when our rapid postwar military demobilization was in high gear. It was the same atmosphere that led Truman to defer approval of the NSC-68 recommendations, even though he appreciated their strategic soundness.

When the Korean War allowed Republicans and Democrats alike to loosen the purse strings a bit for military rearmament, many in the opposition party, now urging a decisive victory in Korea, and willing to follow MacArthur into a general war with China, were ready to claim superior wisdom from having been Mao haters since the middle 1940s. This was virtue through hindsight only. Their new charges that the Truman Administration had been overly feeble in its approach to the China problem a few years back were regarded by Administration policy-makers as gratuitous. These charges conveniently overlooked the fact that the critics themselves cooperated in the enfeeblement process. General Marshall later recalled how he was pressed ad nausium in the early postwar period to give the Communists hell. ". . . I am a soldier and know something about the ability to give hell," he told a Pentagon audience. "At that time, my facilities for giving them hell . . . was [sic] 1⅓ divisions over the entire United States. That's quite a proposition when you deal with somebody with over 260 and you have 1⅓." [17]

Significantly, Marshall did not count among his hell-giving facilities the atomic bomb. If there was to be a military contest with the Chinese Communists, the bomb apparently was of little military utility, nor evidently could it be used as a threat to forestall counter-intervention by the Soviets. This was also a part of the atmosphere of the times—especially with respect to any official contemplation in public of its use against Asians so soon after Hiroshima and Nagasaki.

However, the Korean War also eroded this constraint on United States calculations of usable power in conflict situations. Truman did not unequivocally rule out the use of the bomb.[18] And the Eisenhower Administration went further in actually hinting that it would have to resort to nuclear weapons if the war resumed due to a breakdown in peace negotiations.

If the NSC-68 planners had their way, Korea would have marked the transition to a new era of higher peacetime military budgets, aimed centrally at rectifying local imbalances of power between the Communist and non-Communist nations. The Eisenhower Administration also felt it was beholden to a popular mandate against further Koreas. And alterations in the existing local military imbalances would be an essential requisite for the maintenance of our global commitments and preventing Soviet miscalculations such as Korea. But the plans of the Truman Administration for rearmament were seen to be incompatible with the conventional Republican philosophy of reduced government expenditures.

The most appropriate kind of military power for implementing our now globalized "containment" policy was to remain the primary subject of policy-level debate. But for at least another ten years, the policy itself (however much the Republicans disliked associating themselves with the word), and the premise that an advantageous military balance of power was its essential prerequisite, was taken as fact in official Washington.

The weight of the non-Communist nations in the global balance of power was to be defined, predominantly, as the product of three variables: United States military forces-in-being, United States industrial-economic strength, and the indigenous military-forces in-being of allies of the United States. Significantly, the *economic* strength of other non-Communist nations was not to be directly taken into account, in terms of requiring significant outlays by the United States. To the extent that balance of power considerations would suppress other considerations in United States foreign policy, policies whose rationale was the socio-economic development of other nations would receive only marginal attention by top United States decision-makers.

*Occasional pages of history do record the faces of the "Great De-
stroyers" but the whole book of history reveals mankind's never-ending
quest for peace, and mankind's God-given capacity to build.*

*It is with the book of history, and not with isolated pages, that the
United States will ever wish to be identified.*

DWIGHT D. EISENHOWER

*I don't expect other nations to love us. . . . But I do expect them to
respect us. . . . This means that we abide by our commitments, that
we speak only of what we can do, and do what we speak of.*

JOHN FOSTER DULLES

PART III

THE EISENHOWER
ERA

CHAPTER SIX

A NEW LOOK FOR LESS EXPENSIVE

POWER

*We keep locks on our doors; but we do not have an armed guard in
every home. We rely principally on a community security system so
well equipped to punish any who break in and steal that, in fact, would-
be aggressors are generally deterred. That is the modern way of getting
maximum protection at bearable cost.*

JOHN FOSTER DULLES

In one important respect the Korean War simplified the policy
dilemmas of the Truman Administration. It gave the maintenance of a
balance of power against the Soviet Union and China top spot among
previously competing foreign policy objectives, and it gave primacy to
the military components of power. Yet the Truman Administration
left office without resolving the competing doctrines of effective military power put forward by the military strategists.

The Eisenhower Administration retained the predominantly military
definition of the power balance instituted during the later Truman
years; but it carried the process of simplification even further by selecting one of the competing strategic doctrines—and the most narrowly
specialized one, at that—as the concept that would guide the allocation

of national resources to meet the perceived external threats to the nation. The military definition of the power balance was leavened somewhat, however, by the prominence given in the Eisenhower Administration to the nation's economic health as a critical factor in sustaining the global balance. But here too, the politico-economic doctrines which prevailed in the White House tended toward a simplification and narrowing of the premises governing the choice of overseas programs.

The Eisenhower Administration early came to different conclusions about the necessary military ingredients for maintaining the balance of power than did the preceding Administration. The latest views of the Truman Administration were passed on to the incoming Administration in the National Security Council document 141, a report prepared specially for guidance during the transition, and signed by Secretary of State Acheson, Secretary of Defense Lovett, and Mutual Security Administrator Harriman. The report apparently sustained the NSC-68 premise (see above, pp. 50 f.) that a balanced military establishment, including substantial limited-war forces, was necessary in the face of the anticipated Soviet long-range strategic nuclear capability. So there were no realistic prospects for reduced budgets after the Korean War. Indeed, serious planning to take cognizance of the Soviet strategic threat would require *increases* of about $7 billion to $8 billion yearly, largely concentrated in new systems of air defense for the continental United States. The paper also claimed that expanded programs of military and economic assistance were needed in the Far East, the Middle East, and Africa.[1] Eisenhower's basic reaction to this paper was that it ignored the "connection between national security and fiscal responsibility."[2]

The President, unlike some members of his Cabinet, and the Republican leadership in the Congress, claimed to be unwilling to buy the more extreme proposition that *first* place should be given to reducing taxes and balancing the budget through reduction of government expenditures. Eisenhower recalls telling the "astounded and upset" Senator Taft of the inability of the new Administration to scale down by more than $9 billion the fiscal 1954 budget inherited from the Truman Administration because any further reduction would "endanger the security of the United States" :

. . . I deeply respected Senator Taft's views and his dedication to the nation's welfare, but I could not agree that the country should have, or wanted, a tax cut ahead of a balanced budget or a balanced budget ahead of national security. In answer to Senator Taft I took time to review the international situation and this country's global strategy. I referred to the dangers in Iran and pointed out that Western Europe and the oil of the Middle East must in no circumstances fall to Communism. I reminded him of the alarming news of a new Communist invasion of Laos and the continuing wars in Korea and Vietnam. . . . I did not agree that the proposed budget would ruin Republicans in 1954. . . . "Regardless of the consequences," I said, "the nation's military security will take first priority in my calculations." [3]

Eisenhower was stung by charges from influential Democrats, journalists, scholars, and army generals that his New Look defense policy put domestic economic considerations ahead of national security; and he later devoted a chapter in the first volume of his memoirs to a refutation of those charges. Eisenhower's main contention was that he was providing more security at less cost. He would stand as a military man on the force-posture he was designing, and the strategy for its use. He was concerned only to eliminate *unnecessary* cost: "The brave statement 'America can afford anything it needs for national security' was and is true. . . . But I also emphasized that America could not afford to waste money in any area, including the military, for anything that it did *not* need." [4] Moreover, "long-term security required a sound economy." National security could not be measured in terms of military strength alone. "The relationship between military and economic strength is intimate and indivisible." [5]

However, the Eisenhower Administration's premises concerning the ingredients of domestic economic strength were essentially the premises of the Taft wing of the Republican party; George Humphrey at the Treasury Department, Charles Wilson at the Defense Department, Sinclair Weeks at the Commerce Department, Arthur Burns at the Council of Economic Advisers, and Gabriel Haugue, the President's Administrative Assistant responsible for economic affairs, constituted a formidable phalanx of economic conservatism. The programmatic expression of their economic philosophy appealed to the more homespun philosophy of thrift and solvency that governed Eisenhower's approach to the federal budget. Balanced budgets, fiscal and monetary checks to avoid inflation, tax reductions, and, underlying these, a restoration of

the "free market" economy with a minimum of government interference were defined as the ingredients of economic strength.[6] If the
relationship between military and economic strength was "intimate and
indivisible"—as Eisenhower preached—then he might yet be convinced
that a good deal of the military programs in being were sapping America's strength.

Eisenhower's search for a strategic concept that would satisfy both
terms of this great equation (reduced government expenditures, and
military security in the face of expanding Soviet capabilities) had begun shortly after the November 1952 election, and continued with intensity, at various levels in the Administration, for fifteen months, until
it emerged full-blown in the spring of 1954.[7]

The notion that defense budget economies could be effected by concentrating on strategic airpower was being urged by the Churchill government during 1951 and 1952. The concept propounded was very similar to that being urged by the United States Air Force since 1948:
namely, that strategic air power was now the decisive element in warfare and deterrence, its function being to break the back of enemy
power and will at their source. All other capabilities were subsidiary,
and, to the extent the other capabilities took away from the resources
necessary to maintain strategic superiority over the Soviets, these other
capabilities were wasteful. Such strategic monism went against the
grain of the balanced defense concepts developed in NSC-68, and implemented on an emergency basis during the Korean War; but they fit
in handily with the Republican attempt to exploit popular discontent
and confusion with the frustrating military stalemate in Korea. In a
Life magazine article of May 19, 1952 John Foster Dulles presaged the
doctrine which was worked out more fully later by writing of an "instant massive retaliation" capacity as one that provided the United
States the means of taking "action of our own choosing" in contrast to
Korea-type engagements where terrain and means were chosen by the
enemy.

Eisenhower, at this early stage, still fresh from his NATO role,
where it was his job to convince the allies of the necessity for building
a significant "forward defense" capability in Europe, did not take too
readily to such strategic *avant gardism*. The Presidential candidate is
reported to have insisted that the phrase "retaliatory striking power" be
stricken from the Republican platform, where it appeared at Dulles'

suggestion. However, the General was somewhat enamored of the idea of a mobile strategic reserve based in the United States as the concept for organizing the United States contribution to alliance defense, with the forward positions sustained initially by the forward countries themselves. This hope for allied assumption of the major forward defense burdens had been somewhat dampened by his exposure, as Supreme Allied Commander under NATO, to the economic difficulties the Europeans were encountering in raising and provisioning their armies. As yet, though, Eisenhower himself had propounded no discernably coherent strategic concept which could serve as an alternative to the programs of the Truman Administration.

The initial approach to a new concept is supposed to have begun in earnest in December, before inauguration, as Eisenhower assembled his new Cabinet aboard the U.S.S. *Helena,* on his way back from a trip to Korea. Eisenhower posed the problem: a prolongation of the defense programs then under way would have serious consequences for the American way of life. A free economy with minimal government interference in the life of the citizens would be supplanted by a "garrison state." And the draw upon the resources and finances of the nation would likely lead to serious inflation which would do major harm to the economy. Admiral Radford (soon to be selected by Eisenhower as Chairman of the Joint Chiefs of Staff) and Dulles offered suggestions for effecting savings by more efficient deployment and use of the technologies of atomic-age warfare. Radford is said to have argued that United States military power was overextended—especially in Asia where it could be pinned down. Instead, he favored a "mobile strategic reserve" based in or near the continental United States. Major reliance for initial local defense would be on indigenous forces. Dulles used the opportunity to argue the virtues of a United States posture based primarily on massive strategic striking power whose function would be to *deter* the Russians instead of trying to contain them all around their extensive perimeter.

These ideas evidently made an impact on Eisenhower, but they were not yet sufficiently gelled to constitute a base for resolution of budgetary issues in the spring of 1953. With a passion to effect dramatic slashes in the Truman holdover budget for fiscal 1954, Budget Director Dodge, with the President's blessing, instructed all departments to effect downward adjustments of existing program levels. The Department of

Defense was informed that it was expected to effect reductions of some $4 billion for the forthcoming fiscal year, with a view toward an additional $6 billion reduction for fiscal 1955. The means by which the reductions were to be effected was apparently of little interest to the Bureau of the Budget—that was the business of the defense people; but reductions there must be. Not surprisingly, the Joint Chiefs of Staff reported back to the National Security Council that reductions down to the contemplated ceilings would dangerously effect national security. The civilian officials of the Department of Defense thereupon took matters into their own hands, and largely through not letting any new contracts in 1954 were able to effect paper reductions (actually deferred decisions) to a level somewhat in line with White House requests.

Clearly, a continuation of such leveling off and reduction in expenditures would require a major revision in the concepts by which the military were then generating their requirements.

One of the earliest of the concepts developed at the White House-NSC level was announced by the President at the end of April 1953. This was the so-called "long-haul" basis for military planning, which, presumably, was to substitute for the previous Administration's method of planning toward some selected "crisis year" or "year of maximum peril." Under this "new" concept a broad base for effecting mobilization when and if needed was to be substituted for high military manpower levels; and an industrial-technological base capable of supporting expanded production schedules was to be maintained along with research and development in new systems, instead of attempting to fulfill specific production goals tagged to some specific year, only to be faced with inventories of technologically obsolete weapons. Actually, the "old" system was not the caricature it was made out to be by the new Administration. The target years were meant primarily as a stimulus—as a way of dramatizing the adverse consequences to the global balance of power if corrective action was not well under way by then; and this in no way implied that the provision of mobilization, industrial and research bases for expansion and innovation were to be given short shrift.

The effect of the announcement of the long-haul concept seems to have been primarily to deflate somewhat the sense of urgency underlying existing defense budget levels. This was, of course, part of the effect intended. "It has been coldly calculated by the Soviet leaders," explained Eisenhower, ". . . by their military threat to force upon America and the free world an unbearable security burden leading to economic disaster." [8]

Needless to say, the announcement was very well received in NATO circles, where the NATO Council in its April 1953 session agreed to Dulles' suggestions for a slowdown in the NATO buildup. This was merely a formal recognition of the slackening that had already been taking place in Europe during the previous year; but now their economy-mindedness was dignified as giving emphasis to long-term quality ahead of short-term quantity.[9]

A more drastic revision of strategic concepts was still needed, however, to legitimize the reduced national security expenditures made necessary by the goal of a balanced budget. The vehicle was to be a broad examination of the grand strategy of the United States conducted for the President during the spring and summer of 1953 by three task forces under the overall direction of Undersecretary of State Walter Bedell Smith and Robert Cutler, the President's Special Assistant for National Security Affairs. Each task force was to explore the implications of one of three alternative grand-strategies: (a) continuation of "containment"; (b) global deterrence by the threat of nuclear punishment; and (c) "liberation" of Communist-held areas through economic, paramilitary, and psychological warfare methods. The National Planning Board of the National Security Council was to integrate the best ideas of the three groups into a single coherent policy paper.

The resulting document, labeled NSC-162, was a reasonably coherent policy paper, but a failure insofar as its purpose was to provide the Administration with a new concept that would allow for major reductions in defense expenditures. The policy of containing the Soviet Union—with essentially the kind of balanced forces recommended by the previous Administration—was to be retained, but apparently somewhat greater reliance might be placed on strategic air power for deterrence. The Soviet threat was painted as harshly as ever and likely to continue over the long term. The Soviet hydrogen explosion in August underlined earlier fears that the Soviets would soon have the capacity to hit the United States with a massive nuclear strike. As a consequence, NSC-162 was unable to recommend a reduction in military forces, ground forces included. National security, in the years ahead, would have to take priority over all policy objectives.[10]

Meanwhile, the newly selected Joint Chiefs of Staff, with Admiral

Radford as Chairman, had also been conducting a study under orders of the President, who had made firm his expectation that they would give due weight to domestic economic considerations. Their paper, presented in late summer 1953, purported to be a statement of general premises which should guide further detailed planning. The critical premises here, in contrast to those of NSC-162, were a combination of those advanced by Dulles and Radford aboard the *Helena* the previous December. The Joint Chiefs of Staff were unanimous in their opinion that United States military forces were overextended, and that the local defense of potentially threatened areas such as Korea and Germany should be the primary responsibility of indigenous forces backed by United States sea and air power. United States force posture planning should concern itself first and foremost with two primary functions: defense of the continental United States against strategic bombardment, and the maintenance of a massive retaliatory capability. Mobility, efficiency, and readiness should be stressed for the nonstrategic forces and reserves.[11]

Yet in attempting to carry out these premises in the form of substantial budgetary reductions for fiscal 1955, the Joint Chiefs of Staff found little in their respective service programs that they could bring themselves to cut. In the National Security Council meetings in the fall of 1953, Treasury Secretary Humphrey (very much a Taft Republican) and Budget Director Dodge indicated profound disappointment with the estimates presented by the Defense Department. Admiral Radford reacted at this point by insisting that the only way substantial reductions could be effected would be as a result of a basic decision by the Administration on the *kind* of war to be planned for. If the military planners knew that permission would be forthcoming to use nuclear weapons whenever it was militarily advantageous to do so, then there could be substantial dollar savings, since current planning was on the basis of preparing simultaneously for brush-fire and limited conventional wars, conventional wars on the Second World War model, limited nuclear wars, general nuclear wars, and various combinations of these. Apparently, this argument now made an impact on the entire Cabinet, including the President.

By the end of October 1963 there was a consensus on the Radford line, and the President approved a formal paper, NSC-162/2, which specified the critical assumptions of guidance for planners throughout the military establishment: it was decreed that the military commanders could count on using nuclear weapons, tactical and strategic, when militarily required; and it was implied that the President would issue the appropriate weapons release orders upon request from the commanders in the field. Force posture planning was to proceed on this basis, and on the basis that the fundamental objective of national security was to *deter* Soviet aggression—a function primarily of the massive strategic retaliatory capability of the United States. To the extent that it was necessary to counter local aggression, greater reliance would have to be placed on indigenous allied forces; concurrent with these local buildups there could be some return of United States overseas forces to the United States.[12]

Here, finally, was the set of premises which allowed the Joint Chiefs of Staff to take their "New Look" at the overall level of military spending, and the allocation of resources within the total military budget. The document they submitted in December 1953 refined somewhat the general politico-strategic ideas of NSC-162/2. The massive retaliatory power of the United States was seen as a deterrent to *major* aggression, and as a means of fighting general war. Local limited aggression was still a distinct possibility, for which the bulk of the locally deployed ground forces ought to be provided by our allies; but an "educational" effort was needed to convince the allies that such a specialization of functions would benefit everyone. United States ground forces in forward areas in Europe and Asia would eventually be reduced; and our participation in local defense operations would be mainly through tactical air and sea power, and quickly deployable mobile ground units —these functions, presumably, to be built around the new concepts of tactical atomic warfare. The recommended force posture implementations of these concepts were to begin, on an interim basis, with the fiscal 1955 budget and mature by fiscal 1957, resulting in a 25 per cent drop in military manpower, and a reduction in the nearly $50 billion annual defense bill to a level under $35 billion.

It was only after the internal administrative tug-of-war had been resolved that the New Look was dressed up in a neat package for public display by the Secretary of State and the President. However, the public versions—particularly Dulles'—do distill from the potpourri of considerations that went into its formulation the rather simplified new orientation toward the global balance of power.

73

As Dulles explained on January 12, 1954 to the Council on Foreign Relations:

It is not sound military strategy permanently to commit U.S. land forces to a degree that leaves us no strategic reserves.

It is not sound economics, or good foreign policy, to support permanently other countries; for in the long run, that creates as much ill will as good will.

Also, it is not sound to become permanently committed to military expenditures so vast they lead to "practical bankruptcy."

. . .

We need allies and collective security. Our purpose is to make these relations more effective, less costly. This can be done by placing more reliance on deterrent power, and less dependence on local defensive power.

. . .

Local defense will always be important. But there is no local defense which alone will contain the mighty land power of the Communist world. Local defense must be reinforced by the further deterrent of massive retaliatory power. A potential aggressor must know that he cannot always prescribe the battle conditions that suit him. Otherwise, for example, a potential aggressor, who is glutted with manpower, might be tempted to attack in confidence that resistance would be confined to manpower.

Under the previous policy, maintained the Secretary of State, our military leaders could not be selective in building our military power. We needed to be ready to fight in the tropics, Asia, the Near East, and Europe, by sea, land, and air. Such a strategy, he insisted, "could not be continued for long without grave budgetary, economic and social consequences."

In order for the nation's military planning to be put on a more rational basis, said Dulles, it was necessary for the President to make this basic policy decision which he, Dulles, was now announcing to the world: namely, that henceforth this nation would "depend primarily upon a great capacity to retaliate, instantly, by means and at places of our own choosing." Now our military establishment could be shaped to fit *our* policy, instead of having to try to be ready to meet the enemy's many choices: "That permits us a selection of means instead of a multiplication of means. As a result, it is now possible to get, and share, more basic security at less cost." [13]

In one important respect, Dulles had seriously overstated the plan-

74

ning premises agreed upon within the Administration. He had talked of the massive retaliation capacity as if it were to be the primary military means of defense for the entire free community, neglecting to stress adequately the role of indigenous local forces in blocking aggressions during their initial stages. This led to the widespread impression that United States policy had narrowed the choices of the non-Communist world into either accepting local Communist aggressions or turning every local aggression into general nuclear war. Dulles and other Administration officials were hard pressed to explain that they had no such extreme policy in mind,[14] and that local defense capabilities would still be important to deny the enemy easy territorial grabs. Moreover, these local forces could be buttressed quickly by rapid deployments from the central mobile reserve here in the United States. The Communist powers would now know, however, that they could not count on drawing the United States into a purely local encounter with a limitation on the weapons employed. The choice would be ours as to when and where to respond with weapons of mass destruction. Backing away from the denigration of a strategy of readiness to fight in all theatres, that appeared in the Dulles speech, Administration spokesmen explained that programed reductions in United States military manpower levels were the result of improved local defense capabilities in NATO and the Far East, and the development of tactical nuclear weapons which, it was assumed, would reduce ground manpower requirements.

CHAPTER SEVEN

COMMITMENTS AND COERCION:
DULLES' PSYCHOLOGY OF POWER

The free nations have adopted and implemented two interrelated policies for collective security. The first policy is to give clear warning that armed aggression will be met by collective action. The second policy is to be prepared to implement this political warning with deterrent power.

JOHN FOSTER DULLES

In his "massive retaliation" speech before the Council on Foreign Relations Dulles had undoubtedly resorted to hyperbole. In failing to give sufficient stress to the role of indigenous military forces he underplayed that which he was later to be accused of overplaying. Indeed, Dulles personally was much more interested in this means of enhancing the non-Communist side of the balance than in the diplomatic exploitation of advanced weaponry.

Dulles believed in the virtues of alliance-building for reasons that went beyond the purely military calculus of power. Unity of purpose and coordination of policy were no less important in his view as attributes of strength. The cement for effecting such cohesion was thought to be a shared ideology and economic and military interdependence.

But in the areas of the Eisenhower Administration's most feverish alliance-building activity—the wide arc through the Middle East and Southeast Asia that connects Europe to Japan, and hems in the Communist Eurasian heartland—there was thought to be little basis for cultivating strong economic ties.

In the first place, the Administration, in its determined effort to reduce all but the most essential expenditures, was in no mood to begin new programs of foreign assistance unless these could be shown to be directly related to crucial United States national security requirements. Second, the Eisenhower Cabinet was skeptical of the ability of the new nations to make productive use of purely economic assistance. Consequently, the dominant basis of Eisenhower-Dulles appeals for Mutual Security Funds between 1953 and 1956 was that of the supposed comparative economic advantage to the United States of relying on indigenous local forces rather than United States military manpower in order to contain Communist military expansion.

This narrow basis for alliance-building underlay Dulles' signing up of Pakistan and Iraq as recipients of United States military assistance in 1953–54, in the face of outraged opposition from the Arab states and India, and his fashioning of the South East Asia Treaty Organization during a period of increasingly self-conscious neutralism in Asia.

The efforts to sign up military allies in the Middle East, particularly, illustrate the way in which the policy of containment had become submerged in the effort to add overseas weights to the military balance—a departure from the pre-Korean War days when instances of military assistance to countries on the Communist periphery were defined as stopgap emergency efforts, while the most important contributions expected from these peripheral countries were serious strides in their own socioeconomic development.

The military balance-of-power emphasis to containment in the Middle East was, as in Western Europe, stimulated by the Korean War. The Truman Administration had always regarded the Middle East as of strategic significance; and in the early 1950s its special attributes—the source of two-thirds of the West's oil reserves, the Suez Canal, and the location of important British military bases—were seen as immediately vital should there be a global test of strength. The United States, joined by Britain, France, and Turkey, tried to induce the Arabs to participate in a Middle East Defense Command. But Egypt and the

Arab States had defined the effort as a plot by the imperialist powers to reestablish control of the area. Their fingers burned in this attempt, Truman and Acheson fell back on the Point IV approach, offering technical assistance without "strings" in the hope of maintaining a basis for friendly association.[1]

Dulles, however, was not to be dissuaded by these past failures to fill the Middle Eastern military vacuum. The premises of the New Look gave a new imperative to the organization of indigenous military capabilities. The Middle East may be complicated; but certainly not unmanageable to the skilled diplomatist. In 1953 Dulles made a trip to the area, sounding out, with offers of economic and military assistance, current receptivity to a Middle East Defense Command. Colonel Nasser's unequivocal rejection of the scheme, on the grounds that the new nationalist leaders in the area would be committing political suicide if they entered into external defense alliances, only prompted Dulles to try an end run:

Many of the Arab League countries are so engrossed with their quarrels with Israel or with Great Britain or France [observed Dulles] that they pay little heed to the menace of Soviet Communism. However, there is more concern where the Soviet Union is near. In general, the northern tier of nations shows awareness of the danger.[2]

The most receptive countries were Turkey (already a loyal member of NATO, but concerned, on its own account, with being outflanked on the East by its historic rival) and Pakistan (hardly concerned over Soviet aggression, but willing to exploit the Cold War to redress its local imbalance with India). The United States could make direct deals with these two widely separated nations; but the nations between—Iran and Iraq—would be less likely to risk antagonizing their Arab neighbors and Egypt. The trick was to blur the American role in the Turko-Pakistani association, and then on their own have these nations establish a mutual security arrangement with their neighbors, Iran and Iraq.

In February 1954 the United States military assistance agreement with Pakistan was announced; it was defined only as an arrangement for handling arms aid, without any formal alliance obligations. Paralleling these negotiations with the United States, Pakistan and Turkey entered into a treaty of friendship and cooperation for security, pledging to study means of cooperating to defend against external aggression, and inviting other states in the area to become associated with this effort. Overt initiatives to bring Iraq into the "northern tier" arrangements were Turkey's responsibility. The United States had already effected a bilateral military aid agreement with Premier Jamali; but, again, this involved no formal commitments to participate in collective regional defense. The Turkish-Iraqi agreement signed at Baghdad in February 1955 was very similar in terms to the previous year's agreement between Turkey and Pakistan; now, however, a more concerted attempt was made to draw in other states. The Iraqi leadership, quite openly in competition with Egypt for influence among the Arab states, was anxious to increase its regional bargaining power by extracting the maximum assistance from the West. Britain accepted the invitation to transform its previously bilateral base agreements with Iraq into a part of this expanding regional security system—now called the Baghdad Pact. Pakistan's adherence was a foregone conclusion. The next big plum was Iran. In 1954 there was still much political instability after the deposition of the anti-Western Mosaddegh regime; an obvious pro-Western alignment might reignite the extremist fires. But by the fall of 1955 the Shah felt more secure politically, and was particularly anxious to qualify for the assistance benefits of Pact membership in order to modernize his army.[3]

The result was a local bipolarization of the Middle East, with the north organized into the Baghdad Pact, and the south dominated (through subversion and threat, as well as common ideology and friendship) by Egypt. The new situation was very much the outcome of Dulles' efforts, but he was unwilling to become completely associated with his own handiwork. Financial and military support, and participation in the work of Pact subcommittees, yes; but full membership, no. Perceiving Soviet attempts to exploit the local bipolarization, Dulles felt the necessity of preserving some residue of United States influence with Nasser. Thus the simplification that had been taking place in United States diplomacy—attempting to maintain the balance of power by a somewhat indiscriminate adding of military allies—was beginning to produce its own complications.

The American-sponsored proliferation of alliances in the Middle East overlapped the similar effort in Asia to redress the Communist advantage in military manpower by getting signatures to a multilateral Southeast Asian treaty.

79

The deteriorating French position in Indochina was the immediate stimulus to the attempt to multilateralize, put some military flesh on, and give an indigenous cast to the existing pattern of special relationships between some of the local states and the United States, Britain, and France. Dulles and Eisenhower had been urging a Southeast Asian "NATO" since 1953. The full-fledged push now was in part the result of the military lessons of the Indochina conflict: the tactical irrelevance of United States strategic power, the unavailability of United States ground forces, and the lack of trained indigenous forces. And in part the new momentum for a local treaty association was an expression of the growing perception that resistance to Communism requires support of the indigenous peoples affected, and that this would not be forthcoming if the anti-Communist resistance bore the stigma of colonialism.

The Administration had been claiming that a Communist victory in Indochina would have serious consequences for the global balance of power. To the American people, Eisenhower dramatized the strategic considerations underlying our desire to help the French by comparing Indochina to the first of a row of dominoes, which if knocked over would topple the whole row.[4] To Prime Minister Churchill, in an urgent note requesting the British to join us in the *ad hoc* construction of a Southeast Asian collective defense force, the President wrote that:

If . . . Indochina passes into the hands of the Communists the ultimate effect on our and your global strategic position with the consequent shift in the power ratios throughout Asia and the Pacific could be disastrous. . . .[5]

But however disastrous the consequences of a Communist victory in Indochina, Eisenhower felt that the consequences to our global power position could be even *more* disastrous if the United States took up the major military burden of saving the area.

Various schemes for bringing United States military power into play were being advanced by Admiral Radford and Secretary Dulles. The leading option was an air strike from carriers of the U.S. Seventh Fleet. Eisenhower tended to agree with the majority of the Joint Chiefs of Staff that, in purely military terms, this would not significantly help the French situation on the ground. Yet he admitted to feeling "there was some merit in the argument that the psychological effect of an air strike would raise French and Vietnamese morale and improve, at least temporarily, the entire situation."[6] The real barrier, as far as the Pres-

ident was concerned, was the unwillingness of other countries to associate themselves with us in this or any other military intervention on
the side of the French. Dulles, having failed to arrive at a common
basis for action with Eden, appears at one point to have been willing to
go it alone.[7] But Eisenhower claims to have maintained a consistent
position throughout that "there would be no intervention without
allies." As Eisenhower explained to General Alfred Gruenther, then
NATO Supreme Commander:

> No Western power can go to Asia militarily, except as one of a concert
> of powers, which concert must include local Asiatic peoples.
> To contemplate anything else is to lay ourselves open to the charge of
> imperialism and colonialism—or at the very least—of objectionable pater-
> nalism.[8]

At the climax of the 1954 crisis, with the French under siege at
Dienbienphu, the point of no return for a Presidential choice from
among unpalatable alternatives—negotiate from a position of weakness or unilateral United States intervention—had been reached. On
April 29, in a strategy huddle with his top advisers Eisenhower inter-
posed his military judgment to dispose of all further discussion of
United States forceable intervention:

> I remarked [recounts Eisenhower] that if the United States were, unilater-
> ally, to permit its forces to be drawn into conflict in Indochina and in a
> succession of Asian wars, the end result would be to drain off our resources
> and weaken our over-all defensive position.[9]

Henceforth, the task remained for diplomacy to salvage as much of the
situation as possible.

Although Dulles would not put his signature to the resulting Geneva
accords (which could be read as giving legitimacy to the extension of
Communist control that had occurred) the Administration expected a
worse outcome than the one the Communists accepted: the allowance
(albeit temporary) of a non-Communist government for the southern
half of the country. The dire consequences to the power balance which
had been forecast were, it could be claimed, predicated on the fall of
the whole of Indochina.

Thus, the local balance of power could still be consolidated if the
non-Communist countries in the region worked fast enough in responding to the challenge. Dulles immediately concentrated his efforts
once again, committing the prestige of the United States to the con-

struction of a Southeast Asian mutual defense pact to be based primarily on indigenous capabilities. The result was an agreement somewhat short on the provision of capabilities and somewhat unconvincing in its purpose of giving an indigenous, non-colonial cast to anti-Communism.

The Southeast Asia Collective Defense Treaty, dated September 8, 1954, requires only *consultation* among its signatories in case one of them is the victim of armed attack or subversion. Each member "recognizes that aggression . . . in the treaty area against any of the Parties . . . would endanger its own peace and safety," but each member pledges no more than to "act in that event to meet the danger in accordance with its constitutional processes" (Article IV). The list of signatories to the treaty is revealing in itself: the United States, France, Britain, Australia, New Zealand, Thailand, the Philippines, and Pakistan. At the most the treaty provided, as Eisenhower claimed, "a moral, legal, and practical basis for helping our friends of the region." At the least, SEATO merely formalized pre-existing power relationships in Asia, neither significantly adding to nor subtracting from the three-way balance between the Communists, the anti-Communists, and the nonaligned.

Actually, Dulles and Eisenhower were already beginning to lose any illusions they might have had that formally committed military allies were one of the most relevant factors in the global balance of power. If anything, SEATO was a face-saving monument to the obsolescence of that simpler conception. Yet, along with the Baghdad Pact, it reinforced the "pactomania" stereotype of Dullesian diplomacy. More significantly, these early solemn agreements acted later as a constraint on attempts to implement more flexible premises about the functions of nationalism and nonalignment in Asia.

The enrichment of the Eisenhower Administration's premises about the ingredients of effective international power in Asia was reflected by the Formosa Straits crisis of 1954–55. The ink was still wet on the SEATO treaty when the Chinese Communists opened their bombardment of the offshore islands remaining in the hands of the Chinese Nationalists. The failure of the Communists to launch their threatened invasions of Quemoy and Matsu (they did take the Ta-chen) was proudly attributed by Dulles to those very factors of power with which he was most identified, and for which he was most criticized: formal military alliances, threats of strategic reprisal in response to limited enemy probes, and a willingness to convert a seemingly marginal objective into a life and death matter for our side if this appeared necessary to maintain the objective.

And characteristically, for Dulles, the form, more than the material substance, of power received his closest attention.

SEATO was inapplicable to the defense of Taiwan (Formosa) and the offshore islands defined by the Administration as contingently necessary to Taiwan's defense. For one, Taiwan was neither a member of the Treaty Organization nor covered by the treaty provisions, since there was considerable divergence of policy toward the whole China question among the signatories. All United States moves in the crisis had to be undertaken under the authority of bilateral agreements between the United States and the Republic of China on Taiwan. More important, the definition of the conflict by the United States as vital, involving essential strategic interests of the entire free world, was unacceptable to most of our allies. Yet Dulles attempted to give credit to the spirit, if not the letter, of the multi-nation regional security arrangement:

Its [Communist China's] almost unlimited manpower would easily dominate, and could quickly engulf, the entire area, were it not restrained by the mutual security structure which has been erected. But that structure will not hold if it be words alone. Essential ingredients are the deterrent power of the United States and our willingness to use that power in response to a military challenge.[10]

In a news conference on March 15, 1955 the Secretary was asked to indicate how he expected to apply United States military power to the defense of the offshore islands or other points in the Far East and Southeast Asia. "U.S. policy," he replied, "is not to split that power up into fragments." It was rather to preserve the ability to "use our full power." The most effective contribution the United States could make to the defense of the area was by our "strategic force with a high degree of striking power by sea and air." [11]

Eisenhower has disclosed in his memoirs that such public hints of strategic retaliation, however vague, were regarded within the Administration as more than merely threats. A few days before making the above remarks to the press, Dulles had returned from a two-week Asian trip and reported to the President that the Chinese were determined to capture Taiwan. Gaining Quemoy and Matsu would not end their determination.

"If we defend Quemoy and Matsu," advised Dulles, "we'll have to use atomic weapons. They alone will be effective against mainland airfields."

"To this I agreed," recounts Eisenhower. And in response to Dulles' estimate of "at least an even chance" of war growing out of the situation, Eisenhower recalls that "I merely observed that if this proved to be true it would certainly be recognized that the [war] would not be of our seeking." [12]

To take an even risk of general war with Communist China with such equanimity, Eisenhower had to be convinced of two propositions: that the issue involved was of major importance to the global position of the United States, and that Soviet Russia would refrain from direct involvement. These were the essential propositions of John Foster Dulles. Eisenhower showed his concurrence in two messages to Winston Churchill during the height of the crisis. Never was the Dullesian style and substance more evident.

On the vitalness of the interests at stake:

We believe that if international Communism should penetrate the island barrier in the Western Pacific and thus be in a position to threaten the Phillippines and Indonesia immediately and directly, all of us, including the free countries of Europe, would soon be in far worse trouble than we are now. Certainly the whole region would soon go.

. . .

Only a few months back we had both Chiang and a strong, well-equipped French Army to support the free world's position in Southeast Asia. The French are gone—making it clearer than ever that we cannot afford the loss of Chiang unless all of us are to get completely out of that corner of the globe. This is unthinkable to us—I feel it must be to you.

On the consequences of a failure to stand firm:

There comes a point where constantly giving in only encourages further belligerency. I think we must be careful not to pass that point in our dealings with Communist China. . . .

. . .

. . . we must show no lack of firmness in a world where our political enemies exploit every sign of weakness, and are constantly attempting to disrupt the solidarity of the free world's intentions to oppose their aggressive practices.

And finally, in discounting the likelihood of Soviet intervention:

I do not believe that Russia wants war at this time—in fact, I do not believe that even if we became engaged in a serious fight along the coast of China, Russia would want to intervene with her own forces. She would, of course, pour supplies into China in an effort to exhaust us and certainly would exploit the opportunity to separate us from your country. But I am convinced that Russia does not want, at this moment, to experiment with means of defense against the bombing that we could conduct against her mainland.[13]

The fact that the Chinese Communists decided not to attack after all was for Dulles proof of his premises of power and vindication of his strategic concepts. Emmet Hughes quotes the Secretary of State as claiming, "Of all the things I have done, the most brilliant of all has been to save Quemoy and Matsu." [14] This pride was reflected in the controversial "brink of war" interview he gave late in 1955 to James Shepley of *Life* magazine:

The ability to get to the verge without getting into the war is the necessary art. If you cannot master it you inevitably get into war. If you try to run away from it, if you are scared to go to the brink you are lost. We've had to look it square in the face—on the question of getting into the Indo-China war, and on the question of Formosa. We walked to the brink and we looked it in the face. We took strong action.[15]

Dulles claimed that in all of these situations the ultimate decisions were the President's, which undoubtedly was the case. He also claimed that "The President never flinched for a minute on any of these situations. He came up taut." [16] Again, this may very well have been the case, once the alternatives had been narrowed. But Dulles' intended implication that he and Eisenhower had identical premises about the most effective means of dealing with the nation's opponents bears further examination.

CHAPTER EIGHT

WAGING PEACE: THE EISENHOWER FACE

Quite naturally . . . [John Foster Dulles and I] agreed that a determined pursuit of peace with justice should be . . . the foremost objective of the American government. Such an objective . . . could reasonably be pursued, we knew, only if the United States spoke from a position of power.

But the needed power would have to comprehend not only military strength, the ago-old single criterion of civilizations long since reduced to rubble, but moral and economic strength as well.

DWIGHT D. EISENHOWER

The international posture of the United States during Eisenhower's first term cannot be shown to have flowed directly from the premises of power of Secretary Dulles—neither as consistently as is claimed by his adulators nor as unrelentingly as is charged by his detractors. The policy flexibility (or ambivalence) during the early Eisenhower years seems less attributable to any revision of premises by the Secretary than to the fact that the President had very different attitudes on the prominence to be given coercive tools of power in our diplomacy.

The greatest source of Eisenhower's power—in a personal sense—was that he was so well liked. His inclination as a world statesman was to transfer his likeableness to the nation which made him its leader, to make the personal style the national image.

The observation by Eisenhower's speech writer, Emmet Hughes, that there was a "deep conflict of premises" between the President and his Secretary of State [1] refers primarily to the disagreement about the best means for influencing men and nations.

Both men were apparently aware of the difference from the beginning of their relationship. Dulles put the matter delicately in a private conference before their official association began: "With my understanding of the intricate relationships between the peoples of the world and your sensitivities to the political considerations involved, we will make the most successful team in history." [2] And in one sense they did; the teamwork aspect of their relationship was impeccable. Eisenhower, in awe of Dulles' diplomatic credentials, gave his Secretary of State an unusual amount of authority in policy formulation and implementation. While Dulles, in awe of Eisenhower's tremendous domestic popularity and international prestige, was scrupulously deferential and loyal to the President's convictions, to the extent they were expressed in any particular policy.

However, as both the record and the memoirs of the period suggest, Dulles was much more industrious in translating his own predilections into policy than those of the President. And since such translation of general approach into particular diplomatic moves was, in the Eisenhower administrative fashion, the Secretary's job, not his, the President's general approach often remained unarticulated (in policy as well as speech) while the Secretary's policy premises were well attended. Readers of Eisenhower's own memoirs must fill in a great deal between the lines to glean the essentials of this relationship. With the exception of one or two instances, such as Eisenhower's questioning of Dulles' abruptness in withdrawing the Aswan Dam assistance (see below, p. 103), we are exposed to no differences of opinion. Eisenhower records the version of their relationship which he would like to stand:

It was said . . . that he [Dulles] sought not only to be influential in the conduct of foreign affairs, but to be responsible only to his own convictions and inclinations. What his critics did not know was that he was more emphatic than they in his insistence that ultimate and personal responsibility for all major decisions in the field of foreign relations belonged exclusively to the President, an attitude he meticulously maintained throughout our service together. He would not deliver an important speech or statement until after I had read, edited, and approved it; he guarded constantly against the possibility that any misunderstanding could arise between us. It was the mutual trust and understanding, thus engendered, that enabled me, with complete confidence, to delegate to him an unusual degree of flexibility as my representative in international conferences, well knowing that he would not in the slightest degree operate outside the limits previously agreed between us. The association was particularly gratifying to me because of the easy partnership we developed in searching for the answer to any complex problem. But although behind closed doors we worked as partners, he in all our conversations lived his conviction that he was the adviser, recognizing that the final decision had to be mine.[3]

Sherman Adams too claims that "the Secretary of State never made a major move without the President's knowledge and approval"; but he goes on to make the revealing observation that "the hard and uncompromising line the United States government took toward Soviet Russia and Red China between 1953 and the early months of 1959 were more a Dulles line than an Eisenhower one." [4]

The popular identification of Eisenhower with benign foreign policy postures is more than a myth circulated by critics looking for dissension at the top. The purpose here, in exposing the differences, is to help explain the simultaneous existence of seemingly contrary basic foreign policies at the top levels of the Eisenhower Administration. The putting forward of two faces on basic United States policy was not so much a conscious tactic as the result of a two-headed foreign policy formulation, in which differences were not fully confronted within the Administration.

Each of the prominent "peace" initiatives of the period were generated and formulated by special assistants or staff aides to the President, not by Dulles, in contrast to the usual pattern.

According to the principal drafter (Hughes), Eisenhower's April 1953 "Chance for Peace" address to the American Society of Newspaper Editors went against Dulles' grain. But because the Secretary of State knew how impatient the President was to follow through on a hunch that a dramatic peace probe in the wake of Stalin's death was worth a try, Dulles only objected obliquely to the address. To those working on the speech, Dulles spoke plainly:

. . . there's some real danger of our just seeming to fall in with these Soviet overtures. It's obvious that what they are doing is because of outside

[Western] pressures, and I don't know anything better we can do than keep up these pressures right now.[5]

Dulles' view of the power struggle between the Communist and non-Communist worlds conformed quite closely to what a game theorist would call a "zero-sum" game: that is, anything which could be rated as a plus for one's opponents, such as an increase in their military power, general power potential, or even economic well-being, should be regarded as a minus for oneself—and vice versa. Eisenhower, on the other hand—and this is what worried Dulles—was anxious to reduce the costs and risks of the contest to the United States by finding opportunities for *mutual* gain: by searching for "non-zero-sum" relationships.

Eisenhower's biggest frustrations at this time came from trying to reduce government expenditures. If only the huge burden of arms spending could be reduced significantly, then budgets could be balanced, taxes could be reduced, and private enterprise could flourish with less government interference! To Eisenhower's way of thinking, these effects would in turn lead to a revival of the American spirit of individual initiative which was the basic source of our national strength.

Possibly the new Soviet leaders had analogous problems. Eisenhower recalls that his "hope" was that "perhaps the time had arrived when the Soviet leaders had decided, because of the discontent of their subjects, to turn their factories to producing more goods for civilian use and thus to raise the living standards of the Soviet population." [6]

Dulles' hope was in the other direction—that the gap between the desires of the Soviet people and the policies of the Soviet regime would become so wide that the Soviet Union would eventually collapse. Dulles could, and did, finally go along with the peace probe Eisenhower and his White House advisers were preparing in April 1953, and banked on the result being an intensification of the gap between popular aspiration in the Communist countries and Politburo policy. His most optimistic view of the speech seems to have been that it might be a good weapon of political warfare.

But Eisenhower appears to have meant it when he pleaded publicly with the Soviet leaders for "a few . . . clear and specific acts . . . of sincere intent," (such as a finalization of the Korean armistice, and the conclusion of an Austrian peace treaty) so as to strengthen "world trust." Out of this could grow "political settlements for the other serious issues between the free world and the Soviet Union," and, concurrently, "the reduction of the burden of armaments now weighing upon the world." This last, Eisenhower truly wanted the Soviet leaders to realize, was his deepest aspiration. The core of the speech, and the part to which Eisenhower gave greatest emphasis, tried to convey his appreciation of the mutual benefits to be derived from substantial disarmament:

Every gun that is made, every warship launched, every rocket fired signifies, in the final sense, a theft from those who hunger and are not fed, those who are cold and are not clothed.

The world in arms is not spending money alone.

It is spending the sweat of its labors, the genius of its scientists, the hopes of its children.

The cost of one modern heavy bomber is this: a modern brick school for more that 30 cities.

It is two electric power plants, each serving a town of 60,000 population.

It is two fine, fully equipped hospitals.

It is some 50 miles of concrete highway.

We pay for a single fighter plane with a half million bushels of wheat.

We pay for a single destroyer with new homes that could have housed more than 8,000 people.

. . .

This is not a way of life at all, in any true sense. . . .[7]

Non-Dullesian premises also underlay the Atoms-for-Peace proposal, presented before the United Nations on December 8, 1953. This venture, too, which Eisenhower referred to as "my second major speech in the field of foreign relations," [8] found Dulles on the sidelines. The idea appears to have been very much Eisenhower's own. The President had been gloomy over the early drafts by his special assistant C. D. Jackson for an "Operation Candor" speech on the destructive power of thermonuclear weapons. The Soviet hydrogen explosion in August 1953 only reinforced Eisenhower's conviction that some way had to be found to dampen the tension and suspicion which had now evolved into an ever-more lethal, expensive phase of the arms race. He was disappointed that nothing concrete had come of his speech to the newspaper editors. "I began to search around," Eisenhower wrote to a friend, "for any kind of an idea that could bring the world to look at the atomic problem in a broad and intelligent way and still escape the impasse to action created by Russian intransigence in the matter of . . . inspection. . . ." [9]

While vacationing in Denver the idea occurred to the President that the United States and the Soviet Union could each donate fissionable material to the United Nations from their respective stockpiles, and the donations could be diverted to peaceful projects under international supervision. This would not be disarmament, but "my purpose was to promote development of mutual trust, a trust that was essential before we could hope for success in the . . . [major] disarmament proposals. . . ." To generate such trust it was important:

. . . to get the Soviet Union working with us in a noncontroversial phase of the atomic field. . . . If we were successful in making even a start, it was possible that gradually negotiation and cooperation might expand into something broader; there was hope that Russia's own self-interest might lead her to participate in joint humanitarian efforts.[10]

Eisenhower delegated the major responsibility for translating this idea into action to General Robert Cutler, his special assistant for National Security Affairs, Admiral Lewis Strauss, Chairman of the Atomic Energy Commission, and C. D. Jackson. Dulles, busy with a round of diplomatic conferences, was brought in only during the last minute drafting efforts on the UN speech. But this was not really his cup of tea. "An idealistic venture like the Atoms-for-Peace plan was hardly the sort of thing that would fire the imagination of a man like Dulles anyway," divulges Sherman Adams. "He gave it his tacit approval, but he had some doubts about it." [11]

Eisenhower was to be disappointed again at the lack of a positive Soviet response to his proposals, and nine months later turned Atoms-for-Peace into a project for joint Western cooperation in research on the peaceful uses of atomic energy. Eventually, Eisenhower could take credit for the creation of the International Atomic Energy Agency, which the Soviets did join, for the exchange of nuclear information and limited inspection over the nuclear energy facilities of member nations without weapons programs. But the tension-reducing and trust-building functions of the original proposal were eclipsed by more dramatic events of 1954—the Indochina conflict, the formation of the Asian and Middle Eastern military alliances, the acceptance of a rearmed West Germany in the Atlantic defense system—all of which were conducted in the Dulles style and reflected his premises.

Dulles inherited the Acheson attitude that there were in fact no significant negotiable issues between the Soviets and us. Each side, for the foreseeable future, was likely to adhere to the position "what's mine is mine; what's yours is negotiable." From the standpoint of the United States the potentially negotiable issue was the Soviet illegal absorption of Eastern Europe, or at least a critical segment of that problem: the division of Germany. But both Secretaries of State were convinced that a condition for Soviet willingness to sacrifice some of their control would be a global imbalance of power clearly favoring the West. Acheson does not seem to have had confidence in the emergence of such a condition of obvious Western superiority. Dulles, at least in his rhetoric, looked forward to an advantageous balance of power developing as a result of the collapse of the Soviet economy and social system. Meantime, however, it was essential to maintain the military strength of the West to deter the Soviets from attempting to alter the balance of power in their favor.

To these premises Dulles added the corollary that some amount of East-West tension was an important condition for the maintenance of Western power. As he confided to a State Department colleague:

> If there's no evident menace from the Soviet bloc our will to maintain unity and strength may weaken. It's a fact, unfortunate though it be, that in promoting our programs in Congress we have to make evident the international communist menace. Otherwise such programs as the mutual security one would be decimated.
>
> The same situation would probably prevail among our allies [as a result of a detente]. They might feel that the danger was over and therefore they did not need to continue to spend large sums for defense.[12]

The Soviets, Dulles believed, were aware of this susceptibility of the Western democracies, and were trying to exploit it. Their calls for negotiations, for relaxation of tensions, for disarmament agreements, were a "Trojan horse" technique to defeat efforts at European rearmament—particularly the integration of a rearmed Germany into the Western bloc, as in the European Defense Community.

However, Dulles found that other political leaders in the Western alliance (with the possible exception of Adenauer) felt compelled—partly for domestic political considerations—to make a convincing display of peace initiatives before asking their peoples to support major rearmament. From 1953 to 1955, Churchill, and then Eden, was a leading advocate of a big-power summit meeting. The Administration maintained its position that the Soviets would first have to show by deeds, not by promises, that they were interested in serious attempts to reduce tension. As an example of a sincere deed, Dulles and Eisenhower on a number of occasions mentioned Soviet agreement to an Austrian Peace Treaty. Suddenly, in the spring of 1955, the Soviets reversed their earlier intransigence on Austria and agreed to a mutual withdrawal of troops, demilitarization, neutralization, and a political system contemplating a non-Communist regime. Dulles was apparently surprised and temporarily thrown off balance by the demands for a summit, now increasingly heard from most capitals.[13]

The Secretary of State quickly regained his footing by suggesting that the Soviets' willingness to pay the entry price (the Austrian treaty) for a summit meeting was due to the success of his diplomacy. "It is clear we are seeing the results of a policy of building unity and strength within the free world," he said in his May 24, 1955 press conference. "This policy has produced a radical change in Soviet policy, illustrated by new Soviet attitudes toward Austria and Yugoslavia." [14]

Now, in order to continue to play the role of man out front in Alliance diplomacy vis-à-vis the Soviets, Dulles took an active part during the next few months in clearing the path to the summit. It is doubtful, however, that he believed the Soviets had made a shift in grand strategy. If anything the Austrian treaty was a tactical retreat, and Dulles was determined that it should be shown as such. He was skeptical of any important agreements occurring at the summit, particularly on the key question of Germany; but for that very reason Dulles felt it important to have the matter of Germany a prominent part of the agenda. Soviet unwillingness to barter control of East Germany would be exposed, and Adenauer could then convincingly reply to critics of his rigid policy that the Soviets were not really interested in a reunified Germany even if it were neutral.[15]

Although Eisenhower appreciated Dulles' reluctance to have the President drawn into a high-level charade of mutual accommodation and cordiality with the Soviets, once it was decided to go to the summit Eisenhower's inclinations again found an opportunity for expression. "Unlike Dulles, who entertained no such high hopes," writes Sherman Adams, "Eisenhower went to Geneva seeking to make the meeting a solid beginning of a move toward world disarmament." [16]

Adams' characterization of Eisenhower's purposes and expectations may be a slight exaggeration. The President had been somewhat disillusioned in his optimism by the Soviets' lack of positive response to his Atoms-for-Peace plan; and, in light of this, particularly angered at the Russian pose as the champion of peace and disarmament. A month before the conference, Eisenhower wrote in confidence to his friend Swede Hazlett: "Personally, I do not expect any spectacular results from the forthcoming 'Big Four' conference." [17] But, in contrast to Dulles, he was unworried about the possibility that the Soviets were engaged in a "Trojan horse" tactic to compel the West to let down its guard. If Soviet tactical considerations required a temporary reduction of tensions, Eisenhower seemed concerned only that the Soviets not attempt to take all the credit for the improved atmosphere. Especially in the field of disarmament negotiations the Soviets should not be able to make all the grandstand plays, as they had been doing recently. Although not particularly hopeful of immediate results, the President was at least determined that this time the propaganda battle would not be won by the Soviets.

Eisenhower did agree with Dulles that in his attempt to convince world opinion that the United States was making a major effort toward peace, he should not create overly high expectations in the American people which would then be followed by extreme disillusionment. Even so, in his address to the nation on the eve of his departure for the conference the former General transformed his peace "probe" into a crusade; and this one, like the others he had led, he must *win*:

If we look at . . . [the] record we would say, "Why another conference? What hope is there for success?" Well now the first question I ask you, "Do we want to do nothing? Do we want to sit and drift along to the inevitable end in such a contest of war or increased tensions?"

Pessimism never won any battle, he reminded his listeners.

But also missing from the previous conferences, said Eisenhower, was "an honest intent to conciliate, to understand, to be tolerant, to see the other fellow's viewpoint as well as we see our own." We must change the spirit in which these conferences are conducted, he urged.

Finally, there was emerging "a terrific force"—the common desire for peace on the part of the people of all the world—"to which I believe all the political leaders of the world are beginning to respond. . . ." Throughout the world prayers for peace were ascending. These prayers, said the President, could achieve "a very definite and practical result at this very moment":

Suppose, on the next Sabbath day . . . America, 165 million people of us, went to our accustomed places of worship and, crowding those places, asked for help, and by so doing demonstrated to all the world the sincerity and depth of our aspirations for peace.
This would be a mighty force.[18]

This demonstrative, symbolic aspect of Eisenhower's speeches for peace also appears to have been the aspect which most appealed to him in the "open skies" plan he dramatically unveiled at Geneva.

Again, this plan was conceived by a group more directly responsive to Eisenhower and his slant on the ways of influencing men and nations than to the Dulles line. A panel of governmental and outside experts headed by Nelson Rockefeller, then Special Assistant to the President on Foreign Policy, had been meeting at Quantico Marine base to study various positions which the United States might take at the forthcoming summit conference. The Rockefeller group's terms of reference were very much Eisenhower's: the Soviets were almost sure to offer a disarmament plan at Geneva, and the United States could not afford to appear any less interested in arms control, especially in light of the rising pacifist and neutralist sentiments in Europe. According to the journalist who was given the privilege of writing the "inside" story on the open skies plan, the problem facing the Quantico group was "how the United States could retain its nuclear power but still make it clear for all to see that its purpose was peace." [19] Both of these demands might be met, the panel decided, if the President were to revive and present in a fresh expanded version some of the ideas for mutual aerial inspection and exchange of military information which had appeared in the "control" provisions of United States arms reduction proposals, starting with the Baruch Plan. This time mutual aerial inspection would be presented as a desirable way to reduce the likelihood of surprise attack. The President received the Quantico recommendations on June 10, 1955 and read them with enthusiasm. Dulles was less enthusiastic, but not opposed. After careful discussion, the plan was held in suspension, pending developments at the conference.[20]

When Bulganin tried to attract attention to Soviet disarmament proposals on the first days of the conference Rockefeller pressed Eisenhower to seize the initiative. Eisenhower sought the counsel of Anthony

Eden, who immediately saw the virtues of the proposal. It was decided that the President himself would present the idea to the conference, but exactly when was held in abeyance.[21] The search was for the best moment of maximum impact. Everybody in the United States delegation knew the President was going to make some particularly important statement, wrote James Reston from Geneva. "Photographers were alerted ahead of time for the briefing. Plans were made to publicize his remarks." [22] The situation was made for the grand gesture, and particularly for the Eisenhower personality.

As if seized by an inspiration, in the middle of reading from his prepared remarks to the July 21 meeting of the conference, the President took off his glasses, placed them on the table, faced Bulganian and Khrushchev, and said extemporaneously:

Gentlemen, since I have been working on this memorandum to present to this conference, I have been searching my heart and mind for something that I could say here that could convince everyone of the great sincerity of the United States in approaching this problem of disarmament. I should address myself for a moment principally to the delegates from the Soviet Union, because our two great countries admittedly possess new and terrible weapons in quantities which do give rise in other parts of the world, or reciprocally, to the fears and dangers of surprise attack.

I propose, therefore, that we take a practical step, that we begin an arrangement, very quickly, as between ourselves—immediately. These steps would include:

To give to each other a complete blueprint of our military establishments, from beginning to end, from one end of our countries to the other; lay out the establishments and provide the blueprints to each other.

Next, to provide within our countries facilities for aerial photography to the other country—we to provide you the facilities within our country, ample facilities for aerial reconnaisance, where you can make all the pictures you choose and take them to your own country to study; you to provide exactly the same facilities for us and we to make these examinations— and by this step to convince the world that we are providing as between ourselves against the possibility of great surprise attack, thus lessening danger and relaxing tension. Likewise we will make more easily attainable a comprehensive and effective system of inspection and disarmament, because what I propose, I assure you, would be but a beginning.[23]

The Soviets, possibly sensing the gesture's emotional impact, possibly caught off guard, and quite evidently anxious to allow as much "relaxation of tension" as possible to emerge from the conference, held back their negative response. Contrary to their usual practice, the Moscow papers reprinted the text of the President's speech. Even on the sensitive question of Germany, the Soviets accepted a rather ambiguously worded joint statement that could be interpreted, loosely, as willingness to accept the Western proposals as terms of reference for forthcoming detailed discussions to be held by the foreign ministers in October.

In Eisenhower's final statement at Geneva before the conference adjourned on July 23 he told the assembly, "It has been on the whole a good week." In his judgment, he said, "the prospects of a lasting peace . . . are brighter. The dangers of the overwhelming tragedy of modern war are less." [24] Sherman Adams recalls when the White House staff welcomed the President back to Washington "he spoke to us with feeling that he had accomplished some real good." And the next day the President told Congressional leaders that the Russians seemed to be changing their tactics toward us.[25]

The October foreign ministers meeting confirmed for Dulles his view that there was really nothing to negotiate about, once having descended from the pleasant atmospherics of the summit to the bedrock of incompatible Cold War objectives. On the matters of Germany, and European security, there was no desire on the part of the Soviets in 1955 to trade their de facto control for paper guarantees that a reunited Germany would be rearmed and "neutral" (Germany was no Austria). Nor was there enthusiasm on the part of Dulles or Adenauer to trade the presumed stability of the present German situation (resulting from a tight integration of the Federal Republic into the NATO apparatus) for the highly volatile political cross currents that would be loosed if reunification, under an Austria-type formula, were an immediate prospect. Schemes for local military "disengagement" were no less suspiciously viewed by the two superpowers. The Soviets were afraid of loosening their main means of keeping the satellites in check. But even if the Soviets should seriously want a mutual thinning out of forces along the Iron Curtain, from the Dulles perspective, this would seriously weaken the overall Western diplomatic position in Europe which now, more than ever, depended upon a large German military contribution to NATO. The reduction of Western military strength could only follow a general political settlement in Europe; it should never be countenanced as a means for "reducing tensions." "Open skies" was flatly rejected by the Soviets as another Western scheme for espionage; thus it never had to undergo the hard scrutiny (its effect upon the

97

credibility of United States strategic doctrines, for example) Dulles would have felt compelled to give it were it truly negotiable.

This return to the more rigid level of East-West interaction was to Eisenhower a "disillusionment," a "grievous disappointment," which he attributed to "Soviet duplicity." But one of his purposes, he felt, had been fulfilled. "The record was established: All could now see the nature of Soviet diplomatic tactics as contrasted with those of the Free World." In addition:

Peoples had been given a glowing picture of hope and, though badly blurred by the Soviets, at least the outlines of the picture remained. Moreover . . . the cordial atmosphere of the talks . . . never faded entirely. Indeed, the way was opened for some increase in intercourse between East and West—there began, between the United States and Russia, exchanges of trade exhibitions, scientists, musicians and other performers; visits were made by Mikoyan and Kozlov to the United States, and returned, by Vice President Nixon and my brother Milton, to the Soviet Union and Poland. These were small beginnings, but they could not have transpired in the atmosphere prevailing before Geneva.[26]

The Geneva episode, more than any other event during the Eisenhower presidency, illustrated Eisenhower's sourness with the coercive tools of power of the thermonuclear age, and a diplomacy premised upon their readiness for use. The kind of influence he wanted to wield, personally, and as the symbol of the nation, was influence over others derived from their confidence in our goodwill, and mutual affection. If the people of the world could only know our sincere purposes they would come to trust and like us—and ultimately their rulers (even in Communist countries) would follow suit. This was the underlying secret of power.

CHAPTER NINE

COMPLICATING THE PREMISES:
SUEZ AND HUNGARY

The cement of fear is not so strong to hold us together as it was to bring us together.

JOHN FOSTER DULLES

While Dulles was pointing with pride at his success in deterring the Communists through the organization and skillful manipulation of the *military* ingredients of the balance of power, the Soviets and Chinese were pushing the competition into new channels. The Administration, however reluctant it was to do so, would need to develop a more complex conception of the requirements for maintaining the balance.

Chou En-lai's emergence as the champion of coexistence at the Afro-Asian Conference held in Bandung, April 18-24, 1955, has been hailed by a Dulles biographer as a "notable victory for the Dulles policy of deterrence as tested at the brink of war." [1] Other analysts are more cautious about the cause and effect relationship, and point to the fact that the tapering off of Chinese pressure against Quemoy and Matsu merely *coincided* with Chou's attitude at the Bandung Conference.

If Communist China's sweetness and light at Bandung was regarded as only the cowed performance of a country chastened by a brink-of-war confrontation with the United States, then the intelligence arms of the United States government must have been totally inept. There is, of course, no support for the notion that Eisenhower and Dulles were unaware of what was really going on—Dulles' self-serving rhetoric to the contrary. In fact, Dulles had conjectured to the President and leaders of Congress two weeks before Bandung that, with the Afro-Asian Conference in mind, the Communists might be trying to quiet the straits conflict so as to be accepted as a peace-loving nation.

Since 1953 the Soviets had been quite openly conducting a program of expanded trade and lending with the new nations. (China was of course not as active in the economic field; but this was still the period when, in American policy-making circles, the "Sino-Soviet Bloc" was thought to be practicing a largely coordinated strategy.) By 1956 the network of Communist Bloc trade and credit agreements extended to practically every nonaligned country in the Middle East and Asia, and even to a few countries supposedly a part of the Dulles alliance system—namely, Pakistan, Iran, and Greece.

The problem was not so much one of *recognizing* the shift in Communist tacts to win friends and influence people through cooperative economic ventures instead of coercion as it was one of *what* to do about it. There was pressure within the Administration as early as 1953–54, notably from Mutual Security Administrator Harold Stassen and from Elsworth Bunker, Ambassador to India, to expand United States economic assistance to additional nations, without making membership in an anti-Communist military pact the determining qualification for assistance.

However, in mid-1954, Stassen was replaced at the Mutual Security Administration by John Hollister, whose aim was to reduce foreign aid expenditures. And Dulles gave his newly appointed Undersecretary of State, Herbert Hoover, Jr., overall guidance of foreign economic policy. Innovation was effectively blocked. And orthodox premises were reasserted with even greater adamancy: namely, that economic aid to nations not militarily allied with the United States was an extravagance we could not afford; that such nations were essentially hostile to our purposes anyway, seeking to embarrass us, and to play off East against West for their own material gain; that many of these new nationalist regimes were more interested in following "socialist" models of development, and thus had ideological leanings toward the "other side" in the Cold War despite their protestations of nonalignment; and, finally, that even if we discounted these ideological incompatibilities and extended aid, most of the would-be beneficiaries lacked the administrative and technical talent, economic structure, and will to make significant gains with the additional capital.[2]

In late 1955 and early 1956, with Soviet salesmen in the underdeveloped areas becoming a familiar part of the international scene Nixon and Nelson Rockefeller added their voices to Stassen's in urging a dramatic response by the United States. The same orthodox wall was encountered again.[3] But now the evidence of Soviet economic penetration, particularly in the Middle East, was more alarming. Dulles was specially worried, as he expressed to a Cabinet meeting on September 30, 1955, over the extent to which the "commercial" transactions were involving the provision of obsolete Soviet weapons to the Arab nations.[4] This time Eisenhower and Dulles asked Congress to increase the foreign aid program—then running at about $2.7 billion annually—to $4.9 billion. They also asked for limited authority, in the nature of contingency funds, to support large projects such as Nasser's Aswan Dam.

Yet, economic assistance was viewed primarily as a slush fund to entice the reluctant to "our side" in the bipolar struggle. Interdependencies between progress toward self-sustaining economic growth, social reform, constitutionalism, and resistance to Communist subversion were not yet incorporated into the Administration's premises about the ways to maintain the global balance of power.

However, the premise that the balance of power was essentially bipolar, or ought to be organized on a bipolar basis, was undermined drastically by the Suez and Hungarian crises in the fall of 1956.

The United States insistence that Israel, Britain, and France desist from their military intervention against Nasser was an embarrassing eruption of the centrifugal tendencies which had long seethed beneath the surface of the Atlantic alliance. The premise that differences among the principal allies in NATO were marginal and mainly over tactical questions, involving how to implement the basic shared commitment to maintain a global balance of power against the Communist Bloc, was now shattered. To differ over what was a sufficiently severe threat to require an act of war against a significant Middle Eastern power, and risk provoking direct Soviet counter-intervention, was to differ over a central, not a marginal, issue.

By the time the Baghdad Pact efforts had reached their culmination in 1955, the United States had already begun to act on assumptions antithetical to those underlying its original sponsorship of this "northern tier" alliance system. This network of alliances was based on the premise that the goal of preventing Soviet absorption of the Middle East was best served by building up the indigenous armies of those regimes willing to enter into formal alliance with the West. Nasser's response —the organization of a Pan Arab alliance system and the bartering of Middle Eastern products for arms manufactured by Soviet Union satellites—shook the foundations of the existing United States approach to the Middle East.

The Soviets were seen to be leapfrogging the northern tier with such success that the Administration feared Soviet absorption of the area to the south (including the oil pipelines and the Suez Canal) might occur without a single Communist soldier crossing an international boundary. And, ironically, this was happening through the very device that we had fashioned: the establishment of military-dependency relationships on the part of local regimes toward external big powers. But the Administration was still not ready to throw its established orientation overboard. Rather, its policies increasingly evidenced the unsettled ambivalence of trying to incorporate into overall policy a new major premise contradictory to its established policy premises. The new premise was simply that it was necessary for the United States to convincingly demonstrate respect for the nationalisms of the area in order to avoid the local political alienation from the West which was easing the way for Soviet penetration.

The policy implications of this new premise were expressed in a series of United States moves in 1955–56 which alienated Britain and France, and contributed ultimately to their split with us over Suez. An early manifestation of the new premise was our embarrassed avoidance of formal identification with our own offspring, the Baghdad Pact. The British, who had joined the Pact, felt betrayed by this turnabout which Prime Minister Eden branded an American "failure to put its weight behind its friends in the hope of being popular with its foes." [5] (The British had recently agreed to liquidate their military base at Suez under the assumption that they could still focus military pressure on the area through the instrumentalities of the Baghdad Pact.) France had been disappointed throughout this period in the United

States unwillingness to demonstrate any sympathy for the French position in North Africa. But now, to add injury to insult, the United States in offering financial assistance to Nasser's billion-dollar development scheme, the Aswan Dam, was aiding an Egyptian regime, which in turn was openly giving assistance to the Algerian rebel movement.

From Dulles' perspective, the British and French were the prisoners of their traditional colonial viewpoint as well as their current economic interests in the area. But the United States had the responsibility of keeping its eye on the ball: the East-West balance of power. If the struggle with the Communists for influence in the Middle East was assuming a new form, because of the growth of nationalism and the Soviet attempt to exploit its combustibility, then the United States would have to adjust its policies.

To our European allies, the American "adjustment" was crude, unsophisticated, and ultimately disastrous. First, we demonstrated a magnanimity to Nasser which the wily politician could only define as New-World gullibility. Then, Eisenhower and Dulles, having finally come to the conclusion that Nasser was playing off the United States against the Soviets on the Aswan Dam project, cancelled the project in such an abrupt, back-of-the-hand manner that Nasser was driven to nationalize the Suez Canal. In French and British eyes, this act—the catalyst of their subsequent military intervention—was an overreaction; it could have been avoided were Dulles not so anxious to humiliate Nasser for having taken the United States for a sucker.

Eisenhower subsequently had doubts that "we might have been undiplomatic in the way the cancellation [of Aswan financing] was handled"; and admitted that if the United States had "avoided a showdown on the issue, we would probably have deprived Nasser of a dramatic and plausible excuse for his subsequent actions affecting the Canal." But Dulles maintained that Nasser got the treatment he was asking for.[6]

Dulles' sympathetic biographer, John Robinson Beal, sheds some light on the Secretary of State's attitude, an attitude significant in view of the movement toward greater flexibility on the subject of nationalistic neutralism and economic competition preceding the Aswan cancellation:

For Dulles, a moment of cold-war climax had come. It was necessary to call Russia's hand in the game of economic competition. Dulles firmly believed the Soviet Union was not in a position to deliver effectively on all her economic propaganda offers.

It was necessary to demonstrate to friendly nations, by act rather than by oral explanation, that U.S. tolerance of nations which felt it necessary to stay out of Western defensive alliances could not brook the kind of insult Nasser presented in his repeated and accumulated unfriendly gestures.

It was necessary to make the demonstration on a grand scale. . . .

Nasser combined the right timing, the right geography, and the right order of magnitude for a truly major gambit in the cold war.

. . .

It risked opening a key Middle East country, one whose territory bracketed the strategic Suez Canal, to Communist economic and political penetration. It risked alienating other Arab nations, controlling an oil supply without which Western Europe's mechanized industry and military defenses would be defenseless.

Dulles' bet was placed on his belief that it would expose the shallow character of Russia's foreign economic pretensions and that most nations would accept the thought that there comes a time when tolerance must give way to firmness.[7]

Dulles had conveyed this rationale to the European Allies. But when, in response to Nasser's Canal grab, *they* launched their own "demonstration on a grand scale," Eisenhower and Dulles slapped them down. The motives of the Administration in demanding that Israel, Britain, and France call off their military action were manifold and complex (indeed, so complex that the Europeans appeared to have genuinely miscalculated that the United States would support them). The event is discussed here because of its pertinence in illustrating the complications besetting the Administration's orientation toward the global balance of power.

On the one hand, the old policy of buying military allies through military assistance agreements had reached a point of diminishing return; and the denial of Soviet penetration into the remaining nonaligned areas required a willingess to back the national development efforts of the strident, sensitive, and unpredictable charismatic leaders around whom the new mass national parties tended to form.

On the other hand, if these "a-plague-on-both-your-houses" regimes were to qualify for assistance, the relative value to our alliance partners of joining us in anti-Communist pacts was degraded.

The policies of the United States during the Suez crisis reflected the fact that such considerations had come into play at the highest levels of government, but also that they had not been resolved. First, there was the wooing of the proud Egyptian nationalists from the Soviet embrace; then came the public altercation in response to being two-timed, with a fear of taking action that would drive Egypt and its allies irreversibly into the arms of Russia. This last result would disadvantageously affect the balance of power.

The British and the French, of course, cast their case *for* military intervention in global balance of power terms:

Foreign Minister Pineau [recounts Eisenhower] compared Nasser's action to the seizure of the Rhineland by Hitler two decades earlier. He argued that the West should react promptly and in strength, or else Europe would find itself "totally dependent upon the good will of the Arab powers."

. . .

Anthony [Eden]'s letter went to some length to elaborate on the anxiety of his government about Nasser's ultimate ambitions, and the British conviction that his seizure of the Canal constituted only the first step of a planned program. He compared Nasser's tactics to those of the Soviets. He equated any exercise of allied restraint and patience to the arguments which had prevailed during the rise of Hitler during the years prior to 1939. . . . The British, he wrote, believed that Nasser's plan included the expansion of his power until he could, in effect, hold the Western world for ransom.[8]

But Eisenhower and Dulles by this time were not worried only about Nasser's ambitions, or the extension of his power. A sufficiently strong Arab nationalism might even be a welcome buffer against Soviet penetration. The Europeans were thinking of their own economic well-being, and equating this with the global balance of power. This, it is true, was in accord with the priorities established by the United States during the Marshall Plan era. But times had changed. Not only was the most intense United States–Soviet competition shifting to non-European areas, but the resilience of the European economies in the face of a squeeze on their oil and commerce was not as enfeebled as the British and French were picturing it. "Foster felt that Anthony's fears of being wholly deprived of Middle East oil were exaggerated," explains Eisenhower.[9] To assuage the fears of the Europeans, the Administration worked out an emergency oil pool plan by which the French and British would be supplied by the United States and other nations whose resources were not cut off by the Middle Eastern crisis. A permanent blocking of the Suez to French and British commerce, and an indefinite denial to them of Middle Eastern supplies of fuel might very well have serious consequences for the global balance. The President and Dulles assured the Europeans that this eventuality was a central consideration in all our efforts. The question was *how* to avoid such a consequence, and, of equal importance in United States calculations, how to do it without turning the entire Arab world against the West. "Obviously we were anxious to sustain our continuing relations with our old and traditional friends, Britan and France," writes Eisenhower. "But to us the situation was not quite so simple as those two governments portrayed it." [10]

The debate between the United States and its principal allies over the consequences of resorting to force against Nasser intensified during the weeks leading up to the British and French military intervention. On October 5, Foreign Ministers Pinay and Lloyd met with Dulles and frankly urged the use of force, maintaining that only through bringing Nasser to his knees could Western prestige in Africa and the Middle East be restored. According to Eisenhower's account, "Foster disagreed vehemently . . . setting forth our conviction that Africa, the Middle East, and Asia would be inflamed against the West if we resorted *unnecessarily* to force." [11]

Exchanges of this nature continued between the three governments up to the last minute, when the British and French intervened with troops and planes, ostensibily to separate the Israelis and Egyptians, three days after the Israelis smashed into Egyptian postions in the Sinai. Eisenhower's last pleading cable to Eden remained unsent as on October 31 British planes based on Cyprus struck at Egyptian ports and communications centers. The cable, which Eisenhower quotes in part in his memoirs as an example of his thoughts at the time, stressed again the weight the United States was giving to the new anti-colonial nationalisms:

I must say that it is hard for me to see any good final result emerging from a scheme that seems to antagonize the entire Moslem world. Indeed I have difficulty seeing any end whatsoever if all the Arabs should begin reacting somewhat as the North Africans have been operating against the French.[12]

The United States reaction, once military action had begun, was consonant with the position developed up to that time. The flat unwillingness to support the British, French, or Israeli action and the spon-

sorship of United Nations cease-fire and peacekeeping efforts were defended in Eisenhower's election campaign speeches, and in Dulles' addresses to the United Nations, as being required by our morally-based
adherence to the principles of nonaggression. However, in a letter to
Winston Churchill on November 27, following the acceptance of a
United Nations-controlled cease-fire, the President was more candid as
to our overriding considerations:

Many months ago it became clear that the Soviets were convinced that the
mere building of mighty military machines would not necessarily accomplish their purposes, while at the same time their military effort was severely
limiting their capacity for conquering the world by other means, especially
economic. . . my point [in communications to Eden counseling against
the use of force] was that since the struggle with Russia had obviously
taken on a new tactical form, we had to be especially careful that any
course of action we adopted should by its logic and justice command world
respect, if not sympathy. . . .[13]

The compelling concerns, it should be underlined, had been for the
political repercussions of Western military intervention. But there also
had been a certain degree of concern that the Soviets might make a direct military response. During the height of the crisis, Eisenhower and
Allen Dulles, Director of the Central Intelligence Agency, were worried
that the Soviets might try to stage fighter planes from Egypt. The President asked for high-altitude reconnaissance flights over Israel and Syria
to see if Soviet planes and pilots had landed at Syrian bases. "Our
people should be alert in trying to determine Soviet intentions," he
told Dulles. "If the Soviets should attack Britain and France directly
we would of course be in a major war." [14]

The President ordered the military to implement measures to "pro-
gressively achieve an advanced state of readiness." In general, however,
these were regarded as precautionary signals to the Soviets that the
United States would not be taken by surpise. Admiral Radford, in discussing the strategic military context with the President, observed that
the Soviets would find it extremely difficult to undertake any military
operations in the Middle East. "The only reasonable form of intervention would be long-range air strikes with nuclear weapons—which
seems unlikely." [15]

Eisenhower was suspicious, however, that the Soviets might attempt
some ruse to gain a military foothold in the area without running the
high risks of direct provocation of the United States. He therefore re-

jected the Soviet proposal for joint police action by the Soviets and the United States as "unthinkable." The Soviets, Eisenhower told the White House Staff on November 5, "seeing their failure in the satellites, might be ready to undertake any wild adventure . . . [they] are as scared and furious as Hitler was in his last days. There's nothing more dangerous than a dictatorship in that frame of mind." [16]

The existing military balance of power, based on United States superiority in strategic nuclear striking capabilities, gave the Administration relative confidence that it could control the military dimensions of the conflict—largely by deterring Soviet military moves. But the military balance was seen to be largely irrelevant to the political dimensions of the conflict, and it was these political dimensions that could very seriously affect the global distribution of power.

The Suez crisis thus drove home, and made operational, the premise that in the power struggle with the Soviets the sentiments of the new nationalist regimes were of critical importance. But as yet the policy implications were drawn primarily in the form of guidelines concerning what *not* to do for fear of alienating the nonaligned nationalists. Policies for positive action—for programs to strengthen the ability of these regimes to counter the socioeconomic sources of Communist subversion within their countries—required the acceptance of additional premises which were still unpalatable to the Eisenhower Administration.

Another lesson of the crisis for the Administration was that neither could the biggest weights on the Western side of the global balance of power be manipulated as if the Alliance was a simple hierarchy with the United States at the apex, nor the movement of these weights be restricted to conflicts between the non-Communist and Communist worlds.

The nonhomogeneity of the opposing bloc was another prominent realization of this period. But again, the problem was what to do about it. The need to solve this problem in concrete policy terms, rather than with the sloganeering rhetoric used to cover lack of action during the Berlin uprisings of 1953, was finally forced upon the Administration by the Hungarian uprising. The Eastern European crisis, too, was to have the effect of undermining the reliance by Dulles and Eisenhower on a rather limited set of coercive tools as our primary weights on the Western side of the global power balance.

Events in the Middle East complicated the premises about the utility of United States technological-military resources (reflected in the United States strategic posture, and our military assistance to allies) for solidifyng the anti-Communist side of the balance, and bringing this organized power more under United States direction.

The simultaneous events in Eastern Europe dramatically demonstrated the impotence of these military components for "offensive" operations, including the support of *diplomatic* efforts, to reduce the sphere of Soviet control. It is technically correct that in the rhetoric of the 1952 election Dulles and Eisenhower had explicitly disassociated their "liberation" policy from any incitements to armed revolt. "The people [in Eastern Europe] have no arms," said Dulles in a Chicago campaign speech, "and violent revolt would be futile; indeed it would be worse than futile, for it would precipitate massacre." [17] Yet implicit in Dulles' call to "activate the strains and stresses within the Communist empire so as to disintegrate it" was the premise that the Soviets might be dissuaded from a violent repression of such disintegrating tendencies out of a fear that we *might* feel compelled to take coercive countermeasures. And this in turn would have to be based on the premise that the balance of coercive power, on a global basis, was such that our implicit threat was credible.

The standard Republican attacks against the Roosevelt and Truman Administrations were that the Democrats had been overly respectful of Soviet power. Their contention was that the Soviets could have been prevented from consolidating their control over the occupied countries of Eastern Europe if only the United States had been willing to bring its superior power to bear. This, of course, was the Republican line in hindsight only; since in the 1945–48 period no prominent Republican was advocating that we be willing to fight the Soviets on the East European question. But it was a tough line in 1952 despite the qualifications against the initiation of violence by the anti-Communist side. Republican campaigners around the country pointed to their platform promise to:

. . . end the negative, futile, and immoral policy of "containment" which abandons countless human beings to a despotism and Godless terrorism which in turn enables the rulers to forge the captives into a weapon for our destruction. . . . The policies we espouse will revive the contagious, liberating influences which are inherent in freedom. They will inevitably set up strains and stresses within the captive world which will make the rulers impotent to continue in their monstrous ways and mark the beginning of the end. Our nation will again become the dynamic, moral, and spiritual force which was the despair of despots and the hope of the oppressed.[18]

Campaign hyperbole or not, the premises were carried over into statements Dulles made early in his career as Secretary of State. From his new position of responsibility, in his first public address (January 27, 1953), he again sounded the clarion: "To all those suffering under Communist slavery . . . let us say: you can count on us." [19]

Stalin's death in March 1953, like the loosening of the lid of a steaming kettle, would seem to have compelled the Administration to face up to the immediate *action* implications of its professed policy. Decisions made, and avoided, in the early months constituted an abandonment at the White House level of "liberation" as an operational policy, but the abandonment was concealed by the rhetoric.

Convincing pressure was brought to bear neither against the East Germans, nor the Soviets to dissuade them from their violent suppression of the worker's uprisings in East Berlin and East Germany in June 1953. The allied commandants in Berlin protested "the irresponsible recourse to military force" by the Communist authorities, and demanded that "the harsh restrictions imposed upon the population be lifted immediately," but there was no significant coercive sanction implied in the context of these demands.[20]

The Secretary of State used the occasion of the Berlin uprisings to claim the correctness of his earlier writings that "the Communist structure is over-extended, over-riding, and ill-founded. It could be shaken if the difficulties that were latent were activated." But he also insisted he had been saying all along that "this does not mean an armed revolt which would precipitate a massacre." [21]

The Congress followed up with its concurrent resolution of August 3, 1953. The hollowness of its operative clause juxtaposed with its statement of conditions in the Soviet sphere came close to being a caricature of Administration paralysis on this issue:

WHEREAS the Soviet regime being unable to win the allegiance of the people under its rule, knows no other method of achieving the compliance of the people to their dictatorship than by force of arms, terror, murder, imprisonment, reprisals and mass deportation; and

WHEREAS the cause of freedom cannot be contained and will eventually triumph; Now therefore, be it

Resolved, That the Congress commends and encourages the valiant struggle of these captive peoples for freedom.[22]

The only material encouragement offered by the United States during the crisis was the distribution of extra food to the East Berliners who flooded into West Berlin. The problem begging for decision, however, was whether the United States should prepare itself to act to greater effect in future contingencies of this sort, which, according to Dulles, were only just beginning.

The abandonment of "liberation" as an operational policy seems to have been made, with some consciousness, at a high level during this period in the context of the military force posture planning described above, p. 71. The grand-strategy task forces appointed by the White House in the spring of 1953 to explore the implications of alternative strategies and come up with recommendations included one group specifically assigned to the "liberation" alternative. In the initial terms of reference for this group the concept conveyed a "roll back" of existing Communist frontiers through political, psychological, and economic warfare programs, along with paramilitary measures. But when the reports of the groups were integrated into one document, and presented to the President for approval in October 1953, no part of the "liberation" alternative was incorporated.[23] And it does not seem to have appeared again as a premise for grand-strategy planning during the Eisenhower years.

Yet the official, and officially blessed, propaganda agencies do not seem to have received the message clearly. Their role was critical in keeping alive and inflating expectations between 1953 and 1956 that the United States would somehow interpose against Soviet repressive measures during a period of major uprisings.

In the fall of 1956 the Administration neither had the intention nor capability of intervening in Poland or Hungary. It is possible that Khrushchev's willingness to strike a bargain with Gomulka over the degree of permissible Polish independence from the Soviet Communist Party was in part for fear of United States action if the Soviet Army should actually engage Gomulka's troops in battle. (Gomulka, at the climax of his dispute with the Soviet Party made it clear that if Soviet troops were brought in, as threatened, the whole nation would stand and fight. Khruschchev would have been rash to regard this merely as a bluff, since Gomulka had rallied the nation around him, including the police and the army.)

But if fear that the Administration might feel morally obligated to implement its "liberation" rhetoric was a factor in the Polish situation, it may have been removed prematurely from the Soviet calculus of risks to be incurred by violent repression of the Hungarian revolt. A series of Administration statements from October 27 to October 31 seemed very anxious to indicate we had no intention of intervening. On November 4 the Soviets returned with 200,000 troops and 4,000 tanks to crush the revolt, reversing their October 30 decision to compromise. How the public posture of the Administration was in fact read by the Soviets, and what real effect the statements, concurrent with the Allied split over Suez, had on their calculation can not be known. It is known, however, that as far as Eisenhower and Dulles were concerned, American power was unable to affect the fate of the revolution.

Eisenhower recalls the Administration's stark appraisal of the balance of usable force at the time:

> The launching of the Soviet offensive against Hungary almost automatically had posed to us the question of force to oppose this barbaric invasion.
> . . . I still wonder what would have been my recommendation to the Congress and the American people had Hungary been accessible by sea or through the territory of allies who might have agreed to react positively to the tragic fate of the Hungarian people. As it was, however, Britain and France could not possibly have moved with us into Hungary. An expedition combining West German or Italian forces with our own, and moving across neutral Austria, Titoist Yugoslavia, or Communist Czechoslovakia was out of the question. The fact was that Hungary could not be reached by any United Nations or United States units without traversing such territory. Unless the major nations of Europe would, without delay, ally themselves spontaneously with us (an unimaginable prospect), we could do nothing. . . .[24]

The weight given by the Administration to this essential appraisal of the military situation is corroborated by other writers. Drummond and Coblentz in their book on Dulles tell of a private State Department session at the height of the crisis at which the Secretary of State listed the following reasons against United States military intervention (theirs is a paraphrase, not a verbatim record):

> First, any attempt at limited intervention by the nearest available American troops in Southern Germany would result in their defeat and massacre by the massive Russian forces.
> Second, only a full-scale intervention would be feasible from a military

viewpoint. It would risk a nuclear war with the Russians, and the American government was not prepared to take this risk on the Hungarian issue.

Third, one of the many ghastly results of a full-scale intervention war would be the total annihilation, rather than the salvation, of Hungary, the country for whose sake the war would be undertaken.[25]

Dulles, according to Drummond and Coblentz, went even farther in his appraisal than is reflected in the Eisenhower recollection. "Dulles made clear," they report, "that these considerations would equally have prevailed if the Suez crisis had not been in progress and if the Soviet Union had been the only aggressor on the world stage." [26]

In the aftermath of the Hungarian crisis the tone of Administration public statements on Eastern Europe changed, as did the tenor of United States diplomacy.

There were a few lame recitals of the history of the "liberation" doctrine, recalling the exclusion of "armed revolts" as an American policy objective. But the talk of activating stresses and strains in the Soviet empire so as to bring about its disintegration disappeared from high Administration statements.

The agitational content of both the official Voice of America and the unofficial Radio Free Europe (which was thought to be the main culprit in arousing expectations of American intervention) was cut down.

The most telling change was in the opening of economic relations on a selective basis with the European satellites. Using our experience with Tito since 1948 as the model, the premise was that trade and aid relationships advantageous to a particular Communist regime—Gomulka's Poland was the leading beneficiary of the new policy—could have the short-term result of lessening its need to be subservient to Moscow. In the longer term, greater economic independence in Eastern Europe might affect the global balance of power in our favor. Moreover, the side effects of demonstrating to the people of these areas that the United States had a concern for their well-being and the chance for increased exposure to Western values, might indirectly act to moderate the totalitarian characteristics of these regimes.

Those within the Administration who had been advocating that the United States venture forth with positive inducements rather than threats in attempting to reduce Communist expansion were—somewhat suddenly—encouraged to peddle their premises. Loud talk and the stick were, at least on an experimental basis, to give way to soft talk and the carrot as tools of power. The Soviets too, not only the satellites and Soviet-leaning neutrals, were to be approached in this vein.

This orientation again gave prominence to the Eisenhower face, as opposed to the Dulles face of Administration policy—the face associated with the President's welfare-not-warfare speech to the Newspaper Editors in 1953, with his Atoms for Peace proposal of the same year; and with the smiles, handshakes, and open skies of Geneva 1955.

CHAPTER TEN

SPUTNIK: NEW ATTENTION TO MATERIAL FACTORS OF POWER

I must say to you in all gravity that . . . it is entirely possible in the years ahead we could fall behind . . . unless we now . . . clearly identify the exact critical needs that have to be met. . . . This means selectivity in national expenditures of all sorts.

DWIGHT D. EISENHOWER

The two-year period from mid-1955 to mid-1957 saw United States policymakers beginning, fitfully, ambivalently to restructure their premises of power to take into account the military and political stalemate in Europe and the new force of self-assertive nationalism in the ex-colonial areas. The integration of a rearming West Germany into NATO, the 1955 Geneva summit meeting, and the Soviet suppression of the Hungarian uprising did more than reaffirm the Acheson-Dulles premise that there was no real basis for negotiation with the Soviet Union. These events also allowed for serious consideration of the hypothesis that henceforth *neither* the United States nor the Soviet Union had as an operational objective interference in one another's sphere of influence in Europe. The movement away from coercion to courtship in Communist Bloc relations with the Bandung nations and the deference to Middle Eastern nationalism shown by the United States in opposition to the effort by Israel, Britain, and France to crush Nasser, also registered, in a halting fashion, a symbiotic mutual movement by the two superpowers away from grand strategies of coercive confrontation toward the acceptance of a mutual military standoff, and to non-military modes of competition for the favor of the Third World.

But the dramatic Russian space achievements in the fall of 1957, and attempts by the Soviets to exploit diplomatically their potential military significance,[1] riveted American public and official attention, more than ever before, on the military-technological factors of power. From 1957 to 1960 the Administration was increasingly pressed to answer opposition party charges that it was letting the nation fall behind the Soviets in strategic military power *and* in the domestic economic and technological foundations for such power. The prospect of our losing in the socioeconomic competition to influence the developing nations was now also a part of the policy dialogue, and was reflected in the Mutual Security Agency's renewed emphasis on economic assistance. However, the major controversies surrounding Administration decisions for the allocation of resources had to do with the best means of preventing the Soviets from surpassing us in strategic military power.

The Administration's first public reactions to the Soviet orbiting of their 184-pound Sputnik I on October 4, 1957 were a model of studied nonchalance. The Soviet announcement on August 26 that they had launched an intercontinental ballistic missile had been greeted with skepticism. The satellite was more easily verified. The Soviets were congratulated for their scientific achievement, but its military implications were deprecated. The President explained to an anxious public on October 9 that the United States could have already produced an orbiting satellite if there had been a merging of the scientific space programs with the ballistic missile efforts. But, maintained Eisenhower, such a merger would have been "to the detriment of scientific goals and military progress." The separation was deliberate, as was the priority given to the missile work over the satellite project. "Speed of progress in the satellite project cannot be taken as an index of our progress in ballistic missile work." And discounting any effects of the current Soviet space achievement upon less tangible facets of power, such as prestige, the President said, "Our satellite program has never been conducted as a race with other nations." Its purposes were purely scientific.[2]

In retrospect, Eisenhower recounts, more faithfully than he was willing to for the public at the time, the shock which pervaded the Administration:

The size of the thrust required to propel a satellite of this weight came as a distinct surprise to us. There was no point in trying to minimize the accomplishment or the warning it gave that we must take added efforts to ensure maximum progress in missile and other scientific programs.[3]

When only a month later the Soviets launched Sputnik II, which carried a dog and many instruments, and was more than five times heavier than Sputnik I, the tremendous strides the Soviets had been making in technology required something more than sanguine recognition. "Throughout the United States," recalls Eric Goldman:

. . . a sense of alarm, exasperation, humiliation, and confusion mounted. Sputniks I and II dramatized as nothing else could have done that the chief thing on which Americans had depended for their national security and for victory in a competitive coexistence with Communism—the supremacy of American technical know-how—had been bluntly challenged.[4]

In the next few weeks science, technology, and their military applications received priority attention at the White House. The appointment of James R. Killian, president of the Massachusetts Institute of Technology, as Special Assistant for Science and Technology was announced, a new post described by the President as carrying "active responsibility for helping me to follow through in the scientific improvement of our defense." In addition, Eisenhower gave personal attention to the administrative bottlenecks in the missile program. He directed his Secretary of Defense (Neil McElroy) "to make certain that the Guided Missile Director is clothed with all the authority that the Secretary himself possesses," and announced other changes designed to eliminate overlapping and conflicting service jurisdictions in the rocket and missile programs. These actions were revealed in a major television address on science and defense four days after Sputnik II (the address had originally been scheduled for delivery a week later).

The President's main message was one of reassurance. It was right that the nation should feel concern in light of the Soviet accomplishments. Otherwise, we might become complacent and fall behind. But there was every reason for confidence that *existing* programs, with only marginal modifications, would continue to provide the nation with "both a sound defense and a sound economy." It was his conviction, he said, that "although the Soviets are quite likely ahead in some missile and special areas, and are obviously ahead of us in satellite development, as of today the over-all military strength of the Free World is distinctly greater than that of the Communist countries." He based this conclusion, said the President, on a number of important facts: we were well ahead of the Soviet Union in the nuclear field, both in quantity and quality. Our stock of nuclear weapons was sufficiently dispersed, so that if we were attacked first, "ample quantities would be available for instant retaliation." The United States missile program was well under way, with test shots of 3500 miles already accomplished; and because of our forward system of bases, ringing the Soviet Union, an intermediate-range missile would be "for some purposes, as good as an intercontinental missile." In addition to these offensive components, the nation was protected from direct attack by "a complex system of early warning radars, communication lines, electronic computers, supersonic aircraft, and ground-to-air missiles, some with atomic warheads." He also expressed confidence in the combined strength of the ground and naval forces of the United States and its allies. The essential approach of the so-called "New Look" for serving the nation's security was reaffirmed. It was important to maintain "selectivity" in defense spending, cautioned the President, otherwise we would neglect priorities and "ride off in all directions at once." [5]

The President's expressed confidence in the adequacy of existing premises and programs in the military sphere, which he said was "supported by trusted scientific and military advisers," was not shared at all by one group of prestigeous advisers whose secret report he had just received. The Gaither Committee report had been briefed to the President and the National Security Council on the morning of November 7. Although recommendations in the report were a direct challenge to the New Look, it was the hope of the committee that the shock of the Sputniks would be utilized by the President, somewhat as Truman had used the shock of the Communist attack in Korea, to mobilize public support in back of a larger and more diversified military program.

Though ostensibly secret, the major recommendations of the Gaither Committee, and the premises on which they were based, were known. Newspaper accounts and Congressional speeches described the report in detail and leaders of the Democratic Party demanded its declassification.[6] The Administration refused to release even a "sanitized" version;

but among policy oriented elites there was general agreement concerning its contents. The contemporaneous accounts have since been confirmed as being essentially accurate through comparison with Eisenhower's own account in the second volume of his memoirs.[7]

The Gaither Committee painted the United States as increasingly vulnerable to Soviet strategic power unless significant corrective action was taken, estimated as leading within a few years to annual defense expenditures of at least $8 billion above the current $38 billion. The Soviets were reported to be devoting 25 per cent of their Gross National Product to defense, as compared with 10 per cent for the United States. Thus, taking into account the greater American GNP, in absolute terms both countries were spending just about equal amounts. And on the basis of the more rapid Soviet rate of economic growth, the committee concluded that the Soviets would soon be spending more.

The committee had been charged originally with assessing the worthwhileness of a proposed $40 billion five-year program of blast-shelter construction. The committee quickly found that such evaluation required it to compare the returns expected against alternative usses of the money; and this in turn required a rather broadly based survey of the strengths and gaps in our overall military posture. It was concluded that a multi-billion dollar program of population protection, whether through blast or fallout shelters (the committee did recommend the latter, but as a relatively low priority item), was not the best use of additional defense monies.

Rather, the most critical problem facing the United States, in the eyes of the Gaither Committee, was how to maintain an effective strategic retaliatory capability when, in the early 1960s, the Soviets would have an operational ICBM force. If no corrective action was taken, the Soviets, if they struck first, would be able to destroy the Strategic Air Command. The vulnerability of SAC, rather than its initial destructive capability, was the matter that should be receiving priority attention. Temporary remedies, such as increasing the number of planes on alert status, dispersal to a greater number of bases, and improvements in early warning were recommended. An acceleration in the intermediate-range ballistic missile program was also urged. But these marginal manipulations of present programs would be insufficient to provide an adequate basis for security, warned the Gaither Committee.

Missiles with intercontinental ranges would have to become the foundation of the strategic force. This would have to be primarily designed as a "second strike" force with attention given to its ability to survive a first strike. But the implications of such strategic planning had to be faced: namely, with survivable strategic capabilities on both sides, the non-Communist world would also need to be capable of fighting limited wars. However, for the limited war capability to be significant, as opposed to that maintained by the Communists, the United States would have to maintain much larger ground forces and air-lift capacity than planned for under the New Look.[8]

These proposals, leaked to the press, and given the dramatic context of Sputniks I and II and Soviet claims of an operational ICBM, could not have come at a worse time from the point of view of the Administration. Eisenhower had failed during his first term to keep military expenditures under the New Look ceiling of $34 billion annually. Reluctantly, for the second term, a more realistic ceiling of $38 billion had been agreed upon. But the second term began amid a general price inflation, with the costs of goods and services purchased by the Defense Department rising faster than those of the economy as a whole. Defense Department officials were now telling Eisenhower that even *without* new programs, military expenditures during fiscal 1958 would rise to about $42 billion.[9] Rather than being able to balance the budget, the President would have to ask Congress to raise the statutory limit on the national debt!

In these circumstances Eisenhower was not at all pleased with the recommendations of the Gaither report, and looked more kindly on arguments which showed that with only marginal improvements in existing programs, and possibly even *more* selectivity than had yet been exercised, we could preserve the existing balance of strategic power against the Soviet Union. It also spurred his renewed interest in the Mutual Security program as a means of saving United States defense expenditures by providing for local defense capabilities with the cheaper-to-provision armies of allies.

Unlike the 1950 period, when Secretary of State Acheson helped provide the President with a grand-strategy rationale for devoting a larger portion of the nation's resources to military programs, the post-Sputnik period found the Secretary of State most effective in buttressing the President's effort to quiet the chorus of demands for greater military outlays. Eisenhower was now joined by Dulles in deprecating those who would overemphasize military factors in the balance of power. In a top-level meeting that considered the Gaither Report, Dulles noted that the committee had confined itself to military problems. "But the international struggle," he observed, "is not just military." The United States in overdevoting its resources to defense could lose the world economic competition. And, in a comment with significance for a whole set of New Look premises, Dulles pointed out that the Soviet Union had made its greatest seizures of territory and people "when only the United States had the atomic bomb." [10]

The implied denigration of the utility of United States military-strategic *superiority* in these remarks was more than polemical. Administration defense planners, fending off prods to spend more to keep ahead of the Russians in strategic striking power had, as early as 1956, accepted the essentials of mutual strategic deterrence as an operational guideline. As explained by Secretary of the Air Force Quarles in August 1956, looking a few years ahead:

[The] build-up of atomic power [on both sides of the Iron Curtain] . . . makes total war an unthinkable catastrophe for both sides. . . .

. . .

Neither side can hope by a mere margin of superiority in airplanes or other means of delivery of atomic weapons to escape the castastrophe of such a war. Beyond a certain point, this prospect is not the result of *relative* strength of the two opposed forces. It is the *absolute* power in the hands of each, and the substantial invulnerability of this power to interdiction.[11]

Eisenhower was responsive to suggestions, from the Gaither Committee and other experts, that attention should be paid to maintaining at least this minimum deterrent against a massive Soviet strategic strike, and that hardening, mobility, and dispersal were important components of a survivable deterrent. However, he accepted the counsel that this could be done within existing expenditure levels, with possibly some alteration in priorities among various projects.

As in 1953, the President bristled at suggestions that he was sacrificing national security to economy considerations. But he adamantly refused to be stampeded by those whom he saw as converting every international crisis into larger appropriations for their pet projects:

The problem was not unfamiliar [Eisenhower recalls]. Our security depended on a set of associated and difficult objectives: to maintain a defense posture of unparalleled magnitude and yet to do so without a breakdown of the American economy.

"We must get people to understand that we confront a tough problem," I said, "but one that we can lick." We could not turn the nation into a garrison state.[12]

In retrospect, Eisenhower claims to have seen the Soviet space feats of 1957 as less of a shock to the premises of power underlying the New Look than as a stimulus to the nation's further scientific and technological progress. We were "jarred . . . out of what might have been a gradually solidfying complacency in technology. It caused us to give increased attention to scientific education in this country and ultimately to all phases of education." [13] Yet coupled with the Administration's hold-the-line-on-expenditures attitude, the emphasis on the nation's need to keep from falling behind in science and technology tended to give the government's interest in domestic programs of education and research a "security" cast. Not that they were expected to add directly to the nation's military potential, but the stress given to science, mathematics, and engineering in the President's January 1958 special message on education, and the title and content of the National Defense Education Act indicated that the Eisenhower Administration was willing to launch new federal programs only for the solemn purpose of guaranteeing that the United States would not become a second-class power, materially defined.

Although the President's first reaction to the Soviet space shots was to maintain that we were not in a space race with the Soviets, the United States space effort, centered in the Vanguard project, was accelerated on an emergency basis. The first results were none to happy, with launching pad failures televised before the entire world. Finally, on January 31, 1958 the United States entered space with the launching of Explorer I—an event which the Secretary of State hailed as having "reestablished the prestige of the United States." He had received reactions from around the world and could report that:

Our friends are entirely reassured as to our capabilities in this field. They recognize that the Soviet Union perhaps specialized in this field for a longer time than we have, but the fact that we are already at least close on their heels in a much shorter span of time I think reassures them as to our capacity, if need be, to move on and take the leadership in this field also. The effect in sum has been very reassuring and has strengthened the position of the United States in foreign affairs.[14]

By the summer the race was in full momentum, with successful United States launches of Vanguard I, Explorer III, and Explorer IV. The Soviets continued to launch heavier satellites (Sputnik III, May 15, 1958, weighed 2,900 pounds), but the United States could claim greater sophistication.

In the more immediately critical field, that of long-range ballistic missiles, the competition also began to be equalized by the end of 1958. While the 1500-mile Thors and Jupiters were readied for deployment in England, Italy, and Turkey, the Administration called attention to every evidence of progress in its long-range Atlas and Titan projects. In November an Atlas was successfully tested on a 6,300 mile course. The solid-propellant Minuteman ICBM entered its development phase, and the Polaris program for submarine-launched missiles was begun in earnest.

Yet the Administration had a difficult time in trying to restore confidence. During its last year and a half in office the growing body of defense-oriented intellectuals, journalists, and politicians were circulating and repeating the phrases "delicate balance of terror," and "missile gap." The thrust of the criticism directed at the Administration was that it was overly complacent about the ability of the United States to maintain a retaliatory capability that was not vulnerable to destruction by a Soviet first strike. Journalists, claiming their reports were based on the estimates of high Defense Department officials, predicted a Soviet missile lead of three-to-one for the early 1960s. Administration spokesmen refused to talk "numbers" in public. They insisted that numerical estimates were not as important as the fact that there would be no "deterrent gap,"—a vague concept meant to convey the notion that regardless of the forecast Soviet missile strength, the United States, while constructing its advanced ICBM force, would maintain a diversified capacity (based in part on manned bombers) to inflict unacceptable damage on the Soviet Union in a strategic exchange.

Science, technology, the rate of economic growth, and the esoteric calculus of strategic nuclear deterrence were the dominant terms with which national power was evaluated by Administration defenders and critics during the later Eisenhower years. But underneath this dialogue, forces stubbornly resistant to such material factors of power continued to brew and erupt and undermine the peace on which the American pursuit of happiness depended.

CHAPTER ELEVEN

CONDITIONED RESPONSES TO

NEW CHALLENGES

What attracts attention are the aggressive probings of the Communists and the free-world reactions thereto. That gives the impression that our foreign policy consists primarily of reacting to Communist initiatives.

Nothing could be farther from the truth. The fact is that . . . we are building quietly but steadily . . . the solid foundations of an international order based upon justice and law as substitutes for force.

JOHN FOSTER DULLES

Suez, Hungary, and the rapid development of Soviet intercontinental strategic power produced the beginning of a perception in the highest counsels of the Administration that the international environment was in the throes of a profound departure from the comparatively simple patterns of the early 1950s. The transformation of the general military stalemate from one in which United States strategic superiority balanced Communist military manpower to one of stalemate at the level of full-scale strategic warfare was seen as providing the Communist powers with new temptations to foment local instabilities in the non-Communist world, while preserving their free hand to block all attempts at Western interference in the Communist sphere. The power of the United States and its allies to control events within the non-Communist portion of the world would therefore have to be based on more than the existing global distribution of military power. This surely was an underlying realization determining the United States decision to bridle the efforts of France and Britain to trample Nasser. Similarly the realization that the emerging global distribution of military power canceled whatever leverage United States strategic superiority might provide for Western influence over events in Eastern Europe underlay the beginning, after Hungary, of efforts by the United States to intensify economic relationships with Communist regimes.

But efforts by the United States to develop a more varied set of diplomatic tools to compensate for the muscle-bound state of its military power were retarded by the Administration's felt need to respond decisively to new provocations in the Middle East, Asia, and Germany. Capabilities in being, diplomatic as well as military, rather than the developing concepts of what would be desirable capabilities, determine the management of any particular crisis; and unfortunately for the new concepts, a government's post-crisis analysis sometimes tends to be a morale-building rationalization of its recent performance with existing capabilities and concepts. In such cases, the implementation of new concepts gets delayed until there is a change in personnel.

This pernicious effect of emergency crisis management upon the receptivity to new premises within the Eisenhower Administration was most evident in our Middle Eastern activities during the turbulence of 1957 and 1958.

Dulles and Eisenhower, in opposing the military moves of Britain and France against Nasser in 1956, had taken a very large step in the direction of a United States foreign policy that attempted to work with, rather than against, neutralistic nationalism. They expected applause from the Middle Eastern Nasserites, but instead seemed to be encountering jeers. Rather than having United States restraint interpreted by the Arabs as the product of our respect for their desire to be fully independent, our insistence that force not be used was being defined by the Nasserites and the Soviets as the product of our fear of a Middle Eastern confrontation with the Soviets.

Now with Britain and France thoroughly humiliated in the eyes of the Arabs, and the Baghdad Pact allies more confused than ever as to

United States objectives in the area, Dulles felt it essential to reassert the United States interest and intention of keeping the Middle East out of Communist hands. So instead of translating the events of 1956 into an invitation to the Soviets to cooperate in a mutual Cold War "disengagement" from the Middle East, the Administration redefined the area as a critical weight in the bipolar balance and reaffirmed the nation's resolve to do battle there to keep it on our side. On January 1, 1957 the President met with a bipartisan delegation of Congressmen to generate support for his forthcoming request for authorization to use force in the area when necessary. "The existing vacuum in the Middle East," he told them, "must be filled by the United States before it is filled by Russia. . . . Should there be a Soviet attack there . . . I can see no alternative to an immediate United States move to stop it." [1]

In his special message to the Congress on January 5, Eisenhower went even farther than had Truman in March 1947 in simplifying the United States interest in the Middle East as one of preventing this critical geopolitical region from falling under the control of the Soviets:

Russia's rulers have long sought to dominate the Middle East. That was true of the Czars and it is true of the Bolsheviks. . . .

. . .

The reasons for Russia's interest in the Middle East are solely those of power politics. Considering her announced purpose of dominating the world, it is easy to understand her hope of dominating the Middle East.

Stressing its importance as a transportation and commercial link between the continents, and as a source of two thirds of the world's oil deposits, the President painted the consequences of a Soviet domination of the area in global terms:

Western Europe would be endangered just as though there had been no Marshall Plan, no North Atlantic Treaty Organization. The free nations of Asia and Africa, too, would be placed in serious jeopardy. . . . All this would have the most adverse, if not disastrous, effect upon our own nation's economic life and political prospects.[2]

With the stakes this high, said the President, "Nothing is more necessary . . . than that our policy with respect to the defense of the area be promptly and clearly determined and declared." In the situation then existing "the greatest risk . . . is that ambitious despots may miscalculate. If power-hungry Communists should either falsely or correctly estimate that the Middle East is inadequately defended, they might be tempted to use open measures of armed attack." [3] The greatest insurance against the possibility of major war for control of the Middle East, contended the President, was a Congressional reaffirmation of the vital American interest in the area, and a clear declaration by the Congress of its willingness to have the armed forces of the United States used to help Middle Eastern nations "requesting such aid, against overt armed aggression from any nation controlled by International Communism." [4] The President's address also contained requests for Congressional authorization of economic and military assistance for regimes in the area to use for purposes of economic development and self-defense. But these were subordinate in emphasis to the request for the declaration of intent to employ United States armed forces directly against Communist encroachments in the Middle East.

The urgency of the need for a clear commitment by the United States to defend the Middle East against Communist aggression was presented in starkest outline by the Secretary of State before the Congressional committees handling the proposed resolution:

Soviet ground, naval and air forces are stationed in the areas adjacent to the Middle East—Bulgaria, the Black Sea, the Ukraine, the Caucasus, and Central Asia. These Soviet forces are of a size and are so located that they could be employed at any time with a minimum of warning. This fact is nothing new. But today it takes on new implications.

There has been a change in the possible deterrrent role of certain Western European nations. Until recently they provided a serious deterrent to Communist aggressions against the Middle East. But for a variety of reasons—psychological, financial, and political—this no longer meets the needs.

Another factor is evidence that the Communist rulers may now be thinking in terms of possible "volunteer" operations in the Middle East, such as the Chinese Communists perpetrated in Korea.

No one can reliably predict whether, and if so, when, there would be Communist armed aggression, but three things are known: (1) the Communist capability, (2) the temptation, (3) the lack of any moral restraints.

. . .

There is ample evidence of Communist infiltration into certain areas, particularly organized labor; and there are plottings of assassinations and sabotage to gain Communist ends. Local Communists have recently obtained small arms. . . . Arab refugees . . . are a special target for Communist propaganda.

Thus the Middle East area is at once endangered by potential military threats against which there is now no adequate deterrent, by a rapidly mounting financial and economic crisis, and by subversive efforts which seek advantage from exceptional opportunities arising out of recent events. This adds up to a new and gave danger.[5]

Dulles rejected charges that in focusing on the Communist military threat he was misdirecting our efforts, which should rather be directed at the underlying causes of instability and hatred of the West. He contended that the Administration was conducting a many-faceted approach to the Middle East, including an intensified program of economic assistance (the President had just appointed James Richards to head a mission to the area, and had requested that Congress provide the Administration with flexible authority to spend $200 million in already appropriated funds so that Richards would have a better basis for discussing specific development projects with friendly regimes). The United States believed that no efforts should be spared to tackle the root causes of trouble in the area, said Dulles. "But we do not take the pessimistic view that, unless and until these problems can be solved, nothing can usefully be done to prevent the area from being taken over by international communism." [6]

Congress passed the joint resolution, essentially in the form and words requested by the Administration. Henceforth referred to as the "Eisenhower Doctrine," the Senate and the House of Representatives resolved:

. . . that the President be . . . authorized to cooperate with and assist any nation or group of nations in the general area of the Middle East desiring such assistance in the development of economic strength dedicated to the maintenance of national independence.

SEC. 2. The President is authorized to undertake . . . military assistance programs with any nation or group of nations of that area desiring such assistance. Furthermore, he is authorized to employ the armed forces of the United States as he deems necessary to secure and protect the territorial integrity and political independence of any such nation or group of nations requesting such aid against overt armed aggression from any nation controlled by international communism. . . .[7]

The clumsiness of the instrument for dealing with the intricacies of the Middle East was soon apparent. But rather than asking for a refinement of Congressional intention or refashioning a more flexible public rationale for its policies, the Administration preferred to rest its case for its response to the unanticipated challenges of 1957 and 1958 on the familiar military containment premises of the Eisenhower Doctrine.

The first application of the military clause of the Eisenhower Doctrine could be viewed as a limited success. In April 1957 the Sixth Fleet was ordered to the Eastern Mediterranean as a display of United States support for King Hussein of Jordan, then in severe political trouble following the King's dismissal of his pro-Nasser Prime Minister, Suleiman Nabulsi. Egypt and Syria were abetting the antiroyalist rebels, and to this extent the conflict was more than a purely domestic affair. With the local alignments against the King, his gambit—understandably —was to attempt to redress the balance by bringing in the Cold War. King Hussein claimed that the independence and integrity of Jordan were threatened by "International Communism"; and the Administration in Washington, conditioned to the clang of its own bell, poised itself to respond. In addition to the demonstrations by the Navy, $10 million of emergency aid was promptly granted to Jordan.[8] Egypt and Syria failed to intervene on the side of the rebels, nor did Israel move to pre-empt such intervention, which would have presented Washington with an even worse tangle. In Administration circles, the rapid quieting down of the Jordanian crisis was attributed to the swiftness with which King Hussein was brought under the protective cover of the Eisenhower Doctrine. This was presumed to have given him the leverage needed locally to reconstitute a government and army loyal to him, and to suppress the Nasserite dissidents.

A more plausible case of Communist exploitation of Middle Eastern instabilities occurred in Syria. But this time the Eisenhower Doctrine proved to be an inappropriate tool for effecting countermoves against Soviet penetration. Administration officials were seriously apprehensive over the increasingly close relationships being developed between the Syrian regime and the Soviet Union during the spring and summer of 1957. The Soviets were equipping the Syrian army and, in conjunction with the visit of the Syrian Minister of Defense to Moscow in August, announced large-scale credits for increased trade. The Syrians, meanwhile, were charging the United States with complicity in a plot to overthrow the government in Damascus. Three United States embassy and attaché officials were expelled under allegations that they were involved in the subversive conspiracy. The Syrian Army Chief of Staff, whom Washington regarded as a political moderate, resigned, and his place was taken by a general thought to be a Communist. "The entire action was shrouded in mystery," recalled Eisenhower, "but the suspicion was strong that the Communists had taken control of the government." [9]

Jordan, by comparison, had been easy. Now the Administration was faced with a major test of its proclaimed premise that the United States had a vital interest in preventing the establishment of a Communist outpost in the Middle East. In the Jordanian crisis, the invocation of the Eisenhower Doctrine was simple; it involved only military demonstrations and emergency aid to a regime begging to be saved from Communist subversives. Now, however, although the Communist threat was less of a fiction, the invocation of the Eisenhower Doctrine might back the Administration into a corner in which a failure by the United States to reverse the drift of political loyalties in Syria, by whatever means necessary, would undermine the credibility of our commitments all over the world. The problem was that the means thought necessary for purging Syria of its Soviet-leaning leadership were likely to be very costly and involve risking war. Avoidance of direct United States intervention was based on the legal grounds that the Eisenhower Doctrine stipulated that United States intervention would come in response to a *request* from a threatened government, and also on the lack of sufficient information concerning the real loyalties of the Syrian regime. Eisenhower recounts his considerations at the time: "If the government comprised only radical Arab nationalists and pro-Nasserites, that was one thing; if they were to go completely Communist, that would call for action." [10] The agony and procrastination, however, resulted from the realization that the Syrian leaders were somewhere between these two poles.

Even if it were to be determined that Syria had been definitely taken over by Communists, Eisenhower, for one, was not willing to commit the United States to a reversal of the situation. Asked in his news conference of August 21, 1957 whether it would be tolerable to have in the heart of the Middle East a regime subject to Communist control which at any time could deny the free world a vital part of its oil supply, the President, anxious to leave his options open, replied:

I wouldn't want to speculate, because there are all sorts of degrees. For example, we feel . . . that Tito is in a far different position with respect to the free world than are Communist countries that are directly controlled by Communism.

In other words, it is international communism that spells the greatest danger to the United States, not that we approve of communism anywhere, but international communism and subordination to the views of Moscow are one thing. Independent communism is something else. . . .

I would say that the situation [in Syria] as it develops will be one that has to be closely watched . . . and we must not get into a position that would be intolerable for us.[11]

Yet if there were high risks in doing too much, there were severe embarrassments in not being able to do anything. The Secretary of State was able to evade this dilemma by redefining the crisis as one emanating from the danger of Syrian *aggression* against its neighbors. Assuming that Syria was to become a "nation controlled by international communism," and that nations in the area would request aid from the United States against "overt armed aggression" from Syria, then the Eisenhower Doctrine *would* be most relevant.

To demonstrate the availability of United States military power in case of need, the Sixth Fleet was again ordered to the Eastern Mediterranean, some United States aircraft were redeployed from Western Europe to Adana, Turkey, and the Strategic Air Command was alerted.[12] Deputy Undersecretary of State, Loy Henderson, was dispatched on a mission to sound out officials of Turkey, Lebanon, Jordan, and Iraq. On September 7 Dulles issued a press release describing a White House meeting between the President, himself, and Henderson, who had just returned from his fact-finding mission:

He [Henderson] reported that he had found in the Near East deep concern at the apparently growing domination of Syria and the large build-up there of Soviet arms, a build-up which could not be justified by any purely defensive needs. . . .

. . .

The President affirmed his intention to carry out the national policy, expressed in the congressional Middle East resolution. . . . In this connection, the President authorized the accelerated delivery to the countries of the area of economic and other defensive items which have been programmed for their use.[13]

But if the threshold for United States intervention against the Syrian regime was Syrian aggression against its neighbor nations, there was no compelling reason for Syria to oblige. The regime proclaimed itself Arab-nationalist, not Communist. Lebanon and Jordan were more than willing to accept additional arms shipments from the United States, but having turbulent nationalistic urban masses of their own to contend with, spoke reassuringly of the priority they give to solidarity among the Arab states, and expressed their realization that fights among the Arabs could benefit only Israel. At an Arab summit meeting in Damascus, the Prime Minister of Iraq spoke of a "complete understanding" between his country and Syria. Even King Saud, the Arab leader with whom the Administration had the closest association, claimed to be unable to see any threat to other Arab states from Syria, and pledged, rather, to aid Syria against any aggression.[14]

The Soviets were quick in attempting to turn the situation to their advantage. They accused the United States of planning, in collusion with Turkey, Israel, and others to intervene militarily in Syria, citing the Henderson trip and the White House press release on his return as evidence. "As for the alleged existence of a danger that Syria will take aggressive action against neighboring states," said the Soviet Foreign Minister on September 10, "why doesn't the U.S. government raise this question in the U.N. Security Council if it has such fears?" [15] The United States was clearly being outmaneuvered, and had little recourse but to deflate the war scare that, it must be admitted, was partly of our own making.

Dulles, as dexterous in backing away from the brink as approaching it, used his September 10 press conference to signal the Administration's final realization that it would do no good to make Syria the issue over which there would be a choosing up of sides in the Middle East: "There has been as yet no determination that Syria is dominated by international communism within the meaning of the Middle East resolution," explained the Secretary of State:

There have to be three findings before there is direct armed intervention by the United States. There has to be a finding by the President that one of the countries was dominated by international communism; secondly, there has to be an act of aggression by that country; third, there has to be a request by the country attacked for that aid. . . . And I might say at the present time I don't think it likely that those three things will occur. . . .

. . .

I think the very fact that this [situation in Syria] is being taken seriously affords the greatest likelihood that a peaceful solution will be found. . . .

Certainly we do not believe, there or anywhere else, in peace at any price. The whole purpose of the Middle East resolution was to make clear that under certain circumstances we would act. Now, I believe that the situation probably will work out. . . .[16]

The situation was "worked out," in terms of the appearance and reality of power, on three levels.

On the formal diplomatic level, there was avoidance of a clear test of the letter and spirit of the system of alliances Dulles had spawned in the Middle East, and of the Eisenhower Doctrine itself, by the referral of the war scare to the United Nations, under whose aegis the Middle Eastern countries among themselves agreed to settle their disputes peacefully. The United States could claim that its solemn commitments were still good, as the conditions for intervention had not in fact materialized.

On the level of Cold War atmospherics, the United States and the Soviet Union continued to charge each other with trying to take over Syria. The mutual accusations, of course, were not entirely devoid of genuine apprehension. The United States was viewed as preparing Turkey for an invasion of its southern neighbor, and the United States government in turn feared the Soviets were using the Syrian crisis as a pretext for renewing their traditional pressures, including military threats, against Turkey.

The menacing posture of the Soviets vis-à-vis Turkey allowed Dulles to refurbish the somewhat tarnished visage of American power as the essential deterrent to Soviet aggression in the Middle East. And he leaped at the opportunity. "Mr. Khrushchev . . . now openly threatens Turkey," said a State Department release of October 10, 1957:

He has referred to the fact that the United States is a long way away from the Middle East, whereas the U.S.S.R. is adjacent. Despite distances, he should be under no illusion that the United States, Turkey's friend and ally, takes lightly its obligations under the North Atlantic Treaty or is not determined to carry out the national policy expressed in the joint congressional resolution on the Middle East.[17]

In his press conference a few days later, Dulles was again at home in the strategic high terrain, where the factors in the balance of power stand out starkly: "Certainly, if there is an attack on Turkey by the Soviet Union," he warned, "it would not mean a purely defensive operation by the United States, with the Soviet Union a privileged sanctuary from which to attack Turkey." [18]

But below, in the shifting sands of Middle Eastern politics, the impact of United States behavior upon regional alignments (including the political loyalties of nongovernmental groups), and the possible effects of these on the global balance of power, provided a more questionable basis for a resumption of the militarily-based containment policy expressed in the Eisenhower Doctrine.

It was precisely at the level of the ethnic and socioeconomic bases of political alignments in the Middle East, that the United States found itself without effective means of leverage. The power vacuum, which Eisenhower and Dulles talked of, existed at *this* level. At the military level, Dulles could express confidence that the geographic relationships did not necessarily disadvantage the technologically advanced United States in a potential war. And to this extent, the declaration of intention to interpose our military power against an attempt by the Soviets to absorb the area by overt aggression was not completely meaningless. But it was not particularly relevant to the primary means by which the Soviets were now trying to establish themselves as the big-power influence in the Middle East.

The malappropriateness of the kind of power the United States had been trying to apply in the Middle East was driven home once again during the Iraq-Lebanon crisis of 1958. Considering the United States limitations in Middle Eastern politics, the Administration applied its crude tools with subtlety and skill. In this tactical sense the Lebanon intervention was a success. But as a response to the broader challenge of which the civil war in Lebanon was only a symptom, the United States assistance to the panicky government of Camille Chamoun was a dramatic example of impotence, not power.

Although after the event Eisenhower and Dulles were able to claim success by referring to only the narrowest of the objectives they were trying to accomplish in Lebanon, it is clear that they took the politically risky course of landing United States combat forces on Arab soil out of a desperate sense that *something* had to be done to halt the disastrous train of events in the Middle East. It is doubtful that the United States would have intervened as it did were its only purpose to prop up the pro-Western and Christian President Chamoun against the pro-Nasser rebels in Lebanon.

Eisenhower discloses that when discussing Chamoun's early requests for assistance on May 13, 1958, it was Dulles who this time initially painted the "drastic" consequences of direct United States action:

Foster Dulles felt that if we should send troops into Lebanon there would be a major adverse reaction in the Middle East. He suspected that the pipelines across Syria would probably be blown, the Suez Canal might be blocked, and the wave of resentment among the Arab populations could become so strong that it might be impracticable for the governments of Iraq and Jordan to cooperate no matter how much they might desire to do so. Possible Soviet reaction was another item to consider.[19]

As the discussion went on it became clear that the Secretary of State favored direct action, and that his brother Allen Dulles, the Director of the Central Intelligence Agency, took a more cautious attitude. But we are not told what considerations Foster Dulles threw into the balance to counteract the list of drastic consequences he had just outlined. Clearly, from Eisenhower's account, Eisenhower's top advisers were not at all sure that the expected benefits outweighed the risks, and he was prone to give credence to intelligence reports that showed Chamoun able to control the situation without outside military intervention. Indirect and symbolic military measures were taken, similar to those used in the 1957 crises in Jordan and Syria, but the measures impressed no one. The Administration was pleased to have Chamoun bring before the UN Security Council his charges that Egypt and Syria were arming the rebels, and thereafter—until the July coup in Iraq—United States officials excused our hesitancy by insisting that we did not want to hinder the truce efforts of Secretary General Hammarskjöld. By early July the White House was confident that the Lebanon crisis would pass (President Chamoun had agreed not to run for reelection, and to cooperate in finding a candidate acceptable to both Christians and Arab nationalists) without Western military intervention.

The event which precipitated the Presidential decision of July 14, 1958 to intervene with Marines in Lebanon was the bloody coup in Baghdad that overnight transformed the West's only major Arab ally into a Soviet-leaning Nasserite regime, and, it was feared in those early days, possibly a Communist satellite of the Soviet Union. Yet our response—the Marine landing in Lebanon—was undertaken without any real hope of thereby undoing the coup in Iraq. Nor does it appear that the situation in Lebanon was deemed to require a direct American intervention, despite the renewed requests from President Chamoun.

Analysts of the Administration's behavior in the 1958 crisis had looked forward to Eisenhower's memoirs for additional light on what the Administration thought it was doing and why. But the twenty-nine pages devoted to this episode in *Waging Peace* leave the basis for United States action obscure. At the critical White House meeting where the intervention decision was made, Dulles repeated his earlier warnings that there would be a very bad reaction from most Arab countries, that the Syrian oil pipeline would probably be cut, and the use of the Suez canal denied. What, then, were the substantial benefits to compensate for these critical repercussions? Eisenhower's remarks at the time—by his own account—did not promise very much:

The Iraqi crisis was just another flare-up in the tinderbox of the entire Middle East. As I told my colleagues, "We must all realize that a single move can of itself produce no permanent settlement. Any intervention in Lebanon will put out one fire only; until stable governments are set up and supported locally, the Middle East will never calm down." [20]

Eisenhower kept insisting that it was clear to him that "we had to go in," but just what he thought the consequences of *not* going in would be are never detailed. Presumably, the consequences were self-evident. Thus: "In Lebanon the question was whether it would be better to incur the deep resentment of all of the Arab world (and some of the rest of the Free World) and in doing so risk general war with the Soviet Union or to do something worse—which was to do nothing." [21] In the President's public announcements on July 15, 1958 of his decision to dispatch United States Marines to Lebanon, the action was presented as a means for preserving the "independence and integrity" of Lebanon against "indirect aggression." The source of this indirect aggression was not identified, but there were strong suggestions that it was the United Arab Republic. There was no reference to "international communism" as the source of aggression, nor was the UAR painted as being "controlled by international communism." Soviet radio broadcasts in Arabic were charged with encouraging the Lebanese rebels; but beyond that there was no charge that the Soviets were behind the revolt, or the Iraq coup. Thus some of the necessary conditions for the applicability of the Eisenhower doctrine, conditions absent the previous year in the Syrian crisis and stated by Dulles to be the reason for *non*-intervention, were now bypassed. It was sufficient to establish the fact that the legally constituted government had asked for the assistance of the United States, and to assert, as did the President, that:

I have . . . come to the sober and clear conclusion that the action taken was essential to the welfare of the United States. It was required to support the principles of justice and international law upon which peace and a stable international order depend. . . .

. . .

If ever the United States fails to support these principles, the result would be to open the floodgates to direct and indirect aggression throughout the world.[22]

The last statement above, that the failure to act would encourage aggression, seems to have been the operating premise behind the decision to intervene. The success of the rebel movement in Lebanon would not in itself constitute an alteration in the balance of power, materially or geopolitically. But if the United States were again seen as standing by helpless, as it had in Syria, and as it had in Iraq, a profound psychological ingredient of the power of the non-Communist coalition—the reputation of its leader as one willing to take potentially costly action —would be disastrously undermined. Without a clear conception of what the consequences of action might be, it was nevertheless essential to *act*. The Dulles style was again ascendant. The face of power must exhibit the hard lines of courage and resolve. Without these, the capacity to move nations would be lost.

As it happened, the United States military intervention in Lebanon and the coordinated British intervention to help King Hussein of Jordan incurred less cost and risk than had been contemplated by Eisenhower and Dulles. The Soviets made their usual protests, sent their usual warnings to the Western allies, and made their usual appeals for a summit conference. Nasser, not at all anxious to have a Soviet presence substituted for a Western one, apparently assured the Soviets there would be no requirement for Soviet military intervention unless the Western powers invaded Iraq or the UAR. Moreover, the Egyptian leader kept his assistance to the Lebanese rebels to a minimum, and quickly threw his weight on the side of those who saw gains to be made from a political compromise inside Lebanon. The United States and the Soviet Union had little choice but to fall in behind an all-Arab resolution in the General Assembly affirming the obligation of the Arab states to respect each other's form of government, and asking the Secretary General to help arrange the withdrawal of foreign troops from Lebanon and Jordan.[23]

The Administration was able to claim a major success by retrospectively defining our aims in the Lebanon affair as directed primarily toward keeping Nasser from swallowing up yet another Middle Eastern country, and by attributing Nasser's reluctance to intervene in force to the United States pre-emptive intervention. Eisenhower maintained that one result of the American action was a "definite change in Nasser's attitude toward the United States." Our behavior at the time of the Suez affair had presumably convinced the Egyptian that we would rarely, if ever, resort to force to support our friends or our principles. Now "he certainly had his complacency as to America's helplessness completely shattered.[24]

Eisenhower also claimed that the Lebanon operation was a demonstration—particularly to the Communists—of "the ability of the United States to react swiftly with conventional armed forces to meet small-scale, or 'brush-fire' situations." But he makes the curious point, curious in light of the difficulty he had in identifying the *source* of the "indirect aggression" in Lebanon, that he was now more than ever convinced that "if 'small wars' were to break out in several places in the world simultaneously, then we would not fight on the enemy terms and be limited to his choice of weapons. We would hold the Kremlin—or Peking—responsibile for their actions and would act accordingly." [25]

However, beneath the surface of self-congratulation and reassertion of old strategic doctrine, the Middle East crises of 1957–58 exhibited to those at the helm of United States policy the inadequacy of the predominantly military approach to problems of subversion and "indirect aggression." President Eisenhower's address to the UN General Assembly on August 13, 1958 contained the harbinger of a new orientation toward the sources of effective power in, and over, the revolutionary nationalisms of the ex-colonial and developing areas. "We are living in a time," said the President, "when the whole world has become alive to the possibilities for modernizing their societies." The United States looked with favor upon this trend since "only on the basis of progressing economies can truly independent governments sustain themselves." The President proposed an Arab regional development plan, analogous to the Marshall Plan, to be formulated and managed by the Arab nations themselves, but to be financially and technically supported by the advanced nations. He was ready to pledge United States support now, contingent upon the Arab nations' ability to come up with a plan and willingness to devote their own resources to its implementation. But such an effort would not succeed, warned the President, unless there was simultaneously an elimination from the area of the chronic fear of violence and outside interference in the Arabs' internal affairs. To this end, the United States would support the creation of a United Nations peace-keeping force, so that nations of the area "will no longer feel the need to seek national security through spiralling military buildups. These lead not only to economic impotence but to war." [26]

Walt Rostow, who had been a leading critic of the Eisenhower Administration's earlier policy toward nationalism and neutralism in the developing areas, saw in the President's address a belated surfacing of the premises which "many had sought without success to introduce before the Suez Crisis as well as during and after the formulation of the Eisenhower Doctrine." [27] Rather than focusing on a possible Soviet ground invasion of the Middle East, the new orientation was toward productively exploiting the nationalist ambitions of the Arab world. Economic assistance would no longer be conditioned on membership in the anti-Communist alliance system. Neutralism, and even overt anti-Western postures, would be viewed realistically in its own political context—as more often than not the necessary credentials for Third World political elites who would lead, rather than be swept away by, the mass demands, frustrations, and explosive anger that accompany the removal of colonial overlordship and the enfranchisement of the have-not elements of the population.

It was ironic, but not particularly surprising to those who understood the underlying sociopolitical dynamics, that the region which was the object of the most feverish application of the Dulles policy of providing allied indigenous forces around the perimeter of the Communist world would be the first to benefit from the appreciation that new tools of power were needed to prevent Communist aggrandizement.

Logically, the recognition of the failure of past policies to harness the emotional steam of Third World nationalism, and the search for new tools, particularly economic ones, for channeling this energy toward tasks of internal development rather than external adventures, should have produced a revolution in United States policies for Asia, Africa, and Latin America. However, our policies in each of these areas had yet to undergo the crisis of impotence that faced us in the Middle East before the Eisenhower rhetoric of August 1958 would become the operational premises of our action programs on a global basis.

The delayed reaction to the force of social revolutionary movements in Latin America is probably the clearest example of the Eisenhower Administration's sluggishness in translating its growing perception of the multifaceted nature of power into usable diplomatic instruments. There were few instruments immediately available to the Administration in 1958 when Vice-President Nixon returned from his encounters with anti-American crowds to report that "the threat of Communism in Latin America is greater than ever before." [28]

The regional multilateral instruments at hand were of the traditional kind: agreements among the nations of this hemisphere to come to each other's aid in case of aggression from outside the hemisphere. Moreover, because of the special sensitivity to interference from the colossus to the north, an implication usually carried by such agreements had been explicitly set forth in the inter-American treaties: as stated in Article 15 of the Charter of the Organization of American States, ". . . no State . . . has the right to intervene, directly or indirectly, for any reason whatever, in the internal or external affairs of another State. . . .[29]

When the Administration faced the prospect of a Communist take-over of Guatemala in 1954 by *political* means, Dulles' strategy, on the diplomatic front, had been to get the Latin Americans to make an exception to mutual pledges of nonintervention in the case of Communist regimes. The result of his efforts was the "Declaration of Solidarity for the Preservation of the Political Integrity of the American States Against International Communist Intervention," adopted at the Tenth Inter-American Conference in Caracas, Venezuela, in March 1954. (Guatemala voted against; Mexico and Argentina abstained.) The Caracas Declaration condemned "the activities of the international communist movement as constituting intervention in American affairs," and declared:

That the domination or control of the political institutions of any American State by the international communist movement, extending to this Hemisphere the political system of extra-continental power, would constitute a threat to the sovereignty and political independence of the American States, endangering the peace of America. . . .[30]

Dulles wanted an expansion of the concept of "intervention" to cover political subversion, and this much he got. But he also wanted specific commitments for collective action against the Arbenz regime in Guatemala. In this our Latin treaty partners would not go along. They were not yet ready to define the situation in Guatemala as one in which the "international communist movement" had taken over a country. Nor were they willing to commit themselves to direct counter-intervention when and if such a contingency materialized. A Communist takeover of an American republic would, in the language of Caracas, "call for a Meeting of Consultation to consider the adoption of appropriate action in accordance with appropriate treaties." But to prevent misinterpretation of what had and had not been agreed to, the Latin countries made sure the text of the resolution included the caveat that "This declaration . . . is designed to protect and not impair the inalienable right of each American State freely to choose its own form of government and economic system and to live its own social and cultural life." [31]

Unable to make use of the hemispheric collective security system for toppling the Arbenz regime, the Eisenhower Administration took unilateral action—rather unconvincingly cloaked as aid to Honduras and Nicaragua under the bilateral Mutual Defense Assistance Pacts just negotiated.[32] The June 1954 invasion of Guatemala from Honduras by Castillo Armas with an army of one-thousand men obviously encouraged and assisted by the United States government [33] was so successful, from a tactical point of view, that it discouraged fundamental reassessments in the White House of our approach to the growing militancy of the democratic left in Latin America. The United States apparently did have adequate power at its disposal to handle Communist insurgency or subversion in the hemisphere, if only we would follow the example shown by Dulles in the Guatemalan affair and, unsqueamishly, do what was required. "The rest of Latin America was not in the least displeased," opined Eisenhower.[34]

This being the perception at the highest levels in the Administration of the dimensions of the Latin American "problem," there was only pro-forma attention given to the appeals of others with ties to the President (such as Milton Eisenhower, Douglas Dillon, and Nelson Rockefeller) that we pay greater attention to the socioeconomic conditions creating a fertile field for Communist cultivation. Even the flurry of activity in 1958 following the Vice-President's trip was short-lived, and produced little more than the usual flap of studies and proposals from Washington's Latin Americanists. But programs with a magnitude approaching the dimensions of the problems were, as usual brushed aside. The proposal of Brazil's President Kubitschek for an "Operation Pan America," a hemisphere-wide mobilization of resources to overcome economic and social backwardness, got the conventional response from Eisenhower: banalities about hemispheric solidarity, but no meaningful acceptance, even in principle, of the concept of a major United States investment in development efforts in the form of a massive increase in long-term, low-interest credits. In the wake of the Nixon trip, the only tangible evidence that the United States might be willing to reassess the low rank accorded Latin America in our global priorities was our agreement to the organization of an Inter-American Development Bank, an idea the Administration had rejected in 1955 and 1957.[35]

The shocked recognition that there was need of a deeply cutting reappraisal of U.S. foreign policy toward Latin America came with Castro's overthrow of the Batista regime on January 1, 1959, and the rapid transformation of revolutionary Fidelismo into a harsh totalitarianism as known Communists were given increased responsibility in the Cuban government. Before the year was out, the United States had subscribed $450 million to the new Inter-American Development Bank, and Washington had begun a sweeping policy review.[36]

By early 1960, recalled Eisenhower, the outcome of this policy review was still questionable, but there was "one thing we did know: Fidel Castro was a hero to the masses in many Latin American nations. They saw him as a champion of the downtrodden and the enemy of the privileged who, in most of their countries, controlled both wealth and governments." [37] To counter the Castro *carisma* and the appeal of his programs of expropriation of foreign interests, land reform, and redistribution of the wealth, it would be necessary for the United States to pull out all the stops. The United States would have to demonstrate its concern for hemispheric development and reform in a more dramatic and convincing manner than heretofore. The personality and prestige of the President would have to be closely identified with these efforts. "I decided by early 1960," writes Eisenhower with cryptic understatement, "that the time had arrived for a presidential journey to South America." [38]

Upon his departure for South America the President addressed the nation and the world on the possible sources of misunderstanding between the United States and its neighbors to the South, and on his hopes for a better understanding of one another's purposes. The President observed that Latin Americans sometimes charged the United States with being "so preoccupied with the menace of Communist imperialism and the resulting problems of defense that . . . we neglect cooperation and progress within this hemisphere." But he hoped to make clear, said Eisenhower, that our great arsenals were for one purpose only: "the maintenance of peace, as important to Latin America as to us." And our Mutual Security Program, under which military assistance had been funneled to forty-two nations "makes possible a forward defense for the greater security of all, including our neighbors to the South."

If the United States had been devoting a large portion of its resources to the building and maintenance of "an umbrella of military strength" for the free nations, Latin America should recognize that they, as much as anyone else, had been the beneficiaries. The balance of the speech was a self-congratulatory recitation of the extent of United States investments in Latin America, our collective security commitments, and our historic dedication to the principles of "nonintervention, mutual respect, and the juridical equality of states." There was only passing reference to the problems crying for new approaches —the lack of development capital, wide fluctuations in the prices for Latin American exports, the gulf between wealthy oligarchies and poor masses, and the depressed levels of health, housing, and education.[39]

Upon returning to the United States two weeks later the tone and emphasis of the President's remarks had changed. He talked more about what yet needed to be done and less about what had already been accomplished; he particularly stressed the needs for development capital and more dependable export markets.

But there was still a skirting of the most touchy problem—internal socioeconomic reform, and the close association of the United States with regimes reputed to be resisting such reforms. The President's comments were indicative of the inability of his Administration to revise some rather basic ideological premises:

On occasion I heard it said that economic advance in some American Republics only makes the rich richer and the poor poorer, and that the United States should take the initiative in correcting this evil. This is a view fomented by Communists but often repeated by well-meaning people.

If there is any truth in this charge whatsoever, it is not the fault of the United States. . . .

Moreover, when internal social reform is required, it is purely an internal matter.[40]

In his memoirs Eisenhower discloses that the statement just quoted apparently did not represent his latest thoughts on the relationship between social reform, economic development, and United States influence in Latin America. He claims to have perceived, while on his trip:

that the private and public capital which had flowed bounteously into Latin America had failed to benefit the masses, that the demand for social justice was still rising. . . . Upon my return home I determined to begin planning, and the plans would culminate eventually in historic measures designed to bring about social reforms for the benefit of all the peoples of Latin America.[41]

Evidently his trip had made him an ally of those within his Administration, led by Douglas Dillon and Milton Eisenhower, who saw the dangers in a failure by the United States to identify itself with the forces of social reform. It was the premises of this group which now came to the fore, and provided United States policy with the first manifestation of the orientation that was to receive fuller elaboration and commitment in Kennedy's Alliance for Progress.

At Newport, on July 11, 1960, the Eisenhower face and voice were publicly identified with this new orientation: *change* is the law of life, he said. "Latin America is passing through a social and political transformation. Dictatorships are falling by the wayside. Moderate groups, seeking orderly reform, are contesting with dictators of both right and left who favor violence and authoritarianism. . . ." The choice had narrowed. It was now "social evolution or revolution." It was therefore "imperative that institutions be developed and strengthened sufficiently to permit the peoples' needs to be met through the orderly processes of change." Anticipating the proposals being prepared by Dillon for presentation to the forthcoming inter-American conference at Bogotá, the President listed those matters requiring the urgent attention of "every American nation": land reform, housing, and a wider share of the national product for the bulk of the population; the strengthening of institutions for mobilizing resources and promoting economic growth; and greater respect for human rights, and the will of the people as expressed in democratic elections. "The United States will not, cannot stand aloof." [42]

These ideas were given expression in a new program drafted by Undersecretary of State Dillon, and presented to the special meeting of the economic ministers of the Organization of American States at Bogotá, September 5–13, 1960. Dillon conveyed the offer of the President, backed up by Congressional authorization, of an immediate loan of $500 million for the purpose of inaugurating "a broad new social development program for Latin America." In addition to our steadily increasing programs of economic and industrial development, said Dillon, we must make a "conscious and determined effort to further social justice in our hemisphere." He brought with him to the conference a draft agreement for the establishment of an an inter-American program of social and economic development envisioning:

an overall improvement in the conditions of rural life, through better use of agricultural land, through better housing and community facilities, and through the modernization and improvement of education. . . .

. . .

The agreement also envisages increased contributions to this effort by Latin American governments, particularly through the modernization of tax systems . . . and modernized credit institutions.

"In the light of existing social tensions," continued the Undersecretary to his Latin counterparts, it was obvious that "it is not enough only to construct modern factories, power plants, and office buildings." The benefits from these projects often did not reach down to the ordinary citizen quickly enough:

We must bring fresh hope to the less privileged people who make up such large portions of the populations in many countries of Latin America. We must help them to replace a hovel with a home. We must help them to acquire ownership of land and the means for its productive use.

The administering agency for the allocation of subscribed funds, and for the evaluation of projects in conformity with agreed criteria would be the Inter-American Development Bank. As progress was made through joint and cooperative efforts, the United States would maintain its support with additional funds.[43]

The Act of Bogotá, adopted by the conference on September 13, 1960, incorporated the essential ideas of the Dillon proposal as they appeared in the detailed United States draft. As characterized by President Eisenhower:

"Non-intervention" had given way to a new idea—the idea that *all* American nations had an interest in ending feudalism, the vast hereditary gulf between rich and poor, the system that assured to a handful of families opulence without labor and condemned millions to near starvation without opportunity.[44]

In six short months the White House had moved a long way from its charge that such insidious ideas were "fomented by Communists," and from its insistence that social reform was "purely an internal matter."

The Latin American regimes, however, were not entirely pleased with the new shift in White House thinking. They did not mind the words about social and political reform; these were the standard ritual incantations of all Latin American politicians. What they were most pressing for—behind the scenes—they did not get: namely, guaranteed markets and price supports for their primary products.

Meanwhile the Administration's policy toward Cuba, in reaction to Castro's increasing intransigence, had become steadily more rigid. Repeated attempts by the United States to conciliate Castro, to engage his regime in discussions on the diplomatic level concerning such matters as compensation for expropriated United States companies, met with repeated rebuffs and harangues. It does not appear to have been until about fifteen months after his takeover in January 1959, however, that the United States changed its approach from one of trying to reestablish normal relations to one whose goal was the destruction of the Castro regime. On March 17, 1960, President Eisenhower agreed to a CIA program for the training of Cuban exiles in Guatemala for a possible insurgency operation.[45] In July, the policy of coercion was exhibited publicly in the reduction and subsequent suspension by the United States of the importation of Cuban sugar. And just two weeks before relinquishing the Presidency to John F. Kennedy, President Eisenhower broke off diplomatic relations with Cuba in retaliation for Castro's demands that the United States Embassy in Havana drastically reduce its staff. Even serious critics of the Eisenhower Administration concede that the deterioration of relations after the Castro takeover was not by design of the United States, but a reaction to Castro's increasing pugnaciousness, concomitant with the solidification of his ties to the Soviet Union. Most would agree with Arthur Schlesinger that "the policy of the Eisenhower Administration lacked both imagination and consistency, but it was certainly not one of purposeful hostility." [46]

Also, the White House now apparently believed its own words about the necessity of opposing dictators of the right as well as the left in Latin America. On August 20, 1960, the United States took a leading role at the San Jose, Costa Rica, meeting of OAS foreign ministers in the passage of a resolution condemning the Trujillo government's actions against Venezuela, and calling for a total blockade on the shipment of arms to Trujillo, and a partial economic blockade. The United States promptly complied, cutting most of the Dominican Republic's sugar quota and breaking diplomatic relations with Trujillo.

When the Eisenhower Administration left office, Latin America, the area of greatest lag in the appreciation of revolutionary nationalism as a significant factor in the global power balance, had become the field for the greatest experimentation with new tools and a new ideological stance for influencing global alignments.

There was less flexibility exhibited in the Eisenhower Administration's European and Asian policies during its last two years in office. In part, this was because Dulles had paid much more attention to these areas than to Latin America. But probably just as much influence can be attributed to the fact that, being in close proximity to the sources of Soviet and Chinese military power, the Communist nations were able to threaten the kind of incursions that would seem to call for military responses. Whether calculated, or opportunistic, the Communist tactics in these areas contributed to the perpetuation of the U.S. foreign policy emphasis on military deterrence in Europe and Asia. More creative alternatives for breaking down the rigidity of the opposing blocs in Europe, and for capturing the spirit of revolutionary natonalism in Asia, were deferred.

The summer of 1958, when Washington was reviewing its Middle Eastern and Latin American policies, was the occasion for a renewal of the Chinese offshore island conflict, in the form of threatening deployments and shelling from the mainland. The Administration responded as if, well-conditioned by its repsonse to the same challenge three years earlier, it knew the ropes. However, Eisenhower appeared more worried than Dulles. The Secretary of State seemed as convinced as before that a show of resolve not to give an inch to the Communists was required and would work. Eisenhower was not as confident that the risks—which he now saw as higher than in 1955—were worth the preservation of these tiny islands. The Formosa (Taiwan) Resolution, passed by Congress in the 1955 crisis, was supposed to give him discretion to defend or not to defend Quemoy and Matsu depending on his judgment as to whether their defense was necessary to the defense of Taiwan and the Pescadores. But now:

Chiang Kai-shek had helped complicate the problem. Ignoring our military advice, he had for many months been adding personnel to the Quemoy and Matsu garrisons, moving them forward, nearer the mainland. By the summer of 1958, a hundred thousand men, a third of his total ground forces, were stationed on those two island groups. . . . It seemed likely that his heavy deployment to these forward positions was designed to convince us that he was as committed to the defense of the offshore islands as he was to that of Formosa.[47]

The President was not at all pleased at being boxed in, especially in light of his reading of the changed global strategic situation, in which the Soviets had built up their nuclear striking force. "I did not doubt our total superiority," recalled Eisenhower, "but any large-scale conflict stimulated here was now less likely to remain limited to a conventional use of power." In addition to his fear that the Chinese Communists might consider *us* deterred by the prospect of a two-way nuclear war, the President took special note of the substantial buildup that had taken place over the past three years in Chinese Communist tactical air and artillery capabilities focused on the offshore islands and Taiwan. Clearly the risks were higher than before. But this time, because of Chiang's forcing our hand, we had even less of an option not to fight even if the Communists made very limited moves directed only at the offshore islands.

Under the circumstances, Eisenhower felt that the United States had no other choice but to persuade the Communists that, regardless of the risks, we would actively intervene to throw back an assault, "perhaps using nuclear weapons." For he was still convinced that Taiwan should be kept out of Communist hands to sustain the anti-Communist balance in the Pacific area. If Taiwan fell, said an internal governmental memorandum signed by Eisenhower and Dulles:

Indonesia, Malaya, Cambodia, Laos, and Burma would probably come fully under Communist influence. U.S. positions in this area, perhaps even Okinawa, would probably become untenable, or unusable, and Japan with its great industrial potential would probably fall within the Sino-Soviet orbit. These events would not happen all at once but would probably occur over a period of a few years. The consequences in the Far East would be even more catastrophic than those which followed when the United States allowed the Chinese mainland to be taken over by the Chinese Communists. . . .[48]

Again the strategy of looking determined, of having no alternative but to fight,[49] symbolized by deployments of the Seventh Fleet and destroyer escorts for Chiang's resupply operations, seemed to pay off. But the White House was not sure to what extent the Chinese Communist failure to test our will further was determined by the reluctance of the Soviets to give them promises of counterintervention against the United States.

At the conclusion of the 1958 crisis, Eisenhower was determined that he should not be caught in such a bind again. We would be willing to defend Taiwan, to be sure; but Dulles was instructed to make clear to Chiang that he should reduce his garrisons on the offshore islands. The United States would not be deprived of the decision as to when and if it should go to war should the Communists resume their campaign against Quemoy and Matsu. The Nationalists did thereafter reduce the size of their forces on the offshore islands, "but not to the extent I thought desirable," wrote Eisenhower.[50] It was also important, from Eisenhower's point of view, to make it clear to the rest of the world that the United States rejected force as an acceptable means of regaining the mainland. In this, the President seems to have been less concerned that the Communists would be driven to pre-emptive counteractions than with preventing the Communists from legitimizing their own threats of force. The whole world was watching, and for Eisenhower the opinions of mankind were to be reckoned in the balance of power.

The Administration's response to the Soviet Union's rekindling of the Berlin question and the division of Germany, after a comparatively peaceful nine years, showed the extent to which the military context was still the omnipresent influence in our European diplomacy. With Europe hardened into two blocks, there had seemed little to be gained by deemphasizing Cold War considerations in order to appeal to those who were uncommitted. And with very little economic interdependence (the renewal of East-West trade was just beginning), there were practically no sanctions available except military threats to restrain provocations.

The fact that our diplomatic power in Europe was a direct resultant of the balance of applicable military force was again driven home to the Administration, as it had been during the last European crisis— over Hungary. In that crisis, however, this realization merely clarified the Administration's recognition that the United States, in its operational objectives, was limited to preservation of the existing territorial status quo, and that "liberation" was a vague goal for whose implementation we had no usable tools. Now with a changing military context, for the Administration to shape its diplomatic objectives with direct reference to the balance of applicable force might require a surrender of advanced positions, such as Berlin. The Administration was haunted by such a fear during the 1958–59 Berlin crisis, but seemed too immobilized by past doctrine to do anything to redress the imbalance.

Throughout the spring and summer of 1958, while the United States was embroiled in the Lebanon crisis in the Middle East and the offshore island confrontation with Communist China, the Soviets were gradually beginning to tighten the screws in Europe—combining administrative harrassments of Western traffic to the city of Berlin with calls for a new summit conference to reduce tension. The Warsaw Pact countries also renewed their campaign for a military disengagement from Central Europe.

The United States reactions were initially no more than a stale rehearsal of old positions: we would maintain our rights of access to Berlin;[51] we would not be forced into a summit conference. If the Soviets were serious about reducing tension in Europe, they should be willing to undertake serious negotiations to reduce the sources of such tension —the most outstanding being the unnatural division of Germany. A summit conference would be useless unless there had been substantial progress made toward a resolution of the German problem at the working diplomatic levels. A basis for serious negotiations over the German question had been provided in the Geneva heads of government communiqué of July 1955, namely, reunification on the basis of free elections. But the Soviets had thus far not shown any willingness to negotiate according to those terms.

It seemed that the Soviets were evidently anxious to test the degree of new diplomatic leverage they had gained as a result of their space success and missile claims. Khrushchev announced on November 10, 1958 that the Soviet Union was committed to put an end to the Western occupation of Berlin, and was ready to renounce its Potsdam Agreement obligation unilaterally if the West was unwilling to negotiate an end to the occupation status of Germany and Berlin. Then on November 27, the Soviet Union, in formal notes to the United States, Great Britain, and France, put a time limit of six months for the West to accept their proposals for a termination of the military occupation of Berlin and the "conversion of West Berlin into an independent political unit—a free city . . . demilitarized . . . that . . . could have its own government and run its own economic, administrative, and other affairs." This "free city" of West Berlin, according to the Soviet note, should be guaranteed in its status by the four powers, and possibly by the United Nations. But the immediately responsible nation would be the German Democratic Republic, in whose territory this free city would lie. Thus, in order to guarantee unhindered communications between the free city and the outside world negotiations would have to be undertaken by the four powers with the GDR. The six-months deadline to effect such negotiations read like an ultimatum:

. . . the Soviet Government proposes to make no changes in the present procedure for the military traffic of the USA, Great Britain, and France from West Berlin to the FRG for half a year. It regards such a period as fully sufficient to provide a sound basis for the solution of . . . Berlin's situation. . . .

If the above-mentioned period is not utilized to reach an agreement, the Soviet Union will then carry out the planned measures through an agreement with the GDR. It is envisaged that the German Democratic Republic, like any other independent state, must fully . . . exercise its sovereignty on land, water, and in the air. At the same time there will terminate all contracts still maintained between . . . the Soviet Union in Germany and . . . the USA, Great Britain, and France in questions pertaining to Berlin.[52]

The State Department's response to the Soviet proposals was, of course, negative. But this meant the United States had to face up to the likelihood that the Soviets, in six months, would carry out their threat to abrogate, unilaterally, their Berlin obligations; and this would mean, in turn, that the West would have to deal directly with the East German authorities on all questions of access to Berlin through GDR territory. By such a maneuver, the Soviets apparently hoped to force us to "recognize" the authority of the GDR, thereby legitimizing the division of Germany and presumably demoralizing the Federal Republic. Dulles attempted to provide some basis for sidestepping a "confrontation" by hinting in his November 26 press conference that we might have to deal with the GDR officials as "agents" of the Soviet Union.[53]

If a confrontation *were* to arise on this issue, if after the expiration of the six-months deadline, the East German authorities were to attempt to exercise administrative controls on the access routes to Berlin and not let Western traffic through until we recognized their authority, what would be our response? Would we try to force our way through?

Until now, whenever the West had felt it necessary to threaten a physical challenge to Soviet administrative harrassments on the access routes, the Soviets were able to cease the application of the particular procedure at issue without losing face. The Soviets would usually cover their retreat in advance by claiming that the procedures were made necessary by road repairs or some other temporary technicality.

But with a confrontation in the context of the Soviet ultimatum, the particular technical pretext might be infused for *both* sides with a high political content. The very real possibility that this time the East German officials, backed by the Soviets, would not retreat under our threats to resort to physical means compelled the Administration to reassess the balance of locally applicable force.

Assessing the local military situation, Eisenhower observed that it was "so lopsided as to be ridiculous." He was convinced that if the conflict entered a phase of actual military engagement, "our troops in Berlin would be quickly overrun, and the conflict would almost inevitably be global war." In a White House meeting, critics, particularly leaders of the Democratic party in Congress, tried to paint this situation as a deficiency of New Look defense policies. But the President was no less adamant in insisting that an attempt to balance Soviet ground troops in Europe was a senseless policy:

"The Soviets are engaged in confronting the United States with a series of crises," I said. "The United States has a need for an efficient military system. But it has to be realized that if we program for the sum total of all recommendations for increasing military strength, the mounting burden would call for full mobilization," putting the nation on a wartime footing. I said that we could not have ground forces to match those that the Soviets could mobilize in Middle Europe.

I went on to say that we had no intention of opposing, with ground troops only, a full-out attack by a couple of hundred Soviet divisions, but that we would take care of the situation.

We would be in a Third World War, and "for this type of war our nuclear forces were more than adequate." To Speaker Rayburn, and Lyndon Johnson (then Senate majority leader) the President reiterated his confidence in United States strategic superiority: "In fact, I said, 'If we were to release our nuclear stockpile on the Soviet Union, the main danger would arise not from retaliation but from fallout in the earth's atmosphere.' " [54]

It was obviously necessary to put this confident face on this assessment of the balance of usable force; for, if we had no capabilities or intention of fighting a limited engagement for control of Berlin, the Soviets would have us over a barrel unless we could appear less fearful than they of a general nuclear war. "Possibly, we were risking the very fate of civilization on the premise that the Soviets would back down from the deadline when confronted by force," reflects Eisenhower, "Yet this to my mind was not really gambling, for if were not willing to take this risk we would be certain to lose." [55]

Yet, in actual planning, as far as can be gleaned from Eisenhower's subsequent published description, Eisenhower was very careful to provide himself with alternative courses of action—even in the case of a Soviet refusal to back down. The basic contingency plan which the President approved in late January 1959, included these steps:

(a) A refusal to acquiesce in any substitution of East Germans for Soviet officials in checking the Western occupying powers movement to and from Berlin . . . ; (b) A decision to begin quiet military preparations in West Germany and Berlin prior to May 27, sufficient to be detected by Soviet intelligence but not sufficient to create public alarm; (c) Should there by any substitution of East German officials for Soviets, a small convoy with armed protection would attempt to go through, and if this convoy were stopped, the effort would be discontinued and the probe would fire only if fired upon; (d) transit would then be suspended and pressure would be brought to bear on the Soviets by publicizing the blockade and taking the matter to the United Nations Security Council and, if necessary, to the General Assembly. In these circumstances our further military preparations would be intensified by observable means such as the evacuation of dependents from West Berlin and possibly from all Germany; (e) In the event that this moral and other pressure was not sufficient, use of additional force would be subject to governmental decision. . . .[56]

Meanwhile the West would agree, assuming the Soviets would drop their ultimatum, to engage in high level discussions, but at the foreign ministers level, not the summit. These discussions, according to the Administration, were to provide the Soviets with the opportunity to back away from their November 1958 demands without losing face. Expectedly, the White House and State Department denied any intention to compromise Western rights in Berlin, or to review our refusal to accord the Ulbricht regime any formal or symbolic recognition. Yet we did agree to the attendance of the GDR and the FRG at the forthcoming conference, though not as full participants.

Between January and May 11, 1959, the date of the convening in Geneva of the foreign ministers meeting, the Soviets gave many indications of backing away from their rigid six-months deadline. This made it easier for the West to agree to participate in the foreign ministers meeting, as it diluted the image of the United States being dragged to the conference table under the grip of an ultimatum.

At the start of the May meeting both sides dutifully repeated their mutually unacceptable solutions to the German question. The conference then proceeded to the Berlin issue where, uncharacteristically, the differences between the Western nations and the Soviet Union over future arrangements seemed to be narrowing. But the significant compromises were almost all on the side of the West in the direction of the Soviet position, rather than the other way around. The Draft Agreement handed by the Western Foreign Ministers to Gromyko on June 16 provided that: (a) the United States, Britain, and France would limit the combined total of their forces in Berlin to 11,000 "and to continue to arm these forces only with conventional weapons. . . ." The draft agreement noted that "the Soviet Foreign Minister has made known the decision of the Soviet Government no longer to maintain forces in Berlin"; so the presumption was that only the materialization of this Soviet troop withdrawal would allow the Western governments to adhere to their limitation. On the surface this may have looked like a satisfactory *quid pro quo;* but even if it did come to pass, the Soviets would maintain overwhelming military superiority in the immediate environs of Berlin; (b) the "procedures" for controlling access to West Berlin, "without prejudice to existing basic responsibilities . . . may . . . be carried out by [East] German personnel" (it was stated that the access should be "free and unrestricted," and that "basic" responsibilities should remain in the hands of the four powers; but the legitimizing of operational control by the GDR was a major concession by the West); (c) measures should be taken "to avoid in both parts of Berlin activities which might either disturb public order or or seriously affect the rights and interests, or amount to interference in the internal affairs, of others." (This curb on propaganda and intelligence activities cut hardest against Western operations, and gave in to one of the persistent Soviet complaints against the West Berliners.) [57]

Some analysts have attributed the major concessions by the West to the fact that John Foster Dulles was no longer in charge of United States diplomacy,[58] having resigned on April 15 during the terminal phase of his illness, and having died on May 24. But Secretary of State Herter was not representing a personal position. His was the Administration position, worked out by high officials loyal to Dulles and Eisenhower and responsive to their recognition that the United States had coercive leverage in the Berlin situation only to the extent that our threat to initiate general nuclear war was believed by the Soviets. The point is that the Administration did not *know* if it was believed by the Soviets; and in the event that it was not, lacking an advance indication of some willingness to modify our original negotiating position, concessions by the West at the time of a "confrontation" would have all the attributes of a surrender.

Paradoxically, the Administration was saved the embarrassment of a Soviet acceptance of the Western proposals by Khrushchev's assumption that he could press his advantage to get even more. The Soviet leader had let the six-month "deadline" pass without turning over major Soviet Berlin responsibilities to the East Germans, explaining to Ulbricht, that "conditions are not ripe as yet for a new scheme of things." Finding the West surprisingly malleable, at the June sessions in Geneva, the Soviets extended their deadline for a year, but meanwhile intensified their intransigence at the conference to see if there was even more give in the Western position. This reduced the immediate risks to the Soviets of pressing the West too far too soon, while allowing for the possibility of greater rewards later.

Khrushchev must have been encouraged in the assumption that the West believed it was negotiating from a position of weakness when, before the close of the foreign ministers conference, he received a formal invitation from President Eisenhower to visit the United States.

Another meeting at the summit, it will be recalled, had been built up as a *Soviet* objective; and now the United States was giving in to this also. The fruit on the tree must have appeared to be ripening fast.

Eisenhower had been consistently trying to deflect the growing popular clamor for a summit (considerably amplified by Prime Minister Macmillan's entreaties) with which the Soviets had identified themselves. As the prospect increased of a collapse of negotiations at the foreign ministers meeting, Eisenhower reminded Macmillan of their agreement that substantive accomplishments at the foreign minister's level would have to precede a summit conference. The President confided to his British colleague his fear that "if I surrendered on this point I would no longer have any influence with Khruschchev, who would, thereafter, consider me a 'pushover.' Indeed . . . I would myself interpret such an agreement as an exhibition of weakness." [59]

As Khrushchev pushed his campaign for a summit, Eisenhower thought he found "a device to break the stalemate" in an invitation for the Soviet leader to visit the United States on an "informal basis." This would be no "summit," there would be no "negotiations"; but an opportunity might be provided for an informal conversation on matters of mutual concern.[60]

This "informal conversation," held at Camp David, Maryland, on September 25 and 26, 1959, produced an agreement by Chairman Khrushchev to withdraw his time limit for a Berlin settlement in return for Eisenhower's agreement to a Big Four summit conference in 1960 during which the Berlin issue could be discussed. To purists in the delicate art of German-issue diplomacy, this was an American blunder. Clumsier yet was Eisenhower's press conference remark on September 28 that the Berlin "situation is abnormal." [61] The standard Western formulation was supposed to be that the *division of Germany* was abnormal.

The total breakdown of the 1960 summit, ostensibly over the U-2 reconnaissance issue, and the diplomatic hiatus produced by the impending change in United States leadership, saved the Eisenhower Administration from further negotiations on the Berlin issue. Significantly, the Democrats, watching from the wings, resolved they would not let themselves be caught in a similar diplomatic confrontation without some redressing of the balance of local military capabilities in Europe.

Too long we have fixed our eyes on traditional military needs, on armies prepared to cross borders, on missiles poised for flight. Now it should be clear that this is no longer enough—that our security may be lost piece by piece, country by country, without the firing of a single missile or the crossing of a single border.

JOHN F. KENNEDY

We still tend to conceive of national security almost entirely as a state of armed readiness: a vast, awesome arsenal of weaponry.

We still tend to assume that it is primarily this purely military ingredient that creates security.

We are still haunted by this concept of military hardware.

ROBERT S. MC NAMARA

PART IV

THE KENNEDY-JOHNSON
YEARS

CHAPTER TWELVE

PERCEIVED DEFICIENCIES IN THE
NATION'S POWER

Power is not a matter of arms alone. Strength comes from education, fertile acres, humming workshops and the satisfaction and pride of peoples.
DEAN RUSK

The state of the Union leaves a lot to be desired, the new President informed the nation on January 30, 1961. "Our problems are critical. The tide is unfavorable. The news will be worse before it is better." With the help of more than twenty-five specialized task forces, assembled during and after the election campaign, he had been taking a close inventory of "our whole arsenal of tools," and had been discovering serious gaps—gaps which if not corrected would leave the nation with a deficiency of power for meeting the coming challenges to its very survival. And certainly without attention to the neglected components of our national power, we could not hope to advance beyond these immediate security needs and apply our resources to reduce the misery of others.

The New Frontier's initial analysis of the overall power position of the United States and those components of power requiring remedial attention offered little that was new to those who had kept up with the substance of the informed political dialogue in this country. It was essentially an amalgam of the ideas of two sets of Democrats-in-exile: the Truman Democrats and the Stevenson Democrats. What was strikingly new about the New Frontier was the vital fusion of the hardheaded Cold War orientation of the first with the international idealism of the second. To be sure there had been a good deal of cross-fertilization in ideas and personnel between the two groups in the 1952–60 period. But there were tendencies, and a center of gravity which characterized each, particularly when it came to foreign affairs. What united them was the shared psychology of exile status of experienced men in their prime, oriented toward the public service, but excluded for eight years from its highest counsels. Not unnaturally they applauded one another's findings that the nation's power under Eisenhower had been sadly neglected. They were not always united, however, on remedial programs, or on which of these should be given priority. But neither were their ideas of what to do sufficiently specific for the new President to accept them as ready-made programs. Out of power, without the vast informational resources of the government at their command, analysts, whatever their previous experience, must confine themselves, relatively speaking, to general propositions. President Kennedy, given his practical frame of mind and wide intellectual grasp, was therefore able to accept the analyses of both groups without offending either and fashion fresh programs in which both could see their views reflected.

The first order of business the new Administration set for itself was to attend to the perceived deficiencies in the nation's power to protect its most vital interests. There, the gaps identified constituted a potpourri of the criticisms leveled at the Eisenhower Administration by various Democratic spokesmen during the last few years.

There was the potential "missile gap" that Congressional Democrats, led by Senators Stuart Symington (Secretary of the Air Force under Truman), Henry M. Jackson, and Lyndon Johnson had been harping on since 1958. Kennedy joined in the charge with a major Senate speech in August of that year, systematically outlining the requirements of strategic deterrence. But the intelligence estimates handed over to the new Administration on the United States–Soviet strategic balance showed the standard Congressional Democratic charge of Republican neglect of the strategic arsenal to have been a vast exaggeration. Revised estimates which were being compiled on the basis of newly received information showed, if anything, a missile imbalance in our favor. Actually, the Kennedy Administration found that its predecessor had done a pretty good job in translating the nation's technological resources into actual and projected instruments for the deterrence of stategic attack. The President's State of the Union message, and his Defense budget message two months later, thus told of decisions to "step up" and "accelerate" the missile program, but no new concept for the strategic forces was advanced. Like their predecessors, President Kennedy and Secretary of Defense Robert McNamara, accepted the planning premise for the design of the strategic force that there should be no *deterrent* gap, by which they meant that the force should be large enough to retaliate with "unacceptable damage" against an attacker or combination of attackers, even under the assumption that we had suffered a surprise strategic attack with all the weapons the enemy could launch. An alternative planning premise—namely, that deterrence of attacks upon other areas, particularly Western Europe, required that the United States maintain a "first strike" strategic force, capable of knocking out the Soviet's means of nuclear bombardment of the United States—appears to have been rejected in these early days and never to have been revived.[1] A more usable means of protecting our vital overseas interests against military attack was thought to lie in the improvement of local defense capabilities.

The charge was frequently made by Senator John F. Kennedy that the Eisenhower Administration had left a gaping hole in the United States arsenal of power by failing to provide adequate local defense capabilities for the non-Communist world. Under the prevailing strategic monism we had been, in the Senator's words:

. . . preparing . . . primarily to fight the one kind of war we least want to fight and are least likely to fight. We have been driving ourselves into a corner where the only choice is all or nothing at all, world devastation or submission—a choice that necessarily causes us to hesitate on the brink and leaves the initiative in the hands of our enemies.[2]

The perceived deficiency in the nation's ability to fight "limited," or non-nuclear wars was a rallying point for a wide spectrum of Democrats, however they might differ on other matters. The premise that this deficiency was a critical gap in the overall power of the non-Communist world as opposed to the Communist world had been standard with "security"-minded Truman exiles like Dean Acheson and Paul Nitze, both of whom had been pointing since 1949 to the dangers that would face the United States if we did not remedy this gap by the time the Soviets deployed an intercontinental nuclear capability.[3]

The "conventional" capabilities gap had also become a concern of Adlai Stevenson, Hubert Humphrey, and others who were urging greater United States efforts to control the arms race. This group, in the late 1950s, was increasingly pessimistic about the prospects for *dis-armament*, but were strongly oriented toward "arms control" concepts that stressed a "stabilization" of the nuclear "balance of terror." They perceived that unless the non-Communist world could balance the capabilities of the Communist nations at lower levels of warfare, the United States would have to maintain an obvious superiority at the nuclear strategic level in order to dissuade the Communists from military adventures. And since the Soviets, it was believed, would never accept a position of strategic inferiority, there would be no end to the ever-more-lethal arms race unless a balance of forces could be achieved at the lower levels. As the Soviets were not about to scale down their local war capabilities, the only recourse for the West, therefore—a proposition reluctantly but realistically accepted by the Stevensonians—was to scale up.

Kennedy, characteristically, chose to sidestep the potential contradiction between the Nitze position, which urged superiority across-the-board, and the arms controllers' position which sought parity at all levels. He chose rather to stress their operational similarities as they came immediately to bear on the improvement of conventional capabilities.

The more precise case for the improvement of capabilities for non-nuclear warfare came by way of the Defense Department after the new Administration had settled in, and it remained for the Secretary of Defense and his deputies to articulate the sharpened rationale (see the following chapter).

Analysts with an orientation toward military affairs are prone to pay most attention to the so-called Kennedy-McNamara "revolution" in military policy, as if it were the centerpiece of the Kennedy Administration's foreign policy. But this is to confuse immediacy with high value. At the center of the Kennedy foreign policy was the premise that the competition between the Soviet Union and the United States was shifting to a new arena—the competition for influence over the direction of development in the poorer half of the globe; and it was with respect to this competition that we were in greatest danger of falling behind. Marginal improvements had to be made in our military posture to ensure that the Soviets were not encouraged to try their hand once again in the other arenas of more direct East-West confrontation, such as Berlin. Filing the gaps in our military arsenal, and then vigilance to see that additional gaps did not appear in an era of volatile technology, was the necessary condition for a fundamental retooling in the nonmilitary instruments of power for the vigorous contests in the new arena.

Kennedy's view that the "third world" had now become the decisive field of engagement was shared by most of the Stevensonians, by Senate foreign policy leaders such as J. William Fulbright and Mike Mansfield, and by ever-renewable Averell Harriman. But the Europe-first emphasis remained strong among Truman State Department Alumni, led by Acheson—still the idol of many seasoned top-level career diplomats in the State Department who had survived the Eisenhower-Dulles doldrums. When it came to programmatic expression of the new orientation, the burden of proof would fall on those arguing for allocating a larger proportion of our human and material resources to "containment" in the underdeveloped world. Two weeks before inauguration the supporters of the new orientation received their most effective ammunition from an unexpected source.

Premier Khrushchev, in his historic foreign policy speech of January 6, 1961, displayed the Soviet grand-strategic rationale for focusing Soviet efforts on the underdeveloped areas: due to developments in the technology of warfare, "World Wars" and "local wars" had become obsolete (they would lead to a nuclear holocaust destroying the workers as well as the capitalists), and therefore "unjust." The "just wars" of the contemporary period, the inevitable and necessary wars according to the Marxist-Leninist appraisal of the relation between social and material forces, were "wars of national liberation." The phrase was a catchall for anti-colonial agitations, popular uprisings against established indigenous regimes, and actual guerilla wars. Examples were the campaign of the FLN in Algeria for independence from France, the Castro takeover in Cuba, general efforts to mobilize the leftist forces in

Latin America, and the insurgency in South Vietnam. "The Communists support just wars of this kind wholeheartedly and without reservations," said the Soviet leader.[4]

Here, in Kennedy's view, was an eminently realistic appraisal by the Soviets themselves of where their best opportunities for expansion lay. It conformed with the strategy shift attributed to the Soviets by Walt Rostow, particularly—one of the first in Kennedy's circle of foreign policy advisers to make a serious pitch for a major United States counterinsurgency program. Arthur Schlesinger reports that Khrushchev's January 6 speech "made a conspicuous impression on the new President, who took it as an authoritative exposition of Soviet intentions, discussed it with his staff and read excerpts from it aloud to the National Security Council." [5]

The President was familiar with Mao Tse-tung's aphorism that power grows out of the barrel of a gun. But he knew there was more to guerilla warfare than forming new commando-type units. He appreciated and liked to quote Mao's equally important aphorism: "Guerillas are like fish, and the people are the water in which the fish swim. If the temperature of the water is right, the fish will thrive and multiply." [6] It was critically important to tend the temperature of the water —and as far in advance as possible.

The prophylactic aspects of counterinsurgency provided the link between those in Kennedy's advisory entourage who saw the balance of power primarily in terms of the distribution of coercive capabilities and those who emphasized the more benign components of international influence. When put in this frame of reference, Paul Nitze, Generals Maxwell Taylor and James Gavin, Walt Rostow, Roger Hilsman, Chester Bowels, Averell Harriman, John Kenneth Gailbraith, and Adlai Stevenson could all agree on the necessity for a much larger program of long-term development aid to the many potential targets for Communist insurgency in Asia, the Middle East, Africa, and Latin America.

Having forged agreement that the purpose of foreign assistance was to affect the "temperature of the water" in the recipient countries—to assure those economic, social, and political conditions that are inhospitable to the growth of Communist movements—the next step was to assure application of foreign aid criteria designed by those with credentials in this type of oceanography. The dominant standard that had

prevailed during the Eisenhower period, the degree of overt acquiescence on the part of regimes in power to the anti-Communist orientation of United States diplomacy, was now seen to be hopelessly inadequate. Kennedy accepted the need for a much more "technical"—and
complicated—analysis for determining the utility of the kinds and
amounts of assistance to go to any particular country. As senator and
President-elect he sought the counsel of professionals, and they were
not to be found within the Government. He found them, again mainly
New Deal–Fair Deal exiles (but professional economists all), encamped
along the banks of the Charles River: Galbraith, Carl Kaysen, Edward
S. Mason, David Bell, and Lincoln Gordon at Harvard; Rostow, Max
Millikan, and P. N. Rosenstein-Rodan at the M.I.T. Center for International Studies.[7] Here, during the 1950s, were developed the propositions on economic assistance that became official government policy in
the 1960s: namely, operational criteria for evaluating the worth of any
particular foreign aid program must be stated in terms of a concept of
the socioeconomic modernization process; and the explicit objective of
measures sponsored by the United States should be self-sustaining economic growth for each recipient nation. The concept and objective will
be elaborated in Chapter 14. For the present, it should be noted that
the lack of such a concept and objective for determining the flow of
foreign assistance to the poorer nations was considered by the new
President as probably the most critical deficiency in the arsenal of tools
by which we hoped to influence the international environment.

Kennedy's economist friends were contending that modernization
and the development of greater constitutional democracy and social
justice could go hand in hand; that, indeed, economic development required national planning and reliable administration, and these required the kind of political stability that was best sustained in a constitutional system providing for responsible government according to the
consent of the governed. But Kennedy was also sensitive to the potential gap between the rational political-economy of his advisers and their
Western-trained counterparts in the developing countries on the one
hand, and the combustible character of the "revolution of rising expectations," particularly when exploited by demagogues, on the other
hand. He understood that part of the weakness of the United States in
trying to influence the poorer nations from succumbing to totalitarian
models for modernization was the lack of passion in our commitment

to egalitarian aspects of social justice. We had been only half-hearted in our support for the kind of land reform and tax reform that would bring about the structural economic changes we knew were necessary for modernization. Our excuse, under previous Administrations, had been that an open advocacy of such reform measures would constitute an interference in the domestic affairs of those smaller nations—that it was up to those nations, in their own way, however gradually, to take such social reform upon themselves without outside pressure. The effect of our self-denying ordinance, however, had been to identify the United States with status quo elements in these countries, and to provide social revolutionary elements with confirmation of their suspicion that the State Department was in cahoots with United States private interests who profited from privileges extended them by entrenched local oligarchies. It was from this concern that the Alliance for Progress evolved. As the President put it on the first anniversary of its launching:

For too long my country, the wealthiest nation on a poor continent, failed to carry out its full responsibilities to its sister Republics. We have now accepted that responsibility. In the same way those who possess wealth and power in poor nations must accept their own responsibilities. They must lead the fight for basic reforms which alone can preserve the fabric of their own societies. Those who make peaceful revolution impossible will make violent revolution inevitable.

These social reforms are at the heart of the Alliance for Progress. They are the precondition to economic modernization. And they are the instrument by which we assure to the poor and hungry, to the worker and the *campesino*, his full participation in the benefits of our development and in the human dignity which is the purpose of free societies.[8]

These were strong words. And there might be a problem in seeing that the expectations they might arouse of United States action in support of social reform did not outrun our ability to influence "those who possess the wealth and power in poor nations." But, in Kennedy's view of where the stakes in the global struggle for power then lay, he had little choice but to reidentify the United States with the rising demands of the poor and the disenfranchised.

The idea that essential power relationships among nations were being transformed by these new expectations, passions, and demands was no new preoccupation of Kennedy's. He was one of the staunchest supporters in the Congress of aid to India, during the years when the Administration and many of his own party in the Congress were suspicious of Nehru's socialism and nonalignment. And in 1959, while most of his colleagues were stepping up their polemics on the presumed missile "gap," he took the opportunity to point to another gap "which constitutes an equally clear and present danger to our security":

I am talking about the economic gap—the gap in living standards and income and hope for the future . . . between the stable, industrialized nations of the north . . . and the overpopulated, underinvested nations of the south. . . .

. . .

It is this gap which presents us with our most critical challenge today. It is this gap which is altering the face of the globe, our strategy, our security, and our alliances, more than any current military challenge. And it is this economic challenge to which we have responded most sporadically, most timidly, and most inadequately.[9]

In order to respond to this economic challenge the people of the United States would have to feel confident enough of their own productivity to allow for a diversion of effort to the needs of others. But, reported Kennedy, in his first Presidential address to the Congress:

We take office in the wake of . . . three and one-half years of slack, seven years of diminished economic growth, and nine years of falling farm income.

. . .

Our recovery from the 1958 recession . . . was anemic and incomplete. Our Gross National Product never again regained its full potential. Unemployment never returned to normal levels. Maximum use of our national industrial capacity was never restored.

In short, the American economy is in trouble. The most resourceful industrialized country on earth ranks among the last in the rate of economic growth.[10]

Not only did this lagging state of our economy reduce our capacity and will to provide direct help to the poorer nations, it also reduced another very important aspect of our influence: our reputation for successful management of a largely free economy for the well-being of all our people. "We must show the world what a free economy can do," [11] admonished Kennedy, in recommending a set of economic measures to take up the slack.

Moreover, the United States was placed in a vulnerable diplomatic position with respect to other industrialized nations by its adverse balance of international payments, which Kennedy felt was partly the result of the sluggishness of our own economy in competition with the dynamically expanding economies in Western Europe. "Our success in world affairs has long depended in part upon foreign confidence in our ability to pay," he said.[12] And to intimates he confided his anxiety that the payments deficit was "a club that DeGaulle and all the others hang over my head. Any time there's a crisis or a quarrel, they can cash in all their dollars and where are we?" [13]

For Kennedy, programs to "get the country moving again"—his anti-recession measures of 1961, the Trade Expansion Act of 1962, and the tax cut of 1963—were as much required by global balance of power considerations as they were by considerations of domestic economic well-being. The continued productive growth of the United States was a value in itself, and to be pursued as part of the basic national interest. But it was also regarded as a means toward the more vigorous exercise of power internationally. Unlike the preceding Administration, which seemed to view the requirements of domestic economic productivity as competitive with, and therefore a constraint upon, our overseas commitments (we could not raise additional conventional forces because that might bankrupt us), the New Frontier felt that any gap between our overseas commitments and the existing domestic economic base needed to sustain them was only an argument for expansion of the domestic economy. It was not an argument for reduced defense spending. A contraction in our commitments or an unwillingness to provide ourselves with the widest array of diplomatic and military tools to sustain these commitments would endanger our security in the long run, and currently would further reduce our ebbing global leadership.

Similarly, a continuance of our reliance on protectionist devices in order to protect the home market from growing foreign competition would have adverse consequences on our overall power on the international scene. "Economic isolation and political leadership are wholly incompatible," asserted Kennedy in urging the Congress to grant him the broad tariff-reducing authority requested in the Administration's trade expansion bill of 1962:

In the next few years, the nations of Western Europe will be fixing basic economic and trading patterns vitally affecting the future of our economy and the hopes of our less-developed friends. Basic political and military decisions of vital interest to our security will be made. Unless we have this authority to negotiate . . . if we are separated from the Common Market by high tariff barriers on either side of the Atlantic—then we cannot hope to play an effective part in those decisions.

If we are to retain our leadership, the initiative is up to us. The revolutionary changes which are occurring will not wait for us to make up our minds. The United States has encouraged sweeping changes in free world economic patterns in order to strengthen the forces of freedom. But we cannot ourselves stand still. If we are to lead, we must act. We must adapt our own economy to the imperatives of a changing world, and once more assert our leadership.[14]

Pervading most of President Kennedy's major recommendations to the Congress, for "domestic" no less than specifically foreign programs, was this notion of the power of *movement* itself. The key to leadership on the international scene was a creative exploitation of the currents of change. The surge by the new nations for a place in the sun, the social and economic egalitarianism of the newly enfranchised masses across the globe, and the unconquerable assertion of men that the object of government is to protect and extend the exercise of free choice—this was the very stuff of the new international politics. Leadership in this arena called for a renewal of the dynamics of the American experiment in freedom. Thus, our prestige abroad, our influence upon others—i.e., our power—were seriously weakened by the squalor of our cities, the crime on our streets, the overcrowding and low standards in many of our schools, our shortage of adequate health facilities and medical professionals, and most of all, by the "denial of constitutional rights to some of our fellow Americans on account of race." [15] We had to recapture, Kennedy felt, that pride and nerve to explore uncharted frontiers, without which the nation "would trend in the direction of a slide downhill into dust, dullness, languor, and decay." [16]

As much as to help in the spread of literacy and technical know-how, and to improve the American image abroad, the Peace Corps was directed at improving the quality of life here in the United States. The Peace Corps was typical of Kennedy's integrated and long-term approach to the problem of the nation's power, which would demand from the coming generation of leaders, no less than his own, a willingness to pay a price to secure the blessings of liberty. "A price measured not merely in money and military preparedness, but in social inventiveness, in moral stamina, and physical courage." [17]

President Kennedy's decision, after some hesitation, to stress the competitive nature of the space race with the Soviets, not just the potentials for cooperative scientific exploration, was very much a part of his concern to avoid a flabbiness of the national fiber. The scientific or potential military payoffs from trying to be "first" in space seem to have impressed him less than the intangible effects on the national spirit. Many of the welfare liberals who supported him down the line on other planks in his program cried "Moondoggle." His reply, best articulated in his September 1962 address at Rice University, reflected the New Frontier's intuition of where to probe for that critical vein of adventuresomeness which had once been, and could again be, a special source of national strength:

But why, some say, the moon? . . . And they may well ask, why climb the highest mountain? Why, thirty-five years ago, fly the Atlantic? Why does Rice play Texas? . . .

We choose to go to the moon in this decade, and do the other things, not because they are easy but because they are hard; because that goal will serve to organize and measure the best of our energies and skills. . . .

Many years ago the great British explorer George Mallory, who was to die on Mount Everest, was asked why did he want to climb it, and he said, "Because it is there."

Well, space is there, and . . . the moon and planets are there, and new hopes for knowledge and peace are there.[18]

CHAPTER THIRTEEN

ATTENDING TO THE MILITARY BALANCE

Nuclear and non-nuclear power complement each other . . . just as together they complement the non-military instruments of policy. . . . I firmly believe that the non-nuclear buildup will—by improving and expanding the alternatives open to the Free World—reduce the pressures to make concessions in the face of Soviet threats.

ROBERT S. MC NAMARA

President Kennedy's emphasis on a variegated arsenal of power did not in any way lead him to the conclusion that, short of a major political settlement with the Communists, we could reduce substantially the amount of destructive power at our disposal. In fact, the thrust of his remarks on the nation's military posture, during his years in the Senate and during his Presidential campaign, was that our forces were insufficient across the whole spectrum of warfare. If anything, a greater proportion of the national effort and product needed to be devoted to strengthening and maintaining our military tools than had been the case under Eisenhower.

The required diversion of resources, however, would not have to be away from other public programs, domestic or international; indeed, some of these would have to be expanded. Reallocations, to the extent they were necessary, would be away from private pursuits to public purposes. "Ask not what your country can do for you—ask what you can do for your country." Even so, the New Frontier economists unlike their immediate predecessors, did not believe that expanded government programs (with or without a compensatory tax increase) would slow private investment and consumption. Temporary imbalances in the federal budget, according to the new economics, were often a positive stimulus to the market economy.[1]

The assumption that efforts and resources devoted to the various aspects of the nation's power more often than not complemented each other, rather than detracted from each other, was an essential of the initial Kennedy approach toward the problem of defense spending. To be sure, costs, the size of the federal budget, and the rate of taxation were important considerations, since the nation places a high value on individuals being able to retain as much as possible of what they earn to do with as they like. And balance of payments considerations might suggest special limits on certain types of expenditures abroad. But the notion of the nation bankrupting itself by an increase, say, of 20 per cent in federal spending was regarded as an almost comical superstititon. Kennedy's early instructions to Secretary of Defense McNamara reflected the newer pragmatism: "Develop the force structure necessary to our military requirements without regard to arbitrary or predetermined budget ceilings. And . . . having determined that force structure . . . procure it at the lowest possible cost." [2] The requirements came first.

Kennedy's general premises about the nation's military requirements were well developed before he assumed the Presidency, and were very much reflective of the "conventional wisdom" among Democrats involved in foreign policy matters. But the premises themselves were not the product of partisan politics, however they may have been invoked to that effect. They were the product of a number of strains of strategic thought that had now converged: the ideas generated by Paul Nitze and the Policy Planning Council in NSC-68, the 1960 document reflecting on the military planning implications of the soon-to-come Soviet intercontinental nuclear capability;[3] Air Force–RAND Corporation arguments for a survivable ("invulnerable") strategic retaliatory force (also favored by the Navy as the major rationale for the Polaris submarine-fired missile); the doctrine of "flexible response" put forward within the Eisenhower Administration by Army Chiefs of Staff Mathew Ridgway and Maxwell Taylor in opposition to the strategic monism of Secretary of State Dulles and Admiral Radford; [4] the analysis of the possibilities for limited war in the thermonuclear age by scholars such as William Kaufmann, Robert Osgood, Henry Kissinger, and Bernard Brodie; [5] and the recommendations for a balanced defense posture appearing in the reports of the Gaither Committee and Panel II of the Special Studies Project of the Rockefeller Brothers Fund.[6]

Most reputable American analysts of military policy, by the time of Kennedy's election, were in agreement on at least the following premises:

The temptation of the Soviets and the Chinese Communists to expand into new areas, and otherwise to impose their wills on the non-Communist nations, correlates inversely with their belief in the likelihood of effective counteraction by the leading non-Communist nations.

Effective counteraction, from the perspective of the Soviets and Chinese, would be that which imposes costs disproportionate to their anticipated gain.

The Soviets and Chinese determine the probability of such counteraction on the part of the leading non-Communist nations by attributing to them essentially the same calculus: counteraction will be taken by the non-Communists to the extent that the costs to the non-Communists of such action would be less than the costs of acquiescence in the Communist moves.

Deterrence being the product of these mutual assessments of one another's anticipated costs and gains, an effective strategy and military posture for the United States is one that comprises an ability to respond to each provocation with a degree of violence bearing some reasonable relationship to the value thought to be immediately at stake.

The willingness to incur the amount of destruction to the nation that would accompany total war is not a very believable deterrent threat unless it is posed as a counter to the threat of major direct aggression against our home territory.

To deter provocations short of direct aggression upon the United States, we must therefore be prepared to do at least one of two things:

173

a) to respond effectively at levels of violence well below total war; b) to define the costs of submitting to such provocations as intolerable as the costs we would incur in total war. The latter might work for some of our extraterritorial interests, for example keeping Western Europe from falling to the Communists; but the Communists were unlikely to believe that every inch of territory in the non-Communist world had a comparable value. Conflicts over territorial objectives which during the Cold War had developed a high emotional content for each side might be seen as involving essential psychological components of the overall balance of power. Berlin was one of these conflicts, and with less clarity so were the Chinese offshore islands. But even with respect to these values, the degree of the nation's psychological commitment could fluctuate. In such an eventuality, they might have to be surrendered to our opponents if we lacked effective capabilities for at least initial counter-action at lower levels of violence.

Thus, without capabilities across the entire spectrum of warfare, available for measured application and bearing some relation to the value at stake and the initial intensity of a provocation, our firm diplomatic commitments might ultimately have to be restricted only to that class of extraterritorial objectives clearly required by the global balance of power. The opportunities for enemy probes beneath the threshold of our clearly-defined vital interests would grow accordingly. The non-Communist world would feel increasingly insecure as a result of the uncertainty of our commitment to their defense, and the non-Communist world, including the United States, would become increasingly demoralized out of the recognition of the fickleness of our guarantees. The balance of power itself—composed in large measure of the *reputation* for power among the leading nations—would be seen to be shifting drastically against us. Such a situation would be ready-made for the kinds of miscalculation and irrationality that would bring on the dreaded thermonuclear holocaust.

A few concrete policy implications were drawn from these general strategic premises. Our strategic nuclear capability was to be designed primarily, if not exclusively, as a last resort, as an instrument of retaliation for a direct attack upon the United States. Our capabilities for limited war were to be expanded considerably.

But any number of questions remained, whose answers could not be logically deduced from the above: Would the downgrading of the function of the strategic nuclear forces for deterrence of limited conflicts mean that there would be no contingencies in which the United States might be the first to use these weapons? If the strategic forces were to be primarily retaliatory weapons, what should be their targets? Under such concepts, what should we prepare to do in advance to deal with the possibility of strategic attack upon us despite our capabilities for retaliation? Did we want to limit "limited war" to non-nuclear weapons? If so, how did we propose to enforce such limitations? Did our concept of limiting war mean also localizing it? How would our European allies respond to strategies that seemed to reduce the possible costs to the superpowers of a future war over Europe *in* Europe? The President's early statements on his defense policies skirted many of these complicated issues.

In President Kennedy's March 26, 1961 special message to the Congress on the Defense Budget, there were a number of explicit, and definitely stressed, pledges "not to strike first in any conflict." And these statements were coupled with recommendations for improving the ability of our strategic nuclear forces to survive any attack and strike back with devastating retaliation. The President came closer in this message than had any official spokesman before or afterwards to enunciating a doctrine of no first use of strategic nuclear weapons, but he stopped just short of such an absolute unilateral inhibition. In light of subsequent statements by him and other members of his Administration, the presumption is that his failure to dot the i's and cross the t's was deliberate. Kennedy undoubtedly understood the disadvantage to the West of pledging not to use its strategic nuclear forces unless the opponent did so first. If the opponent was the Soviet Union, and the battlefield was Central Europe, or, say, Iran, the Soviets would then be accorded military superiority, since the applicable forces would only be the local theater forces in which we were, by our own admission, inferior. The attribution of deliberate ambiguity to Kennedy on the matter of whether the United States would ever launch a strategic nuclear strike on the Soviets before they launched one on us is sustained by his insistence in the same early message that:

Our strategic arms and defense must be adequate to deter any deliberate nuclear attack on the United States *or our allies*—by making it clear to any potential aggressor that sufficient retaliatory forces will be able to survive a first strike and penetrate his defenses in order inflict unacceptables losses upon him.[7] (Emphasis added.)

How we might respond to a *non*-nuclear attack on friends or allies was left similarly vague. Clearly, the President was now recommending a major increase in airlift and sealift capacities, and in Army and Marine Corps personnel in order to "increase our ability to confine our response to non-nuclear weapons." The ability to fight "limited wars" should be the "primary mission" of our overseas forces, he told the Congress:

Non-nuclear wars, and sub-limited or guerilla warfare, have since 1945 constituted the most active and constant threat to Free World Security. Those units of our forces which are stationed overseas, or designed to fight overseas, can be most usefully oriented toward deterrring or confining those conflicts which do not justify and cannot lead to a general nuclear attack.

But a potential opponent must know that "in the event of a major aggression that could not be repulsed by conventional forces," we will continue to be prepared "to take whatever action with whatever weapons are appropriate." He must know that our response will be "suitable, selective, swift, and effective":

While he may be uncertain of . . . [the] exact nature and location [of our response], there must be no uncertainty about our determination and capacity to take whatever steps are necessary to meet our obligations. We must be able to make deliberate choices in weapons and strategy, shift the tempo of our production and alter the direction of our forces to meet rapidly changing conditions or objectives at very short notice and under any circumstances.[8]

Not unexpectedly, these statements were not received with enthusiasm by some of our partners in the North Atlantic Treaty Organization. Since the mid-1950s NATO military doctrine, planning, and programs had been based on the premise that any war in response to Soviet aggression upon Western Europe would be general nuclear war; there would be no serious attempt to repulse a major aggression by conventional means. To be sure, under the leadership of NATO Supreme Commander, General Lauris Norstad, the automatic nuclear "trip wire" concept had been abandoned as too dangerous, and in its place was put the concept of the "pause"—an initial response to an enemy probe with non-nuclear weapons to demonstrate our determination to resist, and to provide the enemy with time to decide that he had miscalculated our will; but this new doctrine of a flexible and measured response, coupled with budgetary recommendations for increasing non-nuclear capabilities, immediately aroused suspicions in Europe that in the face of the Soviet inter-continental strategic reach we would regard even a war over Europe as a local war to be fought and won (or lost) in Europe without the United States being subject to devastation.[9] To the Europeans, quite naturally, a war for Europe was total war and they wanted the Soviets to know, in advance, that an attack upon Europe would be just as certainly an act of suicide as an attack upon the United States.

In the context of these growing doubts on the part of our NATO Allies, the Kennedy Administration sought for ways of reassuring them that nuclear weapons would continue to be available for the defense of the entire treaty area. The Administration's main fear was that Germany would attempt to follow the lead of Britain and France and develop its own nuclear capability—one that while possibly too weak to serve by itself as a convincing deterrent to the Soviets could nonetheless make it virtually certain that no war over German soil would remain a limited war. Kennedy appreciated the concerns of his alliance partners, and regarded their leaders as patriotic men conscientiously pursuing their national interests. But his responsibility was to pursue the United States national interest, and that seemed to require that the United States maintain control over the dimensions of conflict in the NATO area.

The campaign to reassure the European members of NATO was waged on two fronts: doctrinal elaborations of "flexible response" by McNamara and his subordinates to show that with its adoption by NATO, deterrence of Soviet provocations in Europe would be increased; and offers by the White House to "share" ownership and control of a part of the United States strategic arsenal.

The Berlin crisis of the spring and summer of 1961 (see below, pp. 242–58) provided the opportunity for the Administration to demonstrate that a buildup of non-nuclear capabilities did not lessen Soviet fears of a general war, but, on the contrary, reinforced expectations on all sides that we would resist a Soviet attack with whatever force was necessary to do the job. Paul Nitze explained the Administration's view of Khrushchev's calculations:

We can ask ourselves the question, what is it that is likely to affect Mr. Khruschchev's judgment on whether aggressive courses of action on his part will likely bring him unacceptably close to the danger of nuclear war. I should think the most important persuader is to be found in Western nuclear capabilities. . . . [But] let us assume two different hypothetical situations [with respect to Berlin]. In the first situation the central NATO front is very lightly covered. It is subject to the risk of deep penetration by Soviet non-nuclear forces starting from a standing start. The only option which the West has, to demonstrate its determination to have its vital interests respected, is to initiate the action with the use of nuclear weapons. In the second situation, the NATO front is firmly held on a continuous line. There are enough reserve forces to mount a really serious non-nuclear probe in the air corridors or along the autobahn. That probe can be thrown back by a full application of Soviet non-nuclear power, but only by involving Soviet and NATO in a major fight.

If you were sitting in the Kremlin, which situation would be considered most likely to bring you face to face with nuclear war? To me, the answer is clear. If I were in the Kremlin I would be most concerned with the second situation; I would consider it much more likely that the West would find it politically possible to initiate action in defense of the Berlin access routes from the second posture than from the first.[10]

To deflect the growing suspicion that the United States was moving toward a "denuclearization" of Europe, the President, in his May 17, 1961 address before the Canadian Parliament, announced that the United States was now committing five Polaris nuclear missile submarines to the NATO Command "subject to any agreed NATO guidelines on their control and use." But anticipating that this would be insufficient—the submarines would still be under the operational command of the United States Navy and direct political control of the United States President—Kennedy took advantage of his Ottawa address to explicitly hold out: "the possibility of eventually establishing a NATO sea-borne force, which would be truly multi-lateral in ownership and control, if this should be desired and found feasible by our Allies, *once NATO's non-nuclear goals have been achieved*." (Emphasis added.) [11]

The purpose may have been reassurance, but imbedded as it was in the precondition of European increases in conventional fighting capabilities, the proposal for a Multilateral Force (the MLF), from its first mention, merely served to reinforce European anxieties. This early statement probably was one of the most forthright on the issue of nuclear sharing by the Administration, representing its real position that flexible intra-alliance arrangements for the management of strategic nuclear weapons were possible as long as there was close agreement on strategy and tactics—this, of course, presupposing that such close agreement would be in terms of the Kennedy-McNamara doctrine, which would shift the burden of coercion in the most likely contingencies to locally applicable non-nuclear capabilities. The European members of NATO found such an ordering of priorities uncongenial: if there was to be any reorientation of NATO plans, deployments, and administrative arrangements, priority, in their view, should be given to the issue of who manages the "deterrent." First, the political control and military command arrangements of alliance strategic nuclear forces must be such as to give prior assurance that when these forces were needed for the defense of *European* soil the required decisions would be made. Then, and only then, could the Europeans agree that current arrangements for nearly automatic strategic retaliation should be supplanted by a flexible tactical fighting capability.

Much has been written about conflicts within the Administration over military arrangements for NATO.[12] But the internal disagreements appear not to have been over the essential United States objectives of filling the non-nuclear–local capability gaps in the global military balance, and of maintaining firm United States control over the dimensions of any conflicts that could become global. The differences of opinion at top policy-making levels concerned primarily *how* to convince the Europeans to accept arrangements that would be compatible with these essential objectives.

The Defense Department tended to stress improvements in capabilities in-being as the primary means of resolving the intra-alliance issues. If our allies in Europe could be shown that it was not too expensive to improve their local war capabilities, if they realized that the Soviets were not as tactically superior on the central front as had been assumed, then the irrational deterrence-only doctrine would give way to the spirit of pragmatic marginalism that characterized McNamara's approach. The rational economic solution was to make marginal improvements where the returns were greatest from each dollar expended. For the Europeans to try to provide protection for themselves with indigneous nuclear arsenals would be to spend heavily only to duplicate what had already been provided by the United States. Any effort the Europeans might make in improving their conventional capabilities would be a valuable increment to NATO's ability to close the gap between Communist and non-Communist local fighting power.

The State Department, attempting to be more responsive to the sentiments of our alliance partners, stressed the nuclear sharing issue. The Europeans, now returning to full participation in the international economy and diplomacy were seen to be signaling, through the strategic debate, that they were no longer content to accept the *dependency* status they had occupied till now. To them, the particularly odious thing about the Kennedy-McNamara military doctrine was its premise of a more or less permanent specialization of function between the United States on the one hand and the Europeans on the other. The United States would retain the grand-strategic tasks while the Europeans would be exclusively "footsloggers" on the front lines. Sensitive to these European concerns, the State Department pressed the view that if the United States wanted to maintain political control within NATO, and over the dimension of any likely conflicts, some formula had to be found that would give the Europeans the status of a true partner in the overall management of alliance affairs, including the matter of strategic planning and operations. We would have to give the Europeans an opportunity to be a partner in joint ownership and management of the nuclear deterrent. If we were worried about control, we need only work out some variant of the double veto system that was already used for the intermediate range missiles we had installed in England, Italy, and Turkey (both the host country and the United States had to approve before these missiles could be launched). The MLF, as finally elaborated in a United States Navy study for a force of Polaris-carrying vessels with crews of mixed nationality, and requiring the affirmative decision of all its national shareholders in order to fire, or of NATO political authorites, seemed admirably suited to this purpose.

On one central facet of the MLF both the State and Defense Departments were in accord. It was a political control device and an arms control device. It was to be designed as a nonuse military system, with "fifteen fingers on the safety catch." From a military point of view, it could be considered an irrelevancy, costly only in the dollars and cents worth of the United States contribution in vessels and weapons, but in no way compromising the essential vast arsenal of strategic nuclear power which would still remain under United States command and control. It was because of its presumed political virtues for holding Europe together that the project generated so much enthusiasm with State Department officials responsible for NATO affairs.

Following de Gaulle's veto of British entry into the European Economic Community, the State Department began more and more to use the promise of United States nuclear sharing with Europe under the MLF scheme as a goad to European efforts to form themselves into a true political union. (See below, pp. 296–307 for discussion of the role of European unity in the Kennedy foreign policy.) Statements by Secretary Rusk and Undersecretary Ball hinted at an eventual relinquishing of our absolute veto on any decision to use the weapons in the MLF *after* the Europeans had made "impressive strides" toward political unity, but this condition was never elaborated in detail.[13]

The President, while never very enthusiastic about the MLF as a military instrument or as a prod to European integration, evidently did see value in the *offer* of the NATO nuclear fleet, or anything similar anyone could come up with as a way of deflecting, or at least deferring West German desires to follow France into the nuclear club.[14] As it turned out, only the Germans were seriously interested; but this was not at all palatable to the White House, where there was sensitivity to the domestic and international political sentiment against anything that smacked of an exclusive military partnership between the United States and Germany, especially involving weapons of mass destruction. Kennedy's dissatisfaction with the enterprise is reported by Schlesinger:

"The whole debate about an atomic force in Europe," he told Spaak of Belgium. . . . "is really useless, because Berlin is secure, and Europe as a whole is well protected. What really matters at this point is the rest of the world." As for the MLF per se, he really considered that, so long as the United States retained its veto (and he never mentioned renunciation as a possibility, though other members of his government did), the MLF was something of a fake. Though he was willing to try it, he could not see why Europeans would be interested in making enormous contributions toward a force over which they had no real control.[15]

Yet in the absence of an alternative for diverting the Germans and symbolizing the ideal of an "indivisible" strategic nuclear deterrent for all of NATO, the President stayed with it. The greatest pressure was directed toward the British. If they would join the scheme, it would avoid the label of a German-American enterprise, would stimulate other members of NATO to join, and, if coupled with a renunciation by Britain of its independent nuclear force, might reverse the anticipated trend toward the spread of nuclear weapons. Simultaneously, the independent nuclear weapons programs of France and Britain were deprecated by Washington, and the "credibility" of our pledges to use nuclear weapons, if necessary, on behalf of NATO's vital interests, was affirmed.

As put by Secretary of Defense McNamara, "relatively weak national nuclear forces" (he could only have been referring to those of Britain and France), when operating independently, are "dangerous, expensive, prone to obsolescence, and lacking in credibility as a deterrent." Such a force was likely to be vulnerable to destruction before being launched, and thus, "if a major antagonist came to believe there was a substantial likelihood of its being used independently, this force would be inviting a pre-emptive first strike against it." In the event of war, the Secretary contended, "the use of such a force against the cities of a major nuclear power would be tantamount to suicide, whereas its employment against significant military targets would have a negligible effect on the outcome of the conflict." [16]

By contrast, affirmed McNamara, "the United States nuclear contribution to the Alliance is neither obsolete nor dispensable." And we would continue to make this power available to the defense of NATO interests on a global basis. Moreover, our strategic forces were sufficiently protected, powerful, and accurate to allow us to use them in a controlled and deliberate fashion against military targets at the outset of a general war, thus providing decision time for both sides before engaging in the ultimate folly of mutual population destruction. By spelling out this strategic concept a bit, McNamara was able to drive home his basic argument on behalf of centralized control of the nuclear capabilities of the Alliance. To a June commencement audience, the Secretary of Defense breezily explained (his real intended audience was, of course, overseas):

The U.S. has come to the conclusion that to the extent feasible, basic military strategy in a possible general nuclear war should be approached in much the same way that more conventional military operations have been regarded in the past. That is to say, principal military objectives, in the events of a nuclear war stemming from a major attack on the Alliance, should be the destruction of the enemy's military forces, not of his civilian population.

The very strength and nature of the Alliance forces makes it possible for us to retain, even in the fact of a massive surprise attack, sufficient reserve striking power to destroy an enemy society if driven to it. In other words, we are giving a possible opponent the strongest imaginable incentive to refrain from striking our own cities.

In such a strategy, explained McNamara, there cannot be conflicting strategies on the part of the NATO allies, nor can there be more than one list of targets. The nuclear campaign would have to be based strictly on centralized direction and control.[17]

We were ready, and would continue to be ready, to fulfill our commitments to the Alliance, whatever this might require, reiterated the Secretary of Defense, and the strategy of controlled strategic response "gives us some hope of minimizing damage" in the event of general nuclear war. But we should not try to avoid facing up to the fact—"the almost certain prospect"—that severe damage would be suffered in such a war.

Thus such a war should not be regarded as a desirable contingency under any circumstances, and we had to do all in our power to insure that lesser conflicts were controlled and stopped short of the commitment to battle of major force by either side. Because of the strength of the Alliance, and the strategy we were enunciating, it was unlikely that any power would attempt to launch a massive attack, nuclear or conventional, on NATO. But for the kinds of conflicts, both political and military, most likely to arise in the NATO area, it was inappropriate, indeed unbelievable, that we should respond at the outset with nuclear weapons. The Soviet superiority in non-nuclear forces "is by no means overwhelming." Moreover, the NATO countries possessed a *potential* for successful defense even against the full Soviet non-nuclear potential. "We do not believe that if the formula, $e = mc^2$, had not been discovered, we should all be Communist slaves." [18]

If prior to these public remarks by the Secretary of Defense the Europeans only suspected that the doctrine of flexible response was to be used to justify the retention by the White House of tight control over the disposition of alliance forces, their remaining doubts were now resolved. General de Gaulle's most apocalyptic visions were seen to be not entirely fantastic ("who can say that if the occasion arises the two [the Soviet Union and the United States], while each deciding not to launch its missiles at the main enemy so that it should itself be spared, will not crush the others. It is possible to imagine that on some awful day Western Europe should be wiped out from Moscow and Central Europe from Washington.")[19]

McNamara's Ann Arbor address may well stand in the history of official strategic thought as a document of seminal theoretical importance, but as an effort at *political* persuasion it was crude, to say the least. It was as if a husband and wife were to try to solve some difference over household management by discussing what they would do in the event the two were lost at sea in a lifeboat with enough food for only one to survive.[20]

Kennedy's instinct was to avoid detailed discussion in public of remote future contingencies, but he was compelled to do so by the course of the ensuing intra-alliance debate over nuclear control. In his news conference of February 14, 1963, he was asked by a reporter whether the government was yet at the stage of making the actual decision to share command and control of nuclear forces with our European allies:

> It is a very difficult area because the weapons have to be fired in 5 minutes, and who is going to be delegated on behalf of Europe to make this judgment? If the word comes to Europe or comes any place that we're about to experience an attack, you might have to make an instantaneous judgment. Somebody has to be delegated with that authority. If it isn't the President of the United States, in the case of the strategic force, it will have to be the President of France or the Prime Minister of Great Britain, or someone else. And that is an enormous responsibility. The United States has carried that responsibility for a good many years. . . .
>
> Now, it is quite natural that Western Europe would want a greater voice. We are trying to provide that greater voice through a multilateral force. But it is a very complicated negotiation because, as I say, in the final analysis, someone has to be delegated who will carry the responsibility for the alliance.[21]

After McNamara's exposition of the need for absolute centralized control and before the statements by Kennedy, both men had come too close for their own equanimity to making decisions in a real and terribly immediate context, rather than in the hypothetical world of strategic theory. The Cuban missile crisis confirmed and refined their premises on the necessity for very tight and unified command arrangements under absolute political control, on the multiplication of risks of awful accidents or miscalculations which would accompany a spread of nuclear weapons to additional powers, and on the importance of denuclearizing the United States–Soviet competition.

It had been the President's hope that, having come so close to the fire over the issue of Soviet missiles in Cuba, the United States and the Soviet Union could cooperate in establishing a fresh tone to the language of diplomacy, resulting in the strategic nuclear balance being pushed into the background where it would still operate as a restraint-inducing factor, but not as a visible element of everyday international discourse. He had looked forward to the December 1962 meeting with Prime Minister Macmillan at Nassau as an opportunity to engage in a wide-ranging where-do-we-go-from-here dialogue in this mood of the Cuban aftermath. Undoubtedly, he would have liked the discussion of United States relations with Europe to have got back to economics—the British role in the Common Market, and a more open trading relationship—rather than defense. But out of the blue came Skybolt, a seemingly technical matter to the President when he reviewed McNamara's defense budget before preparing for his Carribean meeting.

Skybolt, a 1000-mile missile to be carried and launched from a manned aircraft, had been under close scrutiny by McNamara's economists and engineers, and found wanting on "cost-effectiveness" grounds. If its $2.5 billion development costs were invested in other weapons system improvements, a greater increment to our military capabilities could be produced. The U.S. Air Force would, of course, be aggrieved at being denied their best hope of extending the role of manned strategic bombers into the missile age; but McNamara was confident of his ability to manage the generals. The Royal Air Force was also banking heavily on extending the life of its V-bombers through purchase of the American produced missile, as agreed to by Macmillan and Eisenhower in 1960. However, McNamara's confidence that he could placate the British as well as the U.S. Air Force was a gross political miscalculation. The President, evidently unaware of the extent to which it was not only the RAF, but the British Ministry of Defense *and* the Prime Minister himself, whose prestige was staked on maintaining their "independent deterrent" with Skybolt, gave

McNamara the go-ahead to work out some adjustment with British Defense Minister Thorneycroft.[22]

On the plane to his meeting in Nassau with the Prime Minister, Kennedy was warned by the British Ambassador (who was also a close personal friend) that there would be a storm of anti-Americanism in England if the United States pulled the rug from under Macmillan on this issue.[23]

The "agreement" produced by the Nassau conference was a logical monstrosity and almost worthless as a military planning instrument for either government. But as a diplomatic communiqué meant to give the appearance of unity on fundamental issues where there was in fact irreconcilability, it was a masterpiece.

The only concrete agreement was that as a substitute for the Skybolt missile program, the United States would make available Polaris missiles for British submarines (the British would construct the submarines and the nuclear warheads for the missiles). But lest it appear that the United States was now supporting an independent nuclear deterrent for Britain, it was provided that British forces developed under this plan will be "assigned as part of a NATO nuclear force and targeted in accordance with NATO plans" (Articles 6 and 8). These forces and at least equal United States forces "would be made available for inclusion in a NATO multilateral nuclear force" (Article 8). But in Article 7 the "multilateral force" was described as more of an end product of these endeavors, and presumably not identical with the "NATO nuclear force" described in Article 6, which was specifically designated as the command organization for the new force of Polaris carrying British submarines. Moreover, the British contribution to the so-called "multilateral" force was apparently to be taken back under British command in those very situations when it was most likely to be used!

The British Prime Minister made it clear that except where H.M.G. may decide that supreme national interests are at stake, these forces will be used for the purpose of international defense of the Western Alliance in all circumstances. (Article 8.)

If the British were wily in slipping that one in, the Americans could bring something home in the words of Article 10, where:

The President and the Prime Minister agreed that in addition to having a nuclear shield it is important to have a non-nuclear sword. For this purpose they agreed on the importance of increasing the effectiveness of their conventional forces on a worldwide basis.[24]

The statement was a reversal (at least in words) of the standing NATO concept of the non-nuclear "shield" to enforce a limited "pause" on the ground, and the nuclear "sword" for the offensive counterblow.

Macmillan could return to London claiming a victory for the concept of an independent British deterrent, which, of course, the Labour Party was not going to let him get away with. Kennedy and McNamara could forget about Skybolt and leave the State Department to plod through the maze that might eventually lead toward some kind of NATO multilateral force.

But what would de Gaulle say? Almost as an afterthought, the conferees at Nassau extended an offer to de Gaulle to contract for Polaris missiles on terms "similar" to those offered the British. The French promptly and curtly, through their Minister of Information, rejected the offer, pointing out that France had neither the submarines nor the nuclear warheads for the Polaris missiles. Deliberately ignoring the rebuff, Kennedy instructed Ambassador Charles Bohlen to inform President de Gaulle that from our point of view all possibilities were still open for discussion.[25]

By the time Secretary McNamara appeared before the cognizant Congressional committees in the early months of 1963 to defend his department's budget request for the coming fiscal year, de Gaulle had blasted the Anglo-American relationship (using Nassau as a telling exhibit) and had vetoed British entry into the Common Market. Macmillan was on the defensive for his handling of the Skybolt affair, and for his perpetuation of the fiction of nuclear independence while in fact agreeing to become even more dependent upon United States components for England's still-to-be-developed submarine force. Furthermore, Kennedy and Macmillan were both subjected to the charge that it was their ineptitude at Nassau that provoked de Gaulle into excluding Britain from the Common Market. Journalists were portraying the Alliance as being in "disarray."

Many in Congress were ready to attribute all of these difficulties to the attempt by McNamara and Kennedy to shift NATO policy against the will of the Europeans, away from deterrence through the threat of all-out war to a posture that would allow substantial fighting to take place on European soil while the homelands of the Soviet Union and the United States were spared. The standard European argument that this would reduce the risks to the Soviets of an attack upon Western Europe, and thereby increase their temptation to attack, was reflected in questions thrown at the Secretary—particularly by senators and representatives who had in the past been staunch defenders of budgetary requests of the U.S. Air Force.

In defending Administration policy and doctrine against these charges, McNamara went further than any previous spokesman of the government in elucidating official premises about the state of the existing military balance of power, and about intentions for applying our power in future military conflicts. The intended audience for these remarks, quite clearly, was not only the congressional committee members and their constituents, but potential opponents *and* allies who might doubt our capabilities and resolve to live up to our commitments.

Under questioning, the Secretary of Defense maintained that our "current strategic superiority . . . does give us a war-winning nuclear capability, in the sense that we are confident that we can completely crush the Soviet Union if forced to do so." But he cautioned that this fact should not make us overlook the "increasing capability of the Soviet Union to make the United States pay a heavy price for such victories in terms of tens of millions of casualties." [26] Thus when he used the word "win" he meant it only in a special sense, which should be clearly understood:

We would win in the sense that their [the Soviet Union's] way of life would change more than ours [if the strategic forces of both sides were unleashed against each other] because we would destroy a greater percentage of their industrial potential and probably destroy a greater percentage of their population than they destroyed of ours.

Yet if we also calculated the destruction inflicted on Western Europe, the total amount in the West "would exceed that of the Soviet Union." His personal opinion, whichever calculation was made, was that "we cannot win a nuclear war, a strategic nuclear war, in the normal meaning of the word 'win.' " [27]

Members of Congress wanted to know if the Secretary's opinion that there could be no real winners in a strategic nuclear war meant that we were operating under a doctrine of "nuclear stalemate" or "mutual deterrence." And they pressed him to show how we could still deter the Soviets from attacking, especially in Central Europe, where the prize was big and we were presumably still inferior on the ground, if we had convinced ourselves that strategic nuclear war, no matter how we tried to improve our capabilities, would still result in tens of millions of Americans dead.

McNamara rejected the terms "nuclear stalemate" and "mutual deterrence" as inaccurate descriptions of our operating strategy, which he kept insisting was to use whatever force was necessary to defend our vital interests:

For example, we have made it quite clear that the defense of Western Europe is as vital to us as the defense of our own continent and that we are prepared to back up our commitments there with our strategic nuclear power no matter what degree of damage might result should the deterrent aspect of this policy fail. . . . Being realistic, we must admit the Soviets are achieving a growing capacity to inflict damage on the U.S. mainland. . . . This fact makes it increasingly important for us to make clear to the Soviet Union, in advance, those vital U.S. interests which we must support with our total power. The increasing capability of Soviet nuclear forces must not be permitted to lull our Allies, our own citizens, or our enemies into the belief that we would be less willing to defend these vital interests.[28]

But McNamara was not willing to *depend* upon our strategic forces for deterring all Soviet provocations, nor was he sufficiently certain that the Soviets would always get the message in advance concerning what interests of ours were so vital as to make us risk millions of fatalities in their defense. The important question, he explained to the House Armed Services Committee, is what enemy actions can we be certain our strategic forces will deter, and what enemy actions might require other kinds of ready responses to make deterrence work:

Now I feel quite certain that if the Soviets are rational, our strategic forces program will deter the Soviets from launching a first strike against this country.
I say that for the very simple reason that, if they did, we would utterly destroy them, and I mean completely destroy . . . the Soviet Union as a civilized nation.

189

Our strategic nuclear capability, however:

is not a deterrent force in the sense that it will deter all political and military aggression by the Soviets. It did not deter them from putting pressure on Berlin when we had a nuclear monopoly in the early part of the 1950's. It did not deter the Communists from invading Korea. It did not deter them from building a wall in Berlin. It did not deter the Communist . . . attempt to subvert Southeast Asia. . . . It did not deter their attempt to move offensive weapons systems into Cuba.[29]

To the Society of Newspaper Editors McNamara reiterated that it was unrealistic and irresponsible to assume that the possession of great strategic nuclear power alone would deter such "limited" Communist provocations. By the time the Kennedy Administration took office, he said, "It was clear that, unless we were willing to live under a constant threat of having to choose between nuclear holocaust and retreat, we required major improvements in our less-than-all-out war capabilities." [30]

Before the Congressional appropriations committees the Secretary of Defense explained the planning and cost implications of the new strategy. The "general purpose forces," consequently, were being rapidly improved at a new high annual cost of over $19 billion. This included an expansion in manpower (the Army, with 11 divisions from the Eisenhower years, was now being maintained at 16 divisions), improved equipment and munitions, and especially mobility of the "tactical" forces of all three services, and the provision of new, more flexible and functionally integrated command structures, like the multi-service strike command.[31] These programs, McNamara explained, would provide the country with forces that "could, by nonnuclear means alone, counter a wide spectrum of Sino-Soviet bloc aggressions in regions other than Europe."

However, with regard to Europe, "the programmed U.S. forces, together with present forces of other NATO countries, would not be able to contain an all-out conventional Soviet attack without invoking the use of nuclear weapons." [32] It was this latter requirement—the necessity for reliance on nuclear weapons for balancing Soviet military power in Europe—that continued to give the Administration trouble diplomatically, and doctrinally.

Even if the Europeans were to accept the validity of flexible response, and therefore to take the "conventional option" seriously, even if they were to conscientiously fulfill their existing pledges to increase their manpower and equipment levels (we were not asking them to set new goals, only to implement already agreed-upon goals), still NATO could not contain and repulse a determined Soviet attempt to forcibly absorb Western Europe unless we were prepared to redress the local imbalance by turning the war into a global strategic war:

I foresee no period in the future [said McNamara], let's say in the remaining years of this century, when we can, under today's conditions, operate without a strategic nuclear force of the type we are proposing for this five-year period, no matter how large a conventional force we and our allies might build.[33]

If this was indeed the situation in Europe, asked various senators, then why all the emphasis on strengthening non-nuclear capabilities in Europe? If the Soviets could beat us in all-out contest of non-nuclear forces, was it not rational for the Europeans to regard our stress on the conventional option as futile, and not the best use of our or their resources. Reiterating the arguments Paul Nitze had used in connection with the Berlin buildup, McNamara explained that: "The purpose of the increase in conventional forces is to deter certain *low-scale* forms of Soviet political and military aggression which they might be tempted to carry out were they not opposed by the type that are being strengthened."[34] (Emphasis added.)

The Secretary's congressional interrogators were not entirely convinced, and persisted with pertinent questions about Soviet miscalculation of our will to respond with whatever force was necessary. Suppose the Soviets did try to overwhelm our admittedly inferior local forces:

Senator Thurmond. If we were fighting a conventional war and we were about to lose it, we would use tactical nuclear weapons, wouldn't we?
Secretary McNamara. I think a large-scale assault by the Soviet Union and its satellites forces against Western Europe would rather quickly require the use of tactical nuclear weapons in order to preserve the control of Western Europe in the hands of the West. Whether that could be limited to the use of tactical nuclear weapons is an open question in my mind. . . .

. . .

Senator Smith. Are we programming sufficient tactical nuclear capabilities to win such a conflict without carrying it to the point of the ICBM exchange?

Secretary McNamara. Well, I don't want to say that a massive Soviet offensive could be turned back without the use of ICBM's, but we are certainly building up substantial inventories of tactical nuclear weapons that could be used under those circumstances.[35]

McNamara's point was that we needed to be prepared to fight in this middle range of conflict between conventional war and strategic nuclear war, particularly to *deter* the Soviets from escalating to strategic nuclear war, and to that end we already had "thousands" of nuclear weapons in Europe. But we wanted to discourage inflated expectations for the potential role of these tactical weapons in deterring, or repelling, a Soviet nonnuclear attack. As he explained to the House Armed Services Committee in his prepared remarks on the fiscal 1964 budget:

Nuclear weapons, even in the lower kiloton ranges, are extremely destructive devices and hardly the preferred weapons to defend such heavily populated areas as Europe. Furthermore, while it does not necessarily follow that the use of tactical nuclear weapons must inevitably escalate into global nuclear war, it does present a very definite threshold, beyond which we enter a vast unknown.[36]

Some senators pointed to what seemed to be an underlying premise of the whole strategy of flexible response, from its stress on a delayed resort to nuclear weapons through its notion of a city-avoiding nuclear exchange: namely, the premise of a similarly restrained Soviet Union, the notion that our opponent would accept the rules of warfare we wanted to impose. Had the Soviets not rejected the idea of "limited war" in Europe? asked Senator Thurmond, pointing to the newly published book *Military Strategy* edited by Soviet Marshal Sokolovsky, and did not recent Soviet tests of large-yield nuclear weapons indicate a continuation of Soviet strategy to strike large metropolitan areas in the event of a strategic nuclear conflict?

McNamara was careful not to answer categorically these questions of likely Soviet behavior in a military conflict. Indeed, the very reason we were maintaining such a strong nuclear arsenal in Europe was to *deter* the Soviets from taking it upon themselves to cross the threshold into nuclear war. Moreover, he observed a potential contradiction between publicly stated Soviet military doctrine, and their actual military deployments. "You would not think they would maintain a military force structure of 3,200,000 men if they planned to use large numbers of nuclear weapons in any military action." [37]

With respect to the city-avoidance "option" in strategic nuclear war, again, our hope for Soviet restraint was not based on faith in their willingness to "play fair." It was based entirely on the premise that at the moment of truth, despite previous Soviet protestations to the contrary, they would still want to save the Soviet Union from complete devastation. By holding in reserve our vast potential to wipe out their cities, we would be saying: you have not yet lost everything, but whether you do depends on your next move. McNamara was not willing to predict Soviet behavior, only to provide Soviet leaders with an incentive to act more rationally. But this would take advance planning, and he had to admit that, under present circumstances, neither the Soviets nor the United States had the kind of forces in being that would allow them to fight a controlled strategic nuclear campaign as distinguished from an all-out war. McNamara's most careful discourse on this complicated strategic problem was in response to a question by Congressman Leslie Arends before the House Committee on Armed Services:

I do think we should separate the discussion into two parts: one related to circumstances today and the other related to possible circumstances in the future.

Today we know that the great majority of the Soviet strategic forces, both their bombers and their missiles, are in soft [jargon for highly vulnerable] configurations. Under these circumstances it seems almost inconceivable to me that were the Soviets to attack the United States they would attack other than our cities, because they have no possibility of holding in reserve forces for later use against our cities with any expectation that those forces would survive a U.S. attack.

And this leads me to the conclusion . . . that under today's circumstances I personally believe any nuclear attack by the Soviet Union on the United States will include an attack on the major urban areas of the United States.

Now, turning to the future, it is possible, although I think not probable, that . . . Soviet attack might be directed primarily against our military installations. And were that to be the case, it might be advantageous to direct our retaliatory attack primarily against their military installations, thereby giving them an incentive to avoid an attack on our major urban areas. Now, I have emphasized: One, that this circumstance applies to the future and not to the present; and two, I think it a possible, but unlikely situation. But because it is possible, it seems to me that we should develop a weapons system that would permit us to take advantage of that situation. And this weapons system should have two characteristics that weapons systems designed to meet other situations might not have.

The first is that it must be invulnerable, because my set of premises require that we hold back a certain portion of our force, even under attack by the Soviet Union, which means that it must be able to survive that attack . . . .

Secondly, the force must be larger than would otherwise be the case. Because since no force can be completely invulnerable, we will lose a portion of it under those circumstances and we must buy more than we otherwise would buy.[38]

The point was not lost on the congressmen that McNamara's preferred strategic context seemed to be one in which both the Soviet Union and the United States possessed highly invulnerable "reserve" strategic weapons. This meant, quite obviously, that he had abandoned as desirable, let alone feasible, a United States first-strike capability powerful enough to destroy the Soviet capability to inflict unacceptable damage upon the United States.

This was precisely the premise of McNamara's statement to Stewart Alsop in an interview published shortly after the Cuban missile crisis. A nuclear exchange confined to military targets seemed more possible, not less, he emphasized, "when *both* sides have a secure second-strike capability. Then you might have a more stable 'balance of terror.' This may seem a rather subtle point, but from where I'm sitting it seems a point worth thinking about." [39]

Senator Stuart Symington, a Secretary of the Air Force during the Truman Administration, was somewhat disturbed by McNamara's interview with Alsop, "I presume that means the sooner they [the Soviets] have a second strike capability the better. That was the impression I got from the article." McNamara denied that this was a correct interpretation of his remarks. But it was necessary for us to adjust to the new emerging strategic situation in which the Soviets were in fact moving toward a relatively invulnerable missile force. The point of his comment to Alsop, he explained, was that "we should not assume that our position is worsening as they do that. As a matter of fact, it will put less pressure on them to carry out a pre-emptive strike in a period of crisis, and this is to our advantage." [40]

Senator Margaret Chase Smith was worried that the suggestion that we resign ourselves to the coming condition of essential strategic parity with the Soviets was likely to have "serious long-term effects on our national will, our courage and our determination to resist attacks on our way of life."

McNamara did grant that the questions raised by his predictions of increasing Soviet strategic power, and by the Administration's response to this new strategic reality did go "straight to the fabric of national will and determination." But what was it that sustained this national will and determination, and most importantly, the perception by our opponents of our willingness to stand by our commitments? It was our *total* power as a nation, and this was not simply the measurement of our strategic nuclear effectiveness in all-out war as opposed to theirs (the ultimate unlikely contingency which, regardless of relative "margins of superiority," would be disastrous to both sides). The overall balance of power was what really mattered, and:

I don't believe that any time in our lifetime they will reach parity with us in the total power of their system versus ours; particularly, I believe that if you include as an element of that power, the attraction and influence and effectiveness of our political system, but even for the moment excluding that and dealing only with their economic and military power, I don't foresee any situation in which they will reach parity with us.[41]

It was the Secretary of Defense's responsibility to speak in precise terms about the military balance and to elaborate to the Congress and public the sometimes esoteric strategic doctrine that guided his budgetary decisions on the military posture. But his discussions of those matters were often revealingly matter-of-fact and dryly abstract, far removed from the everyday crisis preoccupations of the Administration.

Yet those discussions were an essential background factor to diplomacy, and it was on occasion necessary for the President himself to bring them forward as a reminder to friends and foes alike that we were prepared, if driven to it, to pay the highest price in defending our values. The address the President proposed to deliver before the Dallas Citizens' Council on November 22, 1963 was to be one of these occasions for taking public stock of the various components of the nation's power, "ranging from the most massive deterrents to the most subtle influences." On the military side we had gone far in two and three-quarter years toward closing the "gaps" left by the previous Administration:

The strategic nuclear power of the United States has been so greatly modernized and expanded in the last 1,000 days, by the rapid production and deployment of the most modern missile systems, that any and all potential aggressors are clearly confronted now with the impossibility of strategic victory—and the certainty of total destruction—if by reckless attack they should ever force upon us the necessity of a strategic reply.

In less than three years, we have increased by 50 per cent the number of Polaris submarines scheduled to be in force by the next fiscal year—increased by more than 70 per cent the portion of our strategic bombers on 15 minute alert—and increased by 100 per cent the total number of nuclear weapons in our strategic alert forces.

Our security is further enhanced by the steps we have taken regarding these weapons to improve the speed and certainty of their response, their readiness at all times to respond, their ability to survive and attack and their ability to be carefully controlled and directed through secure command operations.

But the lessons of the last decade have taught us that freedom cannot be defended by strategic nuclear power alone. We have, therefore, in the last three years, accelerated the development and deployment of tactical nuclear weapons—and increased by 60 per cent the tactical nuclear forces deployed in Western Europe.

Nor can Europe or any other continent rely on nuclear forces alone, whether they are strategic or tactical. We have radically improved the readiness of our conventional forces—increased by 45 per cent the number of combat ready army divisions—increased by 100 per cent the procurement of modern army weapons and equipment—increased by 100 per cent our ship construction, conversion, and modernization program—increased by 100 per cent our procurement of tactical aircraft—increased by 30 per cent the number of tactical air squadrons—and increased the strength of the Marines.

As last month's Operation Big Lift—which originated here in Texas—showed so clearly, this nation is prepared as never before to move substantial numbers of men in surprisingly little time to advanced positions anywhere in the world. . . . Finally, moving beyond the traditional roles of our military forces, we have achieved an increase of nearly 600 percent in our special forces—those that are prepared to work with our allies and friends against guerillas, saboteurs, insurgents, and assassins who threaten freedom in a less direct but equally dangerous manner.[42]

A few months after the signing of the Nuclear Test Ban Treaty, in a period of presumed lessening of tension with the Soviet Union, the President was not yet ready to assume that our adversaries had abandoned their ambitions, and we could therefore dispense with or at least substantially reduce our vast arsenal of coercive instruments.

But this need to stay militarily powerful was only a part of the role, thrust upon us "by destiny rather than by choice," to be "the watchman on the walls of world freedom."

To be truly worthy of the power and responsibility that was inevitably ours, the President cautioned, we must "exercise our strength with wisdom and restraint," never in the pursuit of aggressive ambitions, and always in the pursuit of peace and goodwill toward men. "For as was written long ago: 'Except the Lord keep the city/the watchman waketh but in vain.' " [43]

CHAPTER FOURTEEN

NEW TOOLS FOR THE NEW ARENA: OPPORTUNITIES AND OBSTACLES

To bring real economic progress to . . . the less developed world will require . . . a fresh approach—a more logical, efficient, and successful long-term plan—for American foreign aid. . . . I strongly urge its enactment . . . in full awareness of the many eyes upon us—the eyes of other industrialized nations, awaiting our leadership for a stronger united effort—the eyes of our adversaries, awaiting the weakening of our resolve in this new area of international struggle—the eyes of the poorer peoples of the world, looking for hope and help, and needing an incentive to set realistic long-range goals—and finally, the eyes of the American people, who are fully aware of their obligations to the sick, the poor, and the hungry, wherever they may live.

JOHN F. KENNEDY

President Kennedy approached the problem of the economic under-development of large portions of the non-Communist world with a fervor reserved for no other element of public policy. Fresh innovation in policy rationale and programs were possible with respect to this "third" world.

The Truman and Eisenhower Administrations had been concerned about those segments of mankind who, while not Communist, were by no means securely aligned in opposition to the spread of Communism nor inclined toward the kinds of socioeconomic development able to sustain democratic political systems. But this concern had been marginal to the Truman and Eisenhower foreign policies; Kennedy made it a central pillar of his.

The approach of the Truman Administration to the economically backward societies had been primarily one of benevolent protection: we would help them help themselves in their own way through a low-key program of technical assistance; and we would organize whatever coercive responses were required to prevent the Communists from taking over these countries.

The Eisenhower Administration had been pessimistic about significantly affecting socioeconomic conditions in the Third World, and concentrated on lining up existing regimes as military allies. As allies they could qualify for military assistance to build up their own military forces which could be used as forward barriers against attempts by the Communist nations to extend their realm, and as instruments of domestic social control.

In his pre-White House years, Kennedy turned most of his fire on the Eisenhower-Dulles approach to the Third World. The Middle East, particularly, had been the scene of "grave errors":

We overestimated our own strength and underestimated the force of nationalism. . . . We gave our support to regimes instead of to people—and too often we tied our future to the fortunes of unpopular and ultimately overthrown governments and rulers.

We believed that those governments which were friendly to us and hostile to the Communists were therefore good governments—and we believed that we could make unpopular policies acceptable through our own propaganda programs.

.   .   .

We must talk in terms that go beyond the vocabulary of the Cold War—terms that translate themselves into tangible values and self-interest for the Arabs as well as ourselves.

It is not enough to talk only in terms of guns and money—for guns and money are not the basic need in the Middle East. It is not enough to approach their problems on a piecemeal basis. It is not enough to merely ride with a very shaky *status quo*. It is not enough to recall the Baghdad Pact or the Eisenhower Doctrine—it is not enough to rely on The Voice of America or the Sixth Fleet. These approaches have failed.[1]

199

For "terms that go beyond the vocabulary of the Cold War" Kennedy went to his Charles River economist friends (see above, p. 165). They were putting together a doctrine on the relationship between the structure of societies, the availability of external capital, and the modernization process. This was no academic exercise. Most of the economists had either been government officials, were now consultants to the government, or were participants in overseas technical assistance programs of private foundations. They were primarily concerned with applications, and most particularly with affecting the foreign assistance program of the United States government. There were the expected intellectual disagreements among learned men of an inexact science; but there was a notable convergence on a set of propositions with important implications for concrete policy.[2]

The objective of assistance to the underdeveloped nations should be to help them achieve a condition in which economic growth is a normal and self-sustaining process within a democratic political system.

The attainment of a condition of self-sustaining growth for most of the underdeveloped nations will require fundamental modifications of the economic *and* noneconomic structures of their societies.

Procrastinating the fundamental societal modifications until popular demands for change have risen to a high pitch will likely lead to violent upheavals followed by totalitarian rule.

The required structural modifications can be accomplished peacefully if they are begun early, and are translated into carefully coordinated attacks on the particular roadblocks to modernization found in each nation.

Frequently occurring roadblocks are: (a) a lack of sufficient agricultural productivity beyond the subsistence level (sufficient productivity is an important source of investment capital formation); (b) a lack of sufficient investment in social overhead projects (transportation and communication networks especially); (c) the lack of indigenous specialists able to administer these development tasks and to train the rural population in modes of greater productivity; (d) the lack of literacy, which does not allow for the absorption of new values (including population control) and techniques by the population; and (e) the lack of sufficient commitment on the part of elites to greater economic egalitarianism and political democracy.

The isolation of these roadblocks to modernization and the attack upon them will require comprehensive national planning; and since the need for various expensive projects will arise in advance of the market for them, the government in these countries, not the free market, will have to be the major determiner of investment during the early stages of economic growth.

But in many of these countries those people who run the government, who would be responsible for formulating and carrying out national development plans and negotiating for foreign assistance, are themselves very much attached to the existing social structure. Even in those nations where the top political leadership is personally committed to basic structural alterations of their societes (this is particularly likely in the new post-colonial societies where mass nationalist parties were the instruments of the independence movements), their continued authority may rest on the support of those groups in the society who still command the bulk of resources in the countryside, and who continue to staff the civil and military bureaucracies. These latter groups, for material and psychological reasons, may be reluctant to bring on the restructuring that would have to accompany true modernization.

As a source of desired investment capital and foreign exchange, the United States, other developed nations, and international development authorities can exercise some leverage over the otherwise sluggish pace of structural change by making performance in attacking the critical roadblocks to modernization the foremost criterion for continued economic assistance.[3]

Military or ideological alignment with the United States should not be a prominent criterion for the flow of assistance.

Many of the scholars involved in generating these propositions were now brought into the government—on the White House staff, the State Department, and as ambassadors to important underdeveloped countries (Galbraith as ambassador to India, Lincoln Gordon as ambassador to Brazil). From their point of view, and from Kennedy's, they had practically a carte blanche opportunity to reorganize the entire foreign assistance program, its personnel as well as its operational guidelines. All foreign assistance would henceforth come under the direction of one agency whose tasks and functions could be defined afresh. Moreover, a large new foreign aid program for Latin America was to be funded. In Latin America, because it had been largely ignored in the aid programs of the previous Administrations, the new premises would have a proving ground, unencumbered by existing programmatic commitments.

In back of the dry premises of political economy was the competition between the West and the Communists for influence over the mode of modernization in the Third World. This, to the Kennedy Administration, was the arena of most active, international competition, signaled by Khrushchev's emphasis on "wars of national liberation" (see above, p. 164). The Soviets and the Chinese, deterred at the strategic level, and presumably also at the level of overt local aggression across international boundaries, were now seen to be exerting their most intense pressure beneath these levels. It was as if we had been involved with our major adversaries in a gross game of Cold War *de*-escalation. Our effectiveness in this game depended on our ability to block their gains at the next lower level, while sustaining the barriers already erected at the higher levels.

We were still involved in a competition for global strategic ascendancy. But the tactical requirements of success at this current low level demanded the utmost subtlety and skill, since the objects of the power competition by both sides were national societies undergoing rapid transitions in socioeconomic structure and values, where the only predictably persistent value was the emotionally charged commitment to *self*-determination. The most damaging epithet politicians in these countries could throw at one another was that of being some other nation's pawn.

President Kennedy's appreciation of, even empathy with, the highly insecure political base of the leaders of the developing nations was in back of his attempt to expunge Cold War rhetoric, as much as possible, from the public rationale for foreign assistance. He responded positively to the suggestions from Walt Rostow, David Bell, and others to tone down the anti-Communist appeals appearing in the first draft of his March 1961 foreign aid message.[4] From the outset, however, he was the focal point of the tension between two "constituencies" of the foreign assistance program: the overseas recipients of assistance (whose Washington champions were the development economists in Kennedy's advisory entourage); and, opposing them, the neo-isolationist elements in the American electorate, in portions of the business com-

munity, and in segments of organized labor whose congressional bro-
kers have traditionally coalesced to prune Administration foreign assistance requests not carrying a simple "essential for national security"
rationale. The President did have a basic national security rationale;
but it was far from simple. He did see the need to ride with, rather
than against, a good deal of the political turbulence in the recipient
nations, even when it assumed anti-American, quasi-Marxist overtones; but he was too shrewd a domestic politician to assume that his
tactical international apoliticism would get the needed appropriations
out of Congress.

Thus, the President's Task Force on Foreign Economic Assistance in
its 189-page "summary presentation" to the Congress in June 1961,
explaining the Administration's proposed Act for International Development, set forth the basic Cold War rationale, strongly—but in less
than a page:

Communism Exploits the Demand for Change.
One of the most critical circumstances of today is that the underprivileged
masses in less developed areas of the free world have a passionate aspiration
toward economic, social, and political change. . . . This irresistable trend
toward progress is well understood in the Communist bloc; purposeful
Communist programs are underway to exploit the instabilities of the transi-
tional periods and to bring the less developed countries into the Communist orbit.
This is the "Decade of Decision."
We can expect, therefore, that the decade of the sixties will be a period
of continuing crises, characterized by massive social and economic transformation and acute political instability in areas covering half the globe.
We can also expect that it will be a decade of decision, and that the course
of events during this period will determine whether most of the peoples in
the emerging areas will live in open or closed societies.
The Choice is Between Freedom and Totalitarianism.
The controlling fact is that the need of the underdeveloped world for investment capital (and for other resources as well) can be met in only two
ways: by extraordinary external aid or by forced savings. These alternatives
are inescapable. The first alternative leaves the way open for the evolution
of a free society. The second requires a totalitarian political system. Faced
with these alternatives, the only acceptable course for industrialized nations
of the free world is to provide external aid to the underdeveloped world and
thereby to help turn a decade of crisis into a decade of development—of
growth within a free society, of parallel progress in economic, social, and
political life. . . .[5]

There was also a quotation of the "because it is right" passage from Kennedy's Inaugural Address. The remainder of the presentation constituted an exposition in detail of the programmatic implementation of the premises of politico-economic development outlined above.

The contrary ideological requirements of the overseas recipients as opposed to the domestic provisioners bedeviled Kennedy throughout his Presidency, and explains the observed ambivalence in the public rationale of his foreign assistance program—with one tendency represented by the Alliance for Progress, and the other by the Clay Report.

To be sure, the Alliance for Progress was very much a part of the grand strategy of the Kennedy Administration for frustrating Communist penetration of the Third World. But this aspect of the Alliance's rationale was consciously underplayed in the public rhetoric.

As revealed by Arthur Schlesinger, Jr. (who was heavily involved as a consultant to Kennedy on Latin American affairs), the Cold War was a pervasive part of the discussions in the White House on the Latin American aid program. Kennedy's interregnum task force on Latin America (chaired by Adolph Berle [6]) emphasized the Communist threat, describing it as "more dangerous than the Nazi-Fascist threat [to Latin America] of the Franklin Roosevelt period. . . ." The objective of the Communists, said the task force report, was "to convert the Latin American social revolution into a Marxist attack on the United States itself." As this revolution was "inevitable and necessary," the way to counter the Communist threat was to "divorce" the Latin American social transformation "from connection with and prevent its capture by Communist power politics." The United States needed to put itself clearly on the side of the indigenous "democratic-progressive movements . . . pledged to representative government and economic reform (including agrarian reform) and resistance to entrance of undemocratic forces from outside the hemisphere." The truly democratic social reform groups "should be known to have the good will and support of the United States, just as every Communist group in Latin America is known to have the support of Moscow or of Peiping." It was also necessary for the United States to develop its capabilities for paramilitary and military counterinsurgency operations and to be prepared to offer effective military support to progressive regimes such as

Betancourt's in Venezuela. But we should not try to "stabilize the dying reactionary situations." [7]

The aspect of the Berle report which surfaced in the full-blown Alliance for Progress was the insistence that the United States offer a hemisphere-wide long-range economic development plan, based on the kind of coordinated national planning urged by the Harvard and M.I.T. economists. This was the type of action required to avoid the spread of violent insurrectionary movements in Latin America, and also to give credibility to United States professions of being on the side of those working for social justice and democracy.

After the Kennedy inauguration the momentum for a new departure to Latin American policy accelerated. Berle was appointed to head a reconstituted task force on Latin America in the Department of State, where he and Thomas Mann, the new Assistant Secretary for Inter-American Affairs, labored to give the earlier ideas operational content. One of their recommendations was that the President make a major address on United States policy toward Latin America, proposing a ten-year program of continental development.

Richard Goodwin, a member of the interregnum task force, Kennedy's staff man on Latin America during the campaign, and now a member of the White House staff, was given the responsibility for a first draft of the address. Goodwin responded to the challenge by gathering in all the ideas then adrift in Washington on what the content of a fresh approach toward Latin America ought to be. The time was ripe for major emphasis on Latin America (thanks especially to Castro's increasing alignment with Moscow); and there was a growing appreciation, cultivated by the President, that an economic development orientation in our foreign assistance program was our best long-term weapon of counterinsurgency in the hemisphere. The problem was how to sell the economic porpositions at home and in Latin America without injecting the Cold War rationale, which would alienate the reformist elements in Latin America with whom we were trying to align ourselves.

The "solution," as exhibited in the President's proposal of March 13, 1961 for "a vast new ten-year plan for the Americas," was a coupling of the structural approach to economic development that had been advanced by the Charles River economists with the revolutionary idealism of Thomas Jefferson and Simon Bolivar. Kennedy christened the *Alianza* as the contemporary expression of the American revolution (North and South) for the rights of man:

Our nations are the product of a common struggle—the revolt from colonial rule. . . .

. . .

The revolutions which gave us birth ignited, in the words of Thomas Paine, "a spark never to be extinguished. ". . . we must remember that . . . the revolution which began in 1776 and in Caracas in 1811 . . . is not yet finished. Our hemisphere's mission is not yet completed. *For our unfulfilled task is to demonstrate to the entire world that man's unsatisfied aspiration for economic progress and social justice can best be achieved by free men working within a framework of democratic institutions.*[8]

The concrete steps "to complete the revolution of the Americas" were to be presented in detail at a ministerial meeting of the Inter-American Economic and Social Council. But the President's speech gave a preview of the socioeconomic standards which his Administration would insist be applied in evaluating a potential recipient's commitments to the ideals of the unfinished hemispheric revolution. If the Latin American nations were ready to do their part to "mobilize their resources, enlist the energies of their people, and modify their social patterns so that all, and not just a privileged few, share in the fruits of growth . . ." then the United States, "for its part, should help provide resources of a scope and magnitude sufficient to make this bold development plan a success. . . ."[9] Political freedom, said the President, had to accompany material progress, but political freedom must be accompanied by social change:

For unless necessary social reforms, including land and tax reform, are freely made, unless we broaden the opportunity of all our people, unless the great mass of Americans share in increasing prosperity, then our alliance, our revolution, our dream, and our freedom will fail.[10]

This approach, which was to be elaborated five months later at Punta del Este, was a product of the analysis of the New Frontiersmen that the weakest chink in the armor of the non-Communist world was the phenomenon of the entrenched oligarchy holding on to privilege in the face of rising demands for social justice. The approach of the Alliance for Progress was also based on the Administration's fresh premises about which components of United States power were most appropriate for affecting the course of Third World development. By identifying ourselves with the current of social revolution it was thought we

could give it a legitimacy in these countries that would draw responsible professional and middle class elements into the reform movements, and thereby channel pressures into practical demands and non-
violent modes of agitation. Furthermore, by providing an agenda of
practical reforms, and insisting that governments in these countries
make discernible progress in these directions in order to qualify for development loans, we would be providing significant pressure from
above to complement and reinforce the popular pressures we were encouraging from below. Progressive regimes would be strengthened
against conservative elements in their societies; and oligarchical regimes
would be squeezed in an ever-tightening vise. Opportunist leaders
would at least know where their bread was to be buttered.

If the Latin American nations took the necessary internal measures,
Secretary of the Treasury Douglas Dillon told his fellow delegates at
Punta del Este, they could reasonably expect their own efforts to be
matched by an inflow of capital during the next decade amounting to
at least $20 billion. The problem, he said, did not lie in a shortage of
external capital, but "in organizing effective development programs so
that both domestic and foreign capital can be put to work rapidly,
wisely, and well." There were underlying principles to be adhered to:
the loan recipients would have to dedicate larger proportions of their
domestic resources to national development projects; integrated national programs for economic and social development would have to be
formulated, setting forth goals and priorities to insure that available resources were used in the most effective manner; and such national development programs would have to be in accord with the right of all
segments of the population to share fully in the fruits of progress.

To implement these principles, said Dillon, difficult and far-reaching
changes would have to be instituted by many of the Latin American
nations:

It will require a strengthening of tax systems so that would-be evaders will
know they face strict penalties and so that taxes are assessed in accordance
with ability to pay. It will require land reform so that under-utilized soil is
put to full use and so that farmers can own their own land. It will require
lower interest rates on loans to small farmers and small business. It will require greatly increased programs of education, housing, and health.[11]

The assembled delegates of the Latin American republics, except for
Cuba's Che Guevara, responded with enthusiasm to the United States
initiative (we were careful however to point out that we were respond-

ing to the original Latin initiative for an Operation Pan America first proposed by Brazil's President Kubitschek in 1958), and pledged themselves in the Charter of Punta Del Este to: [12]

Direct their efforts immediately toward assuring that the rate of economic growth in any Latin American country was "not less than 2.5 percent per capita per year."

Arrive at "a more equitable distribution of national income, raising more rapidly the income and standard of living of the needier sectors of the population, at the same time that a higher proportion of the national product is devoted to investment."

Achieve more balanced economies, less dependent upon the export of a limited number of primary products.

Accelerate the process of "rational industrialization," with special attention to the development of capital-goods industries.

"Raise greatly the level of agricultural productivity . . . and to improve related storage, transportation, and marketing services."

"Encourage" comprehensive land reform programs, including the:

. . . effective transformation, where required, of unjust structures and systems of land tenure and use, with a view to replacing latifundia and dwarf holdings by an equitable system . . . so that, with the help of timely and adequate credit, technical assistance and facilities for the marketing and distribution of products, the land will become for the man who works it the basis of his economic stability. . . .

Eliminate illiteracy and provide, by 1970, a minimum of six years of education for each school-age child, and to modernize and expand the entire educational system so as to provide the skilled personnel required during rapid economic development.

Improve basic health services and disease prevention and control.

Increase the construction of low-cost houses for low-income families.

Maintain stable price levels.

Promote regional economic integration, with a view to achieving ultimately a Latin American common market.

Cooperate with other nations to prevent harmful effects from fluctuations in foreign exchange earned from exports of primary products, and to facilitate Latin American exports to foreign markets.

In order to avoid offending Latin sensitivities toward "conditions" imposed by the colossus to the North, the United States recommended, and the Charter included, a provision for a panel of nine "high-level experts" chosen by OAS and UN officials "exclusively on the basis of their experience, technical ability, and competence in the various aspects of economic and social development," to evaluate the national development programs of the nations and report their findings to the Inter-American Development Bank and governments prepared to extend aid. The United States government, presumably, would rely on the findings of these nine wise men for determining the flow of our assistance.

It was still of course an *Alianza* mainly at the level of verbalized aspiration. Some observers, like Tad Szulc of the *New York Times* thought:

The United States failed to realize the incredible difficulties lying ahead . . . while the Latin Americans, realizing them fully because they knew themselves and their problems, signed the commitments for self-help and reform without much intention of seriously living up to them.[13]

Schlesinger, on the other hand, claims that "The American [United States] negotiators had no illusions about the mixture of motives, nor did they suppose that setting fine words down on parchment would have magical effects." [14]

According to Ted Sorenson, the President, after a year or so of little progress was disappointed:

. . . what disturbed him most was the attitude of that 2 percent of the citizenry of Latin America who owned more than 50 percent of the wealth and controlled most of the political-economic apparatus. Their voices were influential, if not dominant, among the local governments, the armies, the newspapers and other opinion-makers. They had friendly ties with U.S. press and business interests who reflected their views in Washington. They saw no reason to alter the ancient feudal patterns of land tenure and tax structure, the top heavy military budgets, the substandard wages and the concentrations of capital. They classified many of their opponents as "communists," considered the social and political reforms of the *Alianza* a threat to stability and clung tenaciously to the status quo.[15]

Moreoever, even when there was the will to reform, there appeared to be a conspiracy of history, natural phenomena, and elemental human forces against essential change. The desire to effect at least a 2.5 per cent per capita rate of economic growth just did not conform to the facts. A 3 per cent per annum increase in the gross national product was very impressive for a Latin American country, yet with population growth running at 2.5 to 3 per cent, the per capita increase was usually all but wiped out even in the best of cases. The lack of Latin American economists with experience in integrated national economic planning was another factor making for sluggishness. By the end of 1962 only five countries were able to submit national development plans for review, and of these only those submitted by Mexico and Venezuela were competently done and within the spirit of the *Alianza*. The lack of sufficiently studied and engineered projects meant that the United States government was able to disburse only two thirds of the $1.5 billion it had already pledged for the first year and a half of the program.[16] Nor was the picture brightened by the worldwide drop in basic commodity prices—the major source of national income for most of the Latin American countries.

Was it all worth the effort anyway? Kennedy continued to think so, but without the earlier euphoria. He admitted that the Alliance for Progress "has failed to some degree because the problems are almost insuperable." In some ways, he said, "the road seems longer than it was when the journey started. But I think we ought to keep at it." [17]

A basic purpose of the Alliance, after all, had been to make it clear to all in the hemisphere, and hopefully elsewhere in the Third World, that the United States was not a status quo power working to preserve oligarchical privilege in the backward countries. It was to demonstrate, by putting our money in back of our rhetoric, to whom and to what we were committed. It was to show that we were on the side of change in the direction of a more equitable distribution of wealth within nations and among nations, of greater participation by men, wherever they live, in deciding upon the rules by which they would live, and of a more abundant and creative life for all human beings. And it was to convey the message that we were for all of these things not simply out of compassion for the less fortunate, but out of enlightened self-interest.

"Perhaps our most impressive accomplishment," said the President on the first anniversary of the Alliance for Progress, "has been the dramatic shift in thinking and attitudes which has occurred in our hemisphere":

Already elections are being fought in terms of the Alliance for Progress. . . . Already people throughout the hemisphere—in schools and in trade unions, in chambers of commerce and in military establishments, in government and on the farms—have accepted the goals of the charter as their own personal and political commitments. For the first time in the history of inter-American relations our energies are concentrated on the central task of democratic development.

This dramatic change in thought is essential to the realization of our goals.[18]

The problem was that the dramatic change in thought, if unaccompanied by meaningful changes in government programs in these countries, could create an even larger gap between popular demands and government responsiveness, with governments in turn attempting to stifle demand, and the discontented turning in their frustration to insurgency. Our strategy for effecting a "divorce" between Communist and non-Communist social reform movements, and making the latter more powerful by tangible evidence of the success of their programs, was based on the assumption that governments, under prodding by the United States, would respond to the mounting political pressure more quickly than they had in the past.

The prod, around which the Alliance for Progress was built, was the long-term low interest loan program for development projects administered in accord with the guidelines set forth in the Charter of Punta del Este. But the diffusion of responsibility to internationally appointed technical experts for implementing the conditions in the Charter made it difficult to use this tool as an instrument of reform. Governments could too easily blame their failure to gain the new external capital promised in the Alliance on the bureaucracy and red tape of the inter-American machinery, rather than on their own procrastination. And the United States could be accused of insisting upon complicated technical standards precisely for the reason that it would reduce the projects we would have to support. Before the end of 1962 the governments of the Americas, through their delegates to the Inter-American Economic and Social Council, were recommending that "in order to prevent disappointment both on the part of the countries seeking assistance and of the financing institutions, both national and international, it will be advisable to make the conditions and operations of these institutions more flexible. . . ."[19]

Latin American diplomats also began to press with greater fervor for international commodity price stabilization agreements, arguing that the instability of their countries' foreign earnings, more than anything else, prevented the amount of domestic capital available for investment in development from being increased. This case was not entirely convincing to the Administration, since there was a good deal of "surplus" domestic Latin American private money drawing interest in American and European banks. The people receiving money from the export of basic commodites were very often the same elements least interested in the social reform that would have to accompany true economic development in their countries.

The more conservative Latins, and United States interests unsympathetic to the national planning approach and emphasis upon public investment in the original conception of the Alliance, were able to point to the fact that there had been a decline in the flow of private capital to Latin America since Punta del Este. The obvious implication was that all the talk of dramatic social change, including drastic land and tax reforms, had raised the specter of confiscation of private holdings without sufficient compensation, harrassment of foreign-subscribed private enterprise, and political instability leading to unpredictable radical economic experiments. "Taking into account the limitations to the availability of public funds," said the first-year evaluation report of the IA-ECOSOC, "it is clear that the objectives of the Alliance cannot be achieved without the full participation of the private sector and adequate measures must be taken to assure maximum contribution to growth by the private sector." [20] The forces for stability, recovering from the first shock of seeing the White House seriously identifying itself with the forces for change, had begun to regroup.

The President's response to the conservative counterattack was to show as much favor as possible to leaders like Betancourt and Mateos, and to point his finger at those Latin American forces who, in his view, constituted an alliance against progress:

No amount of external resources, no stabilization of commodity prices, no new inter-American institutions, can bring progress to nations which do not have political stability and determined leadership. No series of hemispheric agreements or elaborate machinery can help those who lack internal discipline, who are unwilling to make sacrifices and renounce privileges. No one who sends his money abroad, who is unwilling to invest in the future of his country, can blame others for the deluge which threatens to overcome and overwhelm him.

But the elements of lethargy, obstruction, and despair were not going to prevail this time, affirmed the President four days before his death.

These forces should know that he was fully committed, and prepared for a long struggle. "Nothing is true except a man or men adhere to it —to live for it, to spend themselves on it, to die for it," he declaimed, quoting from a poem by Robert Frost. More important than money or institutions or agreements was this spirit of persistence in the face of great obstacles.[21]

Whatever the President's real assessment of the chances of implementing the goals of Punta del Este, the Alliance for Progress put forward the face of United States power the New Frontier preferred to emphasize, combining the features of modernity (the new science of development economics) with the gaze of fiery idealism (Tom Paine and Simon Bolivar). Underneath was the hard unsentimental assumption that anything less would allow the Communists to capture, with their "science" and their revolutionary ardor, the revolution of rising demands by the newly enfranchised poor of the Third World. The visage of social reformer, however, was not something put on simply as a Cold War expedient. It was also thought to be the expression of our deeper and better selves, "for America at its best has never wholly lost a sense of the community of human destiny." [22]

The United States has a mixed tradition. Those who claim that altruistic motives are illegitimate considerations of foreign policy trace their lineage to George Washington's farewell address. The Constitution talks of securing the blessings of liberty to ourselves and our posterity; it says nothing of our obligation to extend these blessings to others. This view that the "irreducible national interest" (see Part I, Chapter I) ought to be the *sole* determinant of foreign policy, not just the primary object of policy, had proven a powerful weapon in the hands of the opponents of economic development assistance since the Second World War. And the opponents, by virtue of their control of key appropriations committees, have held an effective veto over Administration proposals. A President asking for an increase in foreign aid thus usually needs to use all of the instruments of leverage at his disposal. But as executive leverage is to some extent an expendable commodity, its use on a particular program has required that the case be made for that program's priority within the Administration as well as to the public and the Congress, since other budget items also need White House backing. The strongest contention is that in the President's judgment program X is essential for national security.

The Kennedy Administration, partly because of its analysis of the sensitivities of the new nations, partly because of its belief that the country was at its best when it gave vent to its altruistic traditions, was initially inclined not to make the national security rationale the be-all and end-all of foreign aid. But gradually, and tragically to some New Frontiersmen, the White House began to trim its approach back to this irreducible national interest as the Congress fell back into its habit of trimming the "fat" from foreign aid requests.

Congress went along with the essentials of the Administration's program in 1961, creating the Agency for International Development, authorizing the Alliance for Progress and the funds requested for this new venture, and increasing the proportion of foreign assistance appropriations devoted to economic as opposed to military projects. But the next year, the counterattack was in full swing, led by Congressman Otto Passman, chairman of the House Appropriations Subcommittee on Foreign Aid.

In 1962, the President asked the Congress for a total of $4.9 billion for the various foreign assistance programs. As Congress began to axe the recommended economic development programs, Kennedy appealed to the legislators in the terms of his preferred public rationale: if we were truly for a world of independent self-reliant nations, if we really believed that weakness and dependence for national societies was not a proper environment for the development of political liberty and individual well-being, then in good conscience we could not reduce these foreign assistance programs any further.[23]

Insufficiently impressed, the Congress trimmed a full billion dollars off of the President's request. There was great disappointment in the White House; AID's first chief, Foweler Hamilton resigned. Schlesinger portrays Kennedy as "convinced that extreme measures were necessary to get the aid bill through Congress in 1963," and deciding upon "the familiar device of a blue-ribbon panel of bonded conservatives set up to cast a presumably cold eye on the aid effort and then to recommend its continuance as essential to the national interest." [24]

The panel was about as bonded a group as could be found. Designated "the Committee to Strenghten the Security of the Free World," it was chaired by General Lucius D. Clay, highly respected in banking and financial circles and famed for his Cold War toughness toward the Soviets over Germany and Berlin. Fiscal responsibility was represented by Robert B. Anderson, Eisenhower's last Secretary of the Treasury, and before that Secretary of the Navy. Robert A. Lovett, a Secretary of Defense under Truman, and the man most identified in the public mind with the New York "establishment," could never be accused of fuzzy liberalism. Organized labor was represented by the militantly anti-Communist George Meany. Edward S. Mason, of the Harvard-MIT economists circle, was added as an afterthought, but largely as a concession to some of the development economists who may not have appreciated the political gamesmanship of the President. The main economic development aura was provided by Eugene Black of the World Bank. Other members were Clifford Hardin, L. F. McCollum, Herman Phleger, and Howard Rusk.

If a blue ribbon was desirable for packaging the 1963 Foreign Aid proposals, the Clay Committee was more than willing to provide the truest blue, in the form of a return to the strict national-security-only criterion that had kept economic development assistance to a trickle since the Korean War, and in its insistence that the "private sector" rather than government-owned enterprises should be the favored recipients of assistance. But rather than squaring the circle by arguing that the nation's security interest and interest in expanding overseas private investment would be best served by a long-term continuation of the level of effort the President was recommending, the Committee did just the opposite:

We believe that we are indeed attempting too much for too many and that a higher quality and reduced quantity of our difficult aid effort in certain countries could accomplish much more. We cannot believe that our national interest is served by indefinitely continuing commitments at the present rate to the 95 countries and territories which are now receiving our economic and/or military assistance. Substantial tightening up and sharpened objectives in terms of our national interests are necessary . . .

. . .

For the present . . . we are convinced that reductions are in order in present military and economic assistance programs. Mindful of the risks inherent in using the axe to achieve quickly the changes recommended, the Committee recommends these reductions be phased over the next three years.[25]

Schlesinger reveals that the final version, quoted in part above, was considerably more positive than the first draft, which he characterized

215

as "sour and niggling." Apparently the President and David Bell, the new AID Administrator had made known their dislike of the tone of the original document, and Clay acquiesced in a revision.[26] The Administration released the report reluctantly, in the knowledge that Clay's support was now politically indispensable, even if only to salvage the 1963 bill after it was torn apart by Representative Passman and his friends.

The Louisiana Democrat could not have been more pleased by the Clay report. And now cautious Republicans like Everett Dirksen and Charles Halleck could vote for cuts in the Administration's aid program while wrapped in the mantle of Establishment patriotism. In August 1963, as the congressional wrecking operation shifted into high gear, the Administration's major lobbying efforts focused upon trying to gain senate ratification of the nuclear test ban treaty. Nevertheless, in a last-minute effort to have some of the cuts restored, the President got General Clay to meet the press with him at Hyannis Port for a final appeal. The General said what was expected of him, claiming that the current reductions had "gone to far." It remained for the President to turn the national security argument around strongly *for* a vigorous foreign aid program.

It was important for the American people to understand, said Kennedy, that this was a matter which involved "the balance of power all over the world." Thus:

It is a matter which involves very greatly the security of our country. This is the same view that was held by President Eisenhower and this is the same view that was held by President Truman, and it is no accident that three Presidents sitting where they do, bearing the responsibility for foreign policy, should all feel that this program is most important, most effective, most essential. . . .

. . .

I think . . . it is as essential a part of our effort as the appropriations for national defense.[27]

But the "national security" standard, as wielded by the Congress, applying narrower concepts of security and the global balance of power, was in 1963 a keener instrument for whittling down than building up. The actual appropriations bill of $3.2 billion, a slash of $1.7 billion from Kennedy's original request, was the lowest since 1958, and the smallest percentage of our gross national product allocated to foreign assistance since the start of the Marshall Plan.

In an Administration that defined the Third World as the major arena of competition, this congressional action was interpreted as a severe curb on the diplomatic power of the United States.

The President, however, was not one to take such defeats without fighting back. If the case for foreign aid had to be made in terms of national security, then that was the way he would make the case. But the connection would have to be more clearly set forth than previously.

In a westward swing through the United States with Secretary of the Interior Udall in the fall of 1963, the President frequently departed from his major theme—the conservation of national resources—to talk about the preservation of the nation as a whole.

At Great Falls, Montana, for instance, he made special note that though Montana was 10,000 miles from Laos, Montanans knew that the Minutemen missiles stationed in their state were only thirty minutes from the Soviet Union. The object of our policy, he said, was "to make sure that those . . . Minutemen missiles . . . remain where they are." That was the reason, the President explained, why we were assisting so many countries to maintain their freedom: "Because I know full well that every time a country, regardless of how far away from our own borders—every time that country passes behind the Iron Curtain the security of the United States is thereby endangered." Most of us grew up in a period of isolation, and neutrality, and unalignment, Kennedy said, which was our policy from the time of George Washington to the Second World War. But then suddenly we became "the keystone in the arch of freedom. If the United States were to falter, the whole world, in my opinion, would inevitably begin to move toward the Communist bloc." [28]

Except for his address during the Cuban missile crisis, probably the hardest-hitting basic national security speech of the President's career was made at the Mormon Tabernacle in Salt Lake City. It was the last week of September 1963. The Senate had ratified the nuclear test ban treaty. There was talk of détente with the Soviet Union. The President, aware that the audience to which he spoke would translate their mood of increasing isolationism first into a disapproval of foreign economic assistance, once again drove home the connections between the security concerns of his audience, the global balance of power, and our array of foreign commitments. This largely extemporaneous address merits liberal quotation:

I know that many of you in this State and other States sometimes wonder where we are going and why the United States should be involved in so many affairs, in so many countries all around the globe. . . .

. . .

I realize that the burdens are heavy and I realize that there is a great temptation to urge that we relinquish them, that we have enough to do here in the United States, and we should not be so busy around the globe. From the beginning of this country . . . we had believed that we could live behind our two oceans in safety and prosperity in a comfortable distance from the rest of the world.

. . .

I can well understand the attraction of those earlier days . . . but two world wars have shown us that if we . . . turn our back on the world outside . . . we jeopardize our economic well-being, we jeopardize our political stability, we jeopardize our physical safety.

. . .

Americans have come a long way in accepting in a short time the necessity of world involvement, but the strain of this involvement remains and we find it all over the country. . . . We find ourselves entangled with apparently unanswerable problems in unpronounceable places. We discover that our enemy in one decade is our ally the next. We find ourselves committed to governments whose actions we cannot often approve, assisting societies with principles very different from our own.

. . .

The world is full of contradiction and confusion, and our policy seems to have lost the black and white clarity of simpler times when we remembered the Maine and went to war.

. . .

The United States has rightly determined, in the years since 1945 under three different administrations . . . that our national security, the interest of the United States of America, is best served by preserving and protecting a world of diversity in which *no one power or no one combination of powers can threaten the security of the United States.* The reason that we moved so far into the world was our fear that at the end of the war, and particularly when China became Communist, that Japan and Germany would collapse, and these two countries which had so long served as a barrier to Soviet advance, and the Russian advance before that, would open up a wave of conquest of all Europe and all of Asia, and then *the balance of power turning against us we would finally be isolated and ultimately destroyed.* That is what we have been engaged in for 18 years, to prevent that happening, to prevent any one monolithic power having sufficient force to destroy the United States.

For that reason we support the alliance in Latin America; for that reason we support NATO . . . for that reason we joined SEATO. . . . And however dangerous or hazardous it may be, and however close it may take us to the brink on occasion, which it has, and however tired we may get of our involvements with these governments so far away, we have *one simple central theme of American foreign policy* which all of us must recognize, because it is a policy which we must continue to follow, and that is *to support the independence of nations so that one block cannot gain sufficient power to finally overcome us.* There is no mistaking the vital interest of the United States in what goes on around the world. . . .

If we were to withdraw our assistance from all governments who are run differently from our own, we would relinquish the world immediately to our adversaries.

. . .

This country has seen all the hardship and grief that has come to us by the loss of . . . Cuba. How many other countries must be lost if the United States decides to end the programs that are helping these people, who are getting poorer every year, who have none of the resources of this great country, who look to us for help, but on the other hand in cases look to the Communists?

That is why I think this program is important. . . .[29]

The New Frontier tried to transcend the vocabulary of Cold War diplomacy, but found it had often to return to this vocabulary when addressing the American public in order to be granted the resources to develop more flexible programs for the Third World.

CHAPTER FIFTEEN

CASTRO, LAOS, THE CONGO: LIMITS ON THE COERCIVE POWER OF THE SUPERPOWERS

There is a limitation . . . upon the power of the United States to bring about solutions. . . . The problems are more difficult than I had imagined them to be.

JOHN F. KENNEDY

During the first nine months of his Presidency, Kennedy was faced with a number of crises that seemed to many of his advisers to require a direct application of United States military power. In each of these situations he held back, confirmed anew in his premise that if our military power was indeed powerful enough it need not be used, provided we were sufficiently imaginative and facile in applying the varied instruments of influence at our disposal.

Kennedy was highly motivated to explore all means short of force, for he perceived the contagious nature of violence and appreciated the awful dimensions it could reach. He also saw the limitations of military power when used as an instrument of persuasion. These limitations were characterized to an academic audience on November 16, 1961: "We possess weapons of tremendous power—but they are least effective in combating the weapons most often used by freedom's foes: subverison, infiltration, guerrilla warfare, civil disorder." Yet, "we cannot, as a free nation, compete with our adversaries in tactics of terror, assassination, false promises, counterfeit mobs and crises." We had been cast in the role of "the most powerful defender of freedom on earth," but we were unable to perform that role "without restraints imposed by the very freedoms we seek to protect." Moreover, not everyone agreed with us in our definition of freedom and human dignity, nor did they possess the same will to defend it. "We send arms to other peoples—just as we send them the ideals of democracy in which we believe—but we cannot send them the will to use those arms or to abide by those ideals."

Kennedy would not have denied these premises nine months earlier, but neither would he have made them a central theme of a major address on public policy. At his inaugural he had exorted his nation to respond to the trumpet call of world leadership. He had cautioned, even in his exultation, that this was to be a "long twilight struggle," requiring great sacrifices, and no prospects of quick reward. But the mood had been one of great confidence in the ability of the new generation of American leaders to mobilize first the nation's and then the world's resources for the mammouth struggle "against the common enemies of man: tyranny, poverty, disease and war itself." Now it was in a considerably more chastened mood that the President counseled:

We must face the fact that the United States is neither omnipotent nor omniscient—that we are only 6 percent of the world's population—that we cannot impose our will upon the other 94 percent of mankind—that we cannot right every wrong or reverse each adversity—and that therefore there cannot be an American solution to every world problem.[1]

The Bay of Pigs fiasco was probably Kennedy's major chastening experience, but he did not come to these premises suddenly in the midst of that crisis. He had decided already in the cases of Laos and the Congo that the least desirable policy options were those that would require United States military intervention, and that we would have to accept barely tolerable outcomes (neutralization for Laos, a flimsy UN presence for the Congo) rather than solutions. The denouement of the Bay of Pigs took place during the Laotian and Congolese crises of 1961. On the one hand, it does seem to have reinforced his skeptical attitude toward plans based on the assumption that by the exercise of our military prowess we would control all of the critical variables in these messy political situations. "Thank God the Bay of Pigs happened when it did," he told Ted Sorenson. "Otherwise we'd be in Laos by now—and that would be a hundred times worse." [2] On the other hand, he was under tremendous pressure to compensate for the demonstration of United States impotence at the Bay of Pigs. As he confided to Walt Rostow, Eisenhower could survive the Communist successes in Indochina in 1954 because the blame fell on the French, but "I can't take a 1954 defeat today." [3]

Though the Bay of Pigs did not determine Kennedy's actions henceforth, it bears special examination as a crisis that made the President more keenly aware of the scope and limitations of the various facets of the nation's power. In this respect it was a more significant event than even the missile crisis of 1962; and certainly what he learned during the Bay of Pigs crisis was central to his evaluation of the various options presented to him for dealing with Cuban missiles (See pp. 258–66).

Kennedy's handling of the Laotian crisis was a product, but also a reinforcement, of his premise that it was of fundamental importance for the superpowers to avoid a direct military clash, and of the corollary that this would often require of both that they accept only tolerable outcomes rather than "solutions." These premises were rooted in an appreciation of the deep ideological gulf that separated the Communist and non-Communist nations, so that a victory for one side, such as a satellite in the Third World, could well be regarded by the other as "intolerable." In such situations, to press for victory could be very risky. The risk, Kennedy further appreciated, was shared by both sides, given the balance of thermonuclear capabilities, but was also difficult to control once a war was underway, since in the heat of battle the pressure to win could easily submerge the more limited objective of merely denying the opponent victory.

The objective of avoiding a direct military confrontation of the superpowers also dominated our considerations during the Congo civil wars of 1960–62. The Soviets were rushing in where angels feared to tread, with military assistance to some of the factions rebelling against the central Congolese government. Pessimistic about the ability of any external power to control the local situation, but unwilling to see the Soviets exploit the chaos unopposed, the Kennedy Administration carried forward the Eisenhower Administration's policy of keeping the Soviets out by putting the United Nations in. Nevertheless, events in the Congo compelled a degree of United States support for UN operations bordering on direct involvement. United States pronouncements and actions were carefully tailored in line with the assumption that expectations about who and what the United States supported in the Congo would critically influence internal Congolese politics. Not that we could determine or control the situation, but rather, important local participants and potential outside meddlers knew that the balance of forces in the Congo depended upon the degree of support various factions could expect from the United States. As it turned out, things went our way more than we expected (see below, pp. 235–41), but not primarily because of what we did. The Congo crisis was not only another lesson to Kennedy on the limits of our own power; it was also a demonstration of the degree to which the Soviets are limited in their ability to exploit Third World instabilities.

President Kennedy hesitated, reversed himself, and was embarrassingly unsure of his footing during his effort to topple Castro in the spring of 1961. But from the outset he was constant, in his basic premise that fundamental United States interests would be ill-served if that effort were to involve the direct employment of our military power. This premise was a part of the ground rules for Central Intelligence Agency contingency planning, as originally approved by the Eisenhower Administration. The condition that there would be no United States military intervention was explicitly a part of the understanding between the White House and the CIA, and was reiterated and stressed during the secret meetings in March and April between the new President and his chief military, diplomatic, and intelligence advisors.[4] This self-denying ordinance against the application of United States military power was reinforced in a pledge by Kennedy, just five days before the exile landing at the Bay of Pigs:

. . . there will not be, under any conditions, an intervention in Cuba by the United States Armed Forces. This government will do everything it possibly can, and I think it can meet its responsibilities, to make sure that there are no Americans involved in any actions inside Cuba.

The basic issue in Cuba is not one between the United States and Cuba. It is between the Cubans themselves. I intend to see that we adhere to that principle and as I understand it this administration's attitude is so understood and shared by the anti-Castro exiles from Cuba in this country.[5]

And it was this prohibition, in the "moment of truth" where he saw what in fact would be required to make the exile operation succeed, that led Kennedy to accept the terrible embarrassment and pain of allowing the 1400 Cuban exiles to be decimated by Castro's forces.

In everything that has thus far been divulged about the Bay of Pigs crisis, the evidence is that the President thought he had approved an operation whose success would *not* require the use of United States military forces. He accepted the intelligence of the CIA that Castro's hold over the people of Cuba was very unstable, and that the majority of the people, including presumably Castro's own army, would rise against him once a small force of exiles had established a beachhead. The President and his military advisers also accepted the CIA's intelligence on Castro's military forces, and the derived evaluation by the Joint Chiefs of Staff, that an insurrectionary beachhead could be established by the Cuban exiles, using the equipment already at their disposal, and without direct United States military support. And at the outside chance that the operation might not succeed militarily, it would have been conducted in such a low-key manner that the exiles presumably could disappear into the hills and reorganize themselves for a longer-term guerrilla operation without having to call on the United States to bail them out.

On all of these critical intelligence and military operational premises the President discovered, after the assault was underway, that he was wrong. A good deal of what has been written about the Bay of Pigs explores the bases of these mistaken premises—poor advice, deliberate deception by operatives afraid to tell the President the truth for fear the whole thing would be called off (but possibly confident that once it was underway the President would be too heavily committed to reverse himself), the failure of the President to draw out advisers who had important doubts, and inexperience on Kennedy's part in knowing how to manage the vast military and intelligence bureaucracies.

Some people, looking back at the calamity, argue that better generalship on our part would have saved the day: a less vulnerable landing site should have been selected; the time of the exiles' air strikes should have been better; supplies of ammunition should have been dispersed rather than concentrated in a single ship which was sunk early in the campaign, and so on. Other critics dwell on the failure of the United States to become militarily involved even in a marginal way—but presumably the critical margin: if the United States had been willing to provide air cover, it is argued, the exiles could have at least established a beachhead from which a major insurgency could have then been mounted.

But as the facts came in, the President apparently was convinced that he and his subordinates had made more than a series of technical and marginal errors: The principal agencies and individuals involved in the planning and direction of the venture had cooperated in constructing a grossly uninformed depiction of the situation in Cuba. Different pictures of Castro's political and military strength were available from British intelligence, and even from our own State Department,[6] not to mention usually responsible American newspapermen.[7] Yet from those within his inner circle, the President received no thoughtful dissent to the most critical premises sustaining the consensus to go ahead, except that offered by Arthur Schlesinger. By Schlesinger's own account, he too was ineffectual in advancing counterarguments at meetings when they might have done the most good. Moreover, Schlesinger seems to have neglected to pinpoint the implication which later, in the midst of the operation, faced the President: namely, that there was no way of avoiding a direct and obvious and substantial United States military involvement if the objective was to take Cuba away from the Castroites.[8]

When the President, belatedly, realized that this indeed was the situation, he was able to quickly regain his perspective and evaluate the remaining options—take on Castro ourselves, or liquidate the Bay of Pigs operation—in terms of their implications for the global balance of power. When viewed in this context, liberated from preoccupation with the tactical factors, he knew what he had to do. He was well aware that he, personally, would be subjected to charges of cowardice, of callous disregard for the lives of the exiles on the beach, and of downright political inepititude; and that overseas these charges would be directed at the nation as a whole. During those critical hours, Kennedy confided to James Reston and Arthur Schlesinger his conception of where the basic national interest lay. In Schlesinger's account:

Kennedy seemed deeply concerned about the members of the Brigade. They were brave men and patriots; he had put them on the beachhead; and he wanted to save as many as he could. But he did not propose to send in the Marines. Some people, he noted, were arguing that failure would cause irreparable harm, that we had no choice now but to commit United States forces. Kennedy disagreed. Defeat, he said would be an incident, not a disaster. The test had always been whether the Cuban people would back a revolt against Castro. If they wouldn't, the United States could not by invasion impose a new regime on them. But would not United States prestige suffer if we let the rebellion flicker out? "What is prestige?" Kennedy asked. "Is it the shadow of power or the substance of power? We are going to work on the substance of power. No doubt we will be kicked in the can for the next couple of weeks, but that won't affect the main business." [9]

The main business—the substance of power—what was it? The main business was still, as it had been since the days of the Truman Doctrine, preventing extensions of Communist control that would constitute a significant change in the global balance of power, but accomplishing containment of Communism, if at all possible, without a major war. We would risk war, even the survival of the United States itself, were that necessary to prevent an imbalance of power against us. But Kennedy, on this score, found himself in complete agreement with the argument of Senator Fulbright who, during the planning stages of the operation, had protested, "The Castro regime is a thorn in the flesh; but is is not a dagger in the heart." [10] If the thorn could be extracted with a tweezer, that was one thing. It was surely not worth hacking to pieces the tissue of hemispheric relations now being nurtured in the Alliance for Progress, nor worth a major diversion of military resources at a time when trouble was brewing in Laos, the Congo, and Berlin. Sorenson recounts the President's calculations:

"Obviously," he [Kennedy] said later, "if you are going to have United States air cover, you might as well have a complete United States commitment, which would have meant a full-fledged invasion by the United States."

American conventional forces . . . were still below strength, and while an estimated half of our available Army divisions were tied down resisting guerrillas in the Cuban mountains, the Communists could have been on the move in Berlin or elsewhere in the world. . . .

When the reports of the failure of the exile brigade demanded Presidential action one way or the other:

He would not agree to the military-CIA request for the kind of open commitment of American military power that would necessitate, in his view, a full-scale attack by U.S. forces—that, he said, would only weaken our hand in the global fight against Communism over the long run. [11]

The global fight against Communism had been shifting to the new arena of competition for influence over the development process in the Third World. To allow ourselves to be panicked into a military intervention in the Americas would, if anything, be playing the game as the Communists wanted us to play it—in the stereotyped style of the hated collossus to the North. The real issue, Castro's betrayal of the ideals of the Cuban revolution, would be submerged in the escalation of battle and emotions. And the dichotomization between left and right, which always gives the Communists their biggest opportunities for exploiting indigenous revolutions, would block the new lines of communication Kennedy was trying to string with progressive reformist groups in Latin America, Africa, and Asia.

In his address before the Society of Newspaper Editors on April 20, the President, while taking full responsibility for the disastrous outcome at the Bay of Pigs, tried to direct the nation's attention to the lessons of the episode. It is clearer than ever, he said, that we face a relentless struggle in every corner of the globe "in situations which do not permit our own armed intervention":

We dare not fail to see the insidious nature of this new and deeper struggle. We dare not fail to grasp the new concepts, the new tools, the new sense of urgency we will need to combat it—whether in Cuba or South Viet-Nam. And we dare not fail to realize that this struggle is taking place every day, without fanfare, in thousands of villages and markets—day and night—and in classrooms all over the globe.

Too long, he said, we had fixed our eyes on traditional military tools for maintaining the balance of power—on armies prepared to cross borders, on missiles posed for flight. "Now it should be clear that this is no longer enough." [12]

In dealing with Castro's Cuba, Kennedy from the outset of his planning rejected the use of substantial United States military power. We were initiating a change in the status quo, and we could set the rules of engagement. In Laos the situation was quite different. Our major opponents were trying to topple the status quo in their attempts to absorb Laos, and their decisions, no less than ours, would determine the dimensions of the conflict.

Kennedy perceived that the question of *who* was trying to change the existing situation was a very important one in our evolving relations with the Soviet Union. The effects of a "war of national liberation," fomented and successfully managed by the Soviets or Chinese, could be considerable on the global balance of power—on its psychological "wave of the future" component affecting the expectations and alignments of men and nations. "The security of all Southeast Asia will be endangered if Laos loses its neutral independence," explained Kennedy in his March 23, 1961 news conference. "Its own safety runs with the safety of us all." Yet when pressed by a reporter to "spell out your views a little further" on the relationship of the security of Laos to the "security of the United States and to the individual American," the President rested his case on our formal treaty commitments and on local geopolitical considerations:

Well, quite obviously, geographically Laos borders on Thailand, to which the United States has treaty obligations under the SEATO Agreement of 1954, it borders on South Vietnam . . . to which the United States has very close ties, and also which is a signatory of the SEATO Pact [actually, only covered by a separate protocol]. The aggression against Laos itself was referred to in the SEATO Agreement. So that, given this, the nature of the geography, its location, the commitments which the United States and obligations which the United States has assumed toward Laos as well as the surrounding countries—as well as other signatories of the SEATO Pact, it's quite obvious that if the Communists were able to move in and dominate this country, it would endanger the security of all and the peace of all of Southeast Asia. And as a member of the United Nations and as a signatory of the SEATO Pact, and as a country which is concerned with the strength of the cause of freedom around the world, that obviously affects the security of the United States.[13]

The possibility that he might not be putting the strength of his commitment to an independent Laos across to the people of the United States and to the Soviets worried the President, particularly after the Bay of Pigs. How could he convince them that he had not ruled out United States intervention against Communism in a tiny kingdom on the other side of the world while he had rejected intervention against a Communist regime ninety miles off our shores in our traditional sphere of influence and military control?[14] He was apparently unwilling to resort publicly to the bald "falling dominoes" arguments Eisenhower and Dulles invoked over Indochina in 1954 and Quemoy and Matsu in 1958. His problem was that anything short of that might not be sufficiently convincing to the Communists.

The President saw that his most important task was to convince the Soviets that we could not and would not accept a Communist takeover of Laos. If that ultimately required a larger diversion of United States resources and even a military engagement, the task of fully convincing the American people and the Congress would be formidable, but he would have to cross that bridge when he came to it. For the present, he was unwilling to whip up war fever over Laos that might then get out of hand and foreclose his immediate diplomatic objective of achieving a cease-fire in Laos and a neutralization agreement backed by the big powers.

One hope of the Administration was to "collectivize" our commitment and any military response, just as the Eisenhower Administration attempted when contemplating intervention in Indochina in 1954. Secretary of State Rusk argued for SEATO assumption of responsibility for intervention at the organization's annual ministerial meeting in Bangkok on March 27. But France was clearly against what it regarded as a resumption of the Indochina war; and Britain, actively engaged in the "honest broker" role of trying to persuade the Soviets to impose a cease-fire on the Communist Pathet Lao prior to the convening of the Geneva peace conference, felt its effectiveness would be compromised by voting for SEATO intervention. SEATO was immobile and served to confirm Mao's thesis that it was a paper tiger.[15] If there was to be any military intervention, the United States would have to assume full responsibility.

The United States commitment, and our resolve to stick by it, had somehow to be conveyed to Khrushchev before the Soviets became overcommitted. Outwardly, they were as yet doing little more than airlifting military supplies to the Pathet Lao from Hanoi, but there was pressure on them too to increase their aid and possibly even to preempt a United States intervention by more direct involvement. It was here that the Kennedy Administration made a shrewd guess as to the Soviets' real motivations in Laos at that particular time: it might very well be that the Soviets were not anxious to become involved in the Laotian insurgency, but felt they had to be the dominant backer of the Pathet Lao for fear of that role—and presence—falling to the Chinese Communists. If this premise about Soviet motives was true, then the Soviets might be seriously interested in a viable neutralization of Laos as a device to take the pressure off them to intervene, and as a buffer against Chinese southwestward expansion. Kennedy saw his job as convincing Khrushchev that whereas our commitment to prevent the Communists from overruning Laos was absolute, even if that required a major military intervention by the United States, we were sufficiently appreciative of the Soviets' interests to accept their bona fides about neutralization.

There remained, of course, the difficult task of getting the Laotians to accept whatever settlement was worked out, since the terms of neutrality would obviously have to include stipulations as to the makeup of the Laotian regime. But at the time this was viewed as a subordinate problem to that of bringing the intentions of the superpowers together on the neutralization outcome.

"I want to make it clear to the American people and to all of the world" Kennedy had said at his March 23 press conference, "that all we want in Laos is peace, not war; a truly neutral government, not a cold war pawn; a settlement concluded at the conference table and not on the battlefield." [16] However for the Soviets to have as much clarity in their intentions, Kennedy understood that they might have to be given more than merely words; this was of course the meaning of the President's deployment of Marines to Thailand simultaneous with his protestations of sincere peaceful intent. In this respect, Kennedy was a traditional diplomatist—unsheathing the arrows while holding forth the olive branch. And this was exactly the posture the President felt was of greatest importance to display before Khrushchev in their meeting at Vienna that June, especially since the Bay of Pigs might have given him the erroneous impression that Kennedy was unwilling to send American boys into battle.

The greatest danger, Kennedy told Khrushchev at Vienna, was the possibility of miscalculation by one side of the interests and policies of the other.[17] Such a miscalculation could lead to situations where, against the intentions and interests of both sides, they might find themselves embroiled in war against one another. One of the purposes of their conversations, then, was to reduce the uncertainty each might have about the other's vital interests and intentions, so that hopefully the United States and the Soviet Union would be able to survive their rivalry.

The "wars of national liberation" which the Soviet Premier had endorsed in January were fraught with such possibilities for miscalculation, maintained Kennedy. Khrushchev insisted that the Soviet Union could not be held responsible for every popular uprising, even when it assumed a Communist coloring. If what Kennedy meant by urging that the superpowers should refrain from challenging each other's vital interests was that the Soviets should refuse to aid those progressive forces trying to rid themselves of capitalist-imperialist domination, then the President was only trying to get him to acquiesce in continued Western intervention. Khrushchev agreed there should be no interference by the superpowers in the Third World against the will of the peoples, especially in the context of the ability of the United States and the Soviet Union to destroy each other, but insisted that it was the United States that was interfering, not the Soviets.

Kennedy attempted to get Khrushchev to agree on the importance of preserving the existing balance of power. The equilibrium would be disturbed, he contended, if additional nations were brought into the Communist camp. The Soviet countered with the observation that if some African country were to go Communist it would be but a drop in the bucket on the Communist side, if that was how the balance was conceived. The point was that it was dangerous to oppose movements toward Communism in any country where it was an expression of the popular will. It was only such popular movements that the Soviets would support anyway. They knew that it was futile to send guerilla troops into a country to support a movement not supported by the people. This was evidently something the Americans had not yet learned.

Much of this dialogue, though not mentioning Laos directly, would seem to have been a dialogue about Laos. Yet in those early conversations at Vienna, Khrushchev seemed to be attempting to avoid the issue whenever Kennedy tried to get down to specifics.

As it turned out, Khrushchev really only had one matter on which he was willing to agree and that was Laos—that is, the necessity for a mutual backing off from a military confrontation and the establishment of a neutral buffer state. But to get to this area of agreement too quickly would have been to avoid the opportunity to intimidate the young President by a more ideological discussion. There were other conflicts between them not subject to resolution, such as Berlin, and it was important, evidently, for Khrushchev to display his toughest side and the depth of his commitments, in order to ward off attempts by the new Administration in Washington to probe for Soviet vulnerabilities. Kennedy did afterwards admit to a rough time, but not to being intimidated.

When the discussion finally got around to Laos, Kennedy led the conversation away from the great issues to the practical problem of decreasing commitments on both sides and establishing a truly neutral and independent country. If a reduction of commitment was now a sincere American objective, then why the threat of sending in U.S. Marines, asked Khrushchev, possibly hoping to exact a pledge of non-intervention. Kennedy denied that any order had been issued to send in the Marines. But he would not play the game Khrushchev's way, and instead drove home the point that all this could be avoided if there were a genuine cease-fire, so that negotiations could begin in earnest. Khrushchev, apparently more readily than expected, did agree that a cease-fire should be the priority item, and that negotiations for an independent neutral Laos should proceed. For his part, the Premier would exert every influence over the Laotians to arrive at a settlement.

Kennedy would never know whether it was mainly the course of the Sino-Soviet conflict itself that led Khrushchev to cooperate to neutralize Laos, or whether it was the result of "getting the message" from Kennedy's intensified diplomatic campaign, and intelligence of military preparations and deployments.

The seventh fleet had been moved into the South China Sea. Helicopter-borne Marines had been alerted for deployment from Japan and Okinawa to Thailand, within quick assault range of the Laotian capital of Vientiane. Reporters wrote of intensive military planning in the Administration, and suggested the planners were contemplating a spectrum of commitment from military advisers to a major assault. Sorenson recalls that Kennedy viewed the "leak" of the military planning as an aid in communicating his intentions to the Communists.[18]

The military deployments and planning were not just for show. Kennedy considered the direct employment of United States military force as *undesirable,* yet possibly necessary. He was unwilling to deny himself bold coercive moves to keep the Soviets and Chinese out of Southeast Asia; but he was highly skeptical of those who recommended such bold moves under the simple assumption that this would scare our opponents off. Moreover, his examination of the contingency plans presented to him by his military advisers, in the context of our still understrength conventional capabilities, and the festering Berlin, Cuba, and Congo crises, made him responsive to General MacArthur's advice that anyone who wanted to commit United States ground forces to the Asian mainland should have his head examined.[19]

The President had had his fingers burned by his uncritical acceptance of self-serving evaluations by the military during the planning sessions for the Bay of Pigs, and was now merciless in puncturing the optimism of their Laos scenarios. Sorenson's account reveals the sharp edge of the President's questioning and his underlying assumption that military means ought to be viewed as last-resort options:

The Chiefs had talked of landing and supplying American combat forces through Laotian airports (inasmuch as the kingdom is landlocked). Questioning now disclosed that there were only two usable airstrips even in good weather, that Pathet Lao control of the nearby countryside could make initial landing difficult, and that a Communist bombing of these airstrips would leave us no alternative but to bomb Communist territory.

If we use nuclear bombs, the President asked, where would it stop, how many other Communist movements would we have to attack, what kind of world would it be? No one knew. If we didn't use nuclear weapons, he asked, would we have to retreat or surrender in the face of an all-out Chinese intervention? The answer was affirmative. If we put more forces in Laos, he asked the Chiefs, would that weaken our reserves for action in Berlin or elsewhere? The answer was again in the affirmative. If neither the royal nor the administrative capital cities fell, and the cease-fire squabble was merely over where the truce was to be signed, would these risks be worthwhile? No one was sure.

Once in, how and when to get out? he asked. Why cannot air and naval power suffice? Do we want an indefinite occupation of an unenthusiastic, dark-skinned population, tying up our forces and not those of the Communists? Is this our best bet for a confrontation with Red China—in the mountains and jungles of its landlocked neighbor? Would forces landing in Vietnam and Thailand end up defending those regimes also? [20]

Fortunately, the diplomatic campaign displaced the urgent military planning, for a while at least, in the aftermath of the Kennedy-Khrushchev meeting at Vienna. The Geneva negotiations, with Averell Harriman leading the United States delegation, took over a year—with infinite patience, and cajolery, exercised by both the Soviet Union and the United States in response to the maneuverings and tantrums of their respective Laotian counterparts. When the United States finally succeeded in bringing around the rightist Phoumi Nosavan (favored by the Eisenhower Administration) to accept a secondary position in a government headed by the neutralist Souvanna Phouma, the Pathet Lao, whose candidate Prince Souphanouvong was also supposed to accept a cabinet portfolio, reopened their military campaign. It was this open violation of the cease-fire that led Kennedy finally to move the Marines into Thailand, but this apparently only under the prodding of Harriman himself.[21] The Pathet Lao called off the new military push, as quickly as it had started, and negotiations resumed.

Finally, on June 12, 1962, Kennedy and Khrushchev simultaneously announced the good news each had received from Geneva that agreement on a coalition Laotian government had been reached. And the Declaration and Protocol on the Neutrality of Laos was solemnly signed on July 23 by the Geneva Conference participants, an impressive array of the aligned and unaligned: Burma, Cambodia, Canada, Communist China, North Vietnam, South Vietnam, France, India, Poland, Thailand, the Soviet Union, the United States, and the Kingdom of Laos itself.[22]

However, the mood of mutual congratulation swiftly turned again to one of mutual recrimination as the Laotian factions fought among themselves, and North Vietnam began to once again openly assist the Pathet Lao while using the corridor the latter controlled, the so-called "Ho Chi Minh Trail", for supplying the Viet Cong in South Vietnam.

The conflict and its resolution, however messy, did provide useful lessons and precedents for the Kennedy Administration, and hopefully for the Soviet Union as well. It demonstrated the paradoxical effect on the objectives of both occasioned by the almost unlimited destructive power at the disposal of each. The mere existence of such destructive potential could serve as a rationale, and indeed an honest motive, for one to refuse to intervene in third area conflicts against the will of the other, and also to provide the pretext for mutual military withdrawal. To this extent the coercive power of the superpowers could be viewed as a stabilizer—making it mutually advantageous for each not to challenge the vital interests of the other. Yet at the same time, it could lead smaller, and still nonaligned, actors on the international stage to defy the will of either superpower, knowing full well that intervention by the defied superpower was forestalled by the threat of counter-intervention by the other; or more unscrupulously, to bribe one superpower by hinting of alignment with the other. To this extent the mutual inhibition felt by the superpowers against intervention in third area conflicts might be destabilizing, in the sense of permitting local conflicts to reach an incendiary stage in preference to intervening.

Under Kennedy's leadership the Administration in Washington was at least cogizant of the uncertainties and did not demand answers or solutions, perceiving that such demand in the absence of a power to bring about solutions might be more dangerous than a groping adaptation to each situation as it arose. "We are taking a chance in all of southeast Asia," said Kennedy of his decision to support a shaky coalition government in Laos, "and we're taking a chance in other areas":

Nobody can make any predictions for the future, really, on any matter where there are powerful interests at stake. I think, however, we have to consider what our alternatives are, and what the prospects for war are if we fail in our present efforts. . . . So . . . there's no easy, sure answer for Laos. . . . And I can assure you that I recognize the risks that are involved. But I also think we should consider the risks if we fail, and particularly of the possibility of escalation of a military struggle in a place of danger.[23]

It was a similar willingness to confront uncertainty, and live with it, that governed Kennedy's reactions to the Congo upheaval during this same period.

For many who were uncomfortable with uncertainty, and the lack of visible solutions, the best attitude toward the Congo crisis was "let Dag do it." Let the Secretary General bear the responsibility and also the onus for what, from all accounts, was a hopeless situation. For Eisenhower the appropriate reactions to "the whole sorry mess" were "dismay and disgust." [24] The New Frontiersmen, however, seemed to regard the situation with all its Byzantine intrigue as a challenge to their own political agility.

The global balance of power considerations that governed the Eisenhower Administration's basic decision for the Congo in the summer of 1960 remained for the most part the premises underlying the Kennedy Administration's actions.

But so tangled had the situation in the Congo become, the United States seeming to support one Congolese faction one day, opposing it the next, the United Nations police action turning into a military operation against the attempt of the pro-Western Katanga province to become an independent African state, that many in the Congress wondered if the Administration had any conception left of where basic United States interests lay.

Secretary of State Rusk felt it necessary to set the record straight on why we supported the UN action in the first place.

He reminded the cognizant senate committee that Einsehower's support of a UN presence for the Congo was primarily a means of keeping the Soviets out. The Congolese army had mutinied during the first week of July 1960 immediately after the Congo became independent, whereupon Belgium announced the return of Belgian troops to protect the life and property of the Europeans still there. The Congolese government was outraged at the return of the Belgian military, and sought help from all quarters—the UN, the Soviet Union, and the United States.

The alternative to United Nations intervention, Rusk recalled, would have been violence, and chaos, and a ready-made opportunity for Soviet exploitation, which the United States would have been compelled to counter. Thus, "if a direct confrontation of the great powers in the heart of Africa was to be avoided," it was necessary to establish a UN presence. "Looking back, gentlemen, it seems obvious now that this was the right choice." [25]

The requirements of preventing a great power confrontation during the early phase of the Congo crisis had been complicated, but did not take any fundamental rethinking of our premises about the nature of the global balance of power. The Soviet Union was pouring personnel, materials, and political agents into the Congo, hoping to establish a foothold in the center of Africa. This was truly an extension of the Soviet presence into a new area, and if they did succeed in establishing a loyal regime in the Congo, they would emerge as the only great power capable of calling the tune for the many new nations south of the Sahara. The result would not be merely "a drop in the bucket," as Khrushchev phrased it, but a new imperial momentum for the Soviets, bringing them eventually to the Atlantic and putting them in command of the great, still unexploited wealth of the vast African continent.

The objective of the United States was simple, before Kennedy assumed the Presidency, and could be easily understood. We had to keep the Soviets out, but without getting in ourselves if at all possible. First, it was important to avoid a direct clash with the Soviets. Second, we wouldn't know what to do once in the Congo, anyway. We were unfamiliar with the intricacies of tribal relationships, and were not about to assume the obligations, politically and financially, for making the new Congo nation a showpiece of United States-sponsored development. All we wanted was a relatively stable authority in the Congo willing to and capable of resisting Sovet overlordship. The United Nations presence was a device to pre-empt the Soviet military assistance which, presumably, was requested by the Kasavubu-Lumumba government in Leopoldville solely for the purpose of giving it the wherewithal to restore order and restore the authority of the central Congolese government. Thus, we supported the unprecedented granting of supranational functions to the Secretariat of the UN—that is, the mandate to establish domestic order within a nation, to act as if it were the national authority in the Congo until an indigenous authority could establish its power and legitimacy over the area.

We did not find it too difficult to dispense with our formal legalistic position in favor of the sovereignty of nations and the inability of the United Nations to act on domestic matters, particularly to take sides in favor of certain contending political factions within a nation. The balance of power was at stake, and we knew where our interests lay.

In the early phase of the crisis, the source of the threat to the balance of power was also the source of the threat to the authority of the central government—or at least, this was our plausible definition of the meaning of the growing Soviet intervention. So the United States support of the UN police force and even the use of the United States Air Force for supplying materials to the UN operation and for flying in troops of the UN force was not a subject of major political controversy in the United States.

When Premier Lumumba objected to President Kasavubu's acceptance of the UN role, and the heavy indirect United States support, the nationalist Congo President dismissed his pro-Soviet Premier, who thereupon became the leader of an insurrection against the central government. Lumumba was captured and murdered, and Antoine Gizenga, his political heir, established himself in Stanleyville as the leader of the insurgency, hoping for major support from the Soviets. Then, in 1960, when the Soviets continued to supply the Gizenga elements with agents and materials, President Kasavubu closed the major airfields to all but United Nations traffic and ordered the Soviet and Czechoslovakian embassies to close.

The chaos once again seemed to have rapidly assumed an order of simplicity consistent with the balance of power premises that Eisenhower used to justify our support of the UN action, and most unfavorable to the Soviets' effort to capture an indigenous African nationalist regime through a low-cost, low-risk, policy of subversion. In order to establish their foothold, the Soviets would have to openly support an insurrection against the legitimate Congolese government, supported by UN forces with contingents from the nonaligned world operating under a mandate of the world organization.

The Soviets now turned their fire on Dag Hammarskjöld's management of the UN operation, and tried to create opportunities for Soviet vetoing of decisions within the Secretariat—the meaning of their notorious troika proposal. But they were clearly on the defensive, and swinging back wildly in their frustration.

During the fall of 1960 and spring of 1961 events in the Congo took a turn, largely self-generated, which denied the new Administration in Washington the luxury of neatly fitting the crisis into the Cold War context.

The troublemaker now was the clever ruler of Katanga Province, Moise Tshombe. Receiving major revenues from the Belgian-owned copper mines in Katanga, which made that province the wealthiest of any in the Congo, Tshombe saw the advantages of turning Katanga into a sovereign state, not having to disipate its wealth throughout the poorer sections of the former Belgian colony. Not surpririsingly, the Belgian copper interests, fearing the consequences of unstable—and possibly radical—rule from Leopoldville, encouraged Tshombe in his dreams of becoming a chief of state.

However, the UN operation and the viability of the Central Congolese Government would collapse if the legitimacy of Katanga's secession were granted. The Congo, after all, was only a potential nation; if each segment, whether because of tribal or economic reasons, was allowed the right to choose only how long and under what conditions it would remain a part of the Union, there would be no Union. Hammarskjöld appreciated this, and certainly, remembering our own Civil War, the United States should have appreciated this. But there was a contrary ideology in the American ethos—self-determination. This unresolved contradiction was exploited by Tshombe and his Belgian supported propagandists in the United States, so that the Kennedy Administration was placed on the defensive in justifying its continued support of UN operations as they began to be directed primarily against the professedly anti-Communist Tshombe. Moreover, the Communist agents still active in the Congo were now most vocal in promoting the use of force against Tshombe to keep Katanga a part of the Union. Hammarskjöld (soon to die in a plane crash in Africa and to be succeeded by U Thant) and Kennedy were caught in a bind, cynically exploited by Tshombe and his European supporters on one side and the Communists on the other.

They knew that the United States was unwilling to intervene in the Congo, but also that it was reluctant to have the UN assume the management of a full-fledged combat operation against Katanga. To have the UN assume this role in such inauspicious circumstances would probably dash forever the hopes of gradually building up its peace-keeping functions through consensus of its member nations, and would probably make it more likely that other nations would support the Soviet scheme for injecting the veto into all major administrative functions of the world organization.

On the other hand, if the United Nations was unable to keep Tshombe in the Congolese union, that effort—the mobilization of African forces for an attack upon Tshombe—might fall by default to the Soviet-backed Gizenga. The Cold War polarization of the Congo crisis would be resumed, but this time with the emotional issues unfavorable to the anti-Communists.

It was Kennedy's sensitivity to the emotional issues involved—which was a part of his orientation to the whole question of "power" in international relations—that led him to reject the counsel of United States neutrality on the Katanga issue. We had to side with the Congolese nationalists, supported as they were on this issue by the extremists, against the Katanga secession, or else the Soviets would be able to pose as the sole champions of the nationalists. As the UN operation was allowed to cross into that hazy area where the distinction between pacification and offensive combat operations breaks down, criticism mounted in the Congress and in Europe. Still Kennedy stood firm in his support of Hammarskjöld, and then U Thant. How far Kennedy was actually willing to go, being committed to the restoration of a unified Congo, no one knew. Schlesinger reports that during the summer of 1962 our ambassador to the Congo, Edmund Gillion (whose advice had been closely followed by the President) was suggesting that UN troops ought to be given the go-ahead to smash Tshombe's army. But in the White House, Carl Kaysen and Ralph Dungan were against a deeper American involvement, which would have been required, at least for logistic support, if major combat ensued.[26] Kennedy, naturally, was up to his strategem of turning the coercive screws while fashioning tempting inducements. But this time, in Moise Tshombe, he was dealing with a man who saw that time was on his side, and also a man who seemed to take a perverse delight in the amount of international mischief he was capable of causing. Tshombe would enter into "negotiations" with United States, British, Belgian, and UN diplomats, and then either break the "negotiations" off, or agree with broad smiles and proceeded to stall. He was apparently bargaining for major concessions from the government in Leopoldville as the price for his return.

By December 1962 the UN, backed by the United States, was reaching the point where its inability to compel Katanga's reintegration was severely undermining the United Nations authority, and pressures by the radical Africans for taking matters into their own hands was increasingly difficult to contain. U Thant was now asking for additional United States transport planes and equipment. Within the State Department he had supporters who were urging that we persuade the Secretary General to accept a squadron of United States fighter aircraft, to be flown by our Air Force, in support of a swift assault by UN forces against Tshombe's strongholds. The President, reports Sorenson, ruled against an immediate move of this sort, pending a survey by a military mission on the combat requirements for an effective defeat of Tshombe's forces. But he did approve U Thant's original request for additional logistics equipment.[27]

A few days before the new year, as a result of confused orders from UN headquarters, attributed by some to a communications foul-up, UN forces in the Congo, evidently provoked by some belligerent action by Katanga, took the offensive, sweeping into a central Katangese stronghold at Jadetville, and breaking the back of Tshombe's military resistance. The sophisticated Tshombe, gracefully bowed to reality, and emerged a few months later as Prime Minister of the unified Congo—an outcome that must have put Kennedy's teeth on edge, with all his appreciation of historical irony. After all, Tshombe could have been the pretext for a major Communist insurgency campaign in the heart of Africa; and now, it seemed that he might only have been playing for little more than personal glory.

Yet somehow, the outcome, like that in Laos, was tolerable. Had we demanded of ourselves that we have more control and certainty over the outcome we might either have washed our hands of the situation earlier, giving other parties a chance to exploit a collapsing UN effort, or we might have intervened prematurely and then have been held responsible for the chaos which still exists.

These efforts to gain tacit Soviet cooperation in a policy of mutual nonintervention in the Third World were made in an experimental spirit. The President was aware of the major risk that a perception by other nations that the superpowers were afraid of becoming embroiled against one another might contribute to the belligerency of the smaller powers: expansionist nations like China and Indonesia, divided nations like Vietnam and Korea, nations with historic animosities, such as India and Pakistan, or the Arab countries and Israel.

Whether the pressure exerted by the superpowers against the "escalation" of local conflicts would win out against the propensity of the lesser powers to take matters into their own hands promised to be the big uncertainty of the coming decade.

CHAPTER SIXTEEN

BERLIN AND CUBAN MISSILES:
DEFINING SPHERE OF CONTROL

. . . this secret, swift, and extraordinary buildup of Communist missiles —in an area well known to have a special and historic relationship to the United States and the nations of the Western Hemisphere . . . is a deliberately provocative and unjustified change in the status quo which cannot be accepted by this country if our courage and our commitments are ever to be trusted again by either friend or foe.

JOHN F. KENNEDY

It was over Berlin and the missiles in Cuba that President Kennedy displayed most clearly his appreciation of the central function played by military power as an arbiter of conflicting goals and wills in international relations. These two crises were also indicators of the gap existing between the reality of a two-sided organization of effective power in the international system and the hope for a pluralistic world based on self-determination. Berlin and Cuba compelled Kennedy, at least temporarily, to renew the bipolar concept as indeed the safer basis for coping with the fierce conflicts in a world armed with nuclear power and without a central system of law and order. He could still hope that on the basis of such a bipolar balance of power, sustained by each superpower's fear of the other's military prowess, a more peaceful phase of competition between the Communists and non-Communists could begin. A period of peaceful competition, based initially on well-defined and mutually respected spheres of control, might *eventually* lead to a depreciation of military power as the currency behind most international transactions, and to a less rigid international order.

The bipolar concept was Achesonian. And it was thus not surprising that Truman's Secretary of State was charged by Kennedy with developing the major position paper on Berlin and Germany for the Administration to consider. But the bipolar concept was sufficiently imprecise to allow for variable applications, depending upon the reading of the dominant forces at work in immediate situations.

On the one side were the true-blue Achesonians who saw the renewed Soviet pressures on Berlin as a constant and central pillar of Soviet diplomacy. In 1961, Khrushchev was once again trying to strong-arm us out of that militarily exposed city, 110 miles inside Communist-controlled East Germany. As a symbol of the potential revival of Germany as a complete and independent nation, Berlin's absorption by the East German Communist regime would demoralize the non-Communists of West Germany, and incline frustrated German nationalists toward "neutralization" and renunciation of the North Atlantic Treaty as the only remaining way to buy reunification and some degree of independence from the Soviets.

All Soviet moves—whether invitations to summit meetings or harassments on the Autobahn—were read by the Achesonians as part and parcel of this basic Soviet offensive strategy. Soviet objectives were nothing less than the removal of the United States from the European power balance, leading to a Soviet takeover of all Europe and global dominance as a result. The current status of Western forces and administrative arrangements in the city of Berlin and along the transportation corridors connecting it with West Germany were the hard-won results of the Truman Administration's policy of refusing to knuckle under to this Soviet offensive strategy. Existing military deployments and detailed bureaucratic procedures were part of this legacy, designed to show, unequivocally, that there could be no alteration of the status of Berlin apart from a final settlement of the future of Germany by the victor powers of the Second World War. There was nothing to negotiate about Berlin unless the Soviets really wanted to negotiate their own withdrawal from East Germany (the Achesonian presumption was that they did not). More important, any attempt by the Soviets to unilaterally alter the status of Berlin arrangements, no matter how tiny each single alteration might appear, had to be resisted. The Soviets would be tempted to take those small steps if we only accepted their definition of such incidents as "local," since the applicable coercive pressure around Berlin would always favor the Communists. It was necessary, therefore, for the United States to expand and generalize each local incident into a symbol of the entire bipolar conflict, known as the Cold War. This was the Western strategy that had worked in the past. There was no reason to believe that anything different was required in 1961. If the Eisenhower Administration had hinted to the Soviets that a changed status for Berlin was possible, it was up to the Kennedy Administration to revive the original Truman policy of standing firm, and making every inch of ground holy.

On the other side, with the Kennedy Administration and among influential Democrats in Congress, were those who regarded the Soviets as essentially defensive in their posture on Germany and Berlin. Whatever may have been the thrust of Soviet ambitions in the immediate postwar period, by now, it was postulated, the Soviets were anxious mainly to hold on to their control over Eastern Europe, so as to prevent it ever again being an invasion path for a revived and revengeful Germany. Our grand strategy, therefore, should be one of reassurance to the Soviets that any European settlement we would subscribe to would provide such guarantees against a renewal of the German *Drang nach Osten*. It was in our interest to involve the Soviets in discussions over the future of Germany and Europe, for it was *we* who were dissatisfied with the status quo. Until we made substantial progress toward a general European settlement, Berlin would continue to be an explosive issue between us. At the outset, we ought to give the Soviets the benefit of the doubt. They might be genuinely afraid that we were using Berlin as an outpost for subverting their control over East Germany, particularly, and Eastern Europe generally. We were of course right in refusing to turn over control of the entire city to the East Germans, since it would then be used by the Communists to bring daily humiliation upon the non-Communist West Berliners, and eventually to drive them out of the city altogether, dashing West German hopes for an eventual reunification of Germany under a non-Communist regime. But Berlin itself should not be the fighting issue. That was to play the Soviets' game. European security was the real issue. And European security was a potentially soluble problem susceptible of negotiation—negotiation to provide mutually acceptable guarantees against aggression and against local armaments imbalances. Tension over Berlin should not be allowed to obscure the real issue or deflect the powers from working toward a general settlement. Therefore, anything that could be done to "defuse" Berlin, without compromisng *essential* Western rights of access, should be pursued. To respond in kind to every Soviet provocation in and around Berlin was, to this school of thought, counterproductive.

Kennedy's position, as revealed by his statements and behavior in response to Soviet demands and provocations, turned out to be more agnostic than that of either the hardliners or the defusers with respect to premises about the underlying Soviet motives. But he was probably more keenly sensitive than either to the great instability of the bipolar balance of terror at its most immediate point of direct contact in Berlin. If he was wrong, in either encouraging the Soviets too much or provoking them too much, he might be wrong for ever. It was easy for advisers to advise; but he bore the responsibility for action taken. Consequently, his steps were smaller, and more tentative than many in his entourage might have liked.

Critics charge the Kennedy Administration with ambivalence and inconsistency on the Berlin issue. Defenders invoke the same record to demonstrate the virutes of pragmatism. The sequence of decisions does display an erratic pattern.

United States official statements on Berlin early in 1961 were few and far between, but conveyed a stiffer posture on Berlin and Germany than had been displayed by the Eisenhower Administration during the last round of negotiations in 1959 (See above, p. 154). In the city, on March 8, 1961, Averell Harriman, the President's roving ambassador, explicitly disassociated the new Administration from the Eisenhower Administration's concessionary proposals of 1959. "All discussions on Berlin," he said, "must begin from the start." [1] At the same time Kennedy, through Ambassador Llewellyn Thompson, had sent a personal note to Premier Khrushchev suggesting a meeting between the two leaders to clear the air. The meeting was not to be for purposes of negotiation, but rather for each side to better understand the other's basic commitments so as to remove any chance of miscalculations that might lead to war.

The final Acheson report on Berlin was not yet in when Kennedy and Khrushchev met in Vienna in June. There had been no great urgency for a full-dress Berlin policy review since the Soviets had refrained from heating up the issue. As it turned out, the Soviet Premier was very tough on Berlin during their meeting, using language close to the tone of an ultimatum: a peace treaty recognizing East German jurisdiction over access to Berlin would be signed in December and wartime occupation rights would be ended. If the West tried to violate the sovereign rights of the Ulbricht regime, force would be met with force. It was up to the United States to choose whether there would be war or peace.[2] And at the close of their talks, Kennedy was handed an official Soviet *aide-mémoire*, somewhat less belligerent in tone, but clearly heralding a resumption of the Berlin conflict.

The Soviet *aide-mémoire* called for the immediate convening of a peace conference to "formally recognize the situation which has developed in Europe after the war, to legalize and consolidate the inviolability of existing German borders [and], to normalize the situation in West Berlin." In the interests of achieving agreement rapidly, said the Soviets, it would not be necessary to tie the conclusion of a peace treaty to the formal recognition of the German Democratic Republic or the Federal Republic of Germany by all parties to the treaty. If the United States was not prepared to sign a joint peace treaty with the two Germanies, a peaceful settlement could be achieved on the basis of two separate treaties. But the peace treaty, or treaties, as the case might be, would have to contain the same kind of provisions on the most important points of a peaceful settlement.

The most important points to be settled, the Soviets made clear, involved the status of West Berlin. At present, said their *aide-mémoire*, "the Soviet Government does not see a better way to solve the West Berlin problem than by transforming it into a demilitarized free city." This "free city" of West Berlin (East Berlin was by implication to remain under the complete control of the GDR) would have:

. . . unobstructed contacts with the outside world and . . . its internal regulations should be determined by the freely expressed will of its population. . . . Token troop contingents of the United States, the United Kingdom, France, and the U.S.S.R. could be stationed in West Berlin as guarantees of the free city.

This, of course, would mean "putting an end to the occupation regime in West Berlin, with all its implications": namely, the peace treaty or treaties which provided for the new status of West Berlin would establish clearly that any questions relating to the use of "communication by land, water or air within the territory of the G.D.R. would have to be settled solely by appropriate agreements with the G.D.R." [3]

The Soviets were proposing, in short, an agreement to legitimize the division of Germany, with East Berlin to be under the complete authority of the Ulbricht regime and West Berlin to become an international city. The Soviets and their allies would be given as much control over the administration of West Berlin as the United States and its allies. Moreover, access to this new international city—located within East Germany—would be controlled by the East German government. Clearly, for the West to make such an agreement would have been to capitulate to the essence of the demands Khrushchev had been making with respect to Germany since 1958.

Why was Khrushchev renewing these demands with such vigor and confidence now? This question bothered President Kennedy and his associates in their post-mortems on the Vienna conference. Did the Soviets feel emboldened by perceptions that the strategic nuclear balance finally was such as to make Communist local military superiority in Central Europe the only relevant factor of power behind the diplomatic bargaining? Had our backing out of the Bay of Pigs adventure and backing away from a superpower showdown over Laos given Khrushchev the impression that with Kennedy the United States would be the first to swerve off the collision course.

The President, in his oral exchanges with the Soviet Premier at Vienna, seems to have sensed that Khrushchev might be capable of underestimating the Kennedy resolve and nerve under pressure. Kennedy was careful to choose the words and demeanor to disabuse him of such notions. Sorenson and Schlesinger both recount Kennedy's response to Khrushchev's final insistence that the decision to change the occupation status of West Berlin by December was irrevocable, whether the United States agreed or not. If that was the case, retorted the President, "it will be a cold winter."

It was also very important that the new Soviet demands, which were broadcast to all the world, were responded to publicly. If the Soviets were committing themselves before the public to move against our will,

247

we must commit ourselves before that same public not to let them get away with it.

Indeed, the Achesonians, in the President's advisory entourage tended to define the issue almost exclusively in terms of a dramatic public test of wills. Our position in Berlin embodied not only our will to prevent any further extension of Communist control, but also our will to ultimately undo the coercive subjugation of peoples in Eastern Europe. Furthermore, if we even sugggested that our position in Berlin was amenable to compromise when the Soviets began to tighten the screws, we were suggesting that the only price the Soviets had to pay for our giving up something of our position was for them to loosen the pressure. We had to be concerned with the effect of such a message on Soviet and Chinese tactics in future conflicts. We also had to be immediately concerned with the effect of such a message upon the people of West Berlin and upon the German government, who had accepted a secure tie to the Western alliance in NATO as the means by which the unity of Germany could eventually be negotiated—from strength. To be committed to the status quo, unequivocably committed in the immediate crisis, was not to be committed to a static and essentially defensive position in Europe, Acheson would argue. Rather it was the minimal basis from which a more dynamic negotiating position could be launched. But first things first.

Acheson's policy advice for the immediate crisis was straightforward: reject the Soviet proposals, reject negotiations, and prepare for the worst, which could mean a military showdown to enforce our right to access to Berlin.

For the latter contingency, Acheson dusted off the favorite ploy of General Lucius Clay (which the National Security Council rejected during the 1948–49 blockade, but accepted in case of trouble after Khrushchev's 1958 ultimatum): dispatch a military combat unit up the Autobahn from the East-West German border toward Berlin. The purpose was to force the Communists to physically interpose their own military forces against ours in order to prevent ours from exercising their right of access to the city. We would keep marching. If the Communist forces did not give way, the battle would start. War would have begun with all its propensities for physical and emotional expansion to the point where it engulfs the societies of the participants.

Of course, the premise behind the ploy was that the Communists would back down short of the actual physical exchange. This was based on the more fundamental premise that the United States had a greater immediate interest to preserve Western access to Berlin than the Soviets had to prevent Western access. Put another way, for the Soviets to deny us access would be to have forced a dramatic change in the status quo. For us to have continued to exercise access would mean only that the Soviets had failed, as yet, to convince us of the need to change existing arrangements. If the Soviets backed away from the confrontation, they could do so under the cloak of rationality in the face of our irrationality. If we backed down, we would be demonstrating that our commitments were less absolute than we had been claiming. The reputation for being absolute, even somewhat irrational, was an important facet of our power, particularly in Europe. The Soviets must know this. They must know that we considered we had much to lose in Berlin, and thus our bravery could not be dismissed as a mere bluff.

Yet all of this was based on a series of surmises about Soviet motives and about Soviet assessments of our motives. If any one of these was wrong, it would mean war. And a war in Germany, if we were not to lose it, would require us to turn rather quickly to a strategic nuclear war. Acheson had to admit that this was so. The implication of this realization for him and others of his persuasion, however, was not the abandonment of contingency plans that might possibly lead to holocaust in favor of alternatives likely to lead to humiliation. Rather it was to argue with more force for the provision of military capabilities that would somewhat rectify the local imbalance in Europe, so that the refusal to surrender to Soviet demands would not require that we step immediately with the Soviets onto an escalator to suicide, with no exit.

Kennedy was to accept the logic of additional military steps—namely, a significant conventional capability—for any military engagement on the central front in Europe. This was in accord with the general strategic recommendations he had presented to the Congress in March. But it was uncongenial to the President's style of dealing with a problem to reduce the Berlin crisis to the Achesonian matrix: successful test of wills, or military engagement. He refused to accept, without further study, the notion that there could not be Western initiatives designed to avoid a test of wills without in the process compromising basic Western interests.

Our expectation of a test of wills was, after all, based on the assumption that the Soviets were in fact going to act unilaterally as threatened in their *aide-mémoire*. Yet they had threatened and then not acted in the past. The search should be for a means of deflecting the Soviets from the one-track course they had outlined. Those who knew the Soviet Union best, as for example Llewellyn Thompson and Averell Harriman, were not at all sure that the Soviets were anxious to follow that course. The status quo in Berlin might be truly hurting them, as suggested by the increasing flow of refugees into the Western sectors; they might feel a change was necessary. Possibly we could cater to their need to demonstrate some movement on the issue without thereby having to accept their terms of negotiation.

The President's instincts were to open up the Berlin issue to a wider set of alternatives, and for the United States, for a change, to set the terms of reference, rather than always reacting negatively to Soviet proposals. But he was unwilling to enter into negotiations with only the increasingly unbelievable "trip wire" military posture in Western Europe to back him up. Accordingly, he put his political advisers, including Acheson, to work on developing an expanded list of political options while he put the Defense Department to work on increasing his military options.

As it turned out, his advisers found it easier to be creative when proposing military measures than when proposing political approaches. The State Department, designed more to implement and reiterate established policy premises rather than to generate new ones, responded characteristically: it took exasperatingly long to reply, but came up eventually with a remarkably thorough statement of our position on Berlin, which turned out to be little more than a marginally updated amalgam of positions developed in the 1950s. Acheson had more of substance to propose, but it was, again, designed primarily for strengthening our hand in preserving the status quo, rather than changing the status quo. Backed by Vice-President Johnson, Acheson urged a Presidential proclamation of national emergency. This could be accompanied by an immediate expansion of military manpower, including the calling up of reserves, a $5 billion increase in the defense budget, plus new taxation and stand-by controls on wages and prices. To openly prepare our people for the worst and visibly begin to make our economy ready for war would demonstrate to Khrushchev, more starkly than any manipulation of our military capabilities in the vicinity of Berlin, that the current Soviet threats were merely stimulating us to enhance our commitments and to more thoroughly involve the national honor in those commitments.

Acheson's national emergency package was opposed by powerful voices within the Administration. Walter Heller and the Council of Economic Advisers were strongly against a tax increase at that time, and argued that there was a real danger of serious inflation resulting from the scare buying that would accompany the proclamation of emergency. Heads of the domestic departments were wary of the effects on the civilian welfare programs. And McNamara, Rusk, and even reputedly "tough" White House advisers like Henry Kissinger, warned against unnecessarily bellicose reactions by the United States, which, rather than indicating unflinching resolve might convey hysteria. Others on the White House staff were concerned that we not over-emphasize the Berlin confrontation by devices like the proclamation, and thereby induce Khrushchev, for considerations of his own prestige, to respond in kind with arms increases and menacing postures in preparation for a showdown.

Kennedy rejected the suggestion for an immediate declaration of national emergency, but incorporated some of the major premises underlying the Acheson proposals into his own planning. He knew that words were not enough to dissuade the Soviets from an easy Berlin *fait accompli*. It was diplomatically unsound to enter into negotiations, with the Soviets assuming we were afraid of and unprepared to handle such a contingency. It was agreed that the military increase which the President had already ordered as a part of his general program for remedying the nation's military deficiencies should perhaps be accelerated under the impetus of the Berlin crisis to convince Khrushchev that his bluster could lead only to the firming up of our backbone. Nor did the President unequivocally reject the more extreme suggestions of a large-scale mobilization and a declaration of national emergency. These might yet have to be used; but they should not be used up so early in a crisis. Our grand strategy should be the classical one of arming to parley; we *wanted* the parley, and we wanted it to take place in an atmosphere conducive to calm deliberation on terribly complicated conflicts of interest. Showdowns could only revive the simplifications of the Cold War, and possibly lead to hot war.

The President's television address on July 25 was designed to be both very tough and more reasonable than previous United States statements on the Berlin issue. We would not be pushed around, and were ready to resist with force, if need be, any unilaterally imposed changes in the status quo. But the status quo was not our objective.

Our presence in West Berlin, and access thereto, cannot be ended by any act of the Soviet government, the President told the world. It would be a mistake to consider Berlin, because of its location, as a tempting target: "I hear it said that West Berlin is militarily untenable. And so was Bastogne. And so, in fact, was Stalingrad. Any dangerous spot is tenable if men—brave men—will make it so." The city had become "the greatest testing place of Western courage and will, a focal point where our solemn commitments . . . and Soviet ambitions now meet in basic confrontation." Berlin was no less protected than the rest of us, "for we cannot separate its safety from our own."

He warned the Soviets not to make the dangerous mistake, that others had made, of assuming that the West was too soft, and too divided in the pursuit of narrow national interests, to fight to preserve its objectives in Berlin. Too much was at stake for the Alliance as a whole: "For the fulfillment of our pledge to that city is essential to the morale and security of Western Germany, to the unity of Western Europe, and the faith of the entire Free World . . . in . . . our willingness to meet our commitments. . . ."

Accordingly, in addition to the supplementary defense buildup the President had asked the Congress to approve in March, he was now asking for an additional $3.25 billion appropriation—most of which would be spent on making certain that we have the capability in being to deploy rapidly to the Central European front without lessening our ability to meet our commitments elsewhere. These additional measures included a trippling of the draft calls for the coming months, ordering to duty certain reserve and National Guard units, reactivating many deactivated planes and ships, and a major acceleration in the procurements of non-nuclear weapons.

It was unwise to call up or send abroad excessive numbers of troops, explained the President. But he wanted to make it clear that "while we will not let panic shape our policy," he was contemplating still more dramatic steps if the situation required them:

. . . in the days and months ahead, I shall not hesitate to ask the Congress for additional measures, or exercise any of the executive powers that I possess to meet this threat to peace. . . . and if that should require more men, or more taxes, or more controls, or other new powers, I shall not hesitate to ask them.

In that message, however, he did request one additional item, separated from the others in his text, and related more to the overall general preparedness of the nation rather than to the Berlin crisis. Yet it was this item—his request for a special appropriation of $207 million for a new start on a Civil Defense shelter program—that came close to creating that national atmosphere of "panic" and overreaction likely to interfere with his efforts to direct attention in this country and the Soviet Union to political alternatives and away from military posturing.

Most of what followed this section in the President's July 25 address was anticlimactic—reversing the emphasis he had intended. The press played up the military measures, including the Civil Defense program, but gave comparatively scant attention to his offer to consider any arrangement or treaty in Germany consistent with the maintenance of peace and freedom, and the legitimate security interests of all nations." The very carefully worded elaboration of this offer was all but ignored in United States new summaries:

We recognize the Soviet Union's historical concern about their security in Central and Eastern Europe, after a series of ravaging invasions, and we believe arrangements can be worked out which will help to meet these concerns, and make it possible for both security and freedom to exist in this troubled area.

He had said that we were "ready to search for peace—in quiet exploratory talks—in formal or informal meetings," but the noisier measures got the headlines in the United States.[4] And it was these that dominated Khrushchev's reaction to the President's speech.

Khrushchev, at the time, was discussing disarmament issues with John J. McCloy. He told McCloy in emotional tones that he was angered by the President's speech, and professed to find in it only an ultimatum akin to a preliminary declaration of war.

By this time, however, the refugee flow from East Berlin to West Berlin was seriously damaging Soviet prestige, and the productive manpower resources of East Gemany. Khrushchev may have welcomed an atmosphere of imminent explosion as the context for his sealing of the boundary between East and West Berlin just three weeks after the Kennedy address.

On August 7, the Soviet Premier delivered one of the most belligerent speeches of his career linking "military hysteria" in the United States with an "orgy of revanchist passions" in West Germany, and warning the West against any intervention under the illusion that there could be anything like a limited war over Berlin. Khrushchev was bestowing honors on Cosmonaut Titov for his space feat, and used the occasion to make pointed allusions to the strategic power of the Soviet Union. "Any state used as a springboard for an attack upon the Socialist camp will experience the full devastating power of our blow." The territory of the United States would be crushed. Intervention, an act of war by the West, would be a suicidal act, spelling "death to millions upon millions of people." [5]

When the East Berlin sealing action was begun six days later, the specter of a thermonuclear holocaust had already been projected as its backdrop. The next move was up to the United States. We could regard it, as the Soviets were claiming, as a stabilizing device to bottle up the combustible passions on both sides of the boundary to within controllable confines. Or we could define it as a unilateral abrogation of established four-power responsibility for the city as a whole, and besides that a shameless denial of free choice to the Berliners, thus fitting into that category of action which the President insisted we would be forced to resist. Khrushchev was gambling on the vividness of the nuclear backdrop as the main barrier to Western action. But it was not such a terribly dangerous gamble for him, since the "wall" at first consisted of double strands of barbed wire and other light barricades, backed up by elements of a motorized division of the East German army at critical crossing points. Western counteraction, if it was to be physical, could have been in the form of a symbolic cutting of the wire, or pushing over of some obstacles. It need not have involved anything as dramatic as a bulldozing operation with tanks and cannon; and the next move would have been up to the Soviets. Khrushchev still had many options. His gamble, of course, was that *we* would not "overreact."

But he did more than simply gamble. The Soviets launched a well-planned diplomatic campaign, calculated to provide the Western nations with a convincing political excuse for doing nothing. On August 13, the Warsaw Pact countries issued a declaration against "subversive activities directed from West Berlin" against the "socialist countries." The Pact members accordingly were requesting the East Germans:

. . . to establish an order on the borders of West Berlin which will securely block the way to the subversive activity . . . so that reliable safeguards and effective control can be established around the whole territory of West Berlin, including its border with democratic Berlin.

And then, in a deft attempt at limiting the issue: "It goes without saying that these measures must not affect existing provisions for traffic control on communications routes between West Berlin and West Germany." [6]

The Ulbricht regime in its implementing decree, issued on the same day, emphasized the point again: "As regards the traveling of West Berlin citizens abroad along the communications lines in the German Democratic Republic, former decisions remain valid." And the decree stated explicitly that no former decisions on transit along these routes were being revised.

On the afternoon of August 13, the United States Secretary of State, after checking with the President at Hyannis Port, issued a statement which, however caustic, signaled that the United States got the message:

Having denied the collective right of self-determination to the peoples of East Germany, Communist authorities are now denying the right of individuals to elect a world of free choice rather than a world of coercion. The pretense that communism desires only peaceful competition is exposed: the refugees . . . have "voted with their feet" on whether communism is the wave of the future.

Available information indicates that *measures taken thus far are aimed at residents of East Berlin and East Germany and not at the Allied position in West Berlin or access thereto.* (Emphasis added.) [7]

Rusk did claim that restrictions on travel between East Germany and Berlin were in direct contravention of the 1949 four-power agreements (signed at the conclusion of the Berlin blockade) and indicated that the appropriate diplomatic protests would be forthcoming. But there was not even a hint that the unilateral imposition of barriers across the city might constitute a fighting issue.

Many in the West were shocked and outraged at the Communist action. The West Berlin leaders who had foreseen the wall in the writing, as it were, felt themselves helpless and suddenly demoralized. Even Chancellor Adenauer at first maintained silence.

Kennedy sought advice from advisers at home and abroad, and found a solid consensus that there was not much we could do apart from issuing verbal protests. Sorenson recounts that "not one responsibile official in this country, in West Berlin, West Germany, or Western Europe— suggested that allied forces should march into East German territory and tear the Wall down." [8] The Mayor of Berlin, Willy Brandt, in a personal letter to President Kennedy, demanded actions of a retaliatory nature, such as a selective ban on imports from East Germany, a refusal to issue travel permits to East German officials wishing to travel to the West, and the taking over of the portion of the elevated railroad system in West Berlin that was still administered by the East. He also called for special actions to demonstrate renewed support by the United States for the West Berliners, many of whom felt that the West's failure to prevent the erection of the wall mean that the balance had been tipped in the Soviets' favor, and it was only a matter of time before the noose would be tightened around the entire city. Among the symbolic actions suggested by Brandt, four were adopted by the White House during the next few days:

a reinforcement of the Allied garrison in West Berlin;

the appointment of General Lucius Clay as the American Commandant;

a movement of allied troops along the Autobahn into West Berlin to demonstrate the continuing rights of Western access;

the dispatch of a high level member of the United States Cabinet to the city (Vice-President Johnson was Kennedy's choice).

The wall remained, and was reinforced with bricks and mortar. There were a number of incidents involving brutal treatment of refugees trying to escape, and a number of dangerous incidents, such as a confrontation of Soviet and American tanks across the barriers, and other rather daring demonstrations of resolve by General Clay.[9] West Berlin remained Western. And the allies continued to exercise their rights of access to the city while refusing to grant recognition to the East German regime. December 1961 came and went and the Soviets refrained from carrying out the unilateral actions threatened in their July *aide-mémoire*.

The situation seemed to be settling down to an uneasy, but basically stable equilibrium, based on what now could be tacitly recognized as more clearly defined spheres of effective control. Meanwhile, the "search for peace—in quiet exploratory talks" that Kennedy had called for in his July address had got underway in the form of periodic meetings between Secretary Rusk and Soviet Foreign Minister Gromyko, and the Soviet and American ambassadors.

In the spring of 1962, a "crisis" of sorts developed, but between the West Germans and the Americans, not between the superpowers, as a result of the United States carrying its "explorations" with the Soviets into considerations of how to design an international authority for controlling access to West Berlin. The Federal Republic leaked details to the press of a supposedly secret Western negotiating position, which had the effect, probably intended by Bonn, of making impossible for the time being any effective bargaining with the Soviets over this kind of arrangement.

Kennedy was willing to live with the situation as it stood, coming around to the realization that a major global settlement was probably the necessary correlate of significant "movement" on the German question. As he put it to President Kekkonen of Finland, "Let the Soviet Union keep Germany divided on its present basis and not try to persuade us to associate ourselves legally with that division and thus weaken our ties to West Germany and their ties to Western Europe." [10] And in his famous interview with Aleksei Adzhubei (editor of *Izvestia*, and Khrushchev's son-in-law) Kennedy was careful to distinguish our basic long-term objective of a reunification of Germany through free elections from our immediate intense commitment to the maintenance of Western rights in Berlin. "Now we recognize that today the Soviet Union does not intend to permit reunification," explained the President, "and that as long as the Soviet Union has that policy, Germany will not be reunified." Furthermore, "we recognize that the Soviet Union can sign any treaty it wishes with the East German Authorities." What we objected to—what was dangerous—was a treaty that attempted to transfer responsibility to the East Germans for controlling access from West Germany to West Berlin. "The problem now," said the President, "is to make sure that, in any treaty which the

Soviet Union reaches with East Germany, the rights of the other powers are recognized in Berlin. That's all we're talking about." [11]

Berlin and the other diplomatic crises of Kennedy's first year could be viewed as tests of the ground rules for coexistence that the President had propounded to Khrushchev during their conversations in Vienna: no action by either superpower to alter the existing balance of power and no attempt by either to interfere within the other's sphere of control. At Vienna there was what looked like mutual assent to these ground rules in principle, but considerable difference over how they might apply in practice. There was no objective definition of the balance of power, nor could the President and the Chairman assent unequivocally to the other's definition of *legitimate* spheres of control. The Soviet Union and the United States still differed importantly over ideology and objectives. The Berlin conflict was the product of these differences, not its cause. Neither side could agree simply to a maintenance of the "status quo." Moreover, with so many new nations experimenting with various types of regimes and still determining their interests and inclinations internationally, there was no such thing as even a de facto status quo in the Third World. Consequently there would be a series of tests in a volatile environment to determine who had effective power over what, and where in fact, at any point in time, the spheres of control lay.

The biggest test during Kennedy's Presidency was to occur once again in the Caribbean, within the sphere of effective control of the United States, but now, according to the Soviets, part of the environment of dynamic change. From the Soviet point of view, there was no reason, in principle, why a Communist regime, aligned with the Soviet Union, should be regarded as an illegitimate penetration into our sphere of control. Khrushchev could easily interpret Kennedy's inhibitions at the time of the Bay of Pigs as the product of a realistic appraisal by the President that acceptable "spheres" have ideological more than geographic dimensions.

Kennedy, of course, was unworried about a Communist Cuba from a strictly geopolitical point of view. His objection to a Communist Cuba was ideological; it was on the grounds that Castro did not rule according to the voluntary consent of the governed that Kennedy regarded his regime as illegitimate. Kennedy's reluctance to apply United States military power to topple Castro was due to pragmatism, not cynicism. He was unwilling to make Castro a martyr to the Cuban people and to the rest of Latin America by sending in the Marines; the more effective method was to allow Castro to fashion his own noose, which would eventually be tightened by the Latins themselves.

What finally moved Kennedy to coercive action during the second Cuban crisis was the balance of power consideration. Khrushchev surely must have known that the President would be compelled to take countermeasures if it was clear that the global balance of power was being threatened. But this is probably why Khrushchev tried to confuse the issue, and, as a hedge, to keep his missile deployments to Cuba clandestine.[12] As it turned out, Kennedy had a clearer notion of the intangible *political* components of the balance of power than Khrushchev anticipated. In a retrospective reflection on the event, Kennedy characterized the Soviet missile deployment as:

. . . an effort to materially change the balance of power . . . not that they were intending to fire them, because if they were going to get into a nuclear struggle, they have their own missiles in the Soviet Union. But it would have politically changed the balance of power. It would have appeared to, and appearances contribute to reality.[13]

It was of course significant that Khrushchev must have thought the President would be constrained from taking counteraction once the missiles became operational, and this continued to bother Kennedy:

What is of concern is the fact that both governments were so far out of contact, really. I don't think that we expected that he would put the missiles in Cuba, because it would have seemed an imprudent action for him to take, as it was later proved. Now, he obviously must have thought that he could do it in secret and that the United States would accept it. So that he did not judge our intentions accurately.[14]

Khrushchev had broken the ground rules. He had not merely penetrated our sphere of control, but he had done so in a manner that, if allowed to stand as a *fait accompli*, would tip the global balance of power against us. Kennedy had been insisting publicly that the United States could not allow Cuba to become a base for Soviet "offensive" weapons. It was as much the fact of this drawing of the line in public as it was the actual military situation created by the Soviet deployments that underlay Kennedy's definition of the deployment as intolerable. Once the line had been so unequivocally drawn, for us to allow Khrushchev to defiantly step over it would have been to appear impotent against the Soviets' attempts to do as they pleased. This was the "appearance" that would have "politically changed the balance of power."

The Administration seemed to fear that the consequences of this apparent change in the balance of power would be felt first in the form of a new Soviet squeeze play on Berlin. Khrushchev had lessened his pressure on Berlin the previous year at about the time it became generally known that recent Soviet missile claims had been greatly inflated, and that the United States still possessed overwhelming superiority in intercontinental strategic striking power. The deployment of missiles to Cuba, which might well appear to redress the balance by extending the Soviet strategic reach, could revive that margin of insurance against a United States strategic response which, presumably, was the necessary and sufficient condition for a Soviet probe in Berlin. Indeed, throughout the crisis, Kennedy and his advisers were very much on edge in expectation of Soviet retaliation in Berlin for our exercising our superiority in the Caribbean (there was some thought that the symmetry of a blockade for a blockade would appeal to the Russians).* This anxiety was eased somewhat by the realization that Khrushchev had clearly indicated he would not reopen the Berlin issue until after the November congressional elections, which suggested that he did not feel safe enough to move on Berlin until the missiles became operational. Still Kennedy felt it necessary to warn the Soviets in his October 22 speech that "any hostile move anywhere in the world against the safety and freedom of peoples to whom we are committed, including in particular the people of West Berlin, will be met by whatever action is needed." [15]

Once the missiles were detected there was no question in the President's mind but that they would have to be removed. The question was how to attain their removal at the lowest cost in United States lives

---

* Arnold Horelick accepts as plausible the hypothesis that the Soviets had Berlin in mind when they decided to install the missiles, but he rejects the notion that there was danger the Soviets would retaliate in Berlin for our toughness over Cuba. His analysis of Soviet behavior and statements in this and other crises over the years leads him to put more credence in the speculation that the Soviets would be particularly reluctant to couple Berlin to a crisis atmosphere over Cuba. Soviet strategy has been to define its Berlin ploys as localized adjustments not worth a global confrontation. A Berlin crisis in the midst of the Cuban crisis would only make it easier for the United States to claim the Berlin issue was central and strategic.

and Cuban lives without in the process bringing on a major war with the Soviet Union. For Kennedy, the corollary to the latter constraint was that we should not attempt to humiliate Khrushchev.

The notion that Cuban lives and Soviet face ought to constrain our plan of action guided the President in his narrowing of options. However, some members of his entourage did not appreciate or share the President's convictions on these boundary conditions. We know the course of action that was finally selected, and how the issue of the missiles (and bombers) was resolved. This course of action was by no means an inevitable derivation from an analysis of the irreducible national interest, the immediate threat posed by the Soviet deployments, and the balance of military capabilities on both sides.

Experienced Presidential advisers with access to the same information as the President came to different conclusions about the actions necessary and most desirable to protect the basic national interest, and preserve the balance of power. Consequently, the intensive dialogue, actually decalogue, conducted by the President and his advisers during the period October 16–28, 1962 heightened the Administration's self-awareness of the sometimes conflicting premises of power underlying its foreign policy, and contributed, in the form of a Presidential choice, to a selection and sharpening of those premises which would govern Administration policy henceforth.

A consideration which the President found he could not ignore, but which was easier for some of his advisers to bypass, was the moral character of our actions.

The arguments in behalf of restraint because of moral considerations were presented most strongly by George Ball and Robert Kennedy in opposing the resort to an air strike against the missiles—the option favored at first by most of Kennedy's special executive committee, including the Joint Chiefs of Staff. Ball argued that, regardless of the military outcome, a surprise attack would be against our best national traditions. The Attorney General supported Ball's stand, offering, "My brother is not going to be the Tojo of the 1960's." [16] Sorenson quotes Robert Kennedy as contending passionately that the sudden air strike would be "a Pearl Harbor in reverse, and it would blacken the name of the United States in the pages of history." [17] To knock out the Cuban missiles and aircraft capable of reaching the United States might mean killing 25,000 Cubans. Castro would become a martyr throughout

Latin America, and the Cuban people would bear a grudge against us for decades.

These arguments, it should be noted, stressed the political value of action consistent with the presumed moral expectations of others, and of our own people. It rested on the premise that the reputation for moral restraint by a great power is an important element of political influence. It was apparently this line of reasoning that swayed a number of influential members of the executive committee away from the air strike. "I had wanted an air strike," recalls Douglas Dillon. "What changed my mind was Bob Kennedy's argument that we ought to be true to ourselves as Americans, that surprise attack was not in our tradition. Frankly, these considerations had not occurred to me until Bobby raised them so eloquently." [18] Robert Kennedy has claimed the ideas which he voiced were really the President's, and has attributed them to his brother's "belief in what is right and what is wrong." [19]

But the detailed accounts of the deliberations during the thirteen days of the crisis show the President to have been less absolutely constrained by such an absolutist ethic than his younger brother, looking back, now claims. The President was not willing to rule out an air strike, not even an invasion of Cuba, if that's what it would take to effect a removal of the "offensive weapons." His position seems to have been that these more costly actions (calculated in part in moral terms) should not be taken until the less costly alternatives had been exhausted. And he ultimately came around to the naval "quarantine" on weapons-carrying vessels as the least costly of potentially effective alternatives, which did not, by its adoption as the first move, prevent us from resorting to the higher cost and higher risk alternatives later. His was an ethic of pursuing the objective, but, patiently, with means least destructive of human life, even though the objective might be more certainly and swiftly attained by alternative means if one did not worry about their destructive side effects.

Such moral questions were involved and taken very seriously by the President. But it would be a distortion to separate them explicitly from the other considerations which weighed heavily upon him. These considerations can be grouped under his general concern for "controlling the risks." [20]

The biggest risk, from the point of view of the President, was to do nothing, to accept the presence of Soviet strategic weapons in Cuba as the new status quo. The Soviets would have achieved a tremendous victory on which they would then surely capitalize to put the squeeze on Berlin or anywhere else that their objectives came into conflict. They would be prone to miscalculate the strength of our commitments and be more than ever tempted to take reckless actions that would compel us to respond in force, possibly at a level where the ability to keep things under control on either side would be severely destabilized.

If there were very high risks in doing nothing, there were also high risks in reacting too massively. The White House was not afraid of a "rational" Khrushchev, but a Khrushchev forced to eat humble pie in public was an unknown. It was important to keep the Soviets reality oriented, to show them that we had the capability and the will to forcibly remove their local threat to our security if driven to it, and to provide them with a less humiliating option than retreat under a public ultimatum. Nor was it thought diesirable to put the Khrushchev pledges to protect Castro under too severe a test by accually invading Cuba. The choices narrowed rather quickly, therefore, to either the naval blockade or the air strikes with the latter finally abandoned by the President—as an initial response, though not ruled out as the next step in case the blockade failed. The President's reasons, according to Abel, Sorenson, and Schlesinger—those reasons which he expressed to his assembled group of advisers [21]—were primarily on the grounds of the immediate risks of the air strike as opposed to the naval blockade. Thus, in Abel's account, in the final review of the alternatives, on October 21:

The President asked General Walter C. Sweeney, Commander of the Tactical Air Force, whether he could be certain that an air strike would take out all the Soviet missiles at one stroke. Sweeney replied that it should be possible to destroy some 90 per cent of them, though he could not guarantee 100 per cent effectiveness. A clean surgical operation, in short, was a military impossibility. The plan called for bombing Castro's military airports, as well as the missile bases, and several of these were in populated areas. Haunted by the thought that thousands of Cuban civilians might be killed, in addition to the Russians manning the missile sites, Kennedy once again vetoed the air strike. Even if only 10 per cent of the missile sites were to survive, he reasoned, they might be fired against the United States.[22]

The blockade, by contrast, offered Khrushchev the choice of avoiding an immediate military clash, by merely keeping his ships away. This would not settle the matter of the missiles already there, but it would, without a direct engagement, establish firmly our intention to maintain control in the Caribbean. Khrushchev could, of course, stall on the matter, but once having turned away from challenging the blockade, the reality of our power would have been recognized. If Khrushchev under these circumstances were to make concessions, they would be temporary concessions to present realities, a tolerable posture for a Bolshevik; it would not have to look like a humiliating and irreversible defeat.

The strongest *public* remarks to Khrushchev were made in the President's dramatic October 22 radio-television address, divulging the fact that we knew the Soviet missiles were in Cuba, and outlining our initial low-level response. The only specific reference to a higher level military response was in connection with the hypothetical contingency of an actual launching of nuclear missiles from Cuban soil: "It shall be the policy of this Nation to regard any nuclear missile launched from Cuba against any nation in the Western Hemisphere as an attack by the Soviet Union on the United States, requiring a full retaliatory response upon the Soviet Union." [23] There was a deliberately vague reference in Kennedy's speech to further action, in addition to the blockade, if the missile preparations in Cuba continued, but nothing even approaching an ultimatum. It was only through *private* channels that the screws were tightened; and then, only in conjunction with our public acceptance of the formula: you remove the weapons under UN supervision; we will give assurances against invasion. Sorenson reports that Robert Kennedy, at the request of the President, when handing a copy of this formula to the Soviet Ambassador, accompanied it with a very tough oral message: the point of escalation was at hand. Unless the President received immediate notice that the missiles would be withdrawn, we were in a position to take strong and overwhelming retaliatory action.[24] That was on Saturday, October 27, six days since the President's radio-television address demanding the removal of the missiles, one day after the receipt of the emotional and surprisingly contrite secret letter from Khrushchev, only hours after a second stronger Khrushchev letter, this one broadcast to the entire world.

There had still been no real confrontation of wills. The installation of the missile sites in Cuba, from components already there, had been continuing at a rapid pace. The naval quarantine was in force, but both sides had avoided a clear test: the President had taken his time in actually implementing the blockade. His speech was delivered Monday night. On Thursday morning, when the Navy hailed a Soviet tanker, Kennedy ordered it to be passed through without inspection, allowing for the possibility that the ship had not yet received its instructions from Moscow.[25] The Soviet cargo ships with their submarine escorts would have arrived Friday. The Navy was urging the President to go far out into the ocean to intercept the Soviets before they reached the Caribbean. But, backed by McNamara, he insisted that Khrushchev be given all possible time to communicate with his ships. The President did, however, find the opportunity to stop a ship to symbolically show our resolve: a dry-cargo freighter, owned by a Panamanian company, Lebanese registered, with a Greek crew, but sailing under a Soviet charter was halted and boarded at dawn Friday, found to be carrying only trucks and spare parts, and allowed to pass.[26] The Soviets, for their part, stopped the progress of their cargo ships, and had actually turned them back toward home port by Friday. But would they stop work on the missiles already in Cuba? And, once these were operational, would the Soviet Navy sail toward Cuba more confidently? Or, would the Communists invoke a counter-blockade around Berlin where they had tactical superiority? As the President dispatched his brother with his final private ultimatum to Khrushchev, these doubts remained intense. Still, Kennedy stood his ground, and refused to be stampeded into the tempting chest-thumping postures urged upon him by some advisers.

Even after the Soviets gave in essentially to our terms and agreed to dismantle the missiles (Khrushchev's message of Sunday, October 28), Kennedy instructed his associates, as Sorenson describes it, that there was to be:

. . . no boasting, no gloating, not even a claim of victory. We had won by enabling Khrushchev to avoid complete humiliation—we should not humiliate him now. If Khrushchev wanted to boast he had won a major concession [no U.S. invasion of Cuba] and proved his peaceful manner, that was the loser's prerogative.[27]

It is tempting to over-define the resolution of the Cuban missile crisis as having reestablished clarity concerning the spheres in which each superpower was to exercise effective control. It is true that the Soviets were effectively kept from establishing an offensive military base in the Western hemisphere. But Castro was not about to accept anything like the "normalization" of relations with the neighboring superpower that the Soviet Union reimposed on Hungary and Poland in 1956 following the threat (which never materialized) of Western intervention in Eastern Europe. Castro would not even allow the UN to verify the dismantling of the Soviet missile sites, the contingency upon which our no invasion pledge was conditioned. For three weeks Castro balked at returning to the Soviets their Ilyushin-28 bombers, which, like the missiles, were within range of the United States. This, not the inspection issue, became the outstanding problem between the United States and the Soviets. When finally the Soviets persuaded Castro to give up the bombers also, we lifted our naval quarantine, and talked in public with the Soviets as if the crisis was now completely resolved. This allowed the Soviets to portray the outcome as one establishing the legitimacy of the Castro regime, thanks to the Soviet missile ploy.

The United States for its part never explicitly affirmed the no invasion pledge, but neither did we deny that we felt bound by it as a tacit agreement. Indeed, many of our actions and statements henceforth suggested that if only Castro would pledge not to export his revolution to other Latin American countries, we would be perfectly willing to establish normal relations with Cuba again, despite the fact that it was a Communist regime and an ally of the Soviet Union. The Communists thus were given an even greater claim to legitimacy in the Caribbean than they were willing to allow the West in Berlin.

Ambiguity remained, but the lines were holding, and had weathered their most serious threat. Henceforth attempts at interpenetration of one another's sphere would be more subtle, and far below the threshold of frontal challenge to the other's military dominance in areas of traditional hegemony.

Possibly also—but this would materialize more in the context of the nuclear test ban negotiations—there could be mutual agreement to refrain from actions, symbolic or material, designed to significantly alter the existing balance of coercive power.

CHAPTER SEVENTEEN

THE TEST BAN: STABILIZING THE BALANCE

On the Presidential Coat of Arms, the American eagle holds in his right talon the olive branch, while in his left he holds a bundle of arrows. We intend to give equal attention to both.

JOHN F. KENNEDY

The unwillingness of the United States to destroy the wall the Communists had built in the festering Berlin enclave and the unwillingness of the Soviet Union to run the blockade the United States had cast around Cuba had parallels that were perceived in the White House. The symmetrical aspects were disturbing and hopeful at the same time.

It was disturbing to have it again made clear that military force, the distribution of physical coercive capabilities, counted more than the nonmaterial factors—ideology, community, loyalty, and even kinship—in defining "power."

But the reassertion of the dominance of the impersonal factors of power, however cruel to those finding their demands factored out of the calculus, allowed for the beginning of a less jittery relationship. Each had demonstrated to the other a "rational" respect of the other's arsenal of massive destruction, each had respected the other's refusal to

267

be dramatically undermined within his existing territorial sphere of dominance, and each had also demonstrated it was not about to allow lesser members of its ideological community to stampede it into an actual test of strength with its giant opponent.

Soviet behavior in the China-India border war, which took place concurrently with the Cuban crisis also could be read as a sign that the Soviets had possibly reached a critical turning point in their global strategy. Instead of demonstrating solidarity with the Chinese Communists, and thereby attempting to gain some of the laurels for the ascendancy of Communist power in that theater, the Soviets maintained an icy neutrality in that conflict, and after the cease-fire entered into negotiations with India to agument their military assistance to the Nehru government. Policies of East-West confrontation were to be avoided in the Third World as well as in Europe; but this might require assisting in the creation of local balances of power so as not to require the direct intervention of either the Soviet Union or the United States on behalf of weaker parties, interventions which would lead to counter-interventions by the other superpower to prevent alterations in the overall balance.

The situation could be perceived as an equilibrium of sorts. Its maintenance, however, would depend upon the perpetuation of the belief by both of the giants that neither was positioning to topple the other.

A modicum of mutual trust was thus an important element in any program for stablizing the equilibrium, at least trust in the other's good sense, and at best (though this was still far in the distance) trust in the other's good intentions. The journey of a thousand miles as stated in the Chinese proverb Kennedy quoted to Khrushchev in Vienna, starts with but a single step. Khrushchev had not been ready to take that step with Kennedy the previous year. He had explored the atlernative path, with its lures of a quick and decisive victory in the Cuban missile deployment, and had almost tumbled into the abyss. Moreover, the President, in an admixture of good grace and prudence, had refrained from the temptation to push the opponent as he lost his balance. Would the Soviet leader's common sense lead him to a more positive response to a fresh invitation from the President? Both Kennedy and another seasoned politician, Prime Minister Macmillan, against the advice of some of their more "sophisticated" advisers, believed it was worth a try, and that the first step ought to be the much offered and much rejected nuclear test ban treaty.

There were clues that Khrushchev might be ready. He seemed to be pushing hard within his own camp to convert the events of October and November 1962 into lessons on the futility of a foreign policy based on military confrontations and an accelerating arms competition. On December 12, in a post-mortem to the Supreme Soviet on the Cuban crisis, he accused the Albanians and the Chinese of wanting "to bring on a clash between the Soviet Union and the United States."

He could not agree with the irresponsible characterization of the United States as a "paper tiger," said Khrushchev: "If it is a 'paper tiger' . . . those who say this know that this 'paper tiger' has atomic teeth. It can put them to work; and it cannot be regarded frivolously." If during the Cuban crisis the Soviet Union had not shown the proper restraint, asked Khrushchev, if instead the Soveit Union had heeded "the promptings of the untrarevolutionary loudmouths," what would have been the consequences:

We would have entered the stage of a new world war, a thermonuclear war. Our vast country would have withstood it, of course, but tens and tens of millions of people would have perished! And Cuba would have simply ceased to exist. . . . Other densely populated countries that do not have vast expanses . . . also would have perished completely. And even those who remained alive, and future generations too, would have suffered incredibly from the consequences of atomic radiation.

Was this the path of mankind's development outlined by Marx and Lenin?

There must be other modes of conducting the competition with the United States. The "sensible norms" of international relations should be strengthened, urged the Soviet Premier. It was necessary to show "more sobermindedness and a greater desire to remove the roadblocks that cause friction and create tension among states." It was necessary to manifest goodwill in the search for mutually acceptable solutions.

One of the areas in which new efforts had to be made to achieve mutually acceptable solutions, said Khrushchev, was in disarmament. And to that end, "We call upon the Western powers to remove the last barriers to an agreement on ending nuclear tests for all time to come." [1]

This time there appeared to be more than rhetoric involved in the Soviet call for an agreement. Khrushchev had been agitating within his Party for some time for a greater concentration of resources and administrative attention on domestic economic problems, especially the shortfall in agricultural production. His November 19 speech to the Central Committee plenum outlining new party and administrative arrangements for attending to the domestic economy was read with care in Washington.[2] It had obviously been the product of much detailed study, analysis, and prolonged debate within the party hierarchy even before the Cuban missile crisis. But possibly to clinch his controversial program now, and solidify the party ranks behind him, Khrushchev needed concrete evidence that a modus vivendi with the United States was feasible.

Chairman Khrushchev's most recent special notes to the President contained what looked like quite sincere attempts to underline the seriousness of his pleas to finalize negotiations on the test ban. "This is a very propitious moment for doing so," he wrote in his December 19 letter. "The period of maximum crisis and tension in the Caribbean is behind us. We are now free to consider other urgent international matters, in particular a subject which has long been ripe for action—the cessation of nuclear tests."

The differences between the two sides, Khrushchev correctly pointed out, had narrowed to the question of how to confirm that suspicious seismic vibrations on the territories of the nuclear powers were not underground tests. Both were willing to rely on existing means of detection for determining violations in space and under water.

Every time the question of inspecting for underground tests had come up, the Soviets had accused the West of using the issue as a pretext for establishing a spy system on Soviet territory. The preferred Soviet formula during the past few years was to include underground tests in a comprehensive ban but to exempt these from inspection, relying instead on an unpoliced voluntary moratorium. In pre-Cuba negotiations at the Eighteen Nations Disarmament Conference in Geneva, in response to the Western scientific evidence that outside seismic detection systems could not identify disturbances below a certain magnitude, the Soviets had accepted the idea of a network of international seismic stations to be installed near the frontiers of the nuclear powers and in their territory. The apparatus in these stations was to be sealed, so as to preclude tampering, but they were not to be manned by international personnel. The West continued to insist that such purely technical means of inspection would be insufficient, and that some degree of human verification would be essential.

Now, however, Khrushchev claimed to be making a further concession:

If . . . it should be considered necessary for foreign personnel to participate in such deliveries of apparatus to and from automatic seismic stations, we could agree to this, taking measures, if required to prevent such visits from being used for espionage purposes. Our proposal for automatic seismic stations thus includes elements of international control. This is an important gesture of goodwill on the part of the Soviet Union.

Having accepted the principle of on-site inspection, Khrushchev then proceeded to define the only outstanding issue between the two sides as being the number of on-site inspections to be permitted each year. "Very well: if this is the only obstacle to agreement, we are prepared to meet with you on this point in the interests of the noble and humane cause of ending nuclear weapons tests." Khrushchev urged that discussions to find an agreed number, already having begun between V. V. Kuznetsov for the Soviet Union and Arthur Dean for the United States, continue posthaste with the intention of coming to an agreement by the first of the year.[3]

Yet when it actually got down during the coming months to arriving at an agreed number of inspections the Soviets seemed to be as recalcitrant as ever. The Soviets had started their post-Cuba negotiations on this issue with the announcement they would accept "two to three" inspections a year on their territory. The United States had been insisting that the minimum number it could now accept (and that due to progress in technical detection devices) was eight to ten. The "bargaining" was actually asymmetrical, since the Soviet maximum was an arbitrary barrier meant to "protect" against presumed espionage, whereas the western minumum was professedly based on a scientific determination of the average amount of normal seismic disturbances each year below the threshold of intensity that could be picked up with the instruments. It was not unreasonable for the President to assume the

Soviets had an acceptance price somewhat different from their asking price. But the Soviets broke off the tripartite talks that had been taking place in New York City during January 1963, without so much as a hint that they might be willing to strike for a middle ground between the Western minimum and their maximum. In April, after considerable debate among the President's advisers, the United States presented a revised minimum of seven, instead of eight to ten, to the Eighteen Nations Disarmament Conference; but the Soviets still wallowed in the mud of two to three, lacing their pronouncements in Geneva with innuendoes of lack of Western good faith.[4]

There were plenty of grounds for pessimism, for assuming the Soviets were up to their old tricks of using the arms limitaiton negotiations as primarily a propaganda forum to generate ban-the-bomb movements in the non-Communist countries while they readjusted their weapons development schedules for a new try at catching, and possibly overtaking, the United States in military power. During the spring of 1963, the five Communist delegations at the Geneva discussions were unrelenting in their attacks upon United States overseas bases, particularly those servicing our Polaris-carrying submarines, upon the Anglo-American weapons sharing agreement of December 1962, upon United States–Canadian joint nuclear defense planning, and upon the Franco-German treaty of cooperation. They also reintroduced their standard proposals designed to force the United States to reject publicly measures which had a powerful "peace" image: namely, a non-aggression pact between NATO and Warsaw Pact countries, a Mediterranean nuclear-free zone, and a ban on the stationing of strategic nuclear weapons on foreign territories.[5]

Furthermore, in the speeches where Khrushchev seemed to be holding the olive branch in one hand, he certainly had not dropped the bludgeon from the other. United States Kremlinologists—many of whom had predicted the Soviets would not dare to deploy offensive missiles to Cuba—were (with a few exceptions) wary this time of banking heavily on the benign aspects of Khrushchev's posture. They felt it was their responsibility to direct the President's attention to belligerent passages in Khrushchev's statements, such as:

If anyone in the West supposes that the Soviet Union renounces its determination to conclude a German peace treaty and on this basis to normalize the situation in West Berlin, he is mistaken. We are for negotiations with the Western powers, but there is a limit to patience, even if the Western powers do not agree to such a treaty it will be signed.

(Speech of December 12 to the Supreme Soviet.)

. . .

. . . the main efforts of the U.S.A. and its NATO partners are directed not at achieving an agreement on general and complete disarmament but at further intensification of the arms race and the creation of aggressive NATO nuclear forces. . . . Even on such a question as a ban on nuclear weapons tests, the United States and Britain are doing everything possible to impede a positive outcome of the talks. (Khrushchev interview with editor of *Il Giorno*, published in *Pravda*, April 24, 1963.)

The *Il Giorno* interview was duplicative of the report by Norman Cousins to the President of his personal conversation with Khrushchev on April 12.[6]

President Kennedy was losing hope, but felt he should still try. If Khrushchev's signals to us were confusing as to his real intentions, could it not also be that he was not completely sure of the meaning of ours? In April and May, through an exchange of letters with Khrushchev, Kennedy and Macmillan persisted in trying to convey the seriousness of their objective to negotiate a nuclear test ban, and both offered to send very senior representatives to Moscow to speak for them on this issue.

The President's position was reinforced in late May by the resolution introduced in the Sentate by Thomas Dodd and Hubert Humphrey to put the Senate on record as favoring (*a*) an agreement to prevent nuclear testing in the atmosphere and under water (where adherence could be adequately verified without new arrangements), and (*b*) a pledged by the United States to refrain from further testing in these environments even in advance of a formal agreement so long as the Soviets also refrained from resuming their tests. Unlike the earlier unpoliced moratorium Eisenhower had agreed to, and Khrushchev had then violated without prior notice in 1961, this mutual abstention would not extend to underground tests in the absence of effective inspection machinery.* President Kennedy, according to Schlesinger, was somewhat concerned that a push for the limited ban now might undercut the narrowing of differences on the comprehensive ban, but was pleased to be able to point to a growing national consensus in favor of some anti-testing agreement.[7]

* The proposed ban on atmospheric tests had been offered by the United States

A momentum was building up which the President was anxious to encourage. Sorenson was set to work on a first draft of a major speech about "peace," to be ready for delivery on June 10 at the President's commencement appearance at American University. "The President was determined to put forward a fundamentally new emphasis on the peaceful and the positive in our relations with the Soviets," recalls Sorenson. "He did not want that new policy diluted by the usual threats of destruction, boasts of nuclear stockpiles and lectures on Soviet treachery." [8]

Two days before Kennedy's American University address, Khrushchev replied in a sour letter that he would receive the high-level emissaries as proposed by the President and Prime Minister Macmillan. It is doubtful that Khrushchev knew he was significantly strengthening the President's hand, but the timing could not have been better. White House correspondents were briefed that the June 10 speech was of major importance. They were not to be disappointed. And, as it turned out, even Khrushchev was impressed.

The President used the American University rostrum to announce two important decisions: the agreement between Khrushchev, Macmillan, and him to have "high-level discussions" take place shortly in Moscow "looking toward early agreement on a comprehensive test ban treaty"; and the decision by the United States Government not to conduct further nuclear tests in the atmosphere so long as other states did not do so. "We shall not be the first to resume." If revealed matter-of-factly in a press conference, these decisions would have been regarded as significant, but not momentous. However, embedded as they were in a dramatic appeal to the nation to reexamine our attitudes toward the Soviet Union, the Cold War, and peace itself, the impression was created of a turning point in United States-Soviet relations with far-reaching implications.

He was speaking of peace, said the President, because of the "new face of war." In an age when great powers could maintain large and relatively invulnerable nuclear forces, total war, to bring about the surrender of an adversary, made no sense. It made no sense to talk about a "Pax Americana enforced upon the world by American weapons of

---

before, under Eisenhower in 1959 and under Kennedy in 1962. Both times it had been rejected by the Soviets as a hypocritical attempt to convince the world that the nuclear arms race was being halted, whereas in reality it was not.

war." He was not talking of "the peace of the grave or the security of the slave":

Today, should total war ever break out . . . no matter how—our two countries [the United States and the Soviet Union] would become the primary targets. . . . All we have built, all we have worked for, would be destroyed in the first 24 hours.

. . .

I speak of peace, therefore, as the necessary and rational end of rational man.

But he was not referring to "the absolute, infinite concept of universal peace and good will of which some fantasies and fanatics dream." World peace did not require that each man love his neighbor; it required only that they "live together in mutual tolerance." Rather than premising our work for peace on a revolution of human nature, and thus inviting once again the incredulous reactions, and the inevitable discouragement:

Let us focus instead on a more practical, more attainable peace . . . on a series of concrete actions and effective agreements which are in the interest of all concerned.

. . .

With such a peace, there will still be quarrels and conflicting interests, as there are within families and nations . . . [but] history teaches us that enmities between nations, as between individuals, do not last forever. However fixed our likes and dislikes may seem, the tide of time and events will often bring surprising changes in the relations between nations and neighbors.

In order to let time work its course, we had to have time, and this, in the thermonuclear age, required some degree of mutual accommodation.

To act in accord with such a prescription we would also need to "re-examine our attitude toward the Soviet Union." We would have to avoid the trap of seeing only a distorted and desperate view of the other side, of regarding conflict as inevitable, and communication nothing more than an exchange of threats:

No government or social system is so evil that its people must be considered as lacking in virtue. As Americans, we find communism profoundly repugnant as a negation of personal freedom and dignity. But we can still hail the Russian people for their many achievements—in science and space, in economic and industrial growth, in culture and in acts of courage.

Among the many traits the peoples of our two countries have in common, none is stronger than our mutual abhorrence of war. Almost unique, among the major world powers, we have never been at war with each other. And no nation in the history of battle ever suffered more than the Soviet Union suffered in the course of the Second World War. . . .

The Soviet Union, and the United States, moreover, had a common interest in relieving themselves of the heavy burden of armaments:

For we are both devoting massive sums of money to weapons that could be better devoted to combating ignorance, poverty, and disease. We are both caught up in a vicious and dangerous cycle in which suspicion on one side breeds suspicion on the other, and new weapons beget counterweapons.

Both sides, therefore, could be regarded as having "a mutually deep interest in a just and lasting peace and in halting the arms race," and "agreements to this end are in the interests of the Soviet Union as well as ours—and even the most hostile nations can be relied upon to accept and keep those treaty obligations, and only those treaty obligations, which are in its own interest."

Our primary long-range interest, maintained the President, was in an agreement for general and complete disarmament. The prospects for a treaty involving such a comprehensive agreement were of course still very dim. But we would continue to work on this effort.

Efforts should be concentrated on the one major area of negotiations where the end *was* in sight: the treaty to outlaw nuclear tests. With less equivocation than he was to display two months later in asking the senate to ratify the treaty, the President catalogued a list of far-ranging implications:

The conclusion of such a treaty . . . would check the arms race in one of its most dangerous areas. It would place the nuclear powers in a position to deal more effectively with one of the greatest hazards which man faces . . . the further spread of nuclear arms. It would increase our security—it would decrease the prospects of war.

Anticipating criticisms at home, as well as driving home the solidity of his intentions to Khrushchev, the President dealt with the risks on noncompliance. He admitted that no treaty, however much it might be to the advantage of its signatories, however tightly it might be worded, could provide absolute security against the risks of deception and evasion, "but it can . . . offer far more security and far fewer risks than an unabated, uncontrolled, unpredictable arms race." [9]

The Soviets broadcast the speech with very little deletion and then rebroadcast it in its entirety. The full text was published in the Soviet press. But there was no immediate response from Khrushchev. Meanwhile, the President made preparations for a European trip to tend to one of the effects of the emerging United States-Soviet strategic standoff—namely, the ability of de Gaulle to sow doubt, particularly in the minds of the Germans, about the credibility of our pledges to bring our strategic capability into play to counter Soviet military provocations in Europe. (See Chapter 18 for an elaboration.)

The Presidential rhetoric (and presumably the private assurances also) designed for West German ears would be somewhat at odds with the tone of the American University speech. There are few clues to indicate if the President and his advisers gave close attention to the apparent contradictions, or whether this was one of those cases where the position papers, having been written in different offices of the government, were never compared. It is possible, but one can only speculate, that a higher statecraft was at work during the summer of 1963: The assurances to the West Germans could be considered as guarantees by the United States to back them up in their conflicts with the Soviets in *hypothetical* situations, which would become more remote under conditions of East-West détente. To work toward the détente with the Soviets while, simulaneously, refurbishing our guarantees to the Germans was thus not a policy contradiction, unless the Soviets or the Germans chose to put that construction on it. Kennedy could reasonably expect that if the Soviets were truly interested in the test ban and other steps toward détente, they would not use our rhetoric toward Germany as a pretext for charging us with bad faith. After all, the Soviets also had their Germany to soothe, and ought to understand the requirements.

Khrushchev evidently did understand and also seemed to appreciate the symmetry involved. On July 2, one week after the President's ringing *Ich bin ein Berilner* reiterations of the identity of United States and West German security interests, the Soviet Premier was in East Berlin lambasting the West for trying to use a nuclear test ban as a means of obtaining access to the socialist countries by "NATO intelligence experts." For that reason, the Soviet government was proposing a test ban that did not involve territorial inspection—that is, an agreement to ban all nuclear tests in the atmosphere, in outer space, and under water, setting aside the ban on underground tests. But this agreement should be combined with "the simultaneous signing of a nonaggression pact" between the NATO and Warsaw Pact countries, he insisted.[10]

Two weeks later the American delegation, headed by Averell Harriman, and the British delegation, headed by Lord Hailsham began their negotiations with Khrushchev and Gromyko in Moscow.

The atmosphere in the city was electric, as the Soviets were just winding up a round of secret ideological talks with the Chinese Communists. The bitterness of the split between the two powers was explicitly displayed on July 14 in the form of an "Open Letter" by the Soviet Communist Party Central Committee to their new Party organizations. The CPSU letter charged that the Communist Party of China was digressing more and more from the common line of the communist movement on basic issues, particularly "the question of war and peace" and the "possibility of averting a world thermonuclear war." The Chinese comrades erred in not realistically appraising the consequences of the "radical, qualitative change of the means of waging war," contended the Soviets. They fail to take account of the fact that "the atomic bomb does not distinguish between imperialists and working people; it hits entire areas and therefore, for one monopolist, millions of workers would be destroyed." The struggle against world war, with its corollary of the peaceful coexistence of states with different social systems, argued the CPSU letter, was derived from this realistic appraisal of the balance of forces. In such a context, general disarmament, and lesser steps in that direction like the nuclear test ban treaty, should not be regarded as mere tactical expedients. They were the historically determined responsibility of any party which wanted to implement the precepts of Marxism-Leninism.[11]

Harriman seems to have shared the President's view that this time Khrushchev was not merely playing to the galleries in professing peaceful coexistence and deep interest in arms limitation measures. At this particular juncture, Khrushchev probably was an anxious as we were for some concrete agreement to result from the test ban negotiations. Betting on the correctness of this hunch, Harriman was steadfast in compelling Khrushchev to stick to the item where agreement was very near at hand—the three-environment test ban—and to defer negotiation on any nonaggression treaty. But allowing for Khrushchev's need to show the other Communist countries that there was room to accomplish a great deal through negotiation as opposed to belligerency, Harriman permitted the implication to stand that we would take up the matter of a nonaggression pact in subsequent discussions. Still, he was careful not to condition the test ban on any agreement to negotiate the matter.*

It took nine days of negotiation to agree on the final text of the "Treaty Banning Nuclear Weapons Tests in the Atmosphere, in Outerspace, and Underwater," initialed in Moscow on July 25, 1963 by Andrei Gromyko, Averell Harriman, and Lord Hailsham. "Yesterday a shaft of light cut into the darkness," said Kennedy in his July 2 radiotelevision address announcing the conclusion of the treaty and explaining its meaning. It signaled not a victory for one side, but rather "a victory for mankind." It reflected "no concessions either to or by the Soviet Union." But he was anxious to avoid raising expectations of a sudden end to the Cold War and the attendant risks of military conflict:

This treaty is not the millenium. It will not resolve all conflicts, or cause the Communists to forego their ambitions, or eliminate the dangers of war. It will not reduce our need for arms or allies or programs of assistance to others. But it is an important first step—a step towards peace—a step towards reason—a step away from war.

Looking toward the need to gain senate ratification of the treaty, the President attempted to show where such a first step could lead as a way of generating a popular consensus for an affirmative vote, but mindful of the tendency of the American democracy to lower its guard at times of good feeling, he was careful to make a distinction between possible effects and predicted effects.

This treaty "can be a step towards reduced world tension and

---

* Robert Kennedy, in recalling this period, gives much weight to the counsel of Harriman in buttressing the President's premises concerning the meaning of Soviet moves. In his forward to a collection of documents built around the theme of the American University speech, Senator Kennedy states that "after the Cuban nuclear confrontation . . . he [the President] felt the world was changed and that perhaps there would be less opposition to a renewed effort for agreement. This view was not shared in many quarters of the government, although it was shared by Averell Harriman, among others. Based on this view and on the encouragement received from Averell Harriman, President Kennedy made the speech at American University . . . from the American University speech and the efforts that followed came the nuclear test ban treaty. . . ." *Toward A Strategy of Peace*, edited by Walter C. Clemens, Jr. (Chicago: Rand McNally, 1965), pp. xiii–xiv.

broader areas of agreement," said the President. Among the measures mentioned were a comprehensive treaty banning tests everywhere, controls on the numbers and types of armaments, controls on preparations for surprise attack, further limitations on the spread of nuclear weapons, progress toward general and complete disarmament ("our ultimate hope"), and even a mutual foreswearing of aggression, direct and indirect. As yet however, there were no indications that the Soviet Government was willing to accept the kind of inspection arrangements such agreements would require: "No one can predict with certainty, therefore, what further agreements, if any, can be built on the foundations of this one."

The President laid special emphasis on the treaty's potential for helping prevent the spread of nuclear weapons to nations not yet possessing them. "This treaty can be an opening wedge in that campaign." It provided that none of the signatories would assist other nations to test in the prohibited environments. But the transference of completed weapons or their parts was not prohibited, nor were currently non-nuclear nations prohibited from producing weapons from the blueprints and test results of the nuclear nations. Kennedy could refer to such eventual comprehensive prohibitions only as a "great obligation" possibly now closer to implementation.

An immediate effect of the test ban treaty, if faithfully observed by at least the United States and the Soviet Union, would be to reduce the fears and dangers from radioactive fallout. But the President did not claim more than a marginal reduction. The United States in recent years had been taking special precautions to restrict the fallout from atmospheric tests to an absolute minimum. And even if there was a large increase in the amount of testing "the number of children with cancer in their bones, with leukemia in their blood, or with poison in their lungs might seem statistically small to some, in comparison with natural health hazards." (This comparison had been important for the President in March 1962 when he was compelled to resume atmospheric testing in response to the Soviet unilateral breaking of the existing three-year-old mutual moratorium). Still, the amount of radioactivity added to the natural amount, even if statistically insignificant was something over which we had control, and therefore responsibility. And "the loss of even one human life, or the malformation of even one baby—who may be born long after we are gone—should be of concern to us all. Our children are not merely statistics toward which we can be indifferent."

Finally, the President directed the attention of his audience to the likely effects of the test ban treaty upon the nuclear strategic balance itself. With the assistance of the Secretary of Defense, this part of the case for the treaty had been very carefully prepared. The Administration anticipated—and, as it turned out, correctly—that domestic opponents of the treaty would turn their fusilades on its implications for the United States-Soviet competition for military ascendancy. If the country was taking too many gambles with respect to the survivability of its nuclear deterrent, this would be prima facie grounds for the treaty's rejection. The Senate Preparedness Investigating Subcommittee, chaired by John Stennis of Misssissippi, had been holding hearings on the military implications of various test ban alternatives since September 1962, and was expected to be sharpening its axe for this one. "Under this limited treaty," the President maintained:

The [still-permissable] testing of other nations could never be sufficient to offset the ability of our strategic forces to deter or survive a nuclear attack and to penetrate and destroy an aggressor's homeland.

We have, and under this treaty will continue to have, the nuclear strength that we need. It is true that the Soviets have tested nuclear weapons of a yield higher than that which we thought to be necessary, but the hundred megaton bomb of which they spoke 2 years ago does not and will not change the balance of strategic power. The United States has chosen, deliberately, to concentrate on more mobile and more efficient weapons, with lower but entirely sufficient yield, and our security is, therefore, not impaired by the treaty I am discussing.

The President also attempted to anticipate the objectives that would be raised about evasions, secret violations, and secret preparations for sudden withdrawal. These he admitted were possible, "and thus our own vigilance and strength must be maintained, as we remain ready to withdraw and resume all forms of testing, if we must." But he insisted that it would be a mistake to assume that there was any significant likelihood of the treaty being quickly broken. Calculated in terms of their own self-interest, the nations that initialed the treaty in Moscow and others whose accession was expected would be more likely to see the gains of illegal testing or evasion to be slight compared to their cost:

. . . for these nations too, and all nations, have a stake in limiting the arms race, in holding the spread of nuclear weapons and in breathing air

THE KENNEDY–JOHNSON YEARS

that is not radioactive. While it may be theoretically possible to demonstrate the risks inherent in any treaty, and such risks in this treaty are small, the far greater risks to our security are the risks of unrestricted testing, the risk of a nuclear arms race, the risk of new nuclear powers, nuclear pollution, and nuclear war.

In closing, the President stressed once again that the "familiar places of danger and conflict" still require "all the strength and vigilance we can muster. Nothing could more greatly damage our cause than if we and our allies were to believe that peace has already been achieved" but:

. . . history and our own conscience will judge us harsher if we do not now make every effort to test our hopes by action, and this is the place to begin. According to the ancient Chinese proverb, "A journey of a thousand miles must begin with a single step." [12]

It was a balanced appeal. It promised neither sudden gains nor the complete absence of risks. It was uncongenial to the President's style to play the demagogue. Besides, the President's experience probably told him that this was the best way to gain bipartisan support in the Congress.

Not surprisingly, in the debates and hearings directed toward senate ratification, it was the potential military risks rather than anticipated political gains which received the most attention from critics and defenders alike. During those two months the Administration's central arguments in behalf of the test ban moved from stressing its value as a first stop toward détente and peace to its utility as a means of preserving our strategic superiority.

The burden of the treaty's defense fell to McNamara. It was his responsibility, he told senators of the cognizant committees, to assess the direction in which the military balance was likely to move under two conditions: the situation of unrestricted testing in all environments had to be compared with the situation under the test ban—testing restricted to underground.

The Secretary of Defense displayed his standard projections of United States and Soviet force postures, based on a comparison of nuclear technology; numbers of weapons and their accuracy; varieties of systems; their dispersal, mobility, and hardening; decoy and salvo techniques; and the possible deployment of an antiballistic missile system. "The net of the relevant factors," he confidently pointed out, "is that the U.S. nuclear force is manifestly superior to the Soviet Union's." The question was how this favorable situation would be affected by the test ban. "I can say that most of the factors will not be affected at all —not the accuracy of missiles, not variety of systems, not their dispersal or mobility, and not numbers." [13]

But there were a few aspects of the strategic balance which McNamara admitted deserved special attention, since they might be affected to some significant degree by the cessation of atmospheric nuclear tests. One was the development by the Soviets of very high-yield bombs, possibly as high as 100 megatons, in contrast to our relative lack of weapons development in these yields. Would the test ban prevent us from catching up? If so, what difference would it make for the strategic balance? Another concern was the survivability of our missiles under various extreme atmospheric conditions. Some weapons scientists were claiming that we needed further testing to be sufficiently confident that our missiles would actually function in the kinds of disturbed physical environments that might accompany a Soviet surprise attack. Finally, there was the question of the effects of the test ban on each side's ability to develop an antiballistic missile, the reverse of this question being the continual ability of each side's offensive missiles to penetrate whatever antiballistic missile system the other might be able to deploy.

Critics, supporting their claims by testimony from distinguished nuclear physicists such as Edward Teller (the "father" of the H-bomb) and John Foster, Jr., Director of the Lawrence Radiation Laboratory, had focused on these particular issues, as they were in fact the grey areas of legitimate scientific controversy. "From the evidence," intoned the report of Senator Stennis's Preparedness Investigating Subcommittee, "we are compelled to conclude that serious—perhaps even formidable—military and technical disadvantages to the United States will flow from the ratification of the treaty." [14]

In attempting to deal with the doubts raised by Edward Teller, Senator Stennis, and others, McNamara and his civilian and military associated in the Department of Defense presented facts to the Senate Committees which, more than any previous presentation by the executive branch, disclosed the technical bases of the Kennedy Administration's strategy and planning decisions for maintaining the nuclear strategic balance.

With respect to the suspected Soviet superiority in nuclear weapons exceeding fifty megatons, the Secretary of Defense granted the Soviet lead, and deferred to those experts who believed that we could not make significant improvements of the kind needed to catch up unless we were to resume nuclear testing in the atmosphere. These, to the best of his knowledge, were the facts. But what was their *military* significance? This was the relevant consideration in agreeing to the test ban agreement. For some years the Defense Department had been examining the possible uses of very high-yield weapons, such as the Soviets were apparently developing. These studies showed, according to McNamara, that there were two military disadvantages to deploying the higher-yield weapons as contrasted with deploying a large number of smaller weapons:

First . . . for most missions directed at military targets, we can achieve a higher confidence of kill by using two or three smaller weapons instead of one very large one; for a given resource input we achieve higher target destruction with our smaller systems.

Second, very high-yield warheads are relatively inferior as second-strike, retaliation, weapons; it is much more difficult and costly to make them survivable—to harden, camouflage or make mobile the huge missiles required to deliver these weapons.[15]

On the matter of whether a sufficient number of our offensive weapons would be able to strike back after having absorbed the worst the Soviets could throw at us, McNamara was not at all troubled. With or without a continuation of tests in the atmosphere, "The U.S. strategic missile force is designed to survive, and it will survive." It was true that large-yield nuclear tests in the atmosphere would help us determine with greater precision the effects of nuclear explosions on hardened structures such as the silos housing our Minutemen missiles. This would only help to somewhat reduce the uncertainty of calculations based on past atmospheric tests and whatever underground testing was to continue. But where there were such uncertainties we would always err in our planning and deployments on the side of overcorrection:

We know, and the Soviets know, that in the event of a surprise Soviet first strike, at least a substantial proportion of our Minutemen will survive. Also, we and they know that the Polaris submarines at sea and many strategic aircraft will survive. We can say with assurance, therefore, that, even after a Soviet strike, the total surviving U.S. strategic nuclear force will be large enough to destroy the enemy.[16]

Some scientists, notably John Foster of Lawrence, felt that we did not know enough about the vulnerability of our weapons and their associated radars to other "blackout" phenomena, and that the Soviets, in their recent series of atmospheric tests, may have accumulated such information.[17] However, Administration scientists claimed that this concern was ill-founded. Harold Brown, the Pentagon's Director of Defense Research and Engineering, maintained that the Soviet and American experience in determining the effects of such induced phenomena on the performance of nuclear weapons "appears to be comparable." Of course, he said, "the more we learned about it, the better we could do. But I want to make the point that this is a useful, but not vital piece of information." [18] It was not "vital," because, as the chairman of the Joint Chiefs of Staff put it: ". . . with regard to the immediate problems of the weapons systems we are contemplating, the general opinion is that we can attain these weapons even with the present uncertainties about this particular phenomenon." [19]

The same kind of criticism and rebuttal characterized the testimony about the implications of the test ban for the development of an antiballistic missile (ABM). Teller was concerned that in the absence of further testing to determine the effects of nuclear explosions on the defensive radars, it would be very difficult for us to develop a reliable ABM. Again, Harold Brown maintained that the United States and the Soviet Union were "roughly comparable" in knowledge in this field, with the United States possibly even somewhat ahead. More important, the ABM did not look like a good system to deploy anyway, since our calculations showed even the most sophisticated systems would be ineffective (at the time they entered the inventory) against the improved offensive systems and "pentration aids" now under development.[20]

Even if we did decide to deploy an ABM system, said McNamara, by analysis of presently available data, and that obtained from underground testing, "we will be able to design around the remaining uncertainties." With or without a test ban, we could proceed with its development. But the "ABM problem is dominated by factors unrelated to the treaty." [21]

Finally, the Secretary of Defense contested the broadside assertion by some senators (notably Barry Goldwater and Richard Russell) that the overall effect of the treaty would be to preserve the Soviet lead in high-yield weaponry while permitting them to catch up with us in low-yield research through a diversion of their test activity underground. "We pay a price: they do not," said Goldwater.[22] The Secretary emphatically disagreed:

> If testing continued indefinitely without limit as to test environment or size of yield, the most likely ultimate result would be technical parity between the United States and the U.S.S.R. . . .
> But, by limiting Soviet testing to the underground environment, where testing is more difficult and more expensive and where the United States has substantially more experience, we can at least retard Soviet progress and thereby prolong the duration of our technological superiority. A properly inspected comprehensive test ban would, of course, serve this purpose still better.
> *This prolongation of our technological superiority will be a principal direct military effect of the treaty on the future military balance and I consider it a significant one* (Emphasis added.)[23]

The Administration's defense of the treaty against its critics was undoubtedly of educational value to the public and their representatives in Congress. Possibly it also helped to communicate to the Soviets the fact that our approach toward strategic weapons planning and strategies was based on security considerations, and not for aggressive purposes; but McNamara's championing of the atmospheric test ban as a means to prolong our military-technological superiority was ammunition for the more paranoid elements in the Communist world.

The dominance, which was probably inevitable, of military issues in the ratification debates gained the Kennedy Administration its "first step," but it meanwhile put a gloomy pall on those who had sensed a straight path to significant arms reductions immediately ahead. The major premises in the President's American University speech seemed in retrospect as if they had been part of a discussion of some entirely different matter.

The hope that the test ban would serve less as an element in the bipolar military competition than a symbol of possibilities for a new political relationship between the United States and the Soviet Union was revived only on occasion by Administration witnesses before the Congress. It remained for Marshall Shulman, an academic Kremlinologist highly regarded by Washington officialdom, to expound on the larger considerations which informed the Administration's attempt to negotiate a mutually acceptable arms agreement with the Soviets.

Shulman portrayed the Soviets as agreeing to the test ban at this time as an aid in moving toward a less hostile and less tense relationship with the United States. It was important to understand the basis of this current Soviet desire to reduce Cold War tensions, and whether this Soviet interest was compatible with United States interests.

Partly, the Soviet interest grew out of the intensification of their conflict with the Chinese, explained Schulman. Khrushchev was making maximum use of the "peace" issue in order to strengthen his position within the Communist world and to further isolate the Chinese. Among Communist parties in other countries, this was the weakest part of the Chinese case, and the Soviet leadership was attempting, through the opportunity offered by the test ban agreement, to make the most of this issue. But it would be incorrect to regard the Soviet search for measures to reduce East-West hostility as only a tactical response to the Chinese challenge to Soviet hegemony within the Communist world. From the Soviet point of view, the issue between them and the Chinese went deeper than that.

The Soviets, in their analysis of recent events, had come to the conclusion that the world situation was for the time being basically "nonrevolutionary." In Eastern Europe, the major preoccupation of the Warsaw Pact members was in the working out of new economic relationships within their own countries, with the Soviet Union, among themselves, and with the non-Communist world. In the non-Communist industrialized nations, the predicted economic contradictions and social crises had not materialized; the Communist parties in these countries were far from being in a revolutionary mood, and were pressing for more national autonomy from the Communist Party of the Soviet Union. Soviet anticipations for the Third World were similarly confronted with a reality that required pragmatic revisions of earlier doctrines. The new nationalist leaders of Africa and Asia were not about to trade their newly gained independence for either political or economic dependency upon the Soviet Union. Despite substantial Soviet investment of resources and personnel, the new nations were exhibiting neither the hoped-for pliancy in international politics nor a responsiveness to Soviet models for economic development. Simultaneous with their experiencing these frustrations to their grand design abroad, the Soviet rulers were harrassed at home by a set of complex problems, including: low agricultural productivity, bottlenecks in economic administration, major reshuffling of Communist Party positions to deal with administration of the economy, and difficulties between the regime and intellectuals and artists over free expression.

The current Soviet emphasis in foreign policy, of which the test ban agreement was only the surface manifestation, could be interpreted as an effort to bring about a more relaxed East-West atmosphere, allowing the Soviet leadership to devote their attention and resources to the resolution of domestic and intrabloc problems—and then return from a stronger base to a more active prosecution of their international objectives. Elaborating, Shulman described the turn in Soviet policy as an:

. . . adaptation . . . in the name of "peaceful coexistence," to a more indirect mode of advancing Soviet interests. . . .

. . .

The purpose is to encourage the fragmentation of the Western bloc, and the attraction of such decisive industrial areas as West Germany and Japan to a closer relationship with the Soviet block.

. . .

In the perspective of another 5, 10, or 15 years, it is argued [by the supporters of Khrushchev's policies], the political face of Europe may be totally changed, and may be more responsive to Soviet political approaches; competitive conflicts within the Western bloc may make Japan more approachable; the Soviet economy will have overcome its difficulties and forged ahead, in contrast to the stagnation anticipated for the United States and Great Britain.

Then, by a combination of political and economic means against a background of an improved power position, the Soviet Union will emerge ascendant. . . .[24]

The question posed by these premises about the Soviet motivation for reducing tension was: why should we help them?

Here too the Shulman statement provided about the fullest elaboration available in the public record of the kind of thinking behind the American University address and the test ban initiatives. What helps the Soviets may not necessarily be to our disadvantage, he observed. The proposed test ban treaty performed a "significant function in dramatizing the fact that what we have with the Soviet Union is a limited adversary relationship." That is:

In certain aspects of our confrontation, the security of each side is interlocked with the security of the other. It is therefore possible to have some measures which the Soviet leaders feel may serve their interests, and which we, for reasons of our own, regard as our interests as well.

We did, after all, share with the Soviets a mutual, or overlapping, interest in survival. To the extent that the Soviets wished to moderate their policies, for whatever motives, in directions that would avoid very dangerous confrontations such as Cuba and Berlin, our interest in avoiding a global war should lead us to encourage that evolution in Soviet policy. Similarly, if the Soviets were interested in significant arms control measures, not only to mitigate the more dangerous features of our competitive arming, but also out of a hope that this might induce us to let down our guard, we need not for that reason reject the safeguards that added to our security. We would want to maintain our vigilance and not allow the Soviets to easily manipulate the international climate without any substantive changes in policy. We would want to convey to them clearly, and to our own people, that they should guard against "euphoria," that there is a difference between an atmosphere of détente and a reduction in the *causes* of tension, and that until the latter occurred no meaningful progress could be made toward a major reduction of armaments. The job was not to rekindle the Cold War because the Soviets had impure motives; rather the job was to do all we could to encourage the Soviets to move in the direction of a genuine reduction in the causes of tension.

In dealing with the Soviets, Shulman pointed out, we ought to realize that for Communists, no less than for ourselves, there may be unintended, but not unpalatable long-term effects from policies originally undertaken for other purposes:

Indeed, the most striking characteristics of recent Soviet foreign policy has been the way in which policies undertaken for short term, expediential purposes have tended to elongate in time, and become embedded in doctrine and political strategy. The shift to a "peaceful coexistence" emphasis, originally a tactical alternation . . . in the new Communist party program . . . has acquired doctrinal underpinnings, related to the possibility of a peaceful transition to socialism, and the noninevitability of war.[25]

Hope for an elongation of the interest in the test ban into a more comprehensive interest in measures to preserve the peace was the central theme of President Kennedy's September 20 address to the UN General Assembly. If we can "stretch this pause into a period of cooperation . . . then surely this first small step can be the start of a

289

long and fruitful journey." [26] Four days later the Senate ratified the treaty by a vote of 80 to 19.

The question now was what should the follow-up measures be? It seemed potentially fruitful to explore additional items of "military stabilization" now that the Soviet Union had modified its all-or-nothing approach to disarmament, and seemed seriously interested in limited measures of mutual benefit. Two agreements that had received relatively little attention at the time of their announcement—the United States-Soviet "hot line" communications link of June 20, and the United States-Soviet agreement of December 5, 1962 for cooperation in the peaceful uses of outer space—when viewed with the test ban, reinforced the picture of a Soviet leadership with little enthusiasm left for military confrontations or a new phase of arms competition. Even the Cuban missile deployment might have been a trick to cover their strategic inferiority rather than an aggressive move. Possibly it was time for the Soviet proposal for a nonaggression pact for Central Europe to be reevaluated in this light, giving it an initial benefit of the doubt as being the product of a search for means of stabilizing the military balance instead of a means of promoting a political disintegration of the Atlantic Alliance.

Another indication that the Soviets were serious about further arms stabilization measures was Foreign Minister Gromyko's September 19, 1962 concession to a major Western concept for general disarmament: namely, that throughout the stages of disarming it would be desirable for both superpowers to retain a limited number of nuclear missiles as a hedge against clandestine violations.[27] But this was a concession in principle only. There were too many obstacles, such as the inspection issue, still in the way of serious negotiation for general disarmament.

Measures for space "arms control" showed the greatest immediate prospects for agreement as this was an area where the nations could refrain from doing something not yet attempted, rather than dismantling military structures and institutions to which various elements in the bureaucracies and societies of both countries and their allies had become attached. On October 17, 1963 the UN General Assembly endorsed a United States-Soviet sponsored statement calling upon all states to refrain from orbiting nuclear weapons in space;[28] and there were signs that further such agreements were in the offing.

Three weeks after the assassination of President Kennedy, Khrushchev announced a reduction in the Soviet military budget and the possibility of a cutback in military personnel. These "unilateral" moves obviously had been planned for some time, and were undoubtedly undertaken primarily for a more efficient allocation of resources; but they also had the intended side effect of a reminder to the new President that a priority item on the international agenda was the continuation of the efforts by the superpowers to level off the arms race. The United States, however, did not have a matching budget or military manpower reduction in the works at the time that would have justified a gesture of "reciprocity."

Khrushchev persisted. On New Year's Eve he proposed to all heads of states that they sign a comprehensive nonaggression treaty, to include four principal agreements: 1) an undertaking by the states that they will not resort to force to alter existing state frontiers; 2) a recognition that the territory of states should not even temporarily be the object of invasion, attack, military occupation, or any other forcible measure; 3) a declaration that no political or diplomatic issue can serve as a pretext or justification for the violation of the territorial integrity of one state by another; and 4) an undertaking to settle all territorial disputes exclusively by peaceful means in accordance with the UN Charter.

This time there was opportunity for a considered reply by the new Administration. Three weeks later President Johnson addressed a letter to Chairman Khrushchev, welcoming the "stated objective" of his December 31 letter, and stating that he agreed with "most of its contents." But he also urged that priority be given to concluding some of the specific arms control agreements on the agenda at the Geneva disarmament conference rather than "confining ourselves to vague declarations of principle that oppose some wars but not all." Your letter singled out, wrote Johnson, the problem of territorial disputes, and concluded that the solution of such disputes by force was not in the interest of any people or any country. "I agree," he said, and then revealed an additional proposal: "Moreover, the United States proposes guidelines to implement this principle which are even broader and stronger than your own:"

First, abstention from the direct or indirect threat or use of force to change international boundaries, other territorial or administrative demarcations or dividing lines established by international agreement or practice, truce or military armistice arrangements, procedures concerning access to, passage across, or administration of those areas where international agreement or practice has established certain patterns; nor shall force be used by any regime to enlarge its control by "overthrowing or displacing established authorities."

Second, these limitations shall apply "whatever the form" these direct or indirect uses of force might take—aggression, subversion, clandestine supply of arms—regardless of the issue, regardless of any differences in political systems. The third point offered by Johnson reiterated Khrushchev's proposal for peaceful solutions, but added the possibility of solution by regional associations as well as the UN. And finally, the President pointed out that any such obligations, if they were to continue, would have to be subject to the inherent right of individual or collective self-defense, as stipulated in Article 51 of the UN Charter, in case of an departure from the mutual obligations to refrain from using force.

"You will note the basic similarity in our positions," wrote Johnson. Obviously, the differences that were more salient than the similarities, and these had and would continue to preclude any explicit comprehensive nonaggression treaty between the superpowers, short of a renunciation by the Soviets of their last claim to Communist militancy: support for "wars of national liberation." But by responding positively with a counterproposal, instead of attempting a direct refusal, the Johnson Administration was able to indicate a desire to continue a nonbelligerent dialogue such as was initiated by Kennedy, while conveying that the time was not yet ripe for negotiations beyond the specific areas of concrete arms stabilization measures.[29]

A potentially significant arms stabilization measure was announced shortly: namely, a pledge by each superpower as of April 20, 1964 to cut back production of fissionable materials. If this were truly adhered to, it might indicate a tacit renunciation by both of entry into the next phase of the arms race—the antiballistic missile, which presumably would require augmented stocks of fissionable material.

But by 1966, the Soviets appeared well on their way toward a serious deployment of their ABM, in violation of the 1964 fissionable materials cutback pledge and the 1963 "spirit of Moscow." Meantime, Khrushchev was removed on October 15, 1964; and the involvement of the United States in Vietnam was putting a strain on the Khrushchev policies for a United States-Soviet détente. The Johnson Administration, at the time of this writing, was laboring under the immense policy issue of whether to respond in kind to the Soviet's potentially "destabilizing" deployment of ABM's, or to make one last diplomatic effort to convince the Brezhnev-Kosygin regime that a new phase in the arms race would only lead to a worsening of Soviet strategic inferiority, let alone heightened international tension in the context of the Vietnam War.

CHAPTER EIGHTEEN

THE BREAKUP OF BLOCS:
THE DECLINE OF IDEOLOGY
AND CONTROL

*Change is underway within the Communist world, as well as within the
free world. Most of the smaller states of Eastern Europe are restoring,
more and more, their historic ties with Western Europe and the United
States. They are recovering their individuality and becoming less rigid in
their internal policies. And these processes are visible within the Soviet
Union too.*

DEAN RUSK

The convergence of Soviet and United States interests on measures
to control the arms race was in large part the product of perceptions by
the leadership in each country that the military buildup had already
approached the point of diminishing marginal returns. If the arms race
were allowed to continue it would consume an excessively large part of
national energies and resources better invested in other elements of international power and domestic welfare. There was also a convergence,
of a sort, in fears by the two superpowers of being "catalyzed" into a
war against each other by the actions of lesser powers. Both appreciated
the value of keeping the secondary states in their respective alliances in
a condition of military subordination. Security for the superpowers required not only that they balance one another's military power, but

that the supply of advanced armaments be kept in as few hands as possible.

Paradoxically, the requirements of acting upon and institutionalizing the mutual United States-Soviet interest in controlling the military capabilities in one's own camp—and encouraging the other side to control their's—were at cross-purposes with one of the most powerful spurs to control: hostility toward the rival's way of life, coupled with the premise that full-scale war between the two sides was a distinct possibility.

Unity of command within an alliance system was tolerable to all members so long as there was unity on the essential purposes for which action was most likely to be undertaken. But as hostility and the threat of war between the two major blocs of allies declined (the hoped-for atmosphere of détente being cultivated) each alliance member was able to rediscover its unique historical, geopolitical national interests and rivalries. And the possibilities for these different interests requiring incompatible strategies, even in interbloc conflicts, accelerated the loosening of bloc ties in the Communist and non-Communist worlds.

Mao's grievance against Khrushchev for the latter's insistence that the nuclear development program in China be conducted under close supervision from Moscow was severely aggravated during the Quemoy and Matsu crisis of 1958–59 when the Soviets failed to back up Communist Chinese actions with counterthreats against the United States implied use of nuclear weapons. In the early 1960s, with Khrushchev and Kennedy insisting that the non-nuclear nations stop their own nuclear weapons development programs, the Chinese could see only collusion between the superpowers to support one another in the perpetuation of their hegemony over their respective allies. Marxist-Leninist ideology, which was supposed to put the interests of all proletarian movements first, was, according to the Chinese, being subordinated to Soviet self-interest. This charge was not without a melodious ring to other Communist parties—particularly in Eastern Europe where there was serious resistance to the Soviet concept of economic specialization within a self-sufficient Communist trading area, which for most East European nations meant economic vassalage.

The United States was in the early 1960s quite well attuned to this bickering among the Communist nations. The question was how to exploit it to the advantage of our long-range interest in a reduction of

Soviet imperialism, without driving the Soviets into a renewal of anti-Western belligerency and paranoia in order to reassert control in their own sphere.

Developments in our alliance system, and the problems these must have posed to Soviet strategists, were viewed by the Kennedyites as somewhat embarrassingly parallel. And it was not beyond some members of the Alliance, notably de Gaulle with his penchant for cariacature, to draw these parallels in bold strokes to a world audience. His apocalyptic visions, such as "some awful day" when "Western Europe should be wiped out from Moscow and Central Europe from Washington" while the two superpowers spared one another, were the currency of intellectual discussion in Europe and the undertone to diplomatic discussion in NATO.

De Gaulle was stating bluntly what Anthony Eden and Guy Mollet had implied as far back as the Suez crisis in 1956. Only temporarily had the threat of bloc vs. bloc war, in the post-Sputnik Berlin crisis, and then again in 1961, suppressed the subterranean strains. Even in the Berlin crises, allied unity was seen by some observers as merely a façade covering intense differences among the allies over military and diplomatic moves for various contingencies. Also during these years, the intensifying centrifugal pulls of national interest were sublimated in esoteric strategic debates over the timing and targeting of nuclear strikes.

Meanwhile, particularly at the substructures of economic and technological development, the currents for division were also eroding the bases of "the community," piously proclaimed by the supranational institution builders in NATO and Common Market headquarters. And the two major Western community institutions were themselves increasingly at cross-purposes, as the latent contradictions in their reasons for existence were exposed.

In the spring and early summer of 1962, with the Third World crises of the previous year no longer consuming so much of its energies, the Kennedy Administration gave special attention to reasserting its leadership of the Atlantic Community within both the military and economic spheres. Experimental projects for a greater European nuclear role in the Alliance were stressed for the former, and the vision of institutional innovation on a grand scale was projected for the latter.

Early in his Presidency, Kennedy had affirmed his intention to commit to the NATO command the five Polaris submarines originally suggested by President Eisenhower.[1] The commitment of the missile-carrying submarines was confirmed by the President in his May 17, 1961 address to the Canadian Parliament (see above, pp. 178–79).

During the first half of 1962 private diplomatic discussions among the NATO members were held on what Secretary Rusk was now calling "a NATO nuclear deterrent" in preparation for the May ministerial session of the North Atlantic Council. There was expectation that some departure in the existing United States policy of keeping unto ourselves exclusive command and control of the Alliance's nuclear forces (with the exception of the British V-Bombers) might be announced at the May meeting. But evidently this expectation was premature. Subsequent clarifications by United States officials showed we had no intention of increasing the number of "fingers on the nuclear trigger." And apparently, within this condition of retaining control in Washington, the French found our porposed arrangements not at all attractive. Not only was there no mention of a new arrangement for nuclear management in the NATO Council communiqué, but reporters were filing dispatches of a secret speech on nuclear strategy by the Secretary of Defense which presumably revived the rigid specialization of roles concept which many Europeans were now beginning to resent. (A somewhat edited version of this Athens speech was delivered by the Secretary to a University of Michigan commencement audience in June. See above, pp. 182–84.) With respect to the possibility of a NATO-owned-operated-controlled missile force, Secretary Rusk could only inform inquiring reporters that:

We did not get into that in any detail here in Athens because it is a very complex matter that requires detailed, highly technical considerations among the governments, but we did instruct our representatives in the Permanent Council in Paris . . . to see whether there is any agreement, any basis on which we should proceed.[2]

One of the "complexities" was given a more open airing by General de Gaulle in his news conference pronunciamento of May 15, 1962. France, he confirmed, was now bringing its own atomic deterrent force into existence. "As regards the defense of France, the battle of Europe and even the world war as they were imagined when NATO was born, everything is now in question." The French atomic force "is changing and will completely change the conditions of our own defense, those of our intervention in faraway lands and those of the contribution that we would be able to make to safeguard our allies." France's defense, he intoned, for moral and political reasons had to "become once again a national defense." [3]

In President Kennedy's presss conference two days later, the status of the disagreement with France was clarified. We believed the existing deterrent system for NATO provided adequate protection, said the President. Once nation after nation begins to develop its own deterrent, "You are moving into an increasingly dangerous situation." "If they [the French] choose to go ahead, of course they will go ahead, and General de Gaulle has announced they are going ahead." There was apparently nothing we could do or say that would dissuade him. However, with respect to the long-range future of the Atlantic Community, and the respective roles of each country within it, the discussions would continue.

Kennedy avoided the immediate temptation to express the full extent of his annoyance with de Gaulle, salvaging instead whatever measure of influence he might retain with the imperious Frenchman, and retaining in view of our other allies the demeanor of the leader who knows his own ascendancy remains unshaken:

. . . I would say, speaking personally, that however difficult becomes this dialogue with General de Gaulle over . . . the Atlantic Community . . . I would think it would be a far more difficult situation if General de Gaulle were not as stalwart in his defense of the West. We do not look for those who agree with us, but those who defend their country and who are committed to the defense of the West. I believe General de Gaulle is. So we will get along.[4]

Despite the gracefulness, it *was* a serious rebuff the United States had suffered, and, at that, in reply to an intendedly magnanimous offer to give the Europeans a greater participatory role in planning and administering the nuclear strategy of the Alliance. Temporarily, our efforts to reforge unity through a new momentum in military planning were stalemated.

The other arena of challenge to United States hegemony was that of international economics, to which the emphasis was quickly shifted. Here the momentum was in Europe. Even Great Britain had made application to join the Common Market, in a major reversal of her historic insular trading position, and at a sacrifice to her special Commonwealth relationships. The Kennedy Administration had prodded the British in this direction, largely to open up the Continental exclusiveness. But there was the risk that Britain would adapt to the protectionist pattern against America, rather than wedge an opening for American penetration.

There was yet opportunity for us to respond to the European economic movement creatively and augment our international influence while promoting our own economic health. The Reciprocal Trade Agreements Act was due to expire in mid-1962. The occasion of congressional action for its renewal could be turned into a major reconsideration of our position in the world economy: an analysis of our adverse balance of international payments in comparison with the dramatically improving balances on the part of members of the European Common Market, and the recommendation of a vigorous new United States trade policy designed to compete with and within the market. The Administration's Trade Expansion Act had been prepared in late 1961 and presented to the Congress in January 1962; but now the time was at hand when a major push for its passage coincided with the need to redefine our attitude to an increasingly independent, and, if de Gaulle had his way, inward looking, Europe.

On the same day he had replied to de Gaulle in his press conference, President Kennedy combined the themes of Atlantic partnership and trade expansion in his address to a national conference on trade policy. It is a "fact of history," he told the gathering of Congressmen and businessmen active in the trade field, "that responsibility and influence—in all areas, political, military, and economic—ultimately rise and fall together." He discounted the fears expressed in Europe that the United States might be abandoning its commitment to European security. But he also wanted to discount "fears . . . on this side of the Atlantic that the United States may be excluded from the councils and the markets of Europe." The "true course of history" was toward "Atlantic unity." He was striking out at the "limited visions and suspicions" on both sides of the Atlantic.

The President had asked the Congress to grant him broad tariff-cutting authority, so that in negotiations with the Common Market countries he would be equipped with a powerful quid for the quo we wanted from them: namely a reduction of their tariffs on United States products. But, for this new era of freer trade Kennedy was trying to bring about, we would have to compete. The end result would be a higher standard of living for all Americans. "Trade expansion will help spur plant moderniaztion. . . . There'll be new employment in our growth industries . . . and less employment in some others." He was confident in the economy's ability to adjust, and some adjustments would probably require government insurance. "But we will be producing more of what we produce best, and others will be producing more of what they produce best. . . .":

To falter now, or become afraid of economic challenges in this country which has been second to none in all of our history in our ability to compete, or become impatient in the face of difficult or delicate diplomatic problems . . . could well undo all the great achievements of this nation in building this great Atlantic Community.[5]

The President was groping for an idea, the Grand Design, that was to emerge full-blown, in all its glorious ambiguity, on July 4 in his ringing call for a "Declaration of Interdependence":

One hundred and eighty-six years ago, in the same hall from which he now spoke, Thomas Jefferson and his colleagues pledged their lives, their fortunes, their sacred honor in support of a declaration whose doctrine of national *independence* "remains the most powerful force anywhere in the world today."

But the idea of national independence had now reached its zenith: "With the passing of ancient empires, today less than 2 per cent of the world's population lives in territories officially termed 'dependent.' " Out of the power of the first idea, as in the American experience, was born its natural antithesis—which also resounded from this hall in Philadelphia across the world—the doctrine of the "indivisible liberty of all":

As this effort for independence, inspired by the American Declaration of Independence, now approaches a successful close, a great new effort—for interdependence—is transforming the world about us. And the spirit of that new effort is the same spirit which gave birth to the American Constitution.

The new spirit was currently exhibiting the greatest momentum on the other side of the Atlantic. The United States, having for the past seventeen years aided this vast enterprise for European unity, looked upon this development with hope and admiration, said the President:

We do not regard a strong and united Europe as a rival but as a partner. . . . We believe that a united Europe will be capable of playing a greater role in the common defense, or responding more generously to the needs of the poorer nations, of joining with the United States and others in lowering trade barriers . . . and developing coordinated policies in all economic, political and diplomatic areas.

But this effort to form a more perfect union in Europe was only the first order of business of the grand effort to build the Atlantic Partnership:

. . . I will say here and now, on this Day of Independence, that the United States will be ready for a Declaration of Interdependence, that we will be prepared to discuss with a united Europe the ways and means of forming . . . a mutually beneficial partnership between the new union now emerging in Europe and the old American Union founded here 175 years ago.

It would be premature, said the President, to present in concrete detail the design of this emerging Atlantic partnership. Great edifices were not simply or cheaply built. They emerged creatively out of the practice and act of building. But "let the world know it is our goal." [6]

However vague the Grand Design, it did serve as an orienting goal and legitimating ideology for policies which, in the face of a decline in enthusiasm for anti-Communism as an orienting principle, were becoming increasingly difficult to defend. Under the Grand Design it was still possible to assert the requirement for a complete coordination of military planning within the NATO alliance, for a unified system of command and control, for a specialization of function according to capability and resources, for the United States to serve as nuclear "trustee" of the West, for a solid front on economic matters toward the Communist world—in short, but never stated so baldly, for the perpetuation of United States hegemony.

The Cuban missile crisis intervened, and diverted high-level discussion away from Atlantic Community matters for a few months. Indeed, so compelling was the need for secrecy of deliberation, rapid dispatch of decisions made, and tight command and control, that allies were informed of all key decisions after the fact, rather than consulted while strategies were being formulated. The heads of state among our allies understood, and, in contrast to the sniping expressed in their parliaments and newspapers, gave President Kennedy every indication that they backed his tight control of the reins of decision during the crisis. De Gaulle openly pledged his complete support, and apparently fully approved of the premise of unilateralism exhibited by the United States actions in the Caribbean crisis. After all, it confirmed his own thesis of self-mastery for the life and death decisions of the national unit. He only wanted the United States to accept that such national sovereignty was legitimate for others as well.

But for Kennedy the lsesons, at least the immediate ones, of the Cuban missile crisis only strengthened conclusions that were diametrically opposed to de Gaulle's with respect to the international management of nuclear weapons. Suppose the Soviets had transferred actual physical control of the missiles to the Castro regime. The fact of divergent national interests between these two Communist allies might then have stimulated a missile launching by Castro. If the United States, in attempting to prod the Soviets to restrain Castro had made the kind of threat Kennedy made on October 22—namely, that the Soviet Union would be the object of our retaliation in case of a missile launched from Cuban soil—the Soviets might be hard-pressed to preempt our "retaliatory" blow by striking us first. At least under the circumstances of a precipitate missile launching by Castro, the Soviets would be extremely trigger-happy, and prone to mistake our precautionary strategic alerts as the beginning of our countdown.

McNamara's preachments in Athens, and then at the University of Michigan, now stood as the essence of strategic wisdom:

Limited nuclear capabilities, operating independently, are dangerous, expensive, prone to obsolescence, and lacking in credibility as a deterrent. . . . [It is essential to have] unity of planning, concentration of executive authority, and central direction. There must not be competing and conflicting strategies to meet the contingency of nuclear war.

During his thoughtful radio-television conversation shortly after the Cuban missile crisis, the President was asked about his views on proliferation of nuclear weapons among our European allies. "We don't want six or seven separate nuclear powers diverting their funds to nuclear power," answered the President, but if they want to do it, "we are not stopping them." The question was whether we should help make France a nuclear power—"then Italy, then West Germany, then Belgium":

How does that produce security when you have ten, twenty, thirty nuclear powers who may fire their weapons off under different conditions? That isn't in our interest, or in my opinion in the interest of peace, or the interest of Western Europe.[7]

The day following the broadcast of these remarks, the President met with Prime Minister Macmillan in the Bahamas to negotiate the Nassau agreement, which was to make the British nuclear deterrent force ever-more dependent upon United States technical and material support, and provided for its incorporation into a NATO multilateral force. (See above, pp. 185–87.) The same type of association was offered to France.

De Gaulle seized the occasion to stage one of his tantrums: Britain was castigated in French diplomatic circles for perfidious double-dealing, of pretending its inclinations were toward Continental association but meanwhile carrying on its "special relationship" with the United States. In January 1963, the French President abruptly halted the Brussels negotiations for Britain's entry into the Common Market, charging that her insular and maritime nature, plus her traditional trading linkages with diverse and distant countries had made it impossible for Britain to accept the primary commitments to the six Continental members of the market that membership would entail. Britain, he implied, was insisting upon unacceptable conditions, presumably the maintenance of Commonwealth trading preferences. If Britain now entered, she would probably be followed by the other members of her European Free Trade Association, with their own special extracontinental relationships. The European Community thus would be confronted with "all the problems" of Great Britain's economic relations with "a crowd of other states, and first of all with the United States." It was foreseeable, said the French President, that the cohesion of the European Community would not hold for long, and that:

In the end there would appear a colossal Atlantic Community under American dependence and leadership which would completely swallow up the European Community.

This is . . . not at all what France wanted to do and is doing, which is a strictly European construction.

Commenting on the Anglo-American agreement at Nassau as a basis for organizing the nuclear forces of the Alliance, de Gaulle rejected it as having any utility for France, or for that matter, he implied, any self-respecting European power:

To turn over our weapons to a multilateral force, under a foreign command, would be to act contrary to . . . [the principles] of our defense and our policy. It is true that we too can theoretically retain the ability to take back in our hands [when supreme national interests were at stake] . . . our atomic weapons incorporated in the multilateral force. But how could we do it in practice during the unheard of moments of the atomic apocalypse? And then, this multilateral force necessarily entails a web of liaisons, transmissions and interferences within itself, and on the outside a ring of obligations such that, if an integral part were suddenly snatched from it, there would be a strong risk of paralyzing it, just at the moment, perhaps, when it should act.

Instead of the Atlantic relationships sponsored by the United States, France was now concentrating on the "more fruitful" rapprochement between France and Germany. "For the first time in many generations, the Germans and Gauls realize their solidarity." [8]

President Kennedy responded moderately to the French allegations and actions in his January and February 1963 press conferences, but he could not help being somewhat angered at the shambles of his Grand Design. The hard and fast reality, he said, was still the fact that the Communist apparatus, controlling more than a billion people, daily confronts Europe and the United States with hundreds of missiles and scores of divisions. The resources essential to the defense against this danger were concentrated overwhelmingly in the Atlantic Alliance. But only in unity did the alliance have ample strength to balance the Communist power. That which serves to unite us is right, he said, "and what tends to divide us is wrong." What kind of Europe did the Europeans want? he asked, "Do they want one looking out or looking in?"

Today, observed the President, Europe is only relatively secure:

The day may come when Europe will not need the United States and its guarantees. I don't think that day has come yet, and we would welcome that. We have no desire to stay in Europe except to participate in the defense of Europe. Once Europe is secure and feels secure, then the United States has 400,000 troops there and we would, of course, want to bring them home.

He admitted concern at the failure of Britain to obtain membership in the Common Market. It had been our policy, and over the last fifteen years we had put $50 billion worth of assistance behind it, to further a stronger Europe. We felt Britain would be an effective member of that Europe. It was still our hope, however, that a "powerful Europe, joined with the power of the North American Continent, would provide a source of strength in this decade which would permit the balance of power to be maintained. . . ." It would be "a disaster if we should divide." [9]

The State Department "theologians" (the name current during this period for United States officials who were fervent disciples of the European and Atlantic integrator, Jean Monnet) were only stimulated to greater proselytyzing by the high-level "confrontation" between the two "Grand Designs." De Gaulle's design was now openly pictured as reactionary—a return to the older pattern of historical national rivalries in Europe, the pattern which had led to two world wars—and dangerous in that it would encourage the spread of independent nuclear weapons, especially to West Germany, who, with her deep urges to reunite Germany, was capable of rash action. The President was persuaded to appoint a special mission, headed by ex-diplomat Livingston Merchant, to tour West European capitals in behalf of a revised multilateral nuclear force whose core owner-members were now to be Britain, West Germany, and the United States, along with any other NATO members who could be induced to join. France was written off as neither a necessary nor desirable participant. This new MLF, a fleet of twenty-five missile-carrying surface ships, each manned by an international crew, was now presented as the "only alternative" to a presumed imminent German decision to build her own nuclear force under French tutelage.

The President allowed this kind of talk to go on, during the very same months he was making his major efforts to negotiate a nuclear test ban with the Soviets, perhaps to strengthen the impression that we were doing all we could to restrict the spread of nuclear weapons. It is doubtful that he was as highly motivated to actually launch the MLF as were the State Department Atlanticists; nor, apparently, did he think the Europeans would really want to join. Sorenson reports that "gradually in 1963 the MLF proposal fell from the top of the President's agenda toward the bottom." Moreover, "Kennedy had never looked upon either MLF or British entry into EEC as pillars of American policy." [10]

Chroniclers of the Johnson Presidency portray him during his first year as the captive of pronouncements of the MLF zealots in the Department of State, who interpreted his lack of personal attention to this matter as approval of the preexisting formal policy line. Philip Geyelin's account suggests that public endorsements of the multilateral force by the President himself on April 20 and June 12, 1964 were probably in the nature of speech ingredients included as part of the standard recipe of foreign policy statements handed up from the bureaucracy. But Johnson, with his instinct for unfettered movement, swiftly cast off these prior commitments, when it came to making more specific decisions on the financing and composition of such a multilateral venture in preparation for his December meeting with Prime Minister Harold Wilson.[11] There were no agreements made with the Prime Minister on either the MLF or the alternative ANF (Atlantic Nuclear Force), which the British came prepared to advocate. The President merely thrust the responsibility back into the lap of the British to work out some mutually agreeable formula with the Germans, which the United States might then be prepared to discuss. This was, of course, only another way of saying we had washed our hands of the whole matter.

The MLF was in fact abandoned, and left to die from Presidential neglect, although in rhetoric it lingered for a while as the centerpiece of the United States concept of Atlantic Partnership; and the virtual institution that had grown up around it in the State Department continued with artificial respiration (the Germans were insisting on the MLF, went the line) to keep up the pretense that the MLF was still everyone's hope for holding together an otherwise crumbling NATO.

A part of the United States political strategy, of which the MLF was only a convenient instrument, was to keep the Federal Republic of Germany oriented toward us rather than de Gaulle. Every opportunity was taken, in rhetoric, in NATO force-planning sessions, in trade negotiations, to remind Germany that what she wanted most—protection against attack from the East, continued access to Berlin, eventual reunification, membership in international bodies, new trading opportunities—would be more likely to be advanced through her close ties with the United States than with France. We were pleased at the German-French reconciliation, we said, but not at all likely to respond kindly to German adopting a Gaullist "inward looking" posture. The post-Adenauer regime of Ludwig Erhard and Gerhard Schroeder at first seemed to size up the situation in this way too; but as the French President began to intensify French-Eastern European trading and cultural contacts, and to show greater cordiality to Moscow, to take specific steps, not just pontificating, toward weaving a greater Europe "from the Atlantic to the Urals," the post-Adenauer politicians of West Germany also began to search for opportunities to demonstrate "movement," away from the static NATO-first concepts propounded by the United States.

The frustrations suffered by the United States government in trying to begin the MLF and other devices of military "integration" as a means for consolidating the Atlantic Partnership produced two contrary reactions in high policy circles.

The first, associated mainly with the Atlanticists in the Department of State, sought to counter the belief propounded by many of our European friends, including the Germans, that the threat of war between the NATO and Warsaw Pact nations was now so unlikely as to render strict unity of command principles obsolete if not irrelevant. Reflecting the formulations of George Ball, Robert Schaetzel, and others in the State Department, Secretary Rusk reminded the spring 1964 meeting of the NATO Council that, although certain tensions in Europe appeared to have been somewhat relaxed and Communist tactics had been modified, "Communist objectives continue to pose a direct threat to the free world." We should not let NATO's success blind us to current dangers, he cautioned: "Certain of these dangers seem to have diminished; but they can reappear suddenly and without warning. The need for a strong alliance of North Atlantic nations remains essential so long as basic Communist aims remain unchanged." [12]

The second reaction to our frustrations in NATO surfaced at first largely in the form of recommendations by prominent unofficial analysts of the Soviet Union and the Cold War that we consider major alterations in our prevailing mode of containing Communist expansion in Europe. George Kennan resigned his Ambassadorship to Yugoslavia in pique at the congressionally imposed restrictions on his attempts to establish flexible bilateral trading relationships with the Tito regime, and returned to argue with his colleagues at the Council on Foreign Relations on the need of fundamentally revising our premises on how to deal with the Communist world in its new phase of "polycentrism." [13] Before that same influential body in 1965, Marshall Shulman argued that "the language and ideas of the Cold War are no longer adequate as a guide to international politics today." [14] And Columbia University's Zbigniew Brzezinski, a highly respected authority on Soviet policies in Eastern Europe, began to lecture and write extensively to officials and opinion leaders on the timeliness of a major new Western effort to increase economic and political ties across the Iron Curtain.[15]

Though differing in the details of their analyses and prescriptions, these prominent analysts gave voice to and advanced a common body of premises that were to make rapid inroads on the still-prevailing Cold War premises, reflected in the dominant aspects of our foreign policy. At the time of this writing, they could not yet be called operational premises, the war in Vietnam being in large part responsible for the delay in their incorporation into specific programs. These fresh premises can be summarized as follows:

A. The so-called International Communist Movement was undergoing significant changes in its political structure, socio-economic bases, and ideology that were not planned or dictated by its leaders, nor forecast in its ideology.

B. The tendencies within the Communist world which appeared to be gaining the upper hand over countervailing tendencies were: (1) the decentralization of authority and power over resource allocation from the Communist Party of the Soviet Union to the national units; (2) decision-making on major policy issues (for managing affairs within the Communist world and for relations with the non-Communist world) being transferred to the arena of interstate diplomacy, that is, Communist national leaders bargaining with other Communist national leaders, and away from reliance on decision-making by the international Party machinery; (3) independent, bilateral foreign relations between nations within the Communist world and by individual Communist nations with non-Communist nations, especially on matters of trade; and (4) powerful segments of bureaucracies and societies in the Communist nations (including the Soviet Union) becoming committed to the perpetuation of the kind of international East-West climate conducive to this decentralization toward national as opposed to "bloc" instrumentalities of decision.

C. If these tendencies were allowed to continue, it was possible to envision a transformation of International Communism from an aggressive centralized movement seeking world domination to heterogeneous Marxist parties attempting to implement their preferred concepts of state socialism within their own countries.

D. None of this would guarantee a mitigation of the harsher aspects of totalitarian rule in these nations; indeed, the transition to national Communism from Soviet-controlled Communism could, in some cases, be accompanied by a tightening of political, intellectual, and artistic control. But the very fact of pluralism in the Communist World, of relief from exclusive dependency upon decisions made at the apex of a rigid hierarchy located in Moscow, and the opportunity for each nation to choose trading and cultural partners in the non-Communist world, could in time lead to a greater pluralism, pragmatism, and genuine democracy within most national Communist societies.

E. These evolutionary tendencies were fully consistent with the central objective of U.S. foreign policy since 1947: namely, to contain Communism without in the process bringing on a Third World War.

On this much there was agreement among Kennan, Shulman, and Brzezinski, and a growing coterie of Soviet specialists and foreign policy analysts, many of whom were consultants to the Departments of State and Defense, and to the White House during the Kennedy years.

The question on which the growing consensus broke down was what could and should the United States do to encourage this evolution in the Communist world. Even before our heavy involvement in the shooting war in Vietnam, the official bureaucracy, more guarded against congressional censure than charges from academic friends of being wedded to obsolete policy premises, lumbered along with programs and rhetoric fashioned in the simpler good guys vs. bad guys phase of the Cold War. Lacking concrete suggestions for altering existing policy, the official rhetoric, for the most part, noted the "hopeful signs" appearing in the Communist world, but held fast to the proposition that this merely demonstrated the correctness of our past policies, particularly with respect to the rebuilding, rearming, and coalescing to Western Europe under our leadership.

There were some exceptions to the official reiteration of standing formulas, however, which extended back to the Truman Administration. The United States had aided and traded with Yugoslavia to strengthen Tito's ability to maintain his independence of the Soviet Union, even though in the early days we were unimpressed with the differences between the Yugoslav socialist system and the Stalinist model. After the East European crises of 1956, the United States moved quickly to provide economic assistance to Poland; Poland as well as Yugoslavia was extended "most favored nation" trading privileges. And during the late 1950s and early 1960s cultural exchanges with the East European countries were intensified, with ballets, symphony orchestras, and popular musical artists leading the East-West traffic.

But even these marginal policies for extending economic and cultural contacts across the Iron Curtain were met with a wall of Congressional resistance, especially when they happened to enter the glare of publicity. The announcement of Tito's October 1963 visit to the United States produced a new wave of articles in magazines such as *U.S. News and World Report* on how the United States was spending billions on those who want to "bury capitalism." The arrival of Tito in Washington so soon after the ratification of the test ban had stirred fears that the White House was moving too fast on its "journey of a thousand miles."

President Kennedy's guarded handling of his decision to allow the Soviets to purchase United States wheat was a product of this perception that influential segments of Congress would only revive the "blood on their hands" accusations against International Communism if it were presented as a détente-enchancing transaction. The President resorted to justifying the wheat transaction as only a commercial undertaking, dictated primarily by national economic self-interest: it would result in savings to the taxpayer by reducing our government-stored surpluses; it would be paid for in gold, and thereby help reduce our balance-of-payments deficit; it would allow us to enter a world market already being exploited by other agricultural exporting countries, many of whom were our allies.

In short, explained the President, this particular decision on sales of surplus wheat to the Soviets "does not represent a new Soviet-American trade policy. That must await the settlement of many matters." [16]

The many Cold War matters still awaiting settlement were set forth by the Policy Planning Council chairman, Walt Rostow, in the October

1963 issue of the internationally read *Foreign Affairs* quarterly. We were at the beginning of a major effort, he cautiously stated, *"to estab-lish whether or not it is possible* for the Soviet Union and the West to live together on this planet under conditions of tolerable stability and low tension." (Emphasis added.) In a sense:

the fundamental diplomatic issues and problems remain precisely what they were in the immediate postwar days. The fundamental issues are arms con-trol and Germany. The fundamental problems are the unwillingness of the Soviet Union to accept the kind of inspection and international control re-quired to get a serious grip on the arms race, and the Soviet unwillingness to accept a clear separation of its legitimate national security interests in Central Europe from its ideological commitment to hold East Germany as a Communist state against the will of its people.

Yet there were signs that the Soviet Union might be coming around to realizing there was a strong "objective case," from the standpoint of basic Soviet interests, for effectively controlling the arms race and "eas-ing the dangers to all" represented by the Ulbricht regime:

These two great unresolved issues pose for those responsible in Moscow the same question which the Chinese Communists have put to them in recent months with such brutal candor: Is the policy of the Soviet Union to be a policy rooted in the interests of the Russian nation and its people? Or is it to be a policy rooted in an abiding effort to spread the cause of Com-munism over the face of the earth? In the end, this remains the relevant question.

But the United States too bore some responsibility for helping the So-viets to answer anew this challenge to their Leninist ideological legacy. The solutions that we propose, counselled Rostow, must encourage the Soviet Union and its allies:

. . . to perceive that the world we in the West are trying to create by our own efforts and by negotiation has a place of dignity for *all* nations which pursue their national interests with integrity, which respect the hard imper-atives of interdependence and the rights of other nations and peoples.[17] (Emphasis added.)

The concept of a "pluralistic world," by which we had been hoping to contain the Communists' effort to impose their system on others, might also be our most effective concept for encouraging a reduction of Soviet domination of the nations of Eastern Europe. But it had a cor-ollary which was somewhat difficult to square with a good deal of our

Cold War rhetoric and policy: it required that we accord a greater degree of legitimacy to national Communist regimes already in existence, provided they were not externally aggressive.

It was also difficult to stress our dedication to "pluralism" based on the nation as the unit and yet react as if de Gaulle was a heretic to *our* "wave of the future" designs for an integrated North Atlantic Community.

In Asia, the Middle East, Africa, and even Latin America we had, since the Dulles era, moved far toward operationalizing this ideology of national self-determination, even where it meant our having to provide economic support to nations more hostile toward us than toward our Communist rivals. But, in Europe, we still regarded the possibility of a major ally turning neutral as being higher stakes. In the Third World, meaning the "underdeveloped" world, nonalignment was a configuration we could live with, and indeed put to the service of our global strategy for maintaining the balance of power. The development of a nonaligned "third force" in Europe was of a different order altogether, especially if that force possessed its own nuclear capabilities and came into existence prior to a general European East-West settlement that would include the reunification of Germany.

In Europe the timing of an evolution toward greater decentralization of control might have to proceed at a different pace on the western side of the Elbe than on the eastern side. But would such a stance by us be combatible with the kind of Soviet acquiescence in the reduced measures of control over her European satellites we were trying to encourage? President Kennedy, as far as is known, had not in his own mind resolved the potentially momentous cross pressures between the requirements of his objective of maintaining control, particularly over the disposition of nuclear forces in the Atlantic Community, and the requirements of effecting a greater decline in Soviet ideological and material control over the nations of Eastern Europe.

A pragmatic exploration of more economic and cultural bridges across the Iron Curtain was on the agenda at the time of John F. Kennedy's assassination. The wheat transaction with the Soviets was yet encountering Congressional obstacles. The overcoming of these obstacles (such as the amendments to the 1964 Foreign Assistance Act denying the Export-Import Bank authority to guarantee loans to the Soviets to purchase the wheat) was a task to which President Johnson became committed—not so much out of conviction that the wheat sale was a good thing, but more as an early test case to establish his control over the Congress. In his successful push to defeat these legislative restrictions on his negotiating authority, the new President discovered that there was less of an emotional popular opposition to fresh commercial transactions with the Communist countries than some congressmen were claiming.

Moreover, the President found considerable enthusiasm among the exporting segments of American industry for greater economic openings to the East, especially since the Canadians and West Europeans were rapidly expanding their commerce with the Communist world. Reflecting this growing sentiment in the business community, the United States Chamber of Commerce gave its endorsement to the efforts of Presidents Kennedy and Johnson to arrange for the sale of wheat to the Soviet Union and called for additional exploration of the possibilities for expanding East-West trade in nonstrategic goods. Organized labor at this point was more hostile to the idea of expanding East-West trade, fearing that the influx of cheap goods made by labor unable to increase its wages through collective bargaining would undercut American labor's ability to bargain for higher wages in the future.

The January 1964 issue of *Foreign Affairs* featured an article by George Kennan calling upon the Western nations to shape their policies in such a way as "to create advantages and premiums for efforts on the part of the satellite governments to extend their relations with Western countries." He urged his readers to recall that the original Marshall Plan concept deliberately left open the possibility of the extension of European economic arrangements to the entire continent, and that the failure of this grander scheme to materialize was due to the self-exclusion of the East European regimes. Now, if as a result of the evolution of interstate relations in the Communist bloc and the gradual loosening of their rigidly controlled economies and totalitarian social structures, the satellite regimes were willing to increase their economic relations with the West, should we not return to our original concept for a revived continent-wide European economy? Although it was too early to talk of a fundamental settlement of the issues dividing Europe, and of a mutual disengagement of military forces from the German demarcation zone, we ought to be doing what could be done to encourage ideological differentiation, polycentric tendencies, and the interpenetration of spheres in the hope that these would be accompanied by a reduction in the military bloc vs. military bloc legacy of the harsher days of the Cold War. Ideally, at the end of the process lay the realization of the dream of the peaceful unification of all of Europe, and the revival of the great European civilization.

Seasoned diplomat Kennan admitted that "Polycentrism may continue to develop, in spite of . . . the face which the West turns to the troubled and vacillating world of Communism." But if we fail to exploit creatively this historic opportunity for greater interaction, he warned, we risk alienating those "tens of millions of people in Communist countries who still look to the West with longing and with hope and who expect from it policies which take account of all the subtlety and contradiction of their position." More than anything else now these people want "contact with the outside world." This—not the continuation of a Western "quixotic commitment to a highly unlikely violent revolution"—was their hope for a relaxation of the severity under which they were forced to live.

The point of Kennan's disquisition was that to provide these millions of Eastern Europeans with the Western contacts they craved, we would have to deal with and through those regimes we and they disliked. To do so, the West would have "to show itself reconciled to the existence of these regimes, without accepting responsibility for them . . . to convey to them that they have nothing to fear from . . . [the West] if they will only refrain, themselves, from hostile and subversive policies." This, of course, was a more explicit departure from the orientation of our previous policy than Congress, with its "captive nation" resolutions, could be expected to endorse in principle. But Kennan's statement was to provide an orienting philosophy for those people in the Executive and the Congress who were campaigning for greater flexibility in our trade and aid relationships with Eastern Europe.

Kennan was no longer in the government, nor could he claim to speak for the unofficial foreign policy establishment. But occasionally the relevance and basic truth of a position, if eloquently stated to those in power, will resound within the decision-making centers of the polity so that the purely academic becomes a political force by the fact of its clear and timely articulation. This was one of those times.

It was incumbent upon the Secretary of State to react constructively to the Kennan thesis. He could not ignore it, nor cavalierly rebut it.

What Rusk did was to show, by his own thoughtful statement on Eastern Europe, that Kennan was actually describing a gradual policy evolution which the Administration was fostering. The government might not be ready to explicitly endorse Kennan's ideas in the form they were stated, nor did it care to give the evolution a fancy name as if to announce a "new" policy. But possibly it was time to provide the public and the Congress with a clearer appreciation of the premises that informed the Aministration's requests to be accorded greater freedom of maneuver in dealing with the Communist world.

"We have always considered it unnatural," the Secretary of State affirmed in his address of February 25, 1964:

. . . for the diverse peoples of Eastern Europe, with their own talents and proud traditions, to be submerged in a monolithic bloc. We have wanted these peoples, while living in friendship with their Russian and other neighbors, to develop in accordance with their own national aspirations and genius.

This had been our objective, and beyond that we had also ardently hoped for the evolution within those nations of "open" societies capable of satisfying the basic human needs, including the enjoyment of individual freedom. However much these might be our objectives, explained the Secretary, our capacity to influence trends within the Communist world was very limited. This was particularly so during the period of Stalinist terror:

But in recent years an important new trend has been perceptible: some of the Communist governments have become responsive, in varying degrees, if not directly to the aspirations of their subjects, at least to kindred aspirations of their own. *The Communist world is no longer a single flock of sheep following blindly behind one leader.*

.   .   .

The smaller Communist countries of Eastern Europe have increasingly, although in varying degree, asserted their own policies. . . . Most of them are increasing their trade and other contacts with Western Europe and, to some extent, with us. (Emphasis added.)

In light of these recent trends, Rusk outlined the approach the Administration favored for implementing "our policy to do what we can to encourage evolution in the Communist world toward national independence and open societies":

We favor more contacts between the peoples behind the Iron Curtain and our own peoples. We should like to see more Soviet citizens visit the United States. We would be glad to join in cooperative enterprises to further mankind's progress against disease, poverty, and ignorance.

And informing the particular applications of this general policy of encouraging peaceful contacts and cooperation, claimed the Secretary of State, was the conviction that "we can best promote these objectives by adjusting our policies to the differing behavior of different Communist states—or to the changing behavior of the same state."

This discriminating approach, Rusk tried to show, was not new. When Yugoslavia challenged Stalin's monolithic control in 1948 we extended military and economic assistance to the Tito regime. A good deal of the national autonomy and domestic liberalization that the Poles won in 1956 persists, and for these reasons Poland for some years has merited more cordial treatment than other Soviet block states. "We apologize to none for our efforts to help the brave people of Poland to preserve their national identity and their own aspirations." On the other hand, as a result of Bulgaria's role in the suppression of the Hungarian revolution, we had not maintained an embassy there since 1956; and we had refrained from establishing any diplomatic relations with Stalinist Albania. More recently, Rumania had asserted an independent attitude, reflected in its expansion of trade and other contacts with the West, and we had been responding in a generally positive manner to her desire to improve relations with us. Even relations with Hungary were improving as the Kadar regime had "turned to a more permissive policy of national conciliation." We are watching these developments with close attention, said the U.S. Secretary of State.[18]

To be sure, the principles of U.S. foreign policy in past years did not exclude such a policy of differentiated contacts. But the prevailing premises of containment during the Truman-Stalin period virtually cut off all significant interaction between the Communist and non-Communist worlds (with the exception of Yugoslavia) that was not of a hostile nature. And in the pre-Hungary period of the Eisenhower Administration, the Dulles-liberation premises rejected the notion that any Communist satellite regime was a legitimate member of the diplomatic community. Even our establishment of closer ties with Poland after 1956 had strong liberationist overtones which Dulles did little to dissipate, and it had a decided anti-Soviet edge. Now, despite Rusk's claim of a constant thread, the new wrinkle was that an intensification of interaction, "using every kind of peaceful contact available" (to quote Harriman [19]), was emerging as a central thrust, not just a marginal probe, of our East European policy.

Rusk's speech was well received in this country and in Western Europe, with the exception of the West German government who feared it might imply a move on the part of the Johnson Administration toward diplomatic recognition of the Ulbricht regime.

President Johnson, evidently impressed by the lack of any significant outcry even from politicians with East European descendants prominent in their constituencies, sounded the theme of East-West reconciliation once again when dedicating the George C. Marshall Research Library at the Virginia Military Institute on May 23, 1964. As if paraphrasing George Kennan's *Foreign Affairs* article, the President recalled how to General Marshall "permanent peace depended upon rebuilding all European civilization within its historic boundaries." The correctness of Marshall's conviction had not changed, said the President:

Today we work to carry on the vision of the Marshall Plan. First, to strengthen the ability of every European people to select and shape its own society. Second, to bring every European nation closer to its neighbors in the relationship of peace. This will not be achieved by sudden settlement or dramatic deed. But the Nations of Eastern Europe are beginning to assert their own identity.

The time had apparently arrived to convey explicitly that there was a shift in emphasis taking place in our responses to events in Eastern Europe, and a concept was found to give this shift the look of a coherent policy:

We will continue to build bridges across the gulf which has divided us from Eastern Europe. They will be bridges of increased trade, of ideas, of visitors, and of humanitarian aid. We do this for four reasons: First, to open new relationships to countries seeking increased independence yet unable to risk isolation. Second, to open the minds of a new generation to the values and visions of the Western civilization from which they come and to which they belong. Third, to give freer play to the powerful forces of legitimate national pride—the strongest barrier to the ambition of any country to dominate another. Fourth, to demonstrate that . . . the prospects of progress for Eastern Europe lie in a wider relationship with the West.

The President was clearly saying things that would again raise the West German government's fear of according legitimacy to the Communist regime in East Germany. But this time, he was prepared to take the offensive, tying "building bridges" to the reunification of Germany, but suggesting the former was a *means* to the latter, that reunification would not simply emerge full-blown in some grand negotiated settlement—which no one thought was really feasible anyway. America and Europe have achieved sufficient strength and self-confidence, contended the President, to follow a course based on hope and opportunity rather than hostility and fear. Of course, our commitment to the defense of Europe and to the reunification of Germany was unalterable; but:

> . . . it is also our belief that wise and skillful development of relationships with the nations of Eastern Europe can speed the day when Germany will be reunited. We are pledged to use every peaceful means to work with friends and allies so that all of Europe may be joined in a shared society of freedom. In this way I predict the years to come will see us draw closer to General Marshall's bold design than at any time since he stood at Harvard and began to reshape the world.[20]

East-West trade was seen as the most fruitful possibility for building the bridges. The ideological issue could be muted; even West Germany, it could be pointed out, was a very active trader with Eastern Europe; and the temptations of American business to get into a new market could be played off against the emotional reactions of "trading with the enemy" that still resided in scattered segments of the American population. The important thing was not to provoke the opposition party to exploit the residue of emotionalism. This probably explains Johnson's ignoring of this issue during his 1964 Presidential Campaign.

The barrier to an expanded program of East-West trade was the Congressional legislation of 1951, denying the Administration authority to apply the same tariff schedules to goods from Communist countries as to identical goods from other countries. In other words, the "most favored nation" principle of our general reciprocal trading program, whereby all our trading partners become the beneficiaries of tariff reductions we may negotiate with any partner, could not be applied to the nations of Eastern Europe except as authorized by Congress. The Congress was persuaded to exempt Yugoslavia from this restriction, and later Poland. But the Administration now wanted to be accorded the authority to remove existing high-tariff restrictions against particular Communist countries in the process of its trade negotiations with them, without having to return to Congress in each case for a great debate over the legitimacy of the regime of each country as a precondition for extending "most favored nation" treatment.

Before formally requesting the Congress for a revision of the existing law, the President was careful to strengthen his bases of support within the business community. J. William Miller, chairman of the board of the Cummins Engine Company, was appointed chairman of a carefully selected blue-ribbon panel of business, labor, and academic leaders. The Miller report, submitted to the President in the spring of 1965, came out strongly for an expanded program of peaceful, nonstrategic trade "as an important instrument of our national policy" toward the Communist nations of Europe, one that would advance "our national welfare and world peace." The single most important step in this new policy, said the report, was to give the President discretionary authority over the granting or withholding of nondiscriminatory tariff treatment to individual countries of Eastern Europe.[21]

In the fall of 1965, the Administration further accelerated its campaign to prepare the ground for such legislation. The fullest exposition of the emerging policy came in an address to the Salesmanship Club of Dallas by the Assistant Secretary of State for Economic Affairs, Anthony M. Solomon. He attempted to show how American industry could only profit by the expansion of East-West trade, but these potential economic benefits to the United States, he explained, "are not the major reason" for the new policy. The economic returns would be marginal even under the most successful program of East-West trade, as the natural trading partners for the East Europeans were located in West Europe. The significant value of such expanded East-West trade lay in its potential political effects:

It is the contribution such trade can make to the lessening of tensions, fears and suspicions that isolation encourages, and the support that trade can give toward the progressive opening of the Iron Curtain—it is these that we value and should recognize as the critical gains from such trade.

Elaborating, Mr. Solomon contended that the Sino-Soviet split had given the countries of Eastern Europe more room for maneuver and an opportunity to assert their national interests. It is the Chinese Communist thesis, he said, that peaceful coexistence, in its true sense, is not possible between the free world and the Communist world. Should we accept the Communist Chinese dogma, he asked, and constrict the flow of peaceful goods, persons, and ideas—especially in Eastern Europe "where these can influence change in our direction?" Were we to accept so rigid a view, said the State Department official, "we would be aiding Chinese Communist foreign policy which is based entirely on looking down the gun barrel." The United States, of course, was not at a comparative disadvantage in this type of coercive diplomacy, but:

. . . while it is the case that we have more and bigger guns, and will continue so long as necessary to multiply these guns, to rely solely on them is to risk Armageddon. Surely the better course is to use other instruments available to us as well—and peaceful trade is one of them—prudently and wisely, to encourage the forces now at work toward peaceful intercourse and more normal relations.

The case for trade with the Communist nations, as then presented by Assistant Secretary Solomon, went beyond its usefulness as an instrument to pry loose the Eastern Europeans from Soviet control. It was also potentially a means to influence the evolution of the social systems in those countries in directions more compatible with our basic human values, and also, presumably, less likely to support foreign policies of external aggression and aggrandizement. For this reason we were not only anxious to support increased trade with the Soviet satellites; we were also anxious to expand mutually beneficial economic relationships with the Soviet Union.

The Soviets were in a period of critical self-examination, and experimentation with new forms of economic organization that gave a greater role to profits and permitted managers of enterprises some discretion in wage payments and incentives to labor. These reforms did not go so far as a number of reforms recently introduced in Eastern European countries, explained Solomon, "but they are a hesistant first step in the right direction." In this period of groping within the Soviet Union:

The presence of American factories, machinery, and equipment in the Soviet Union surely can be a means of demonstrating the efficiency and excellence of American products and American technology . . . [and] the superiority of the Western system of economic organization.

Consideration should also be given to the implications of Soviet trade in civilian goods for the allocation of Soviet resources to consumer goods, as opposed to military goods, urged Solomon. If more attractive consumption items and luxury goods become available to the Soviet citizens "it becomes difficult then for the regime to reverse direction without generating widespread . . . dissatisfaction. Luxury becomes necessity; and barring emergency situations, resources committed to civilian requirements continue to be so committed."

Another effect of increased trade with the Soviet Union might be to encourage her to adopt "Western standards of international behavior," including the observance of rules of arbitration, protection of industrial property and copyrights, and limitations on freedom to engage in disruptive trade practices. "If the USSR wanted to increase its trade with the West substantially, it would have to being its trade practices into line with those of the established world trading community."

Not since some of President Eisenhower's early speeches had an official spokesman of the government come so close to propounding the thesis, caricatured as "A Fat Communist is a Good Communist." The Assistant Secretary of State was careful, however, to throw in the caveat that "the normalization of behavior in economic intercourse" toward which we were tending "would not, of course, entail a reorientation in political thinking and political objectives" on the part of the Soviet Union. "But is it unreasonable to believe that small steps toward more normal intercourse might over the longer term have a cumulative beneficial effect in reducing the aggressive thrust of Soviet policy?"

Nor was the State Department going to allow the policy it was advocating to be facilely dismissed as playing into Soviet hands by letting down our guard and allowing the Communist bloc to strengthen its power to mount foreign offensives and subversive activities abroad. "We should . . . remember," said Solomon:

. . . that trade which can be encouraged when the time and circumstances are right can also be withdrawn when circumstances change. To move toward a more liberal trade policy with Communist Europe on a selective basis does not commit us in perpetuity to continue that policy. We do not give hostages to fortune. We are in full control.[22]

These were the range of considerations underlying President Johnson's rather cryptic, but very widely noticed remarks in his 1966 State of the Union message:

The . . . most important principle of our foreign policy is support of national independence—the right of each people to govern themselves—and to shape their own institutions.

. . .

We follow this principle by building bridges to Eastern Europe. And I will ask the Congress for authority to remove the special tariff restrictions which are a barrier to increasing trade between the East and the West.[23]

Gradually, somewhat fitfully, the nation was moving toward the European policy Zbigniew Brzezinski had been advocating since 1961, and had been calling "peaceful engagement." This was an alternative to simple containment, which implied an indefinite perpetuation of a partitioned Europe, or to Acheson's negotiation from strength which was predicated vaguely on some kind of Soviet submissive roll back of her Iron Curtain because of the overwhelming military superiority of the West, or to Dulles' "liberation" which assumed a collapse, possibly violent, of the Communist societies due to their internal contradictions. The policy of "peaceful engagement" assumed the capacity of Communist societies for evolution in the direction of greater pluralism internally and a more benign posture toward the outside world—if they were provided the proper environment and inducements to evolve in that manner.

The proper environment and inducements comprised:

The maintenance of Western military strength sufficient to deter Soviet provocations to Western interests (such as access to Berlin).

But abandonment of any posture, military or political, that conveys an intention of inducing a *defection* to the Western side by any of the current Soviet allies or economic partners East of the Elbe.

A shifting of our timetable for German reunification, making it the end result of the mending of the split of Europe, rather than the precondition for a European settlement. This need not imply an acceptance for the time being of the legitimacy of the Ulbricht regime; but it did mean the abandonment of the rigid West German policy, reflected in the "Hallstein Doctrine" of refusing to have cordial relations with other states that recognized East Germany. It was important for West Germany to cultivate good relations with such states, particularly Poland and Czechoslovakia, in order to eventually isolate East Germany, and show the obsolescence of a Soviet policy based on Germany's perpetual division.

A vigorous expansion of economic ties and cultural contacts between the West and Eastern Europe, the latter always insisted upon as being the necessary concommitant of closer commercial relations. An increasingly free flow of people and ideas, not simply a narrow economic quid pro quo, should be the explicit aim of our trade policy; and thus we should bargain hard on credit extensions, most-favored nation treatment, and the like to gain more openness in the East-West exchanges of literature, art, political journals and newspapers, intellectuals, scholars, and students. It would be such exchanges, not simply the alteration of material consumption patterns in the Communist countries, that would restore the vigor of the greater European civilization and render anachronistic the ideological division of the continent.

In 1965–66 the writings of Brzezinski and others, speeches by Administration spokesmen, the formal introduction into Congress of an East-West trade bill, and a series of limited accords including an agreement on the peaceful uses of outer space, the opening of direct air flights to the Soviet Union, the removal of more than 400 nonstrategic items from export control, the allowance of commercial credits to all the East European nations except Albania and East Germany, the extension of consular and cultural exchange agreements with the Soviet Union, the upgrading of our Bulgarian and Hungarian legations to embassies, the beginning of formal discussions in NATO on ways to increase contacts with Eastern European countries—all of these signaled the early phases of an adjustment of United States policy premises to the more pluralistic world we claimed to want: a world where the cement of friendship is more than ideological orthodoxy, and where the dominant lines of institution building are determined by more than considerations of military security, a world where power is a measure of one's ability to contribute creatively to the welfare and development of all.

Yet this tendency was upstaged by the more dramatic events in the external relations of the nation during the same period. The headlines, the rhetoric, and the allocation of resources were focused on crises that called for, or at least so it seemed to the leaders, a visible resort to the coercive instruments of power.

CHAPTER NINETEEN

VIETNAM AND THE DOMINICAN REPUBLIC: REASSERTION OF THE FUNCTIONS OF MILITARY POWER

The world has changed and so has the method of dealing with disruptions of the peace. . . . As a matter of fact, some people urged me to hurry in the marines when the air became hot on a particular occasion recently. . . . The people of the world . . . prefer reasoned agreement to ready attack. And that is why we must follow the Prophet Isaiah many many times before we send the marines, and say, "Come now and let us reason together."

LYNDON B. JOHNSON

On two central planks of the Kennedy foreign policy—arms control and a reduction in the hostile aspects of the United States–Soviet competition—President Johnson seemed able to credibly honor his pledge of November 1963 to continue in the path of his predecessor. In these fields, as pointed out in previous chapters, the essential groundwork had been laid, the implementing dialogue had started, and the critical factor in the environment, the Soviet Union's willingness to reduce the coercive content of her diplomacy, augured well for a period of peaceful coexistence.

But it had not been a premise of the Kennedy foreign policy that the thawing of the icy confrontation in Europe and suppression of military

324

conflict would end the intense power competition between the Communist and non-Communist worlds. Rather, the locus and the modes would shift, but the power contest would persist. Kennedy had often told the Soviets that if they would only be concerned with their own security and not with communizing the world, there would be no disagreements between them and us. But this had been offered more in the nature of a rhetorical point. He did not really expect a return to tranquillity, if indeed there ever was such a condition in international relations. The power struggle, in international no less than domestic politics, was a fact of political life, especially between the giants. Kennedy had delighted in being President at a time when the United States was unequivocally a giant; while appreciating the terrible responsibility of his position, he obviously relished full participation in the game.

Lyndon Johnson, on the other hand, did not seem to bring with him to the White House any well-developed premises about the workings of the international political system, nor any particular enthusiasm for the diplomatic game. With Kennedy's key foreign policy lieutenants assisting him in the details of maintaining the détente and negotiating arms-control agreements, Johnson could hope to devote his unique political skills to major innovations in domestic welfare policy. Foreign affairs were either an annoying distraction from his penchant for manipulating the domestic political system, or, if anything, conducted in response to a domestic political alignment rather than to an international one.

To this extent Johnson could be expected to act very much in the tradition of American nationalism, striving to avoid complicated foreign entanglements, but, when finally nagged into international action, coming out of the domestic hearth with a roar, legitimizing brutish entry into the arena with sweeping moralisms and pronouncements on our indispensability for the survival of the right and just. This describes a *style* of behavior and public posturing; it shows Johnson a reluctant warrior in international politics and Kennedy, by contrast, a happy one. Much of an entertaining nature has been written about the difference in style between Kennedy and Johnson. Yet did the difference in style reflect, or make for, a difference in policy?

The central question is whether any of Johnson's critical decisions (nonaction can also be a decision) were based on a different set of premises about the power of the United States in relation to other communities than the premises this writer believes to have animated the Kennedy foreign policy. Where was the constancy? Where the change? Differences in style may make for a difference in substance, but what does the record reveal?

Two moves by Johnson warrant special analysis: his decision, or series of decisions, to involve the United States as an increasingly active military participant in the Vietnam War—especially his ordering of a systematic bombing of North Vietnam; and his decision to intervene in the Dominican Republic with United States troops to prevent "another Cuba."

No one knows what Kennedy would have done in similar phases of the Vietnam conflict, or in response to the civil disorder in the Dominican Republic. There has been much speculation, with defenders of Johnson usually concluding that Kennedy would have had to make essentially the same decisions, and critics contending that Kennedy would have successfully managed both situations with generally less depletion of our global political assets and specifically without a direct involvement of United States combat units. But this is largely guesswork, and more often than not the guesses are transparently the products of more emotionally grounded pro- or anti-Johnson sentiment.

What Johnson did is known, and a rather rich public record can be pieced together to tell *why* he took certain actions rather than others. From the actions and their rationale a good deal can be ascertained about Johnson's premises concerning the global political environment and the most useful instruments for influencing the behavior of the various elements in that environment. At this level of inquiry, it may be possible to make valid comparisons with the Kennedy foreign policy without having to speculate about what Kennedy would have done.

Vietnam became a crisis for Johnson at about the same time the Dominican situation came to a head—1965, Johnson's first Presidential year after having been elected to the office. Vietnam had been a problem for American policy since the early 1950s, and intermittently during the following years it had faced successive Presidents with agonizing decisions. Johnson inherited the problem; but he had avoided, or postponed, the most difficult unresolved inherited choices of the problem until after the 1964 campaign. Even the air strike he ordered against North Vietnam in August 1964 as a reprisal for the North Vietnamese

PT-boat raid on United States ships in the Gulf of Tonkin was more in the nature of a reflex action than a fundamental decision with vast implications, and therefore in need of the fullest airing.

The decisions to widen United States participation in the war and to extend the area of bombardment to North Vietnam as a matter of policy were made, by all accounts, in late 1964 and early 1965. The taking of counsel on an intensive basis and the actual choices involved in these decisions faced the President with the need to choose between deeply valued national objectives, which he had not done in his earlier decisions. Thus, it was only now that the war in Vietnam became for him—and for the nation—a policy crisis, the center of things on which so much turned.

Previous escalations by the Kennedy and Johnson Administrations could be presented as marginal increments to commitments and levels of effort already established in order to implement our policy of supporting the South Vietnamese government in its fight against the Communist insurgency.

"In the final analysis it's their war," said President Kennedy in September 1963, preserving our options to scale up or down our supporting efforts depending upon the extent to which the Diem Government in Saigon demonstrated the political as well as military capability of sustaining its counterinsurgency effort. "We can help them, we can give them equipment, we can send our men out there as advisers, but they have to win it—the people of Viet Nam—against the Communists." [1] This was still President Johnson's definition of the situation a year later. His Republican opponents, he said, were "eager to enlarge the conflict." "They call upon us to supply American boys to do the job that Asian boys should do." [2] As far as he was concerned, said the President:

I want to be very cautious and careful, and use it only as a last resort, when I start dropping bombs around that are likely to involve American boys in a war in Asia with 700,000,000 Chinese. So just for the moment I have not thought that we were ready for American boys to do the fighting for Asian boys. . . .[3]

During the windup of the election campaign, he reiterated unequivocably, "We are not going to send American boys nine or ten thousand miles away to do what Asian boys ought to be doing for themselves." [4]

Even when the Vietcong, on November 1, 1964, in a surprise attack on the Bien Hao air base, killed five Americans, wounded seventy-six, and destroyed six B-57 bombers, Johnson continued to adhere to the escalation restraints. Philip Geyelin reports that below Johnson, principal Administration foreign policy experts did consider the Bien Hao attack worthy of at least serious consideration as a direct challenge, at least as serious as the challenge in the Gulf of Tonkin, and therefore deserving our military reply. There was a sufficiently significant disagreement among the President's advisers to warrant passing the differing recommendations up to the White House for resolution.

The President's advisers were split over the effect of our response or lack of response upon the strategies of the other members in the international system. Ambassador Maxwell Taylor argued from Saigon that not to respond decisively by an air attack against North Vietnam would cast United States resolve even more in doubt. On the other hand, some of our top Soviet experts, particularly Ambassador Llewellyn Thompson, were wary that such escalation at this time might provoke the post-Khrushchev leadership (whose inclinations we still had little time to assay) into a realignment with Peking to counter a determined United States thrust at the Eurasian rim. But apparently the President's key White House aides, aware of Johnson's view of Vietnam as primarily an aspect of *domestic* politics, decided to defer bringing to him the full international ramifications of the increasing Vietcong escalations until after the election.[5]

It was only after the 1964 votes were in that Johnson convened his first full-dress review of our overall Vietnam policy and strategies, which operationalized as policy the previously debated premise that the Vietnam conflict was the current flash point of the global conflict between the Communist and non-Communist worlds—the major corollary being that as leader of the non-Communist side the United States had to assume full responsibility for assuring that the Communists did not win. Our commitment, the price we would be willing to pay, was henceforth to be unqualified and open-ended. This change in premises was exhibited in a series of events and decisions during the first half of 1965.

On February 7 a reprisal raid was undertaken by United States fighter-bombers on North Vietnamese military barracks areas north of the 17th parallel in response to Vietcong mortar attacks on United States installations earlier in the day, particularly at the Pleiku airstrip where 7 Americans were killed, 109 wounded and at least 20 aircraft destroyed or damaged. We have every reason to believe, McNamara explained to reporters, "that the attack on Pleiku, Tuyhoa, and Nhatrang was ordered and directed and masterminded directly from Hanoi." Undersecretary of State George Ball backed him up in the joint State–Defense Department press conference on the day of the raids. There is no question, said the diplomat (reputed to be the leading Administration "dove" on Vietnam), that "this was a deliberate, overt attempt by the regime in Hanoi to test the will of the South Vietnamese Government . . . and the Government of the United States." This was a situation in which "we could not fail to respond without giving a misleading signal to the . . . regime in Hanoi" as to the strength of our purpose.[6]

The basis of the Administration's conviction that Hanoi was masterminding the campaign in the South obviously needed further elaboration. Accordingly, on February 28, the State Department issued its so-called White Paper entitled "Aggression From the North: The Record of North Vietnam's Campaign to Conquer South Vietnam."[7] The sixty-four-page text, released to all news media, claimed to contain "massive evidence of North Vietnamese aggression." It did document an increase, especially during 1964, of military aid from the North, in the form of weapons and key advisory personnel; but it was certainly no more massive than our increase in "supporting assistance" to Saigon during the same period.

The "advisers" on *both* sides were on their way to transforming themselves into belligerents. Hanoi used our increasing involvement as its justification for increasing its infiltration into the South. And we pointed to the evidence of this increasing infiltration as the reason for bringing coercive pressure upon Hanoi and dispatching more men and materials to South Vietnam to redress the deteriorating military balance.

Washington could correctly argue that we had no desire to be in Vietnam, and that if the North Vietnamese would only leave the South, and Laos, to determine their own futures (without, of course, the Vietcong insurgency) there would be no reason at all for the American military presence on the Indochinese peninsula. But Hanoi could retort, also with some validity, that the National Liberation Front and its insurgency arm, the Vietcong, were on their way to winning the "civil war" but for the intervention of the United States; and, moreover, when in 1956 there might yet have been a chance of determining by *elections* who should rule in the South (according to the terms of the 1954 Geneva agreement), it had been President Diem, with United States backing, who had refused to hold elections. Administration experts were able to point out that the blockage of Vietnamese elections had been just as much the result of Ho Chi Minh's failure to live up to the Geneva accords, and his unwillingness to have internationally administered elections in *all* of Vietnam.

But at the top levels, the Administration was painfully aware that our legal-political case was lacking in the clarity of purpose and centrality of national interest usually demanded by the American polity as a condition of our involvement in war. Furthermore, in the existing global context, our active involvement in such an overseas conflict carried with it the risk of escalation to thermonuclear holocaust. Undoubtedly, it was Johnson's appreciation of this simple popular wisdom that underlay his election campaign to keep the nation out of war and let Asians fight Asians. What, then, served to undercut that which, according to most expectations, was a fundamental political boundary condition for the President?

The explanation probably lies in the fact that the undercutting had been well underway, and had proceeded too far already in the form of actual diplomatic commitments and momentum established by our military participation, when Johnson took the matter under full consideration in late 1964. His lack of a continuing interest in the complexities of foreign affairs, prior to their reaching a crisis state, allowed subordinate levels of the government, under the assumption that they were implementing existing guidelines, to make tactical moves required by exigencies of the moment and to transmute, almost imperceptibly, differences in degrees of commitment and participation to a difference in kind.

This subtle transmutation from discrete increases in degree to a change in the nature of our role in Vietnam is, in retrospect, strikingly evident in the way we went about changing the size and tasks of United States ground forces in South Vietnam.

At Kennedy's death Johnson had inherited an American "advisory" force in Vietnam numbering somewhat short of 16,500. By August 1965, before the impact of the major increments ordered that year had been felt, there were already about 125,000 U.S. troops in the field. And decisions made in 1965 and 1966 meant that, barring a political settlement, the number of United States military personnel in South Vietnam could exceed half a million sometime in 1967.

The shift in the mission of these U.S. troops from "advisers" to the main offensive force also occurred between 1963 and 1966. The process of expanding the advisory role was underway before Johnson assumed the Presidency, and the dates of the different steps along the way are difficult to pinpoint. But the pattern of metamorphosis—which Johnson approved by default if not by design—is not at all obscure, and is logical from a narrow military point of view. Our advice to the South Vietnamese to make extensive use of the helicopter for reconnaissance, troop support, and troop transport required, at least at the outset, the establishment of training and maintenance bases staffed by Americans. But the existence of these bases also established a requirement for protecting them (they were obviously lucrative targets for the Vietcong). The South Vietnamese proved incapable of providing the kind of security needed, and so contingents of U.S. Marines were called to help, and eventually to take over, in the base security role. At this stage the United States became willy-nilly, an active co-belligerent, albeit only in "defensive" situations. The next step, as the Communists increased their military units and their firepower, was for us to expand the perimeter of security for our bases. The actual operations involved in expanding the perimeter were, of course, very much the same as they would be in offensive combat missions. What was indistinguishable in operations easily became indistinguishable in purpose, and we swiftly drifted into a full participation in the "clear and hold" missions designed to reduce the proportion of South Vietnamese territory controlled by the Vietcong. Finally, as political instability in Saigon diverted the South Vietnamese military to political tasks, including the suppression of Buddhist civil disobedience, the United States found itself the dominant combat force in the Vietnam War.

When Johnson took the situation under intense scrutiny in late 1964, he found that the commitments already entered into, and the deployments already underway, were about to make a mockery of his campaign pledges not to let American boys fight Asian boys. To fail to approve the increased deployments now being asked for by the Secretary of Defense would be to fail to rectify the deteriorating military situation—it would mean accepting a humiliating military defeat. On the other hand, the increases in infiltration from North Vietnam, which parallelled our increased involvement during the past year, gave little hope that the increases in our troops would accomplish anything more than to drive the ground war to higher levels of intensity.

Sufficiently detailed accounts of White House deliberations during this period are lacking, and speculation must suffice as to why the President now chose the path of dramatic escalation—a systematic bombing of North Vietnam—that he had so adamantly opposed just weeks earlier. What follows, therefore, is only a hypothesis as to the basis for Johnson's subsequent actions in the Vietnamese conflict. Many more records will have to be declassified and then untangled, and detailed memoirs will have to be published before the accuracy of this reconstruction can be confirmed.

From what is known of Johnson, the political animal, it would be surprising to find that he would allow himself to be trapped into presiding over a slow war of human attrition on the Asian mainland and the long test of endurance it required. For one thing, we were likely to be hurt more than our adversaries who (assuming China was drawn in) had a practically unlimited supply of expendable manpower. For another, the 1964 election results convinced Johnson that he embodied the great American consensus for getting on with the job of tending to the national welfare. The people were tired of the foreign entanglements we had been sustaining since 1947, particularly those like Vietnam where the connection with our own security was complicated and tenuous. Some means would have to be found for bringing a rapid conclusion to this war. Yet Johnson also sensed that the majority of people were overwhelmingly against Goldwater because he embodied the pugnacious aspect of American nationalism that risked further expenditure of blood and treasure in "confrontations" with our adversaries around the globe. Goldwaterism, as the elections showed, was just not the dominant temper today.

But here he was, after having successfully made political capital out of Goldwater's pugnacity, seriously contemplating the very escalation strategies that Goldwater had been advocating. The contradiction is at least partially resolved by attributing to Johnson-the-electioneer the very real belief that bombing North Vietnam *would* lead to the larger war (possibly through the entry of the Chinese) that he knew the American public did not want. Whereas, Johnson the Commander-in-Chief, looking in detail at the developing military situation in late 1964 saw that we were already heavily implicated in a rapidly expanding ground war which could easily lead to the intolerable and larger Asian land war unless some way was found to break out. Marginal increments to our forces in the South, then being recommended by the military command in Saigon and endorsed by McNamara in Washington, might not be sufficient to convince North Vietnam and China, and possibly even the Soviet Union, that an expansion of their commitments to Vietnam would involve them in a "deeply dangerous game." In 1961, Maxwell Taylor and Walt Rostow had foreseen the stage we were now in, and had advocated a selective bombing of the North to disabuse the Communists of the notion that they could support this "war of liberation" in South Vietnam without suffering dearly. President Kennedy had rejected the plan as premature, but now Taylor and Rostow, backed by the Joint Chiefs of Staff, were in a position to point to the strategy's efficacy.

These essential considerations were hidden behind the bombing and subsequent troop buildup. The Administration's announcements of major troop increases came in March, and then again in mid-summer. Actually, these were only ratifications of more basic earlier decisions that the war on the ground could not be lost, and also of a series of commitments entered into before 1965 that were thought of as being only implementations of existing policy. The only new major policy decision was to remove the sanctuary status from the North.

But the way the decision to bring the North under aerial attack was announced and implemented obscured the underlying rationale, and possibly interfered with its utility as a signal to the Communist powers. The bombing raid across the 17th parallel following the Vietcong attack on Pleiku—like our airstrike in response to the Tonkin incident —was defined as a reprisal. The implication was: don't do what you just did or we'll bomb again. But three days later, on February 10, the Vietcong again found their mark. This time a United States billet at Quinhon was blown up, killing 23 Americans. Now three times as many aircraft were used in our retaliation, and the targets were further north, but still in the southern part of North Vietnam. It could appear as if we were trying to establish a let-the-punishment-fit-the-crime pattern, with the crime being attacks on *our* installations. However, the White House attempted (probably deliberately) to blur this impression in its communiqué of February 11 which cited, in addition to the

Quinhon incident, Vietcong ambushes, raids, assassinations, etc., against South Vietnamese personnel and installations as well as Americans. It was these "continued acts of aggression by Communist Vietcong under the direction and with the support of the Hanoi regime," said the statements issued from Washington and Saigon, that were the reasons for the current air strike. This came a bit closer to displaying the central strategic rationale for commencing the bombing—namely, at least an "equalization" of the pain suffered by the North as compared to the suffering caused by their agents in the South, as a way of convincing Ho Chi Minh that if he continued the insurgency the price would henceforth be much higher than it had been. The selection of targets further north and the increase in intensity were also supposed to communicate that the first blows were only a harbinger of much more dangerous blows to come. Yet the full and explicit announcement of this rationale was evidently thought to sound too much like an "ultimatum," with all the risks that would involve of provoking counter-ultimatums, even by parties not yet involved. Consequently, in the coming months, as bombing of the North became a regular feature of the war, it was increasingly justified on the narrower grounds of its usefulness in "interdicting" the transport of men and material from the North to the South.

As the insurgency and terror in the South continued and the infiltration from the North increased, the Administration was criticized heavily by domestic and foreign opponents of the bombing. The United States had expanded the war, it was charged, putting pressure on the Soviet Union to aid Hanoi with at least air defense equipment, and incurring the risk of an even greater direct clash with the giant Communist powers, and what did we have to show for it? An even higher level of warfare in the South. The flimsy argument that we had to bomb the North to buttress the shaky authority of each successive military junta in Saigon was even less convincing.

Meanwhile, with no discernable moves by the opponents to scale down their insurgency, the frequency, scale, and type of target we were bringing under aerial bombardment were increasing. We were, in this phase of the conflict too, using up our fresh options, and settling into a pattern of mutual injury, at a higher level of destruction than that of a few weeks ago. Hundreds of thousands of American boys were being sent overseas to fight Asian boys, the casualty lists were growing, the costs were in the billions, and still the end was no closer in sight.

Johnson's instinct to break out of the pattern now resulted in a series of flamboyant peace moves. Up to the spring of 1965 it had been our stance (in reply to promptings from de Gaulle, the UN Secretary General, Asian neutrals, and academic polemicists in this country) that there was nothing to negotiate except the cessation of the violent insurgency by the Communists; and—in any case—negotiations would have to follow a bona fide cease-fire. In April 1965 the White House appeared to be suddenly changing its tune, or at least to be willing to play the counterpoint of negotiations and planning for peace against the continuing din of bombs and mortar and the calls from "hawks" to expand our targets in the North. Some pundits suspected this was another Johnsonian ploy of playing off the hawks against the "doves" to preserve his options for tactical maneuver in the long and messy conflict that now seemed to stretch endlessly ahead. But the ring of sincerity in his Johns Hopkins address lends greater plausibility to the "break out" hypothesis.

The case for "why we are there" was reiterated, with considerable eloquence, by the President at Hopkins on April 7. There were the references to the "deepening shadow of Communist China," presumably the real stage manager of the insurgency in Vietnam. "It is a nation which is helping the forces of violence in almost every continent. The contest in Viet-Nam is part of a wider pattern of aggressive purposes." There were the invocations of the promises made by "every American President" since 1954 "to help South Viet-Nam defend its independence." There was the catalogue of consequences that would befall the world from a failure to honor these promises now: Around the world, "from Berlin to Thailand," the confidence of people "in the value of an American commitment and in the value of America's word" would be shaken. "The result would be increased unrest and instability, and even wider war." There were the homilies about appeasing the appetite of the insatiably hungry aggressor. "To withdraw from one battlefield means only to prepare for the next. We must stay in Southeast Asia—as we did in Europe—in the words of the Bible: 'Hitherto shalt thou come, but no further.'" And there was the posture of unflinching resolve: "We will not be defeated. We will not grow tired. We will not withdraw, either openly or under the cloak of meaningless agreement."

But once this is clear, said the President, "it should also be clear that the only path for reasonable men is the path of peaceful settlement." In a surprise formulation he suggested an acceptable outcome to such a settlement and a range of flexibility in negotiating formats—both a thawing from what seemed to be our pre-existing frigid stance. The "essentials of any final settlement," he said, are "an independent South Viet-Nam—securely guaranteed and able to shape its own relationships to all others—free from outside interference—tied to no alliance —a military base for no other country."

This was a considerable departure by the White House from its scornful response to de Gaulle's suggestions for a "neutralization" solution. Moreover:

> There may be many ways to this kind of peace: in discussion or negotiation with the governments concerned; in large groups or in small ones; in the reaffirmation of old agreements or their strengthening with new ones.
> And we remain ready with this purpose for unconditional negotiations.

The peace we want, insisted the President, ought not to be incompatible with the desires of the North Vietnamese. "They want what their neighbors also desire . . . progress for their country, and an end to the bondage of material misery." Their Communist ideology and alignment with China were evidently not a bar to their peaceful association in regional economic development schemes, "We would hope that North Viet-Nam would take its place in the common effort just as soon as peaceful cooperation is possible."

Meanwhile, work could begin on projects for regional economic development with those nations among whom peaceful cooperation was now possible. To that end, reported the President, he would ask the Congress to contribute a billion-dollar investment to a program of Southeast Asia economic development to be organized initially by UN Secretary General Thant. Our participation would be inaugurated by a team of Americans headed by Eugene Black. "And I would hope," said Johnson, "that all other industrialized countries, including the Soviet Union, will join in this effort. . . ."

These hopes for the development of the rest of the world, and his dreams for an end to war, claimed the President, were deeply rooted in his childhood experiences. The rural electrification, which brought cheer to the ordinary people along the Perdanales—was there any reason why it should not bring cheer to the sufferers along the Mekong? Why, that vast river could provide food and water and electricity "on a scale to dawrf even our own TVA." That would be impressive:

We often say how impressive power is. But I do not find it impressive at all. The guns and the bombs, the rockets and the warships, are all symbols of human failure. They protect what we cherish. But they are witness to human folly.

A dam built across a great river is impressive.

. . .

Electrification of the countryside—yes, that . . . is impressive.

A rich harvest in a hungry land is impressive.

The sight of healthy children in a classroom is impressive.

These—not mighty arms—are the achievements which the American nation believes to be impressive. And if we are steadfast, the time may come when all other nations will find it so.[8]

Meanwhile, the mighty arms, which were the symbols of human failure and the witnesses to human folly, had to be fully committed "to protect what we cherish." During the month of April the pounding of the North intensified, with 1500 air sorties against military targets recorded.[9] And in the month following the overture to peace at Johns Hopkins, 15,000 additional United States combat troops disembarked in South Vietnam, the largest increase yet for any month. The big buildup was proceeding apace.

This was precisely the wrong way to get Hanoi to the negotiating table, charged critics at home and abroad. To bargain with us while under increasing bombardment would look like surrender. Lester Pearson of Canada, Senator Fulbright, and numerous newspaper editors argued for a bombing pause to convince the Communists of our sincerity. The Administration took counsel and decided to give this gambit a try.

From May 12 to May 18 the bombing raids ceased. Hanoi was informed in advance via diplomatic channels that the pause was coming and that we would be watching to see if there were "significant reductions" in actions by the Communist military units in South Vietnam. The message suggested that such reciprocal action would allow us to halt our bombing, and thus meet what was assumed to be the essential North-Vietnamese precondition for beginning peace talks. When the air attacks on the North were resumed on May 18, the Administration claimed disappointment that there had been no reaction from the other side.

But the critics were not silenced. Surely six days was not long enough to give Hanoi an opportunity to make a considered assessment of our intentions and arrange for an appropriate response. In June, Secretary Rusk told the Foreign Service Institute that all our government received from Hanoi and Peiping were denunciations of the pause as a "wornout trick" and a "swindle." More recent reports, he said, contained clear proof that "Hanoi is not even prepared for discussions unless it is accepted in advance that there will be a Communist-dominated government in Saigon." [10] It was only in November that the State Department admitted it had received a negotiating offer from Hanoi via the French government just a few hours after the six-day May pause ended. The French government is reported to have suggested that the bombings should cease again after the message had been received but apparently the United States government did not regard the response as a sufficiently serious negotiating offer. The Administration was now subject to the charge of being difficient in its credibility. [11]

The failure of the North Vietnamese to give a satisfactory response to our peace overtures in the spring of 1965 was stressed by the President in his July 28 "this is really war" speech, announcing an immediate 75 per cent increase to our fighting strength in Vietnam. Fifteen efforts with the help of forty nations, he said, had been made to attempt to get the "unconditional discussions" started. "But there has been no answer." We were going to persist in our efforts to bring about negotiations, but meanwhile we would also persist on the battlefield, if need be, "until death and desolation have led to the same conference table where others could now join us at much smaller cost." [12]

The President was speaking at a time of extremely low morale on our side. Another civilian government had fallen on June 11, and Air Vice-Marshal Ky had assumed the reigns of power in the face of increasing anti-Government and pro "neutralism" agitation by the Buddhists. Support for neutralism, the new military junta announced, would be punishable by death. It was the beginning of a new time of political troubles in Saigon that would consume the energies of the South Vietnamese military while the United States began to assume the major combat functions. "We did not choose to be the guardians at the gate," said the American President "but there is no one else." [13]

Thus, by the summer of 1965, the full character of the United States political-military involvement in Vietnam had matured; and its underlying premises had been revealed:

A. Global balance of power considerations demanded that we do all that was required to prevent the Communists from taking over South Vietnam. Our failure to honor our commitments to South Vietnam would weaken resistance to Communist expansion all around the globe—a resistance critically dependent upon the belief by the non-Communist societies that the United States, when called upon, would help them to prevail in their anti-Communist struggles.

B. If we did not defeat the Communist insurgency in South Vietnam now, we would surely have to fight them again to stop their expansionist drive in the less developed countries, very likely in a bigger war and possibly closer to our shores. For the Communist world, Vietnam was a test case for the strategy of expanding through "wars of national liberation." They had been pretty well convinced to abandon a strategy of direct military aggression by our stands in Europe and Korea. If this strategy of disguised aggression by paramilitary means were now allowed to succeed, those within the Communist camp who favored the coercive modes of expansion would be vindicated. If this "war of national liberation" were now convincingly defeated, however, those elements within the Communist world who believed in peaceful forms of competitive coexistence would be strengthened.

C. Those directing the insurgency in Vietnam could be induced to call it off only if they were convinced it would cost them too dearly to continue it and that, even with the higher-cost efforts, they would not succeed. Our strategy in Vietnam, therefore, despite its turns and twists had an underlying consistent objective: to increase our opponents costs and diminish their prospects of success. Previous failures to adequately convince them (with only our *support* of South Vietnam) that their costs would be excessive and their prospects of success very low led to our more direct involvement, and this at increasingly higher levels of violence. We had no desire to have American soldiers again fight Asians or to widen the war to include the North, but as lower levels of conflict failed to convince the Communists that we were determined to frustrate their designs, we were compelled to make our determination even clearer.

D. The strategy of steeadily increasing the costs to our opponents carried with it the need to increase our human and material costs; thus, our staying power demanded, increasingly, a national consensus in this country without which the President could not get the congressional majorities needed to provision the war. Consequently, domestic dissent on our involvement in Vietnam became an ingredient in the test of strength and endurance with our opponents. Hanoi, it was feared, would exploit our desire to negotiate an end to the violence with a view toward maximizing dissent in the United States. And they would interpret such dissent as an indication that further persistence by them on the battlefield would soon bring about a condition in the United States where a majority could not be found to approve the continued high costs of the war.

It was probably this latter premise about our opponents' perceptions of the meaning of domestic dissent in this country, and the consequences of these perceptions for our opponents' will to persist in the struggle that was at the root of the increasing erraticism in the Administration's public posture during the following year.

As the buildup in Vietnam by the United States was met by increased Northern infiltration into the South, public criticism intensified. Students and professors held stop-the-war "teach-ins"; and artists, intellectuals, and religious leaders joined with standard peace-movement groups in petitioning the government, or marching on Washington to demonstrate against the bombing and for negotiations. Hanoi cooperated with hints through third parties that it might be willing to negotiate; and each of these were picked up in the press, sometimes some months after they had been made, and thrust at the Administration as further proof of official dishonesty in saying that we were constantly seeking to induce Hanoi to the conference table. The American leaders were uninterested in negotiations, charged the critics.

The Administration's response to the domestic criticism was at first testy and tight-lipped. But in the second half of 1965 the White House changed tactics and began to talk back to the critics, to take them seriously—some observers thought too seriously—and to send Administration representatives to the teach-ins to present the full Administration case. The case included the major premises summarized above, including the last one about the danger of too much dissent. This was a tactical blunder on the part of the Administration, as it would be for any Administration in the American democracy, particularly as the argument against too much argument was only valid if all of the other premises were valid. And serious critics disputed them all.

The President's worst fears of being driven to higher levels of warfare abroad without a sufficient consensus at home to support the greater resource drain seemed to be materializing. He and his aides were irritable and carping. But at the end of 1965, he resorted again to a break-out-of-the-pattern move. This time it was a razzle-dazzle peace offensive the likes of which the diplomatic community had never seen. Prominent American officials made a whirlwind tour of world capitals while the military campaign was dramatically tuned down.

Responding to a Vietcong initiative for a Christmas Eve cease-fire, the United States halted air action over North Vietnam simultaneously with the start of the twelve-hour truce on the ground. A similar "natural" truce would be coming up on the Buddhist Lunar New Year ("*Tet*"), January 20–24.

The Administration used the month-long interval of military de-escalation to press its diplomatic offensive, meanwhile not resuming the air attacks. This time the critics could not say the pause was too short for Hanoi to make serious contacts. Secretary Rusk issued publicly our fourteen points for negotiation in response to Hanoi's four points, with the claim that the two positions were really not so far apart. Certainly, there was reason for negotiation on the basis of both positions. But the Administration's credibility with its domestic critics, already seriously undermined by its past policy ambivalence and rhetorical excesses, was now injured even further by its frantic efforts, probably wholly sincere, to build a world consensus in back of unconditional discussions between the belligerents. Moreover, doubts were raised as to the "unconditional" nature of our appeals for discussions as it became clear that we were quite sticky on the point of *who* was a legitimate spokesman for the other side. "If the Vietcong come to the conference table as full partners," said Secretary Rusk, "they will . . . in a sense have been victorious in the very aims that South Vietnam and the United States are pledged to prevent." [14]

Claiming again to have received no serious offer from Hanoi to negotiate, the Administration resumed the air attacks with even greater punch on January 28. The domestic critics, at least those who were patriotic in motive, must now finally realize there was no alternative but to rally in back of our military efforts. And certainly, if our boys *had* to be over there to hold the ground, who could criticize our efforts to negate as much of the danger as possible by destroying enemy power while it was still on the trails in Laos, on the bridges above the 17th parallel, or in the storage depots near the factories?

But the new jingoism in the Administration's statements accompanying the resumption of bombings in January 1966, particularly the implication that anything less than enthusiastic support was unpatriotic, provoked patriotic men in the President's own party, like Senators Fulbright, Hartke, and Church, to an even greater attack on Administration policies. Senator Fulbright's Foreign Relations Committee became the staging ground for this new phase of the domestic debate.

The most significant function of the Senate Foreign Relations Committee hearings in 1966 was to provide respectability for the serious criticisms—as distinguished from the emotional harangues of the so-called "New Left." Ostensibly convened for the purpose of requiring the Administration to justify its requests for supplemental foreign assistance monies (needed to finance the military and economic assistance to Vietnam over and above the amounts previously authorized in the fiscal 1966 budget), these hearings exposed the nation and the world to the profound doubts about our Vietnam policy held by some of our most experienced former diplomats and military men and some of our most respected scholars.

General James Gavin testified before the Fulbright committee that he feared "the escalation in southeast Asia . . . [will] begin to hurt our world strategic position." This might have "tremendous significance" in the long run, he said. "When we begin to turn our back on what we are doing in world affairs . . . to support a tactical confrontation that appears to be escalating at the will of an enemy we are in a very dangerous position in my opinion. . . ." [15]

This policy, offered George Kennan, "seems to me to represent a grievous misplacement of emphasis in our foreign policies as a whole." Not only were great questions of world affairs not receiving the attention they deserved, said the author of the Containment Policy, but "assets we already enjoy and . . . possibilities we should be developing are being sacrificed to this unpromising involvement in a remote and secondary theatre." Elaborating, he claimed that:

Our relations with the Soviet Union have suffered grievously . . . at a time when far more important things were involved in those relations than what is ultimately involved in Vietnam . . . And more unfortunate still, in my opinion, is the damage being done to the feelings entertained for us by the Japanese people. . . . As the only major industrial complex in the entire Far East, and the only place where the sinews of modern war can be produced on a formidable scale, Japan is of vital importance to us and indeed to the prospects generally of peace and stability in Asia. There is no success we could have in Vietnam that would warrant . . . the sacrifice by us of the confidence and good will of the Japanese people.

If we had kept our eye on these larger strategic considerations Kennan suggested, we would have had no reason to become involved in Vietnam as we were today. And, challenging a central pillar of the Administration's case, he contended that:

. . . even a situation in which South Vietnam was controlled exclusively by the Vietcong, while regrettable, and no doubt morally unwarranted, would not, in my opinion, present dangers great enough to justify our direct military intervention.

Given the situation that exists today in the relations among the leading Communist powers, and by that I have . . . in mind primarily the Soviet-Chinese conflict, there is every likelihood that a Communist regime would follow a fairly independent course.

Yet we were involved now, Kennan granted, and thus our prestige had become heavily implicated. This raised "new questions" which had to be taken into account. "A precipitate and disorderly withdrawal could represent in present circumstances a disservice to our own interests, and even to world peace. . . ." He did, however, feel that we should not rely on the "prestige" or "honor" excuse as a way of avoiding the search for fall-back positions (possibly a retreat into coastal enclaves, as recommended by General Gavin) from which a more orderly reduction of our commitment and presence might take place. In a courageous statement for a man of Kennan's close establishment associations to make before a congressional committee in the full glare of the television cameras, Kennan confessed that:

I . . . find it difficult . . . to believe that our allies, and particularly our Western European allies, most of whom themselves have given up great territories within recent years, and sometimes in a very statesmanlike way, I find it hard to believe that we would be subject to great reproach or loss of confidence at their hands simply because we followed a defensive rather than an offensive strategy in Vietnam at this time.

In matters such as this, it is not in my experience what you do that is mainly decisive. It is how you do it; and I would submit that there is more respect to be won in the opinion of this world by a resolute and courageous liquidation of unsound positions than by the most stubborn pursuit of extravagant and unpromising objectives.[16]

The President, anticipating what was in store in the February sessions of the Fulbright committee, felt it necessary to reassert once more his peace aims as well as his war aims for Vietnam. It was time to show that he meant business about the greater impressiveness of agricultural productivity, rural electrification, and schools than strike aircraft, flamethrowers, and the tremendous military logistics networks. It was also possible he wanted to take some of the spotlight away from the Fulbright hearings.

The television coverage of the Administrator of the Agency for International Development, David Bell, before the Foreign Relations Committee was interrupted on February 4 for President Johnson's announcement of his trip to Honolulu to meet with Prime Minister Ky and President Thieu of South Vietnam. To emphasize that the main purpose of the meeting was to explore plans for the peaceful reconstruction of Vietnam the President announced he was taking along John Gardner, Secretary of Health, Education and Welfare, and Orville Freeman, Secretary of Agriculture. There would of course be strategy huddles with General Westmoreland and the Vietnamese military, but the theme was to be socioeconomic development. And this was the emphasis in the *Declaration of Honolulu* issued by both governments from Hawaii on February 8. The Government of South Vietnam pledged itself to "a true social revolution," to policies designed to "achieve regular economic growth," and to "build true democracy" through the formulation of a "democratic constitution" and subjecting it to ratification by popular ballot. The United States pledged itself to full support of these aspirations. And to demonstrate their seriousness of purpose, President Johnson persuaded the Vietnamese leaders to extend an immediate invitation to Secretaries Gardner and Freeman to survey the social and economic situation and suggest practical courses of action. Upon setting foot again on the continental United

States on the evening of February 8, the President told of this reconstruction mission to Vietnam and announced that Vice-President
Humphrey was leaving immediately for Saigon to join the other cabinet members and to meet with South Vietnamese officials to discuss
these matters. The White House would be represented directly by Mc-
George Bundy and Averell Harriman, both of whom would be going
along with the Vice-President.[17]

The President did get the headlines and the television coverage with
this swoop into Asia with Health, Agriculture, and the idealism of
Humphrey. But the image came across somewhat differently than he
had hoped. The tone of the television commentators and journalists
who covered the event suggested rather strongly that this was Johnson
hucksterism more than substance. Juxtaposed against the good-works
backdrop was the indelible picture of LBJ embracing Prime Minister
Ky as if he were a Democratic Party loyalist in the Texas statehouse.
Ky, who had been installed recently by a military coup, was cracking
down with authoritarian methods on the Buddhist agitators, and had
been making asides to the effect that any negotiations with the Communists would be useless. Rather than Ky's endorsement of the Great
Society, Saigon style, the picture that critics chose to display was that
of Johnson's committing himself to support Ky's irresponsible brand of
jet-set militarism. Whatever Johnson did now his domestic critics
would turn it against him.

But now, also, with Johnson's domestic consensus drooping more
severely than ever before, the military situation, because of the great
United States buildup, began to improve considerably. It was possible
to think, for the first time, of negotiation from a position of strength;
it was also possible to think of accomplishing our objective of keeping
South Vietnam out of Communist hands by virtue of having reestablished physical control over most of the country. Negotiations, therefore, could be approached with more equanimity. If the Communists
wanted them—fine; we were in a good bargaining position. But if for
that reason they didn't want them—fine again. There was no urgency.

Dean Rusk's confident February 18 appearance before the Fulbright
committee probably reflected the Administration's growing confidence
in the military situation. The Secretary was on the offensive against his
critics. He was reasonable, willing to consider all diplomatic alterna-

tives, and effective in picturing the characterizations of Administration policies by Fulbright, particularly, as straw men. Why are we in Vietnam? he asked:

Certainly we are not there merely because we have power and like to use it. We do not regard ourselves as policemen of the universe. . . . But we are in Vietnam because the issues posed there are deeply intertwined with our own security and because the outcome can profoundly affect the nature of the world in which we live. . . .

. . .

What are our world security interests involved in the struggle in Vietnam?
 . . . we must recognize that what we are seeking to achieve in South Vietnam is part of a process that has continued for a long time—a process of preventing the expansion and extension of Communist domination by the use of force against the weaker nations on the perimeter of Communist power.

This was obviously a definition of the problem directly at variance with George Kennan's assessment. The Secretary did not label it as such, but continued:

This is the problem as it looks to us. Nor do the Communists themselves see this problem in isolation. They see the struggle in South Vietnam as part of a larger design for the steady extension of Communist power through force and threat.

I have observed in the course of your hearings that some objection has been raised to the use of the term "Communist aggression." It seems to me that we should not confuse ourselves or our people by turning our eyes away from what that phrase means. The underlying crisis of this postwar period turns about a major struggle over the very nature of the political structure of the world.

What then of the notion, propounded by Rusk himself, that there are many kinds of Communists, and there have been profound changes occurring in International Communism since Stalin's day? He would of course grant that "movement is occurring on both sides of the Iron Curtain":

Communism today is no longer monolithic; it no longer wears one face but many, and the deep schism between the two great power centers of the Communist world—Moscow and Peiping—is clearly one of the major political facts of our time.

. . .

Over time the same process [of evolution most evident in Eastern Europe] hopefully will work in the Far East. Peiping, and the Communist states living under its shadow, must learn that they cannot redraw the boundaries of the world by force.

But we should not delude ourselves out of hope as to how deep this transformation in the Communist world already runs.

There may be differences within the Communist world about methods, and techniques, and leadership within the Communist world itself, but they share a common attachment to their "world revolution" and to its support through what they call wars of liberation.

. . .

A war of national liberation, in the Communist lexicon, depends on the tactics of terror and sabotage, of stealth and subversion. It has a particular utility to them since it gives an advantage to a disciplined and ruthless minority, particularly in countries where the physical terrain makes clandestine infiltration from the outside relatively easy.

At the same time the Communists have a more subtle reason for favoring this type of aggression. It creates in any situation a sense of ambiguity that they can exploit to their own advantage.

We should not allow the Communists to delude us into believing that the war in Vietnam is merely an indigenous revolt. The evidence is overwhelming, Rusk reiterated as unequivocally as ever, "that this is . . . one further effort by a Communist regime in one-half of a divided country to take over the people of the other half at the point of a gun and against their will."

"Are we bound to fight Communism wherever it exists?" asked Senator Aiken.

"No, sir, no, sir, we are not, we are not," said the Secretary:

We are not talking about fighting communism for the purpose of destroying communism as such as a social or political organization, if that is what people want. But what we are talking about, I believe, Senator, is that where Communist countries undertake to commit aggression against those to whom the United States has undertaken a clear *commitment* in an alliance, that there we have a *duty* to assist our allies to meet that aggression. (Emphasis added.)

Commitment? Duty? asked skeptical senators. We—the Senate—gave no commitment to defend South Vietnam, insisted Senators Fulbright and Morse.

347

But Rusk was right back at them with the Truman Doctrine, to assist free peoples who are the victims of attempted subjugation by armed minorities or by outside pressures, with resistance to Communist aggression in Korea to prevent the unilateral abrogation of borders or truce lines established by solemn international convenant, by the SEATO treaty, by President Eisenhower's letter to Premier Diem, by Kennedy's 1961 pledges of support, and particularly by the Congressional Resolution backing Johnson in his reprisal for the Tonkin provocation—a resolution which reaffirmed just seventeen months ago the whole package of commitments. Approved by the overwhelming vote of 504 to 2, that resolution said "that the United States regards as vital to its national interests and to world peace the maintenance of international peace and security in southeast Asia." And it declared that:

. . . the United States is, therefore, prepared, as the President determines, to take all necessary steps, including the use of armed force, to assist any member or protocol state of the Southeast Asia Collective Defense Treaty requesting assistance in defense of its freedom.[18]

Yes, that was what he voted for, admitted Senator Fulbright. And only now did he see the error of his ways. He did not foresee that this pledge would be used to involve us in a war without a declaration of war, without a full congressional debate as to its wisdom, as to the value of the objective to the people of the United States. Now, however, the Secretary was telling us that the objective was to honor our commitment, lest the world doubt us at our word and our alliances crumble across the globe. Were we in truth so heavily committed that it was too late to examine the soundness of the original commitment, or to revise the commitment as the nature of the conflict assumed its true form? Who knew anything, really, about Vietnam, Fulbright asked plaintively, until we began to send American boys to fight over there? Who cared until now? And now we were told we were there because we were there because we were there! Could we not follow George Kennan's noble counsel and liquidate an unsound commitment?

But most responsible critics, however much they lamented the stumbling into a full and seemingly endless commitment to pay a high price and risk wider war defending the self-determination of a people who had never really been asked what they wanted in twenty years of bloodshed—however differently they might travel if they knew where the road would lead, still they had to concede that now we could not allow ourselves to be pushed out by force. As put by Richard Goodwin, White House aide to John F. Kennedy, and now a persistent gadfly to the Johnson Administration:

Our future policy in Vietnam must follow two parallel roads—the road of negotiation and the road of combat. Past miscalculation should have humbled us to the awareness that each specific step may have larger consequences than we can foresee.

But:

Each [future step] should be tested against a single standard: Does it serve or injure the bedrock vital interest of the United States? That interest is to establish that American military power, once committed to defend another nation, cannot be driven from the field.[19]

We were neglecting and even wasting many of our nonmilitary assets of power in the Vietnamese conflict. This, Johnson undoubtedly felt as much as his critics. But being President of the only nation on earth to whom victims would come running for protection in case the Soviets or Chinese should resume their strategy of coercive blackmail, he sensed that to lose in a military power struggle anywhere would be to tip the overall balance of power dangerously against us.

Peace negotiations were fine, so long as they did not register a military defeat. Thus, as the military situation improved we were even willing to contemplate "political" solutions for Vietnam that might eventually bring the Communists into the government in Saigon. That, however regrettable, would be recorded as a failure of non-Communist Vietnamese nationalism. The face of *our* power we still had to save was the military face.

Juxtaposed with Johnson's swift resort to force in the Dominican Republic, the evolution of our Vietnamese strategy cast doubt on his protestations that he, in contrast to Mao Tse-tung, believed that power came from the pipes of an irrigation system rather than the barrel of a gun. The emerging popular view of Johnson—the militarist—was, of course, an unfortunate oversimplification. But, as an inspection of his public posturing at the time of the Dominican crisis shows, Johnson was himself somewhat responsible for perpetuating such gross popular caricatures of the reasons for our behavior.

The public rationale for our military intervention in the Dominican Republic in April and May of 1965 points to two distinct kinds of threats and, accordingly, two phases to our military response, each with a different objective.

The first threat was to the security and lives of United States citizens and other foreign nationals resulting from the civil violence which broke out in Santo Domingo on April 24. On April 28 Dominican law enforcement and military officials formally informed our embassy in Santo Domingo that the situation was out of control and that the police and the government could no longer guarantee the safety of United States or other foreign nationals.

We had "no desire to interfere in the affairs of a sister Republic," explained President Johnson, but on April 28 "there was no longer any choice for the man who is your President":

I was sitting in my little office reviewing the world situation with Secretary Rusk, Secretary McNamara, and Mr. McGeorge Bundy. Shortly after 3 o'clock I received a cable from our Ambassador, and he said that things were in danger; he had been informed the chief of police and government authorities could no longer protect us. . . . At 5:14 . . . we received a cable that was labeled "critic," a word that is reserved for only the most urgent and immediate matters of national security.

. . .

Ambassador Bennet [said] . . . in that cable . . . that only an immediate landing of American forces could safeguard and protect the lives of thousands of Americans and thousands of other citizens of some 30 other countries. Ambassador Bennet urged your President to order an immediate landing.

. . .

When that cable arrived, when our entire country team in the Dominican Republic . . . said to your President unanimously: Mr. President if you do not send forces immediately, men and women—Americans and those of other lands—will die in the streets—well, I knew there was no time to talk, to consult, or to delay. For in this situation delay itself would be decision —the decision to risk and to lose the lives of thousands of Americans and thousands of innocent people from other lands.[20]

The Presidents' prompt dispatch of 400 Marines on April 28, followed in the next three days by 1500 men from the 82d Airborne Division and additional Marine detachments, was an action—according to

White House public statements of April 28, April 30, May 1, and May 2—dictated solely by the requirements of efficiently conducting the human rescue operation.[21] The limited objective, as stated, was impeccable, and presumably the means chosen were necessary (international machinery was simply too sluggish for such a swift *ad hoc* response), although there was already some wonderment expressed in the United States press at the size of the contingents dispatched for the rescue effort. President Johnson was acting properly within his executive responsibility of assuring protection to United States nationals and diplomatic missions abroad, just as President Eisenhower had done in ordering helicopters to rescue the Nixons' party from Caracas crowds in 1958.

However, the White House definition to the public of the objective of our intervention was rapidly expanded within the next few days as "Communist leaders, many of them trained in Cuba, seeing a chance to increase disorder, to gain a foothold, joined the revolution . . . and took increasing control." Almost overnight, therefore, we were openly intervening in force (with an additional 6500 men, and hints of more to come) to "prevent another Communist State in this hemisphere." We were not intervening to prevent change. Indeed, we were for major social transformations in the Dominican Republic. Nor were we intervening simply to prevent violent revolution, however much we were opposed to violent change. Maintaining his fidelity to the noninterventionist conventions of the Inter-American System, the President reaffirmed the proposition that "revolution in any country is a matter for that country to deal with." But "it becomes a matter calling for hemispheric action only—repeat, only—when the object is the establishment of a Communist dictatorship." [22] In justifying his expanded military response to the situation, President Johnson felt impelled to show that he was acting in accord with our solemn obligations to our neighbors, and in defense of our own security, and therefore as any United States President, including Kennedy, would have acted:

The American nations cannot, must not, and will not permit the establishment of another Communist government in the Western Hemisphere. This was the unanimous view of all the American nations when, in January 1962, they declared, and I quote: "The principles of Communism are incompatible with the principles of the Inter-American system."

This is what our beloved President John F. Kennedy meant when, less than a week before his death, he told us: "We in this hemisphere must also use every resource at our command to prevent the establishment of another Cuba in this hemisphere. . . ." [23]

However, the last-quoted remark of President Kennedy was lifted out of a speech stressing the dire need for nations in the Alliance for Progress to take seriously the goals of social reform in order to avoid the kind of despair that led to Castroism.[24] It had quite a different connotation in Kennedy's speech than it did in the Johnson justification of his swift resort to *military* resources. Kennedy had talked of "every resource," as a way of stressing that military response to new Castroite or Communist possibilities was surely a last resort, and, if anything a confession of the failure by nations of this hemisphere to avail themselves of all the resources at their command to lessen the appeals of the Communists.

Johnson was undoubtedly correct in his identification of himself with Kennedy insofar as this referred to Kennedy's not ruling out the use of force if its use was necessary and likely to prevent another Communist takeover in the Caribbean. But the tricky concept here is that of "necessity"; its determination in any situation involves a set of premises about the political and social forces at work in the particular case, and the alternatives short of the use of force available for influencing them.

It is not at all clear that the premises Johnson availed himself of in determining the configuration and strengths of the various political and social forces in the Dominican Republic were similar to the premises with which Kennedy approached the analysis of instability in the contemporary Latin American context. There has been much speculation about the timing of Johnson's public announcement that he was intervening in the Dominican situation to prevent a Communist takeover in addition to protecting American lives, with prominent journalists and some members of Congress revealing evidence that suggests Johnson thought from the start that he was intervening against a leftist (and potentially Communist) takeover, but used the rescue operation as a less controversial diplomatic pretext that would allow him to move troops in immediately.[25] The more significant question, however, is why in any case he thought it necessary for the United States to move in so quickly to prevent the leftist factions from winning in the civil conflict. A hint that he thought that Kennedy might not have intervened in the same way was contained in his defensive extemporaneous remark during a rally-round-the-flag speech on May 3 that "what is important is . . . that we know, and that they know, and that everybody knows, that we don't propose to sit here in our rocking chair with our hands folded and let the Communists set up any government in the Western Hemisphere." [26]

The dire consequences of a failure to act decisively continued to be the rationale invoked by Administration spokesmen to exonerate those responsible for the United States decisions from their remarkable causalness with the facts and double-dealings with prominent Dominican leaders, as our departures from international rectitude were exposed by some of our most respected journalists and Senators Fulbright and Clark.[27] The presumably "unimportant" things, such as the credibility of the Administration's public statements and private guarantees, just had to give way temporarily to the requirements of acting swiftly to prevent the Communists from coming to power in Santo Domingo. If that larger responsibility were fulfilled, history would absolve us of our smaller lapses.

But the Administration's view of its larger responsibility also bears examination. That view rested on the following critical premises: (a) Another Communist regime in this hemisphere would be intolerable. (b) The Communists would very likely come to power in Santo Domingo without our military intervention. In invoking this rationale, what was the Administration really saying about the reasons for its specific acts?

A. The establishment of another Communist regime in this hemisphere was intolerable. This oft-repeated assumption went unchallenged during both the Kennedy and Johnson Administrations, but, as a result, also remained unelaborated. Presumably, the event of another Communist takeover would be dangerous to vital United States interests; but which interests?

Certainly the existence of Communist Cuba did not by the fact of its being communist prevent the people of the United States from enjoying the blessings of liberty, except possibly for those few whose investments in pre-Castro Cuba were expropriated. There was no self-evident reason why one more small Communist nation in the Caribbean should constitute a threat to our security. Of course, if the Soviets

353

would try to make it into an offensive military base, that would be another matter entirely; but we had already demonstrated in October 1962 that it was a mistake for the Communists to try this gambit.

Was the denial of liberty to the Dominicans intolerable? If so, the value we gave to Dominican liberty had been suddenly inflated. For thirty years we acted indifferently to the harsh dictatorship of Trujillo, and only after he was assassinated in 1961 did we throw our support, temporarily, behind democratic constitutionalists in Santo Domingo. Kennedy threatened a Marine landing to prevent an attempt by the Trujillo family to grab back power in November 1961; but when the democratically elected Juan Bosch was deposed by a military coup after having been in office only seven months, Kennedy's strongest actions were to suspend diplomatic relations and to halt economic aid. Diplomatic recognition and economic aid were reextended promptly by the new Johnson Administration as the Dominican junta promised to hold general elections in the spring and summer of 1965. Self-determination by democratic choice for our Caribbean neighbors, was a preference we might strongly indicate, but we were not about to take it upon ourselves to *assure* it to them.

Yet if the denial of political liberty was to come through the establishment of another Communist regime, that evidently *was* intolerable. To whom? Why? United States officials were not pressed to give an answer to this question—a phenomenon which is in part a clue to its answer: the nation generally still took for granted the premise that an extension of Communism is, by definition, an increase in the power of the opposing "bloc" or alliance system, and, in proportion a decrease in our power. Moreoever, our inability once again to oppose such an extension in our traditional sphere of control, after having been duped by Castro, would be taken as a fundamental failure of our capability and will to quarantine the Third World against Communist takeovers— with reverberations sure to be felt in Vietnam, among other places.

It was all a part of the same basic conflict, said the President to the congressmen he assembled at the White House on May 4, 1965 to plead for a $700 million supplemental military budget required now by the increase of our effort in Vietnam simultaneously with the Dominican intervention. By our actions in these two conflicts, he said, we will be signaling to the world that:

. . . we are going to spend every dollar, we are going to take every action, we are going to walk the last mile in order to see that peace is restored, that the people of not only the Dominican Republic but South Viet-Nam have the right of self-determination and that they cannot be gobbled up in the 20th century and swallowed just because they happen to be smaller than some of those whose boundaries adjoin them.

I think it is well to remember that there are a hundred other little nations sitting here this moment watching what happens. . . .[28]

The fusion, sometimes apparent confusion, by Johnson of Santo Domingo with Saigon during these weeks possibly reflected an intention to demonstrate to the world, particularly to the larger Communist powers who might be contemplating increased assistance to Ho Chi Minh, that despite our escalation by carefully modulated steps in Southeast Asia, our patience could wear thin, and we *might* even over-react.

B. If events in Santo Domingo were allowed to take their course during April and May 1965, without significant U.S. military intervention, the probability was very high that a Communist regime would quickly gain control of the Dominican Republic. In the official rhetoric, the simple fact of a rebellion against the civilian junta of Reid Cabral would not have been sufficient to justify a United States intervention. Indeed, President Johnson granted in his statement of May 2 that the April 24 uprising "began as a popular democratic revolution, committed to democracy and social justice." The threat to our interests came, he said, when this legitimate revolution "very shortly moved and was taken over and really seized and placed into the hands of a band of Communist conspirators." [29]

Critics, most prominent among them Senator Fulbright, have charged that this is an inaccurate reconstruction of the real basis of our decision to intervene. The decision, it is contended, was actually forced upon President Johnson by our diplomatic mission in Santo Domingo and conservative Latin Americanists in the State Department who were determined to prevent Juan Bosch's reinstallation by the "popular democratic revolution" but realized Johnson would not act to prevent the revolution from succeeding unless it was clear that the pro-Bosch forces had fallen under Communist control. "The principal reason for the failure of American policy in Santo Domingo," asserted Senator Fulbright, "was faulty advice given to the President by his representa-

tives in the Dominican Republic at the time of the acute crisis. . . .
On the basis of the information and counsel he received, the President
could hardly have acted other than he did." [30] This was an assertion
resting on more than speculation.

The detailed closed hearings conducted by the Senate Foreign Relations Committee during the summer of 1965 had corroborated a number of facts already placed in the public domain by journalists such as
Szulc of the *Times,* Kurzman of the *Washington Post,* and Geyelin of
the *Wall Street Journal:* namely, that the United States diplomatic
mission on the scene in Santo Domingo had refused to mediate in the
dispute between the violently contending factions of the Dominican
military when the Bosch factions were losing (between April 26 and
April 28). Then, as the pro-Bosch factions, under Colonel Caamano
Deno appeared to be turning the tide on April 28, the U.S. Embassy
cabled Washington recommending that we furnish the anti-Bosch
forces with communications equipment from Defense Department
stocks in Puerto Rico. The Administration was reluctant to grant this
request so quickly on the heels of earlier reports that the "loyalists"
were putting down the Bosch rebels. Ambassador Bennett persisted in
his appeals to Washington, painting in more extreme colors with each
cable the consequences of our failure to come to the help of the anti-
Bosch military units. One of the April 28 cables that found its way into
the press captures the trend of the Bennett messages:

I regret that we may have to impose a military solution to a political
problem. . . . While leftist propaganda will fuzz this up as a fight between the military and the people, the issue is really between those who
want a Castro-type solution and those who oppose it.

I don't want to overdramatize, but if we deny the communications
equipment, and the opposition to the leftists lose heart, we may be asking
in the near future for a landing of Marines to protect U.S. interests and for
other purposes. What does Washington prefer? [31]

Frantically, the Embassy in Santo Domingo and the State Department now tried to find the proper legal formula for landing a contingent of U.S. Marines in time to prevent a rebel victory. Meanwhile,
the President had asked the C.I.A. to inform him concerning the extent of Communist infiltration in the pro-Bosch military and political
leadership. The rescue operation rationale apparently got to Johnson
before he had fully resolved his doubts about the credibility of the anti-

Communist rationale, so he moved on the basis of the former; but added the Communist threat in a few days and made it the reason for his expansion of U.S. troops there to an eventual 20,000, and for his insistence upon a political solution satisfactory to the Organization of American States as a precondition for the withdrawal of our military forces.

What was the prospect of a Communist and/or Castroite takeover of the rebellion as perceived by the White House? On the basis of subsequent releases to the press and public statements by the President and the Secretary of State it would appear that these perceptions were fragmentary and uncertain even while the President was telling the nation unequivocally on May 2 that the "popular democratic revolution" had been "taken over" by "a band of Communist conspirators." As journalists writing from Santo Domingo punctured this hyperbole, there ensued probably the most notorious Washington "numbers game" of recent years. The first list to be released publically had been handed out by Ambassador Bennett to journalists in Santo Domingo on April 29. It contained 53 names of individuals in the rebel movement who were supposedly known by the Embassy to be Communists. But the journalists soon discovered that the Embassy had no reliable evidence of the connection between these individuals and the Caamano leadership of the rebel movement in Santo Domingo or Juan Bosch who was then in Puerto Rico. On May 1, a list of 54 was leaked to the press corps in Washington. The version of this list published in the *New York Times* on May 6 identified only 20 of the 54 as having taken part in the current revolt; others were on the list simply for being known Communists or Castroites. Six weeks later another list was leaked to the press, this time containing 77 names. Journalists who checked out these lists carefully discovered them to contain some individuals who were in prison at the time of the violence, others who were not even in the Dominican Republic at the time, and others who were obviously not Communists but had been vocal in their anti-United States sentiment. James Goodsell of the *Christian Science Monitor* maintained that nearly 40 per cent of the original list of 54 could not have played active roles in the April-May uprising.[32] Comparing the list of 54 with the June list of 77, Theodore Draper found that ten names had been dropped from the old list, but obviously it was the oroginal list and not the revised one that was supposed to have formed the basis of the Administration's perceptions of the Communist threat at the end of April.[33]

Clearly the President's May 2 statements were simplifications. However, the Administration, while quickly backing off from its posture of fear of an imminent Communist takeover, rested its case on the argument that such a takeover was sufficiently probable as to warrant the intervention. On May 4, in his description to congressional leaders of the considerations underlying his April 28 intervention decision, Johnson added some confusing, yet revealing, embellishments:

As reports came in, as they do every few minutes, it developed there were eight of those who were in the movement that had been trained by Communist forces. Alerts were set up, and our men continued to ferret out and study the organization. Up to yesterday they had the names and addresses and experience and numbers and backgrounds of some 58. As those 58 came forward and cream began to rise on that crock of milk, they came to the surface and took increased leadership in the movement and the leaders and friends of ex-President Bosch were more or less shoved in the background and stepped aside.[34]

But the Administration was not about to allow itself to be pinned down to any specific figure of known Communists in the rebel movement as the threshold to be passed before intervention was justified. Dean Rusk led the counterattack against the critics, dusting off another one of his famous Munich analogies. "I am not impressed," he said:

. . . with the remark that there were several dozen known Communist leaders and that therefore this was not a very serious matter. There was a time when Hitler sat in a beer hall in Munich with seven people. And I just don't believe that one underestimates what can be done in . . . a situation of violence and chaos, by a few highly organized, highly trained people who know what they are about and know they want to bring about.[35]

It was precisely this kind of reasoning by the Administration that was the target of Senator Fulbright's criticism in his major speech of September 15, 1965.

Intervention on the basis of Communist *participation* as distinguished from *control* was a mistake in my opinion which also reflects a grievous misreading of the temper of contemporary Latin American politics. Communists are present in all Latin American countries, and they are going to inject themselves into almost any Latin American revolution and try to seize control of it. If any group or any movement with which the Communists associate themselves is going to be automatically condemned in the eyes of the

United States, then we have indeed given up all hope of guiding or influencing even to a marginal degree the revolutionary movements and the demands for social change which are sweeping Latin America. (Emphasis added.) [36]

Pundits were now asking whether the Truman Doctrine of assistance to free peoples resisting subjugation by armed minorities or outside pressures had been supplemented by a Johnson Doctrine of military intervention to nip militant beer-hall crowds, or other embryos of insurgency, in the bud. The decisions regarding the Dominican Republic had to be made under great pressure and on the basis of inconclusive information, Fulbright offered. "In charity, this can be accepted as a reason why the decisions were mistaken." What especially galled the Senator, however, were the Administration's attempts to convert the rationalizations for its hasty action into a philosophy of contemporary statecraft.

But possibly there was a philosophy of sorts behind the action—a philosophy that was a carry-over from the Dulles-Eisenhower period of U.S. foreign policy toward Latin America, now expressing itself in the person of a holdover from the Eisenhower period, himself a participant in the Guatemala affair of 1954, Johnson's key Latin America man, Undersecretary of State Thomas C. Mann. It was Mann's speech of October 12, 1965 before the Inter-American Press Association that henceforth served as the text of the basic Administration defense of the Dominican intervention, and, not incidentally, the rebuttal to Fulbright. The landing of troops in addition to the number required to protect and evacuate foreign personnel, contended Mann, was necessary in view of the "clear and present danger of the forcible seizure of power by the Communists." All of those in our government who had full access to official information were convinced of this, he maintained. And the evidence we now had, he argued, showed that we were right, since at the time of our intervention "the para-military forces under the control of known Communists exceeded in military strength the forces controlled by the non-Communist elements within the rebel movement." Equally important, claimed the Undersecretary, "Is the fact that these non-Communist elements were working hand in glove with the Communists." [37] Thus, an injection of external military power, initially from the United States, was necessary, first, to rectify the balance of forces within the country, but also, presumably, to save the rebels from absorption by the Communists in their own ranks. This stands as the official elaboration of the premise that a division-size United States military contingent in the Dominican Republic was essential to the prevention of a Communist takeover of the country.

The philosophy articulated by Mann was simple: in dealing with a Communist insurgency situation (potential or actual) the really critical question is what is the immediate balance of coercive capabilities that can be exercised in the situation? If this is taken care of to our satisfaction, the more complicated political questions can then be attended to, and will eventually work themselves out in a not intolerable manner.

It is not at all clear that President Johnson himself thought he was buying such a stark philosophy in approving of the intervention in the Dominican Republic. But he did follow recommendations in the particular circumstances which implied such premises.

His actions in Vietnam in the spring of 1965 also implied such premises. They implied a belief in the harsh counterinsurgency philosophy that winning the hearts and minds of the people through constructive action must take second place on a scale of action priorities to establishing a satisfactory balance of coercive power—the notion being that only when terror is denied to the opponent as a weapon can the competition for the affection of the populace be the determining aspect of politics.

Yet for this doctrine to serve as a guide for U.S. foreign policy in Third World situations of civil disorder, we must know who are the opponents as far as our interests are concerned. Obviously, any stable sovereign government must have at its command a monopoly of the moblizable coercive power in its country. Subverison, sometimes becoming overt insurgency, is an effort by other groups to undermine the government's monopoly of coercive power, and eventually to overmatch it, either by gaining control over the nation's armed forces through infiltration or conversion, or by defeating the "loyalist" factions by battle in the fields and cities. The question in any situation where we contemplate intervention, therefore, becomes: are we for the "loyalists," who want to maintain the existing regime's monopoly of coercive power, or are we for the rebels, who want to transfer the monopoly of coercive power to other hands. The critical question determining our policy either to strengthen another government's military position against insurgency, or to allow the insurgents to overmatch the government's power is whether we consider the preservation of the existing government more compatible with our interest than the establishment of an alternative government by the insurgents. A posture of nonintervention when the insurgents are losing can be just as much an "intervention" in the domestic affairs of a given country as is overt intervention to help the government forces reestablish the "balance" when the insurgents are winning. The political question cannot be avoided. We have been unable to settle it by saying that our interventions are for the purpose of putting an end to the violence. The consequences of our intervention or nonintervention for the struggle for control over the violence capabilities within a society—that is the question.

To conduct our "Third World" foreign policy without reference to the question of the distribution of coercive powers in these societies is an illusion. Kennedy knew this. It was in back of his threat to land Marines in the Dominican Republic to prevent the return to power of the Trujillos. But he also knew that it was folly to attempt to alter the coercive balance in another country without having a policy for the other domestic political questions in that country: namely, who was fit to rule by virtue of nationwide appeal and, hopefully, legitimation by popular election? Since we had no such policy for Cuba, the bloody and expensive Bay of Pigs operation was folly, and Kennedy called it off as soon as the real costs became manifest.

The blood-and-treasure costs were not as high for the Dominican operation, and other costs—namely, our prestige within Latin America —were evidently not accorded special weight at the time of the intervention decision. But Johnson and his advisers quickly grasped that the adventure could turn into a political disaster unless they developed a policy for legitimating a political regime in the Dominican Republic. The political disaster would be that otherwise the Dominicans would have to be subject to an externally imposed civil order *indefinitely*. And we were not prepared, nor did we have the stomach for managing that kind of imperial order in this hemisphere, unless, of course, it became necessary to preserving a global balance of power against those wanting to overcome us.

Our political policy for the Dominican Republic eventually turned out to be, paradoxically, very similar to the political policy of the pro-Bosch forces whom we had refused support and against whom we intervened because of the White House conviction they were being taken over by the Communists. The basic platform of the Bosch elements was not Bosch himself, but the Constitution of 1963, under which Bosch had served, with its provision for orderly succession, according to the free determination of the Dominican people, and on the basis of universal suffrage. The election of the moderate rightist Joaquin Balaguer to the presidency in June 1966 and the defeat of Juan Bosch was hailed by the White House as a vindication of Johnson's policies. The world diplomatic community, almost universally, admired the masterful way in which the President's hand-picked political trouble-shooters, McGeorge Bundy, and then Ellsworth Bunker, went about their delicate tasks of selecting a provisional government acceptable to the Dominicans for the task of administering the elections, and transferring provisional enforcement authority to the Organization of American States. But the violence-free election of 1966, the victory of Balaguer, and Bosch's gracious acceptance of the outcome—however precarious the political stability that was to ensue—was ironic. Balaguer and Bosch were both in back of the revolution to overthrow Ried Cabral in 1965 and return the country to constitutionalism. A Balaguer youth group fought with the rebels. And Balaguer, also in exile in New York at the time of the 1965 violence in Santo Domingo, publicly opposed the United States intervention.[38] Our puzzled observers could only shake their heads on the intricacies of Latin American politics.

The Administration would of course claim that the outcome, far from being ironic, was very much in accord with what we had in mind from the start of the intervention. The May 1965 statements of President Johnson and Secretary Rusk find them insisting that "we support no single man or any single group of men in the Dominican Republic. . . . The form and the nature of the free Dominican government . . . is solely a matter for the Dominican people. . . ."[39] The essential task of our military intervention, it was claimed at the time, was to make it possible for the Dominicans to establish "a broadly based provisional government which can accept responsibility for the affairs of that country pending elections and pending full return to the democratic and constitutional processes."[40] This hoped-for state of affairs did essentially materialize within the year following our military intervention. But historians of the episode would continue to debate whether it came about because of the military intervention or despite it. The important datum for purposes of our analysis is that the Administration claimed to be vindicated in its swift application of military force to stabilize and clarify a chaotic situation.

The reassertion of the continuing utility of force as an essential instrument of organization in situations of political chaos—a utility which it was important to appreciate if for no other reason than that our major opponents appreciated it and were not at all squeamish in applying it—was the salient effect of the Vietnam and Dominican crises in policy circles. Whatever the eventual return in these localities to socioeconomic and more benign political means of influence, the record would state that these peaceful modes came after force had clarified the situation.

Lyndon Johnson could legitimately claim that the resort to force to move men and nations was the exception, not at all the norm, of his foreign policies. His preferred mode of influence was that of the prophet Isaiah: "Come now and let us reason together."

It was reason, Johnson would insist, that brought about the solution of the Panama Canal crisis of 1964-65, and not simply the reason of the weak in accepting the dictates of the strong. The United States Government, under Johnson, went further toward recognizing Panama's sovereignty over the Canal Zone, and in according Panamanians equitable treatment in United States zone installations than had any previous administration.

It was reason, the objective consideration of the advantages and disadvantages of alternative courses of action, that Johnson could claim to have brought to bear upon the Greeks and Turks to forestall their impending war over Cyprus, and upon the Indians and Pakistanis to persuade them to cease their war over Kashmir. The fact that the United States was in a position to affect the anticipations of advantage and disadvantage of the involved parties (the perquisites and protections of NATO membership to Greece and Turkey, the flow of military and economic assistance to the South Asian countries) was, of course, at the heart of the President's appeals to substitute reason for passion.

Johnson had also shown an ability to practice restraint in situations of extreme local instability, such as in Indonesia, Rhodesia, and the Middle East where it might have been tempting for a great power to intervene. Rather than attempting to play the world policeman, he prudently allowed events to take their course in response to lesser influences.

The United States support for the Alliance for Progress had been extended indefinitely. Constructive development schemes had been sponsored from the Amazon to the Mekong. The Peace Corps continued to receive the wholehearted support of the White House. A non-proliferation treaty and other arms control accords had been spurred by the personal solicitude of the President. New economic and cultural bridges were being built to Eastern Europe. West Germany had been encouraged to depart from its rigid legalisms vis-à-vis the East. And not a harsh word had been heard to come from the President against the Soviet regime, despite the many opportunities to retaliate for anti-United-States diatribes from the Kremlin.

The arts of conciliation and compromise, in the Johnson Administration's self-image, were the facts of our power now, more so than at any time since the start of the Cold War.

Yet an administration cannot escape the massive impressions created on domestic and foreign observers by its most dramatic actions. Regardless of intention, large doses of force in the international environment create a noise level that drowns out the sound of other signals. This remained the condition within which the Johnson Administration was attempting to get friends and adversaries to reason together.

The effort to get messages through the uproar of violence, unfortunately, appeared to have stimulated a revival of the more histrionic aspects of postwar U.S. foreign policy—the resort to ideological hyperbole, to moralizing about the basis of our overseas commitments, to lecturing neutrals about *their* vital interests, and to threats of more violence to come if the enemy persists in his course. The central question was whether the ability of our government to sustain a constructive approach toward the Soviet Union on outstanding East-West issues would outlast the atmosphere produced by the war in Vietnam.

CONCLUSION

CHANGES IN THE FORMS
OF RELEVANT POWER

The record of United States policymaking and crisis behavior from Truman to Johnson shows each Administration relying heavily on the tools of physical coercion—sometimes only as a background factor, sometimes as a visible and active ingredient in a particular situation —in order to control external threats to our national interests. It also shows major efforts by each Administration to enlist dependable allies in the struggle to prevent the Communist nations from extending their control into new areas; in many cases the objective was to have such allies share the burden of providing the coercive power we and they might need to implement this shared interest in containing the Communists. Each of the Administrations considered it necessary to be able to marshall sufficient power globally to balance, and if possible to outweigh, the power any combination of potential adversaries could mobilize. And each Administration considered the military power immediately mobilizable by the United States, and whatever advance commitments of loyalty from other nations we could obtain, as essential ingredients of the global balance of power. To this extent there was constancy over the period in some of the necessary means of foreign policy, as well as constancy in fundamental purposes as shown in Part I of this study.

365

However significant this consensus on some of the necessities of power, the developing recognition at top policy levels of the insufficiency of military preparedness and alliances for maintaining an advantageous balance of power is no less an important aspect of U.S. foreign policy since the Second World War. It is the course of this latter groping for relevant tools of nonmilitary power that constitutes the "change" counterpoint to the constancy theme, and is the analytical thread running through Parts II to IV.

Despite short-term oscillations, there has been a dominant direction to the change. Our foreign policy has become, in its operational energies, oriented increasingly "southward"—toward the less developed Third World. There the objects are still to be influenced; there the weights in the global balance are still to be distributed.

This is not to say that the balance between the two superalliances of industrialized nations has requred less and less attention. That sometimes delicate balance, the deterrence of each by each from significant unilateral alterations in the political-military status quo, has needed tending all along. The technologically spurred arms race has continued, with each side warily eying the other for signs of a decisive new weapons breakthrough. And the unnatural parceling of the volatile German nation into two opposing military alliance systems has kept the terms of a potential German reunification the most critical issue between the United States and the Soviet Union, fusing it intimately with questions of the United States-Soviet military balance.

But the experience on both sides of rather successfully managing the unstable equilibrium in the northern hemisphere, while having to forego any hope of victory there, formed the background condition that made possible a shift of emphasis to the Third World. There the Soviets, prodded by their rivalry with the Chinese, began to seek new victories; and there, we began to fear, we might lose the struggle.

It is difficult to date the shift to this new arena for conducting the power struggle. The Korean War took place there physically, but politically it was conducted as part of the central competition between the two superpowers for control of the older industrialized areas of the globe. At least this was the Truman Administration's definition of what the Soviets were up to, and thus the President refused to expand our commitment (and resources) in Asia for the objective of beating Communist China.

366

For essentially similar reasons President Eisenhower would not follow the advice of some of his advisers to make the United States an active belligerent in Indochina in 1954. Eisenhower was concerned about our inheriting the French mantle of colonialism in Southeast Asia, but his dominant consideration, yet, appeared to be the endless drain on our resources he foresaw from a war on the Asian mainland, and his fear that this was a trap the Communists had set for us in order to weaken us for the big contest they were preparing in Europe. Our efforts in the Third World still ought to be relatively low-commitment, low-cost efforts such as SEATO in Asia and the Baghdad Pact in the Middle East.

The Eisenhower Administration also assumed that the Soviets were operating under a similar calculus of priorities. Thus, we easily faced down the Chinese Communists during the first Quemoy-Matsu crisis and we arranged for the toppling of the Arbenz regime in Guatemala without running any high risks. Our underdeveloped opponents were held at bay or squelched by the threat of our military prowess, and the Soviets, we believed, felt the stakes were much more important elsewhere. Dulles was, of course, gambling much more on Soviet prudence in the China situation than in Central America where the Communist world had less invested, but he felt on firm enough ground to pretend to drag Mao to the "brink."

It was in the Middle East, in the mid-1950s, that the insufficiency of military deterrence and militarily-based alliances for affecting power relationships first became a serious factor for the Eisenhower Administration and suggested major modifications of existing policy premises. It was here that we perceived we were sometimes backing the wrong contenders; that combustible populist nationalism, the social egalitarian passions of the new urban masses, and the heady iconoclasm of the burgeoning student population were undermining the political foundations of pro-Western regimes. It was here we perceived that in the Third World, at least, those who were most ready to formally ally themselves with us against International Communism were often out of tune with the popular currents in their own countries, sometimes holding on to the reigns of government for dear life, and were using the economic and military benefits of alliance for the purpose of redressing their weakening domestic power base. It was often a losing game, we began to realize, both for the local leaders we were backing, and for us, internationally, since the Soviets were ready to back the radical nationalists.

The shock of recognition, the perception that this was the emerging situation in the Middle East, and that policies based on alternative premises were wrong, hit our top policymakers with fullest impact when France and Britain joined Israel in an attempt to topple Nasser by force. To support, or even countenance, that action would be to to put ourselves squarely against what we now perceived to be the popular tides in the Middle East. A defeat of Nasser would only be temporary. Nasser-*ism* was on the rise, and the Soviets would be riding the next wave.

To those who equate rhetoric with policy, the shift in U.S. Middle Eastern policy might appear as the outcome of the conflict between two moral premises of Dullesian diplomacy: the immorality of Cold War "neutralism" as opposed to the immorality of "aggression"—with the latter, in this case, the determining factor. Actually, as the material in Part III of this study shows, Dulles the decisionmaker, as distinct from Dulles the preacher, always kept his eye on the power relationships, as he saw them. It was a change in his reading of these relationships, not a sudden change, but one emerging gradually out of his experience, that determined his choices at this "moment of truth."

The Administration's adaptation to the complexity of immediate and long-term power relationships in the Middle East was fitful and erratic, as evidenced by our behavior in subsequent crises, particularly Syria and Lebanon. The continuing tension between the older institutionalized premises and the newer premises concerning the most appropriate tools of influence in the Middle East was exhibited by the coexistence on the one hand of the "Eisenhower Doctrine," pledging our armed intervention on behalf of regimes threatened by Communist aggression, and, on the other hand, the new emphasis in United States economic assistance policies in the Middle East (announced by Eisenhower in 1958 before the United Nations) to support socioeconomic modernization rather than ideological loyalty in the Cold War.

Similarly, a tension between the requirements of influencing those who would be our loyal allies in the Cold War as opposed to the requirements of influencing those pushing for major socioeconomic reforms in the less developed world came to the surface in the Eisenhower Administration's Latin American policies after 1958. The challenge by Milton Eisenhower and Douglas Dillon to the dominant premises underlying the Caracas Declaration and our Guatemalan proxy intervention was reflected in the Act of Bogotá in 1960, through which the United States pledged support for programs of internal socio-economic reform. In this case, it was Castro who provided the shock of sufficient impact to the more sanguine assumption that the Pax Norte-americano, based primarily on our obvious military umbrella, would be essentially all that was needed to keep our global power rivals out of the Western Hemisphere.

Thus, by the time the Kennedy Administration assumed office, the stage was set for a full-dress inaugural of a fresh set of premises of our national power, and for a restatement of the relationships created with and among the existing premises. This was the central function of many of the early state papers of the New Frontier: the President's Inaugural Address, and his first State of the Union Message, the Foreign Assistance Act of 1961, and the Alliance for Progress. And the operational effects of these fresh restatements of the utility of our tools of power on the international scene were exhibited in the President's decision to call *off* the Bay of Pigs intervention, his acceptance of a neutralization formula for Laos, his threatened intervention on behalf of the anti-Trujillo forces in the Dominican Republic, his new grants of economic assistance to radical African nationalists such as Sékou Touré, and his initially strong anti-militarist stance in response to coups and threatened coups in various Latin American countries.

The Third World policy that Kennedy was trying to institutionalize was based on the primary premise that these undistributed weights in the global power balance would either remain unaligned, become satellites or dependent allies of one of the superpowers, or, in less direct ways, facilitate the use of their territory and resources by one side or the other more as a result of the basic processes of politics *within* these countries than as a direct result of favors granted or threats made by the superpowers to existing regimes.

A secondary premise in the new Third World policy was that the political balance of power within these countries, as literacy and exposure to global communications spread within their populations, would be weighted on the side of leaders and groups sponsoring wide redistributions of wealth and political authority—i.e., the idea of social justice was assuming real political flesh.

369

The conclusion drawn for U.S. foreign policy was that the United States would lose influence in these nations, and over their ultimate choice of friends and benefactors in the international system, unless we identified ourselves with those social and political forces demanding greater social justice.

To the extent that the Third World was now a more important arena of competiton for influence between the superpowers, and to the extent that the mode of competition was changing to one of providing attractive models for, and assistance in, social transformation, the premises concerning the most immediately relevant tools of our power were bound to change.

The capacity to deter aggression by our major adversaries, and a fighting capability to deny them territorial grabs in case deterrence failed, were still necessary ingredients of power internationally. But these ingredients would have to receive *relatively* less attention than previously. Their influence over the course of social transformation in the Third World was seen to be very small, except for areas under threat of direct overt aggression, for even the violent conflicts in these areas would be primarily of a paramilitary kind in which factors other than our great wealth and weapons superiority would determine the outcome.

The trend, however erratic, since the mid-1950s has been to increasingly operationalize these premises of power in our policies toward the Third World, and to give this aspect of our overall foreign policy increasing prominence.

But toward the end of the period of this study a number of developments appear to be complicating the implementation of the premises.

First, the decline in the ideology of the Cold War—from one point of view, a healthy outcome of the stalemate in Europe—has removed from the Administration probably its most effective arguments for prying loose external assistance monies from stingy Congresses. If the Soviets are no longer out to conquer the world, if there are many forms of Communism, if the "bloc" is in a phase of its own disintegration, then why all the worry over whether one or two small nations out there go Communist? Certainly, so a frequently heard argument runs, such events will not affect the global balance of power in a way to threaten our security. Without the Cold War rationale, there is little political steam for foreign aid or concessionary trading arrangements. Altruistic impulses exist in the American body politic, but it is difficult to channel them overseas when our own cities are in social crisis and economic deterioration.

Second, our experience in affecting the conditions within the Third World through economic assistance and other diplomatic pressures on behalf of social justice has not left the policy community with a great deal of confidence in (a) our ability to understand what is really going on within these countries, (b) our ability to significantly effect such events anyway. We have been disappointed to find our faith in supposed "progressives" misplaced. Nasser and Sukarno showed themselves to be more ready to recklessly pursue international glory than to tend the mundane tasks of domestic modernization.

And finally, where we do seem to have had a demonstrable effect on events in the Third World, our interventions have been of the dramatic military sort, where we have depended most on our technological-military prowess to prevent outcomes we have defined (officially) as intolerable. The Dominican intervention and the Vietnam War, as they have been managed by the Johnson Administration, seem to point to a revival, again relatively speaking, of the reliance placed on the tools of physical coercion for influencing events. Whether or not our conduct in Santo Domingo and Vietnam would represent only a temporary deviation from the general trend toward a more flexible reliance on other tools of influence would be revealed by events which unfolded after the writing of this book.

In 1961, an optimistic breed of young men had come to office, chastened by personal experience in war, knowledgeable about the role of coercion in the affairs of men, but determined to show the way to an increased reliance on voluntary cooperative modes of international behavior, and to keep the United States pre-eminent in this altered atmosphere by an imaginative exploitation internationally of the postive psychological and economic inducements that seemed to work so well in our domestic politics. The hope was to substitute the housing development for the aircraft carrier as the visible symbol to the developing nations of United States power; and thereby to help alter the conception of other nations as to what they ought to want for their own face of greatness. Five years later that hope was but a brief flame flickering in the wind.

Men, in and out of positions of responsibility, continued to pay homage to that flame. But would they take the opportunity when the current brutish storm had subsided to reassert and reapply its fundamental message: that the peaceful mode of managing conflict demanded vigilant and precise attention to the sources of conflict, a concern for the details of the politics of other lands, not just our own, and a willingness to become involved, to take sides, if need be, well before the shooting starts.

A style of Presidential politics which tended to leave the details of the international environment to others until the Commander-in-Chief's function was required would probably find this function required more often than a President who cultivated a facility with the rich arsenal of international inducements and sanctions at this nation's disposal, and would directly oversee their application in pursuit of our multiple interests across the globe. The White House, the entire nation, was fully implicated in this interdependent world. There was no escape from responsibility.

NOTES

Chapter One: *The Irreducible National Interest and Basic Premises About World Conditions*

1. Address by President Johnson to The Associated Press, April 21, 1965, in the *New York Times*, April 22, 1965.
2. State of the Union Message by the President, January 5, 1956.
3. See, for example, Walt W. Rostow, "The Third Round," *Foreign Affairs* (October 1963), pp. 1–10.

Chapter Two: *Larger Interests and the Balance-of-Power Consideration*

1. Inaugural Address, January 20, 1961; Department of State *Bulletin*, February 6, 1961, pp. 175–76 (emphasis added).
2. Address by President Johnson to the American Bar Association, August 12, 1964, in the Department of State *Bulletin*, August 31, 1964, pp. 298–301.
3. For the period from McKinley to Franklin Roosevelt, see Robert E. Osgood, *Ideals and Self Interest in American Foreign Relations* (Chicago: University of Chicago Press, 1953).
4. Quoted by McGeorge Bundy, *The Pattern of Responsibility* (Boston: Houghton-Mifflin, 1951), p. 42, from Acheson's speech to the American Society of Newspaper Editors, April 22, 1950.
5. Address by the Secretary of State to the Congress of Industrial Organizations, November 18, 1953, in the Department of State *Bulletin*, November 30, 1953. pp. 741–44.
6. State of the Union Message by the President, January 30, 1961.
7. State of the Union Message by the President, January 11, 1962.
8. Walt W. Rostow, *The United States in the World Arena* (New York: Harper, 1960), p. 178.
9. Harry S. Truman, *Memoirs: Years of Trial and Hope* (New York: Doubleday, 1955), II, 62, 91.
10. Address by the Secretary of State to the Congress of Industrial Organizations, Cleveland, Ohio, November 18, 1953, in the Department of State *Bulletin*, November 30, 1953, pp. 741–44.

Chapter Three: *The Shattering of Expectations*

1. Harry S. Truman, *Memoirs: Year of Decisions* (New York: Doubleday, 1955), I, 70.
2. *Ibid.*, p. 71.
3. William D. Leahy, *I Was There* (New York: McGraw-Hill, 1950), pp. 351–52.
4. Truman, *Memoirs*, I, 85–87.
5. See especially Gar Alperovitz, *Atomic Diplomacy: Hiroshima and Potsdam* (New York: Simon and Schuster, 1965).

6. The quotations are from Truman's letter to Byrnes of January 5, 1946. Truman, *Memoirs*, I, 551–52.

7. Truman, *Memoirs: Years of Trial and Hope* II, 11.

8. Walter Millis, *The Forrestal Diaries* (New York: Viking, 1952), p. 102.

9. *Ibid.*, p. 129.

10. *Ibid.*, pp. 135–40.

11. Truman, *Memoirs*, II, 95.

12. *Ibid.*, pp. 96–97.

13. Truman, *Memoirs*, I, 551–52.

14. John C. Campbell, *Defense of the Middle East: Problems of American Policy* (New York: Praeger, 1960), p. 33.

15. Truman, *Memoirs*, II, 100.

16. Address by the Secretary of State at Princeton University, February 22, 1947.

17. Joseph M. Jones, *The Fifteen Weeks* (New York: Viking, 1955), pp. 138–41.

18. *Ibid.*, pp. 157, 162.

19. Address by President Truman to the Congress, March 12, 1947.

20. Quoted by Harry Bayard Price, *The Marshall Plan and Its Meaning* (Ithaca: Cornell University Press, 1955), p. 22.

21. The fullest quotation from this section of the Policy Planning Staff memorandum is provided by Jones, pp. 251–52.

22. In the Department of State *Bulletin*, June 15, 1947, pp. 1159–60.

23. Price, pp. 24–29; Walt W. Rostow, *The United States in the World Arena* (New York: Harper, 1960), pp. 209–13.

24. X (George Kennan), "The Sources of Soviet Conduct," *Foreign Affairs* (July 1947), 566–82.

25. *Ibid.*, passim.

Chapter Four: 1948–1950: Internal Dialogue on the Components of the Balance of Power

1. Walter Millis, *The Forrestal Diaries* (New York: Viking, 1951), p. 341.

2. This interpretation of Marshall's views relies heavily on Warner R. Shilling's thorough study, "The Politics of National Defense: Fiscal 1950," in Warner R. Shilling, Paul Y. Hammond, and Glenn H. Snyder, *Strategy, Politics, and Defense Budgets* (New York: Columbia University Press, 1962), pp. 5–266, passim.

3. Millis, pp. 240, 350.

4. *Ibid.*, 350–51.

5. This review is the subject of a detailed monograph by Paul Hammond entitled "NSC-68: Prologue to Rearmament," and published in Schilling, Hammond, and Snyder, *Strategy, Politics, and Defense Budgets*, pp. 271–378. My account of the substance of arguments and activities surrounding NSC-68 relies heavily on the Hammond monograph.

6. See Edward S. Flash, Jr., *Economic Advice and Presidential Leadership: The Council of Economic Advisers* (New York: Columbia University Press, 1965), pp. 39–52.

7. Coral Bell, *Negotiations From Strength* (New York: Knopf, 1963), pp. 6–10.

Chapter Five: The Primacy of Balance-of-Power Considerations During the Korean War

1. Samuel P. Huntington, *The Common Defense: Strategic Programs in National Politics* (New York: Columbia University Press, 1961), pp. 59–61.

2. Harry S. Truman, *Memoirs: Years of Trial and Hope* (New York: Doubleday, 1956), II, 341.

3. *Ibid.*, p. 380.

4. *Ibid.*, pp. 387–88.
5. *Ibid.*, pp. 397–98.
6. *Ibid.*, p. 403.
7. *Ibid.*, p. 408.
8. *Ibid.*, p. 432.
9. U. S. Senate, Committee on Armed Service and Committee on Foreign Relations, *Hearings: Military Situation in the Far East*, 82nd Congress, 1st session, 1951, pp. 731–32, 1219.
10. Truman, *Memoirs*, II, 437.
11. See Robert E. Osgood, *NATO: The Entangling Alliance* (Chicago: University of Chicago Press, 1963), pp. 78–79.
12. *Ibid.*, pp. 70–71.
13. *Hearings: Military Situation in the Far East.*
14. For the full text of Acheson's remarks see his January 12, 1950 speech before the National Press Club, Washington, D. C., in the Department of State *Bulletin*, January 23, 1950, pp. 111–18.
15. Department of State, *United States Relations With China* (Washington: GPO, 1949), p. 383.
16. Quoted by Tang Tsou, *America's Failure in China, 1941–1950* (Chicago: University of Chicago Press, 1963), p. 363. Dr. Tsou thoroughly documents the prevailing U. S. consensus of the late 1940s that the stakes on the China mainland were not worth a U. S. military combat intervention.
17. Quoted by John C. Sparrow, *History of Personnel Demobilization* (Washington: Dept. of Army, 1951), p. 380. See also Tang Tsou, p. 366.
18. Press conference of November 30, 1950, see Truman, *Memoirs*, II, 395–96.

Chapter Six: A New Look for Less Expensive Power

1. Paul Y. Hammond, in Schilling, Hammond, and Snyder, *Strategy, Politics, and Defense Budgets* (New York: Columbia University Press, 1962), pp. 359–61; Glenn H. Snyder, in *ibid.*, p. 407.
2. Eisenhower, *ibid.*, p. 74.
3. Dwight D. Eisenhower, *Mandate for Change: The White House Years 1953–1956* (New York: Doubleday, 1963), pp. 172–73.
4. *Ibid.*, p. 535.
5. *Ibid.*, pp. 534, 541.
6. Edward S. Flash, Jr., *Economic Advice and Presidential Leadership: The Council of Economic Advisers* (New York: Columbia University Press, 1965), pp. 100–2.
7. The period of the formulation of the New Look is described in detail by Snyder, *ibid.*, 386–456; Charles J. V. Murphy in a series of *Fortune* articles (January 1953, September 1953, November 1953, December 1953, January 1956, February 1956, and March 1956) and in Donovan, *Eisenhower: The Inside Story*, pp. 17–19, 55–59. The following discussion is a brief amalgam of these various accounts.
8. Radio address, March 19, 1953, in the *New York Times*, May 20, 1953.
9. See Robert E. Osgood, *NATO: The Entangling Alliance* (Chicago: University of Chicago Press, 1963), pp. 89–90.
10. For details on the formulation and contents of NSC-162, see Snyder, pp. 406–10.
11. Snyder, *ibid.*, 414–15.
12. *Ibid.*, 436–38.
13. John Foster Dulles, "The Evolution of Foreign Policy," address to the Council on Foreign Relations, January 12, 1954, in the Department of State *Bulletin*, January 25, 1964, pp. 107–10.
14. John Foster Dulles, "Policy for Security and Peace," *Foreign Affairs* (April 1954), pp. 353–64.

Chapter Seven: Commitments and Coercion: Dulles' Psychology of Power

1. See Richard H. Nolte, "United States Policy in the Middle East," *The United States and the Middle East*, an American Assembly Book, edited by Georgiana G. Stevens (Englewood: Prentice-Hall, 1964), pp. 156–58.
2. John Foster Dulles, "Report on the Near East," in the Department of State *Bulletin*, June 15, 1953, pp. 831–35.
3. John C. Campbell, *Defense of the Middle East: Problems of American Policy* (New York: Praeger, 1960), pp. 49–62.
4. Press conference of April 7, 1954, in the *New York Times*, April 8, 1954.
5. From Eisenhower letter to Churchill, April 4, 1954. Quoted by Eisenhower in *Mandate for Change: The White House Years 1953–1956* (New York: Doubleday, 1963), p. 346.
6. *Ibid.*, 354.
7. See Chalmers Roberts, "The Day We Didn't Go To War," *The Reporter* (September 14, 1954).
8. *Mandate For Change*, p. 352.
9. *Ibid.*, p. 354.
10. John Foster Dulles, Radio-TV address, March 8, 1955, in the Department of State *Bulletin*, March 21, 1955, p. 463.
11. In the Department of State *Bulletin*, March 28, 1955, pp. 526–27.
12. *Mandate For Change*, pp. 476–77.
13. Quotes are from February 1955 Eisenhower letters to Churchill, appearing in *Mandate For Change*, pp. 470–75.
14. Emmet John Hughes, *The Ordeal of Power: A Political Memoir of The Eisenhower Years* (New York: Atheneum, 1963), p. 208.
15. James Shepley, "How Dulles Averted War," *Life* (January 16, 1956), pp. 70 ff.
16. *Ibid.*

Chapter Eight: Waging Peace: The Eisenhower Face

1. Emmet John Hughes, *The Ordeal of Power: A Political Memoir of the Eisenhower Years* (New York: Atheneum, 1963), pp. 343–44.
2. Quoted by Sherman Adams, *Firsthand Report; The Story of the Eisenhower Administration* (New York: Harper, 1961), p. 89.
3. Dwight D. Eisenhower, *The White House Years: Waging Peace, 1956–1961* (New York: Doubleday, 1965), II, 365.
4. Sherman Adams, *Firsthand Report; The Story of the Eisenhower Administration* (New York: Harper, 1961), p. 89.
5. Hughes, p. 109.
6. *Mandate For Change*, p. 149.
7. "The Chance for Peace," Address by the President, April 16, 1953, to the American Society of Newspaper Editors, in the Department of State, *Bulletin*, April 27, 1953, pp. 599–603.
8. *Mandate For Change*, p. 251.
9. *Ibid.*, p. 252.
10. *Ibid.*, pp. 251–255.
11. Adams, p. 112.
12. Quoted by Andrew Berding, *Dulles On Diplomacy* (Princeton: Van Nostrand, 1965), p. 24.
13. See Roscoe Drummond and Gaston Coblentz, *Duel at the Brink* (New York: Doubleday, 1960), pp. 134–39, for a vivid description of Dulles' reactions to the cheering throngs and Soviet embraces during the May 15, 1955 signing ceremonies at Beledere Palace in Vienna.

14. See Coral Bell, *Negotiation From Strength: A Study in the Politics of Power* (New York: Knopf, 1963), p. 127.
15. *Ibid.,* pp. 111–23 passim.
16. Adams, pp. 176–77.
17. *Mandate For Change,* p. 506.
18. Radio-Television address, July 15, 1955, in Department of State, *American Foreign Policy 1950–1955: Basic Documents* (Washington: GPO), II, 2005–8.
19. Robert J. Donovan, *Eisenhower: The Inside Story* (New York: Harper, 1956), pp. 345–46.
20. Donovan. See also Adams, pp. 177–78.
21. Donovan, pp. 348–49.
22. *New York Times,* July 22, 1955.
23. Proposal by the President at the Geneva Conference of Heads of Government, July 21, 1955, in Department of State, *American Foreign Policy 1950–1955: Basic Documents,* II, pp. 2842–43.
24. Statement by the President at the Geneva Conference of Heads of Government, July 23, 1955; *ibid.,* p. 2014.
25. Adams, pp. 178–79.
26. *Mandate For Change,* p. 530.

Chapter Nine: Complicating the Premises: Suez and Hungary

1. John Robinson Beal, *John Foster Dulles: 1888–1959* (New York: Harper, 1959), p. 228.
2. See Walt W. Rostow, *The United States in The World Arena* (New York: Harper, 1960), pp. 364–65.
3. Robert J. Donovan, *Eisenhower: The Inside Story* (New York: Harper, 1956), p. 388.
4. Sherman Adams, *Firsthand Report; The Story of the Eisenhower Administration* (New York: Harper, 1961), p. 245.
5. Anthony Eden, *Full Circle* (London: Cassell & Co., 1960), pp. 374–75.
6. Dwight D. Eisenhower, *The White House Years: Waging Peace, 1956–1961* (New York: Doubleday, 1965), II, 33, 34 *n.*
7. Beal, pp. 258–60.
8. *Waging Peace,* pp. 36, 49–50.
9. *Ibid.,* p. 50.
10. *Ibid.,* p. 38.
11. *Ibid.,* p. 53.
12. *Ibid.,* p. 80.
13. *Ibid.,* Appendix, p. 680.
14. *Ibid.,* p. 91.
15. *Ibid.,* p. 91.
16. *Ibid.,* p. 90.
17. Speech to Council on Foreign Relations, October 6, 1952. Quoted by Beal, p. 312.
18. Quoted by Beal, pp. 311–12.
19. Radio-Television address, in the Department of State *Bulletin,* February 9, 1963, pp. 207–16.
20. Message from the Allied Commandants in Berlin to the Representative of the Soviet Control Commission, June 18, 1953, and letter from the Allied Commandants in Berlin to the Soviet Military Commander in Berlin, June 24, 1953; texts in Department of State, *American Foreign Policy 1950–1955: Basic Documents* (Washington: GPO), II, 1744–45.
21. Press Conference, June 30, 1953, Department of State, *ibid.,* pp. 1745–46.

22. *Ibid.*, p. 1750.
23. Schilling, Hammond, and Snyder, *Strategy, Politics, and Defense Budgets* (New York: Columbia University Press, 1962), pp. 407–9.
24. *Waging Peace*, pp. 87–89.
25. Roscoe Drummond and Gaston Coblentz, *Duel at the Brink: John Foster Dulles' Command of American Power* (New York: Doubleday, 1960), pp. 180–81.
26. *Ibid.*, p. 181. See also Andrew Berding, *Dulles on Diplomacy* (Princeton: Van Norstand, 1965), pp. 115–16.

Chapter Ten: *Sputnik: New Attention to Material Factors of Power*

1. See Arnold L. Horelick and Myron Rush, *Strategic Power and Soviet Foreign Policy* (Chicago: University of Chicago Press, 1966).
2. White House press release, October 9, 1957, in the Department of State, *Bulletin*, October 28, 1957, pp. 673–74.
3. Dwight D. Eisenhower, *The White House Years: Waging Peace, 1956–1961* (New York: Doubleday, 1965), II, 205.
4. Eric F. Goldman, *The Crucial Decade—And After: America, 1945–1960* (New York: Random House, Vintage edition, 1960), pp. 309–10.
5. Radio-Television address, November 7, 1957; see *Waging Peace*, pp. 223–25.
6. The most complete description, compiled from numerous open sources, is by Morton H. Halperin in his "The Gaither Committee and The Policy Process," *World Politics* (April 1961), pp. 360–84.
7. *Waging Peace*, pp. 219–23.
8. Halperin, passim.
9. Huntington, The Common Defense, p. 94.
10. From Eisenhower's account of November 1957 NSC deliberations, *Waging Peace*, pp. 221–22.
11. Quoted by Huntington, p. 101.
12. *Waging Peace*, p. 222.
13. *Ibid.*, 226.
14. Reply by the Secretary of State to a question at a news conference, February 11, 1958, in the Department of State *Bulletin*, March 3, 1958, p. 335.

Chapter Eleven: *Conditioned Responses to New Challenges*

1. Dwight D. Eisenhower, *The White House Years: Waging Peace 1956–1961* (New York: Doubleday, 1965), II, 178.
2. Department of State, *American Foreign Policy: Current Documents* (Washington: GPO, 1957), pp. 784–85.
3. *Ibid.*, p. 790.
4. *Ibid.*, pp. 787–90, passim.
5. Statement by the Secretary of State before the Committees on Foreign Relations and Armed Services of the Senate, January 14, 1957; *ibid.*, pp. 796–97.
6. *Ibid.*, p. 800.
7. Public Law 85–87, 85th Cong., 1st sess., H. J. Res 117, *American Foreign Policy: Current Documents, ibid.*, pp. 816–17.
8. Documents Nos. 298–303, *ibid.*, pp. 1023–28. See also John C. Campbell, *Defense of the Middle East: Problems of American Policy* (New York: Praeger, 1960), pp. 127–31.
9. *Waging Peace*, p. 196.
10. *Ibid.*, p. 197.
11. White House news conference of August 21, 1957, *Current Documents*, p. 1036.
12. *Ibid.*, p. 199.
13. White House press release, September 7, 1957, in the Department of State *Bulletin*, September 23, 1957, p. 487; also in *Current Documents*, pp. 1037–38.

14. Campbell, p. 133.
15. *Current Digest of the Soviet Press*, Vol. IX, No. 37, p. 23.
16. Department of State press release, September 10, 1957, in the Department of State *Bulletin*, September 30, 1957.
17. *Current Documents*, p. 1046.
18. *Ibid.*, p. 1047.
19. *Waging Peace*, p. 266.
20. *Ibid.*, p. 271.
21. *Ibid.*, p. 274.
22. Address by President Eisenhower to the Nation, July 15, 1958. Also Special Message of President Eisenhower to the Congress, July 15, 1958. Both in the Department of State, *Current Documents*, 1958, pp. 965–67, 969–72.
23. Campbell, *Defense of The Middle East*, pp. 142–44.
24. *Waging Peace*, p. 290.
25. *Ibid.*, pp. 290–91.
26. Address by the President to the Third Emergency Session of the UN General Assembly, August 13, 1958; *Current Documents*, 1958, pp. 1032–39.
27. Walt W. Rostow, *The United States in the World Arena* (New York: Harper, 1960), p. 363.
28. Eisenhower, *Waging Peace*, p. 520.
29. OAS Charter.
30. Res. XCIII; Tenth Inter-American Conference, Caracas, Venezuela, March 1–28, 1954, Department of State, *American Foreign Policy, 1950–1955: Basic Documents* (Washington: GPO), I, 1300–2.
31. *Ibid.*
32. Edwin Lieuwen, *U.S. Policy in Latin America: A Short History* (New York: Praeger, 1965), pp. 88–92.
33. Eisenhower's candid discussion of the intervention in his *Mandate For Change*, pp. 504–11, details most of the essentials.
34. *Ibid.*, p. 511.
35. Tad Szulc, *The Winds of Revolution; Latin America Today—and Tomorrow* (New York: Praeger, 1963), pp. 114–17.
36. Lieuwen, p. 113.
37. Eisenhower, *Waging Peace*, p. 525.
38. *Ibid.*, p. 525.
39. Radio-Television address by the President, February 21, 1960, in the Department of State *Bulletin*, March 7, 1960, pp. 351–53.
40. Address by President Eisenhower to the Nation, March 8, 1960, Department of State *Bulletin*, March 28, 1960, pp. 471–74.
41. *Waging Peace*, p. 530.
42. Statement by the President, July 11, 1960, in the Department of State *Bulletin*, August 1, 1960, pp. 318–19.
43. Statement by Undersecretary of State Dillon, September 6, 1960, in the Department of State *Bulletin*, October 3, 1960, pp. 533–37.
44. *Waging Peace*, p. 539.
45. *Ibid.*, p. 533.
46. Arthur M. Schlesinger, Jr., *A Thousand Days: John F. Kennedy in the White House* (Boston: Houghton Mifflin, 1965), p. 222.
47. Eisenhower, *Waging Peace*, pp. 293–94.
48. Memorandum re Formosa Strait Situation, dated September 4, 1958, Appendix O, *Waging Peace*, pp. 691–92.
49. For an analysis of the way the Eisenhower Administration went about limiting its own options, see Morton H. Halperin and Tang Tsou, "United States Policy Toward the Offshore Islands," *Public Policy* (1966), pp. 119–38.
50. *Ibid.*, p. 304.

51. For a description of the U.S. responses to procedural harrassments on the access routes to Berlin during the spring and summer of 1958 see Jean Edward Smith, *The Defense of Berlin* (Baltimore: Johns Hopkins Press, 1963), pp. 157–60.

52. Note from the Soviet Foreign Ministry, November 27, 1958, in the Department of State *Bulletin*, January 19, 1959, pp. 81–89.

53. *New York Times*, November 27, 1958.

54. Quotations are from *Waging Peace*, pp. 334–49, *passim*.

55. *Ibid.*, p. 342.

56. *Ibid.*, p. 341.

57. Western Proposal on Berlin (Draft Agreement), June 16, 1959, Department of State account of the Geneva *Foreign Ministers Meeting*, May–August, 1959, pp. 312–13.

58. See, for example, Smith, p. 204.

59. Eisenhower's own paraphrase of his confidential letter to Macmillan (sent sometime between July 15 and 20, 1959), in *Waging Peace*, p. 402.

60. *Ibid.*, pp. 405–12.

61. Text in *New York Times*, September 29, 1959.

Chapter Twelve: Perceived Deficiencies in the Nation's Power

1. However, see page 193, for discussion of the refinements in planning premises for the strategic forces instituted by the Department of Defense under McNamara.

2. John F. Kennedy, *The Strategy of Peace*, edited by Allan Nevins (New York: Harper, 1960), p. 184.

3. See discussion of NSC-68, pp. 49–54, above. Nitze, the chief author of this prescient document, headed Kennedy's preinauguration task force on national security matters.

4. N. S. Khrushchev, "For New Victories for The World Communist Movement," *World Marxist Review: Problems of Peace and Socialism* (January 1961), pp. 3–28.

5. Arthur M. Schlesinger, Jr. *A Thousand Days* (Boston: Houghton Mifflin, 1965), p. 302.

6. See Theodore C. Sorenson, *Kennedy* (New York: Harper, 1965), pp. 629–33; and Schlesinger, pp. 340–42.

7. See Schlesinger, pp. 585–91.

8. Address by the President, March 13, 1962, in the Department of State *Bulletin*, April 2, 1962, pp. 539–42.

9. *The Strategy of Peace*, pp. 45–54.

10. State of the Union Message by the President, January 30, 1961.

11. *Ibid.*

12. *Ibid.*

13. Quoted by Sorenson, p. 408.

14. Address by President Kennedy to the Congress, January 25, 1962, in House Document 314, 87th Congress, 2nd sess.

15. See early sections of the 1961 State of the Union Address for this catalog of domestic deficiencies.

16. *The Strategy of Peace*, p. 4.

17. *Ibid.*

18. Quoted by Sorenson, p. 528.

Chapter Thirteen: Attending to the Military Balance

1. See Semour E. Harris, *Economics of the Kennedy Years, and a Look Ahead* (New York: Harper, 1964).

2. Quoted by William W. Kaufmann, *The McNamara Strategy* (New York: Harper, 1964), p. 48.

3. See above, pp. 49–54.

4. General Taylor recounts these doctrinal battles, and advances the doctrine of "flexible response" in his *The Uncertain Trumpet* (New York: Harper, 1960).

5. See William W. Kaufmann (ed.), *Military Policy and National Security* (Princeton: Princeton University Press, 1956); Robert E. Osgood, *Limited War* (Chicago: University of Chicago Press, 1957); Henry A. Kissinger, *Nuclear Weapons and Foreign Policy* (New York: Harper, 1957); and Bernard Brodie, *Strategy in the Missile Age* (Princeton: Princeton University Press, 1959).

6. See above, pp. 118–21, for recommendations of the Gaither Report. The Rockefeller Panel report, "International Security: The Military Aspect," was first published in January 1958, and then republished as a part of *Prospect for America: The Rockefeller Panel Reports* (New York: Doubleday, 1961).

7. *Public Papers of the Presidents of the United States: John F. Kennedy*, 1961, p. 231.

8. *Ibid.*, pp. 231–32.

9. See Henry A. Kissinger, *The Troubled Partnership: A Reappraisal of the Atlantic Alliance* (New York: Anchor Books, 1966); especially pp. 106–28. See also Raymond Aaron, *The Great Debate* (New York: Doubleday, 1965).

10. Remarks of Assistant Secretary of Defense, Paul H. Nitze, to the Institute for Strategic Studies, London, December 11, 1961, quoted by William W. Kaufmann, *The McNamara Strategy*, pp. 109–10.

11. *Public Papers of the Presidents: John F. Kennedy*, 1961, p. 385.

12. See, for example, Alistair Buchan's excellent article, "The Multilateral Force: A Study in Alliance Politics," *International Affairs* (October 1964), pp. 619–37.

13. See Seyom Brown, "An Alternative to the Grand Design," *World Politics* (January 1965), pp. 231–42.

14. See Theodore C. Sorenson, *Kennedy* (New York: Harper, 1965), p. 567, and Arthur M. Schlesinger Jr., *A Thousand Days* (Boston: Houghton Mifflin, 1965), pp. 872–73.

15. Schlesinger, p. 872.

16. Remarks of the Secretary of Defense Robert S. McNamara at the Commencement Exercises, University of Michigan, Ann Arbor, June 16, 1962, in the Department of Defense News Release No. 980–62.

17. *Ibid.*

18. *Ibid.*

19. Press conference of the President of France, November 10, 1962, in the *New York Times*, November 11, 1962.

20. I am indebted to Herbert Dinerstein for the domestic analogy.

21. *Public Papers of the Presidents: John F. Kennedy*, 1963, pp. 174–75.

22. Sorenson, p. 564; Henry Kissenger, *The Troubled Alliance*, pp. 82–83.

23. Schlesinger, p. 863.

24. Joint Statement following Discussions with Prime Minister Macmillan—the Nassau Agreement, December 21, 1962, *Public Papers of the Presidents of the United States: John F. Kennedy*, 1962, pp. 908–10.

25. Schlesinger, pp. 865–66.

26. Testimony of the Secretary of Defense before the Senate Committee on Armed Services, February 20, 1963.

27. Testimony before the House Subcommittee on Appropriations, 1963; quoted by Kaufmann, *The McNamara Strategy*, p. 95.

28. McNamara, answering a question by Senator Margaret Chase Smith, before the Senate Committee on Armed Services, February 20, 1963.

29. Testimony before the House Committee on Armed Services, February 1, 1963.

30. Speech to the American Society of Newspaper Editors, April 20, 1963.

31. Testimony before subcommittee of the Senate Committee on Appropriations, April 24, 1963.

32. *Ibid.*
33. Testimony before Senate Committee on Armed Services, February 20, 1963.
34. Testimony before Senate Committee on Armed Services, February 21, 1963.
35. *Ibid.*
36. Testimony before House Armed Services Committee, January 30, 1963.
37. Testimony before Senate Committee on Armed Services, February 20, 1963.
38. Testimony before House Armed Services Committee, February 1, 1963.
39. "McNamara Thinks About the Unthinkable," *Saturday Evening Post* (December 1, 1962), pp. 13–19.
40. Testimony before Senate Committee on Armed Services, February 21, 1963.
41. *Ibid.*, February 20, 1963.
42. *Public Papers of the Presidents of the United States: John F. Kennedy*, 1963, pp. 890–94, and 892.
43. *Ibid.*, p. 894.

Chapter Fourteen: New Tools for the New Arena: Opportunities and Obstacles

1. From an address at La Grande, Oregon, November 9, 1959, in John F. Kennedy, *The Strategy of Peace*, edited by Allan Nevins (New York: Harper, 1960), pp. 107–8.
2. The most comprehensive policy-oriented statement to come out of this group was the book by Max Millikan and Walt Rostow, *A Proposal—Key to an Effective Foreign Policy* (New York: Harper, 1957). A more theoretical treatise is Rostow's *The Stages of Economic Growth: A Non-Communist Manifesto* (London: Cambridge University Press, 1960). Some refinements are added by John Kenneth Galbraith, "A Positive Approach to Foreign Aid," *Foreign Affairs* (April 1961), pp. 444–57.
3. The Foreign Assistance Act of 1961 gave legislative sanction to the injection by the President of this criterion when negotiating development loans. The President, in the language of the Act, was to take into account "the extent to which the recipient country is showing a responsiveness to the vital economic, political, and social concerns of its people, and demonstrating a clear determination to take self-help measures." (Title I, Sec. 201, *Foreign Assistance Act of 1961*, 87th Congress, 1st session, August 30, 1961.)
4. Arthur M. Schlesinger Jr., *A Thousand Days* (Boston: Houghton Mifflin, 1965), p. 592.
5. Department of State, *An Act for International Development*, Summary Presentation, June 1961.
6. The interregnum task force on Latin America, in addition to Berle, included Richard Goodwin, Lincoln Gordon, Teodoro Moscosco, Arturo Morales-Carrion, Robert Alexander, and Arthur Whitaker.
7. Task force quotations are taken from Schlesinger, pp. 195–96.
8. Address by President Kennedy at a White House Reception March 13, 1961, in the Department of State *Bulletin*, April 3, 1961, pp. 471–74.
9. *Ibid.*
10. *Ibid.*
11. Address by Secretary of the Treasury Douglas Dillon to the Inter-American Economic and Social Conference, Punta del Este, Uruguay, August 7, 1961, in the Department of State *Bulletin*, August 28, 1961, pp. 356–60.
12. Title I, Charter of Punta del Este, signed August 17, 1961.
13. Tad Szulc, *The Winds of Revolution: Latin America Today—and Tomorrow* (New York: Praeger, 1963), p. 242.
14. Schlesinger, p. 764.

15. Theodore C. Sorenson, *Kennedy* (New York: Harper, 1965), p. 535.
16. Szulc, pp. 243–44.
17. Quoted by Sorenson, p. 535.
18. Address by President Kennedy at the White House, March 13, 1962, in the Department of State *Bulletin*, April 2, 1962, pp. 539–42.
19. Evaluation of the First Year of the Alliance for Progress by the Ministerial Representatives of the Inter-American Economic and Social Council, meeting in Mexico City, October 22–27, 1962, in the Department of State *Bulletin*, December 10, 1962, pp. 897–901.
20. *Ibid.*
21. Address by President Kennedy to the Inter-American Press Association, Miami Beach, Florida, November 18, 1963, in the Department of State *Bulletin*, December 9, 1963, pp. 900–4.
22. Millikan and Rostow, p. 151.
23. Address by President Kennedy to the Congress, March 13, 1962: House Document 362, 87th Congress, 2nd session.
24. Schlesinger, p. 597.
25. *Report to the President of the United States from the Committee to Strengthen the Security of the Free World: The Scope and Distribution of United States Military and Economic Assistance Programs*, March 20, 1963 (published by the Department of State).
26. Schlesinger, p. 598.
27. From "Transcript of Kennedy-Clay Press Conference," in the The *Washington Post*, August 31, 1963.
28. Remarks at the High School Memorial Stadium in Great Falls, Montana, September 26, 1963; *Public Papers of the Presidents of the United States: John F. Kennedy*, 1963, pp. 727–29.
29. Address in Salt Lake City at the Mormon Tabernacle, September 26, 1963, *Ibid.*, pp. 733–38. (Emphasis added.)

Chapter Fifteen: Castro, Laos, the Congo: Limits on the Coercive Power of the Superpowers

1. Address in Seattle at the University of Washington's 100th Anniversary Program, November 16, 1961, *Public Papers of the Presidents of the United States: John F. Kennedy*, 1961, pp. 725–26.
2. Theodore C. Sorenson, *Kennedy* (New York: Harper, 1965), p. 644.
3. Quoted by Arthur M. Schlesinger Jr., *A Thousand Days*, (Boston: Houghton Mifflin, 1965), p. 339.
4. See Schlesinger, pp. 240–43; and Sorenson, p. 297.
5. Press conference, April 12, 1961, in *Public Papers of the Presidents of the United States: John F. Kennedy*, 1961, pp. 258–59.
6. Sorenson, p. 305.
7. For a perspective on how large was the gap between what competent U.S. journalists knew about Cuba and the assumptions underlying our official moves, see Tad Szulc and Karl E. Meyer, *The Cuban Invasion: The Chronicle of a Disaster* (New York: Ballatine Books, 1962).
8. Schlesigner, pp. 252–95.
9. Schlesinger, p. 276.
10. Quoted by Schlesinger, p. 251.
11. Sorenson, pp. 297, 307.
12. Address to the American Society of Newspaper Editors, April 20, 1961, *Public Papers of the Presidents of the United States: John F. Kennedy*, 1961, pp. 304–6.
13. Press Conference March 23, 1961, *ibid.*, pp. 213–20.
14. See Schlesinger, p. 339.

15. See Arthur J. Dommen, *Conflict in Laos: The Politics of Neutralization* (New York; Praeger, 1965), pp. 194–95.

16. *Public Papers*, p. 214.

17. My reconstruction of the conversation at Vienna, as it relates to the Laotian conflict, is an amalgam of the accounts of Schlesinger, pp. 358–74, and Sorenson, pp. 543–50.

18. Sorenson, p. 643.

19. Schlesinger, p. 339.

20. Sorenson, p. 645.

21. Schlesinger, p. 516.

22. Department of State, *American Foreign Policy: Current Documents* (Washington: GPO, 1962), pp. 1072–85.

23. *Public Papers*, 1962, pp. 18–19.

24. Dwight D. Eisenhower, *The White House Years: Waging Peace, 1956–1961* (New York: Doubleday, 1965), II, 574.

25. Statement by the Secretary of State before the Subcommittee on African Affairs of the Senate Committee on Foreign Relations, January 18, 1962; Department of State, *Current Documents*, 1962, pp. 820–21.

26. Schlesinger confesses to siding with his White House colleagues, approvingly quoting the remark, "Every nation has a right to its own War of the Roses," *Schlesinger*, p. 577.

27. Sorenson, p. 638. Schlesinger, p. 578, says that Kennedy had decided to approve the fighter planes, if they were requested.

Chapter Sixteen: Berlin and Cuban Missiles: Defining Spheres of Control

1. Jean Edward Smith, *The Defense of Berlin* (Baltimore: The Johns Hopkins University Press, 1963), p. 230.

2. Theodore C. Sorenson, *Kennedy* (New York: Harper, 1965), pp. 584–86.

3. Quotations are from the text of the *aide-mémoire*, handed by Chairman Khrushchev to President Kennedy at Vienna on June 4, 1961, in the Department of State, *American Foreign Policy: Current Documents* (Washington: GPO, 1961), pp. 584–86.

4. The full text of the President's Address of July 25, 1961 appears in *Public Papers of the Presidents of the United States: John F. Kennedy*, 1961, pp. 533–40.

5. Quoted by Smith, pp. 254–55.

6. Department of State, *American Foreign Policy: Current Documents* (Washington: GPO, 1961), pp. 619–20.

7. *Ibid.*, pp. 620–21.

8. Sorenson, p. 594.

9. General Clay's virtuosity in brilliantly staging a "confrontation" to counter attempted Communist "salami slices" is well described in George Bailey's "The Gentle Erosion of Berlin," *The Reporter* (April 26, 1962), pp. 15–19.

10. Quoted by Schlesinger, p. 399.

11. Transcript of Interview with the President by Aleksei Adzhubei, November 25, 1961, *Public Papers of the Presidents of the United States: John F. Kennedy*, 1961, pp. 741–53.

12. See Arnold L. Horelick, "The Cuban Missile Crisis: An Analysis of Soviet Calculations and Behavior," *World Politics* (April 1964), pp. 363–89.

13. Radio-Television Interview, December 17, 1962, *Public Papers of the Presidents of the United States: John F. Kennedy*, 1962, pp. 897–98.

14. *Ibid.*, p. 898.

15. *Ibid.*, pp. 808–9.

16. Quoted by Elie Abel, *The Missile Crisis* (New York: Lippincott, 1966), pp. 64–65.

17. Sorenson, pp. 684–85.

18. Abel, pp. 80–81.

19. Quoted by Abel, in footnote p. 64.

20. The title of an insightful essay on the missile crisis by Albert and Roberta Wohlstetter. See their "Controlling the Risks in Cuba," *Adelphi Papers* (April 1965), Institute for Strategic Studies, London.

21. Robert Kennedy continued to maintain that his brother could not order an air strike because the contemplated attack without warning against a small nation would offend the American conscience. See Abel, p. 88.

22. Abel, p. 101.

23. *Public Papers of the Presidents of the United States: John F. Kennedy,* 1962, p. 808.

24. Sorenson, p. 715; see also Abel, p. 201.

25. Sorenson, p. 710.

26. Abel, p. 174; Sorenson, p. 710.

27. Sorenson, p. 717.

Chapter Seventeen: The Test Ban: Stabilizing the Balance

1. N. S. Khrushchev, "The Present International Situation and the Foreign Policy of the Soviet Union," Report at the December 12, 1962 session of the Supreme Soviet, in the *Current Digest of the Soviet Press* (January 16, 1963), pp. 4–8, (January 23, 1963), pp. 3–10, 56.

2. For text, see *The Current Digest of the Soviet Press* (Dec. 12, 1963), pp. 3–8, 14.

3. Letter from Chairman of the Council of Ministers to the President of the United States, December 19, 1962, Department of State, *American Foreign Policy: Current Documents* (Washington: GPO, 1962), pp. 1306–8.

4. For an account of the Soviet negotiating positions on the test ban from late 1962 through the summer of 1963 see Lincoln P. Bloomfield, Walter C. Clemens, Jr., and Franklin Griffiths, *Khrushchev and the Arms Race: Soviet Interests in Arms Control and Disarmament 1954–1964* (Cambridge: Massachusetts Institute of Technology Press, 1966), pp. 185–200.

5. *Ibid.,* pp. 188–89.

6. Schlesinger, pp. 897–98.

7. *Ibid.,* p. 900.

8. Theodore C. Sorenson, *Kennedy* (New York: Harper, 1965), pp. 730–31.

9. Commencement Address at American University, Washington, D.C., June 10, 1963, in *Public Papers of the Presidents of the United States: John F. Kennedy,* 1963, pp. 459–64.

10. See Current *Digest of the Soviet Press* (July 31, 1963), pp. 3–9.

11. "Open Letter of CPSU Central Committee to All Party Organizations and All Communists of the Soviet Union, July 14, 1963," *Two Major Statements on China* (New York: Cross Currents Press, 1963), pp. 3–49.

12. Address to the American People on the Nuclear Test Ban Treaty, July 26, 1963, *Public Papers of the Presidents of the United States: John F. Kennedy,* 1963, pp. 601–6.

13. Robert S. McNamara, testimony of August 13, 1963 before the Committee on Foreign Relations, Committee on Armed Services, and Senate members, the Joint Committee on Atomic Energy, *Hearings: Nuclear Test Ban Treaty,* 88th Congress, 1st Session, pp. 97–100. (Hereafter cited as *Hearings.*)

14. Preparedness Investigating Subcommittee of the Committee on Armed Services, U.S. Senate, *Interim Report on the Military Implications of the Proposed Test Ban Treaty,* 88th Congress, 1st Session.

15. *Hearings,* p. 101.
16. *Ibid.,* pp. 102–3.
17. John Foster, Jr., *Hearings,* p. 637.
18. Senate Committee on Foreign Relations, *Report on the Nuclear Test Ban Treaty,* 88th Congress, 1st Session, pp. 15–16.
19. General Maxwell B. Taylor, quoted in *ibid.,* p. 16.
20. *Ibid.,* pp. 14–16.
21. *Hearings,* p. 104.
22. See Sept. 19, 1963 speech by Barry Goldwater explaining his vote against the treaty, in *The New York Times,* Sept. 20, 1966.
23. *Hearings,* pp. 104–5.
24. *Hearings,* p. 794.
25. *Ibid.,* pp. 796–800.
26. *Public Papers of the Presidents of the United States: John F. Kennedy, 1963,* p. 366.
27. Bloomfield, Clemens, and Griffiths, p. 191.
28. UN General Assembly Resolution 1884 (XVIII), *ibid.,* pp. 191–92.
29. Full texts of both the Khrushchev proposal of December 31, 1963 and the Johnson reply of January 18, 1964 appear in the Department of State *Bulletin,* February 3, 1964, pp. 157–63.

Chapter Eighteen: The Breakup of Blocs: The Decline of Ideology and Control

1. Special Message to Congress, May 25, 1961, Department of State, *American Foreign Policy: Current Documents* (Washington: GPO, 1961), p. 31.
2. Replies by Secretary of State Rusk, Columbia Broadcasting System interview, Athens, May 6, 1962, in *American Foreign Policy: Current Documents* (Washington: GPO, 1962), pp. 543–44.
3. Press conference of the President of France, May 15, 1962, in ibid., pp. 544–45.
4. Press conference, May 17, 1962, in *Public Papers of the Presidents of the United States: John F. Kennedy, 1962,* pp. 401–2.
5. Address to the Conference on Trade Policy, in *ibid.,* pp. 408–12.
6. Address at Independence Hall, Philadelphia, July 4, 1962, in *ibid.,* pp. 537–39.
7. Television and Radio Interview, December 17, 1962, in *Public Papers of the Presidents of the United States: John F. Kennedy, 1962,* pp. 889–904, at 903.
8. Quotations from Press conference, by President Charles de Gaulle, January 14, 1963; pertinent excerpts are reprinted in the Council on Foreign Relations publication *Documents on American Foreign Relations 1963* (New York: Harper, 1964), pp. 168–80.
9. *Public Papers of the Presidents of the United States: John F. Kennedy, 1963,* pp. 92–100, 148–55.
10. Theodore C. Sorenson, *Kennedy* (New York: Harper, 1965), p. 572.
11. Philip L. Geyelin, *Lyndon B. Johnson and the World* (New York: Praeger, 1966), pp. 167–74.
12. Dean Rusk, Statement to North Atlantic Council, May 12, 1964, in the Department of State *Bulletin,* June 1, 1964, pp. 850–52.
13. See George F. Kennan, *On Dealing with the Communist World* (New York: Harper), 1964.
14. Marshall D. Shulman, *Beyond the Cold War* (New Haven: Yale University Press, 1966).
15. Zbigniew Brzezinski, *Alternative to Partition: For a Broader Conception of America's Role in Europe* (New York: McGraw-Hill, 1965).
16. Press conference, October 9, 1963, in *Public Papers of the Presidents of the United States: John F. Kennedy, 1963,* pp. 767–75.

17. Walt Rostow, "The Third Round," *Foreign Affairs* (October 1963), pp. 1–10.
18. "United States Policy and Eastern Europe," address by Secretary of State Rusk, February 25, 1964, in the Council on Foreign Relations, *Documents on American Foreign Relations* 1964, pp. 144–49.
19. See Brzezinski, p. 112.
20. Lyndon B. Johnson, address of May 23, 1964, in the Department of State *Bulletin*, June 15, 1964, pp. 922–24.
21. Text of Miller Committee recommendations in the Department of State *Bulletin*, May 30, 1966, p. 845.
22. Address by Anthony M. Solomon, Assistant Secretary of State for Economic Affairs, October 21, 1965. Department of State Press Release No. 249.
23. The President's message before Congress, January 12, 1966, in the *Weekly Compilation of Presidential Documents*, January 17, 1966, p. 34.

Chapter Nineteen: Vietnam and the Dominican Republic: Reassertion of the Functions of Military Power

1. President Kennedy's interview by Walter Cronkite of the Columbia Broadcasting System, in the *Public Papers of the Presidents of the United States: John F. Kennedy*, 1963, p. 652.
2. Address to the American Bar Association, August 12, 1964, *Public Papers of the Presidents of the United States: Lyndon B. Johnson*, 1963–64, Book II, p. 953.
3. Remarks in Manchester, New Hampshire, September 28, 1964, in *ibid.*, p. 1164.
4. October 21, 1964, *ibid.*, p. 1391.
5. See Philip L. Geyelin, *Lyndon B. Johnson and the World* (New York: Praeger, 1966), pp. 193–202.
6. Press conference, by Secretary of Defense McNamara and Under-secretary of State Ball, February 7, 1965, in the *New York Times*, February 8, 1965.
7. State Department Publication 7839, February 1956.
8. Address by President Johnson at Johns Hopkins University, April 7, 1965, in the Department of State *Bulletin*, April 26, 1965, pp. 606–10.
9. See the President's message to Congress, May 5, 1965.
10. In the Department of State *Bulletin*, July 12, 1965.
11. *The New York Times*, November 18 and 19, 1965.
12. In the Department of State *Bulletin*, August 16, 1965, pp. 262–65.
13. *Ibid.*
14. In *The New York Times*, January 29, 1966.
15. Senate Committee on Foreign Relations, *Hearings: Supplemental Foreign Assistance Fiscal Year 1966—Vietnam*, pp. 230–31.
16. *Ibid.*, pp. 331–36.
17. The Declaration of Honolulu and accompanying statements are published in *Weekly Compilation of Presidential Documents*, February 14, 1966.
18. The quotations and various positions summarized here are gleaned from Secretary Rusk's testimony and interrogation by Senators on February 18, 1966, *ibid.*, pp. 563–684.
19. Richard N. Goodwin, *Triumph or Tragedy: Reflections on Vietnam* (New York: Vintage Books, 1966), p. 38.
20. From President's statement of May 2, 1965, Department of State *Bulletin*, May 17, 1965, pp. 744–45.
21. *Ibid.*, pp. 738–48.
22. President's statement of May 2, 1965, *ibid.*, at pp. 745–47.
23. *Ibid.*, p. 746.
24. See *Public Papers of the Presidents of the United States: John F. Kennedy*, 1963, pp. 872–77.
25. Most of the evidence is documented in Theodore Draper's detailed account,

"The Dominican Crisis: A Case Study in American Policy," *Commentary* (December 1965), pp. 33–68.

26. *Public Papers of the Presidents of the United States: Lyndon B. Johnson,* 1965, p. 480.

27. See Dan Kurzman, *Santo Domingo: The Revolt of the Damned* (New York: Putnam, 1965); Tad Szulc, *Dominican Diary* (New York: Dell edition, 1966); Barnard Collier's articles in the *New York Herald Tribune* during late April and May, 1965; James Goodsen's article in the *Christian Science Monitor,* May 19, 1965, and Philip Geyelin's article in the *Wall Street Journal,* June 25, 1965. Senator Fulbright's major speech on the Dominican crisis appears in the *Congressional Record,* September 15, 1965, as does Senator Clark's on September 17, 1965.

28. Senate Committee on Foreign Relations, *Background Information Relating to the Dominican Republic,* July 1965, p. 63.

29. In the Department of State *Bulletin,* May 17, 1965, p. 745.

30. *Congressional Record,* September 15, 1965.

31. Quoted by Szulc, p. 54.

32. *Christian Science Monitor,* May 19, 1965.

33. In *Commentary* (December 1965), pp. 53–55.

34. Senate Committee on Foreign Relations, *Background Information Relating to the Dominican Republic,* July 1965, p. 62.

35. Press conference, May 26, 1965, in *ibid.,* p. 78.

36. *Congressional Record,* September 15, 1965.

37. Address by Undersecretary of State Thomas C. Mann, San Diego, October 12, 1965, Department of State Press Release, No. 241.

38. See Dan Kurzman, "Dominican Constitutionalism," *The New Leader* (July 18, 1966), pp. 9–10.

39. President Johnson, May 2, 1965, in the Department of State *Bulletin,* May 17, 1965, p. 746.

40. Secretary of State Rusk, May 26, 1965, in *Background Information Relating to the Dominican Republic,* p. 77.

INDEX

Abel, Elie, 263
Acheson, Dean, and altruistic U.S. interests, 16; and Truman Doctrine, 40-41; and NSC-68, 50; and Korean War, 56-57; as adviser to Kennedy, 162, 243-51
Adams, Sherman, 91, 93-94
Adenauer, Konrad, 97, 256
Advisory role of U.S. in Vietnam, 330-31
Adzhubei, Aleksei, 257
Agency for International Development, 203-19 *passim*
Aiken, George, 347
Airborne Division, 82d, dispatch of to Dominican Republic, 350-51, 357
Air Force, strategic doctrines of, 68, 172; in Congo crisis, 240; in Cuban missile crisis, 263
Albania, 269, 316
Alliance for Progress, 26; roots in Eisenhower Administration, 144; as major program of Kennedy Administration, 166, 201-2, 204-13, 226; extension by Johnson, 364
Alliances, Dulles system of, 76-83; *see also* Baghdad Pact; North Atlantic

Treaty Organization; South East Asia Treaty Organization
Alsop, Stewart, 194
Altruism, as U.S. motive, 15-27, 371
American University speech by President Kennedy, 274-77, 279n
Anderson, Robert B., 215
Antiballistic missile, 282-83, 292-93
Arbenz, Guzmán Jacobo, 141
Arends, Leslie, 193-94
Aswan Dam, 103
Atlantic Community, 181, 296-307; *see also* Common Market; Multilateral force
Atlantic Nuclear Force, 306
Atlas missile, 123
Atomic bomb, *see* Nuclear weapons
Atomic Energy Commission, 91
Atoms-for-Peace, 90-91
Australia, 82
Austrian Peace Treaty, 93

Baghdad Pact, 79
Balaguer, Joaquin, 362
Balance of payments, 168-69, 172
Balance of power, concept of, 12-13; as determinant of U.S. priorities, 15-27,

389

and Vietnam conflict, 327, 322; *see also* Sino-Soviet split

China, Republic of (Formosa), strategic significance of, 57; and Quemoy and Matsu, 82-85, 147-49

Chiang Kai-shek, 57, 85

Chou En-lai, 99

Church, Frank, 342

Churchill, Winston S., "Iron Curtain" speech, 38; suggestions for settlement with Soviets, 51, 92; as Eisenhower correspondent during Suez crisis, 107

Civil defense, 253

Clark, Joseph S., 353

Clay, Lucius D., 214, 248-49, 256

Clay Report (on economic assistance), 204, 214-16

"Clear and hold" operations in Vietnam, 331

Clemens, Walter C., Jr., 279n

Committee to Strengthen the Security of the Free World, *see* Clay Report

Common Market, 168-69, 181, 296, 298-301, 303-5

Congo, 221-23, 235-40

Consent, and political power, 1-2

"Containment," Kennan's concept of, 44-45, 50; globalization of, 59; carry-over into Kennedy Administration, 226; as consideration in Vietnam conflict, 339

Control of nuclear weapons, 35, 182-85, 271, 295, 297-98, 301-3

Conventional option, strategic concept of, *see* Limited war

Costa Rica, 147

Council of Economic Advisers, 51, 67, 251

Council on Foreign Relations, 74, 307

Counterforce, McNamara doctrine of, 183, 193-94

Counterinsurgency, *see* Insurgency

Cousins, Norman, 273

Cuba: Bay of Pigs crisis, 20, 221-27, 361; U.S. relations with under Eisenhower, 142, 146-47; missile crisis, 184-85, 258-66, 269, 301-2

Cutler, Robert, 71, 91

Cyprus, 106, 363

Czechoslovakia, 322

Dallas Citizens Council, Kennedy's intended speech at, 195-96

Dean, Arthur, 271

Declaration of Interdependence, 300-1

Democracy, as U.S. objective for developing countries, 15-27, 200; for South Vietnam, 344

De Gaulle, Charles, 183-84, 187, 277, 296-99, 302-5, 312, 335

Deño, Caamaño, 356-57

Détente with Soviet Union, 217, 274-82, 286-93, 294-323, 324, 364

Deterrence, as a strategic concept, 11, 69, 73, 74-75, 83, 85, 173-74, 370; effectiveness in 1961 Berlin crisis, 249

Diem, Ngo Dinh, 327, 348

Dienbienphu, 81

Dillon, Douglas, 141, 144-46, 207, 262

Dirksen, Everett M., 216

Disarmament, policy of the Truman Administration, 35; policy of the Eisenhower Administration, 90-92, 94-98; ideas of Democrats in the late 1950s, 162; policy of the Kennedy Administration, 171, 269-90,

"Disengagement," 97, 178

Dissent, Johnson Administration attitude toward, 340-41

Dodd, Thomas J., 273

Dodge, Joseph M., 69, 72

Dominican Republic, 1965 U.S. intervention in, 326, 349-63

Draper, Theodore, 357-58

Dulles, Allen, 107, 135

Dulles, John Foster, on self-determination, 17; policies as Secretary of State, 65-156, 367-68

Dungan, Ralph, 240

Economic assistance program, overview of, 22, 199-200; and Truman Doctrine, 39-42, 43; of Marshall Plan, 42-44, 47, 312; of Eisenhower Administration, 165-66, 199-219; of Kennedy Administration, 198-219; of Johnson Administration for Southeast Asia, 336

Economics, of Truman Administration,